THE FOUR GOSPELS
OF JESUS THE CHRIST

THE FOUR GOSPELS OF JESUS THE CHRIST

Living Here and Now

Robert Luthmers

Library of Congress Control Number: 2010918841
ISBN: Hardcover   978-1-4568-3632-0
                   Softcover   978-1-4568-3631-3
                   Ebook   978-1-4568-3633-7

This book was printed in the United States of America.

Rev. date: 05/18/2013

Acknowledgements

Frank Zimmermann, *The Aramaic Origin of the Four Gospels*, KTAV, 1979. Stephen M. Wylen, *The Jews in the Time of Jesus: An Introduction*, Paulist Press, 1996. Neil Douglas-Klotz, *The Hidden Gospel*, Quest Books—Theosophical Publishing House, 1999. George M. Lasma, *Gospel Light*, Holman Bible Publishers, 1967. George M. Lasma, *Idioms In the Bible Explained and A Key to the Original Gospels*, HarperSanFrancisco, A Division of HarperCollinsPublishers, 1985. Jean-Yves Leloup, Joseph Rowe, trans. *The Gospel of Mary Magdalene*, Inner Traditions, 2002. Rabbi Berel Wein, *Echoes of Glory*, Shaar Press, 1995. Stevan Davies trans., Andrew Harvey ed. *The Gospel of Thomas: Annotated & Explained*, Skylight Paths Publishing, 2002. Esther A. De Boer, *The Gospel of Mary: Listening to the Beloved Disciple*, Continuum Books, 2005. George M. Lasma, *Holy Bible: From the Ancient Eastern Text*, HarperSanFrancisco for A. J. Holman Company, 1968. Ester De Boer, *The Mary Magdalene Cover-Up: The Sources Behind The Myth*, T & T Clark, 2006. John Bowden, trans. *The Revell Concise Bible Dictionary*, Flemming H. Revell Company, 1991. Jean-Yves Leloup, Joseph Rowe trans., *The Gospel of Thomas*, Inner Traditions, 2005. John P. Meier, *A Marginal Jew: Rethinking The Historical Jesus, Volume Two: Mentor, Message and Miracles*, Doubleday, 1994.

To order additional copies of this book, contact:
Xlibris Corporation
1-888-795-4274
www.Xlibris.com
Orders@Xlibris.com
83503

Contents

Notes

Bibliography

Index

PREFACE

The purpose of this book is to feature the Gospels of Jesus the Christ in an authentic canon apart from the patriarchal language framework of the New Testament. By this I mean that the Gospels have been translated into a language framework that clarifies their truth by eliminating the bias and obscurities of patriarchy, gender, anti-Semitism and the sixteenth century's distortions inherent in King James I's promotion of the divine right of kings. From the discoveries and research over the last fifty years I have been inspired by the Gospel of Mary, the Gospel of Thomas, and writings on the Aramaic basis of the Gospels where the authentic voice of Jesus is made accessible.

This is not a traditional commentary in that the comments are not in the margins but are inherent in the language of the gospels. For example, I have translated the word kingdom into kin-dom because Jesus wasn't a king and refused to become one. He is the kin to all people and the title "King of the Jews" was used by Pilate to justify crucifying him. A snapshot image of a king takes up most of the American Declaration of Independence from King George of Great Britain. Kin-dom is a play on kingdom that evokes an inclusive spiritual community, not a hierarchical construct of set relationships. The heart of Jesus' teaching is that the kin-dom of God (heaven)[1] is within you, a part of you inseparable from yourself even if you are lost in the errors of a corrupt worldly life.

Jesus' gift is to help you find this joy of the Christ (the consciousness of God or God essence) within you. God sent his spiritual Son to teach and form his Christ for humanity as a spiritual Saviour of the worldly and a healer led by the Spirit of Truth. Following your personal version of the Christ helps you to purge error in your life, before a human death, and to be fruitful in the world. The language of this book facilitates this central basic truth.

I have spent most of the last two decades studying and working on this book. I have spent the last twenty-five years working with children in a day care setting. Throughout the writing of this book, I have been able to keep focus on real life by teaching and being taught in my work with young children. When free to choose within limits, they are full of love, joyful, forgive you without being asked, seek the truth, live in the present, absorb knowledge, and radiate the Holy Spirit. Their no means no and their yes means yes.[2]

Mark 10:13–16

> They brought little children to him that he might touch them but his disciples rebuked those who brought them. When Jesus saw it he became indignant, saying, **"Let the little children come to me! Do not hinder them for the kin-dom of God belongs to such as these little ones. Truly I tell you, whoever does not receive the kin-dom of God like a little child will never enter in."**[3] Jesus took them up in his arms, laid his hands on them, and blessed them.

Luke 7:31–35

> The Saviour said, **"To what shall I compare the people of this generation? What are they like? They are like children sitting in the marketplace and calling to their friends, 'We played the flute for you and you would not dance! We have wailed to you and you would not weep!' John came neither eating bread nor drinking wine and you say, 'He must be crazy!' The Son of humanity**[4] **came eating and drinking so you say, 'Behold a glutton and an alcoholic,**[5] **a friend of tax collectors and sinners.'**[6] **Wisdom is justified by all Her children."**[7]

Read, listen, understand, and believe the Good News of this divine, nonviolent, human Teacher, and Saviour. The words of life from this great prophet will help you to understand your own personal truth as you feel the Wisdom of God come through every chapter. Let the wonderful sayings in the Gospels of Jesus wash over you repeatedly, leading to the amazing inspired enthusiasm from the Holy Spirit and the Sacred Father within your own kin-dom of heaven. Truth will remove error learned from the worldly and reveal the original goodness of your sacred heart.

Introduction

My father was a secular Catholic who took on the sin of sending me to public schools but my Lutheran mother raised me as a Catholic. I believe that my viral encephalitis or the drugs used to treat it at age six resulted in an unrecognized hearing impairment in both ears. This caused social and personal problems for me until hearing aids in the early 1980s lessened my difficulty. As I grew up, I became aware of the social problems of alcoholism and prescription drug abuse including suicide, other self-destructive behaviors, and the suffering they caused. All my moral and spiritual teachings came into doubt, but with my protective brother's guidance, I began the serious study of different religions, philosophers, freethinkers, revolutionaries, and the his-tory of war. Later, I focused on her-story, studied various scriptures, and attended many different churches in my search for the truth. The Catholic church had taught me to rely on the nuns, priests, bishops, and popes to read and interpret the Gospels of Jesus. I was born anew in the Spirit by accepting Jesus into my heart. I began reading the King James red-letter edition of the Holy Bible and its repeated study led me to the deeper truth beyond the words of Jesus.

Observations

Jesus was an apocalyptical prophet with a twist. In three days, he set up a new temple revealed in every living body with the kin-dom of heaven within and the Christ available to all who believe. A builder's son built the temple of the Spirit within each person, a truly monumental accomplishment because he opened up access to God for all people.

The church fathers took this notion of our God within *away from humanity* and they put *themselves* between the people and Jesus. They developed a set of rules and erected a new earthly temple where church became a building, while Jesus' spiritual church is a verb. As in Judaism, the Christian church fathers installed another male clergy hierarchy, they wrote new traditions of the elders, they demanded another mandatory tithe, and they wove a new veil to separate people from realizing God through Jesus.

Many of the scholars and teachers of the Christians are like many of the scribes of the Pharisees, so locked in detail that they miss the quantum childlike leap of faith needed to know the spiritual kin-dom of heaven within. These scholastic leaders can't let go of the ego embedded in their mind and body. This ego attaches them to the material world. God and Jesus are reduced to mere Lords and even a queen, a dictator, or a president has a higher rank.

God is the Infinite, the Eternal, the All, Supreme Being, the Absolute without attributes, and the Source of the Source *before* God's role as Creator, Divine Parent, Word, Truth, Wisdom, Life, and Love. A person realizes God (becomes enlightened) through their human spirit, unattached to the demands of their body and things. They show their faith in practice by being a true human being who loves unconditionally like Jesus the Christ and Mary Magdalene the beloved disciple.

The apocalyptic end of the world that Jesus preached (Mark 9:1, Mark 13:30, and Mark 15:62) did happen when Jesus built a new temple in three days through his death, resurrection, and Glory from God. This temple is the consciousness of God in the kin-dom of heaven which is already inside you and outside you. This temple is not an earthly one of strict rules of behavior and there is no need for priests to mediate between God and yourself. A person can escape the living hell attached to the material world by a change of heart. In a quantum leap of spirit the soul is freed and grows to know God within and we learn our own expression, our work, and service to the world.

Process

A loving spouse, a child, your neighbor, a stranger, some traumatic near-death event, a serious illness, or even a pet can open your heart to life and the divine mercy, forgiveness, and loving-kindness of our Creator. Many people, even a sister or brother, can guide you out of your living hell to begin to love your life anew. As a vision-impaired, hearing-impaired, brokenhearted, sick, poor, angry, lost, alone, afraid, dying, low-energy person in my early thirties, I gave up on my human spirit and thought of death to end my living hell. At the urging of a friend, the Light of Jesus penetrated my crust of despair and being born anew in the Spirit enabled me to live in hope as a child of God while removing error.

Jesus (Yeshua in Hebrew), the Son of humanity, is Glorified as a spiritual human being to show and teach the way to unconditionally loving one another. Jesus teaches the God within and lives the Christ so a person can follow their Christ with or without a place of worship, study, and prayer. The Spirit of truth becomes your priority in removing error to become a true human being before earthly roles of female and male, mother and father, sister and brother, or any job. Jesus said in Mark 1:15, **"The time is fulfilled, the kin-dom of God is at hand, repent, and believe in the Good News!"**

Return to the original goodness known by all children before being corrupted by the world into the reactions and choices that separate their human spirit from God in a living death. Live eternal life in the present where God lives: "I AM" not "I should be." Enter now your eternal life reborn in the Spirit and don't worry about your afterlife.

In most bible tracts that I have read, the often used quotes of Jesus are combined with Peter-Paul-Revelation teachings and some Hebrew Bible quotes in a mix, surrounded by the writer's words. With their belief in the equality of all the New Testament scriptures; religious teachers and my experiences in church left me confused. Jesus wants people to follow him before Peter, Paul, and the writer of Revelations. He wants people to receive the consciousness of God (Christ) and know that he was sent by God to deliver and preach the Good News of the kin-dom of heaven within.

Results

The process of assembling a variety of sayings and arranging them in tracts without narrative helped me work through what was going on in my life. Persistent study resulted in providing authentic alternatives to the gender injustice, glorification of royalty, and anti-Semitism embedded in the language of the Gospels. Seeing through trifocal glasses, hearing though two hearing aids, and understanding with help of speechreading; I believe in the gospel of Jesus the Christ. Reading some scripture (selected from all religions) in the morning is like washing my hands and face, brushing my teeth, or doing my exercises. Great understanding and divine inspiration come to me from Christian preaching, teaching, scriptures, and people in a church setting. When staying with close friends or family, I rarely feel the need to read scripture because I connect with the Jesus in the other person. All this doesn't make me any better than a toddler, ten sparrows, or most people who are righteous anyway. I consider myself a follower of the Light of Jesus the Christ, a true human being who is the Son of God adopted at John's baptism (Luke 4:21–22). Although God blessed him like a king in the tradition of King David (Psalm 2:7) at John's baptism, he is greater than a king and his throne is the Good News and example of the Christ. Jesus is kin to all people given to him by God and the spiritual Saviour of the worldly, here and now.

Experience this Word of God as a complete guide to salvation, truth, and problem solving in your new life in the Spirit. I hope the reader, even an atheist or an agnostic, will see clearly the beauty of the words, the variety of sayings, the completeness of his system of understanding, and the modern relevance of Jesus' sayings. *The Four Gospels of Jesus the Christ: Living Here and Now* is for those who find themselves living single, afraid, lost, and alienated during times of profound changes in their lives so they can live alone without being lonely. The private spiritual wisdom in this book is for those in a family or group who need time alone to become whole, complete, love themselves, cleanse their body as well as their spirit, and unite with God so they may peacefully love one another unconditionally.

THE GOSPEL ACCORDING TO MATTHEW

Matthew 1:1–25

1 This is a record of the genealogy of Jesus the Christ, the son[1] of David, the son of Abraham. Abraham was the father of Isaac and Isaac the father of Jacob, and Jacob the father of Judah and his brothers, and Judah the father of Perez and Zerah by Tamar, and Perez the father of Hezron, and Hezron the father of Aram, and Aram the father of Aminadab, and Aminadab the father of Nahshon, and Nahshon the father of Salmon, and Salmon the father of Boaz by Rahab, and Boaz the father of Obed by Ruth, and Obed the father of Jesse, and Jesse the father of King David. King David was the father of Solomon by Bathsheba (the wife of Uriah), and Solomon the father of Rehoboam, and Rehoboam the father of Abijah, and Abijah the father of Asa, and Asa the father of Jehoshaphat, and Jehoshaphat the father of Joram, and Joram the father of Uzziah, and Uzziah the father of Jotham, and Jotham the father of Ahaz, and Ahaz the father of Hezekiah, and Hezekiah the father of Manasseh, and Manasseh the father of Amon, and Amon the father of Josiah, and Josiah the father of Jechoniah and his brothers, at the time of the deportation to Babylon.

12 After the time of deportation to Babylon: Jechoniah was the father of Shelatiel, and Shelatiel the father of Zerubbabel, and Zerubbabel the father of Abihud, and Abihud the father of Eliakim, and Eliakim the father of Azor, and Azor the father of Sadok, and Sadok the father of Achim, and Achim the father of Eliud, and Eliud the father of Eleazar,

and Eleazar the father of Matthan, and Mathan the father of Jacob, and Jacob the father of Joseph the husband of Mary of whom Jesus was born, who is called Christ.[2] There were fourteen generations in all from Abraham to David, fourteen generations from David to the deportation to Babylon,[3] and fourteen generations from the deportation to Babylon to the Christ.

18 The beginning of Jesus the Christ took place in this way. When his mother Mary was acquired for a price[4] by Joseph but before they came together, she was found pregnant of the Holy Spirit. Her husband Joseph was a pious man and did not wish to make it public, so he was thinking of divorcing her secretly. While he was considering this, an angel of God appeared to him in a dream, saying, "Oh Joseph, son of David, do not be afraid to keep Mary as your wife for the child conceived in her is of the Holy Spirit. She will give birth to a son and you will call his name Jesus for he will save his people from their sins." All this happened so that what was spoken by God through the prophet would be fulfilled, *"14 Therefore, God will give you a sign; behold, a young woman[5] will conceive and give birth to a son who will be called Immanuel.* (Which is translated, 'God be with us.')[6] *He will eat butter[7] and honey[8] that he may know how to refuse the evil and choose the good."9* When Joseph woke up from his sleep, he did just as the angel of God told him. He took Mary as his wife and purely was he dwelling with her before she gave birth to their firstborn son whom they called Jesus.

Matthew 2:1–23

1 When Jesus was born in Bethlehem of Judea during the reign of King Herod the Great, wise men[10] came from their country to Jerusalem, asking, "Where is the child who is born to be king of the Jews?" "We have seen his star[11] shine more brightly and we have come to pay him homage." When King Herod the Great heard this, he trembled and all Jerusalem with him. So he gathered all the chief priests and scribes[12] of the people and he kept asking them where the Christ would be born. They told him, "In Bethlehem[13] of Judea for so it has been written by the prophet Micah: *'2 But you Bethlehem of Ephrathah who are one of the little clans of Judah, from you shall come forth a ruler in Israel whose origin is of old, from Ancient Days. Therefore, God will deliver them until the time when she who was in labor gives birth; then the rest of his kindred will return*

*to the children of Israel. He will stand and feed his flock in the strength of God, in the majesty of God's name. They will live secure for now his dominion will extend to the ends of the earth, and he will be the one of peace.'"*14

7 Then Herod called the wise men secretly and learned from them at what time the rising star appeared to them. He sent them to Bethlehem and instructed them, "Go and inquire very carefully about the boy. When you have found him, come back and let me know so that I may go and pay him homage." After hearing the king, they set out and ahead of them the star that they had seen before in their country had stopped just over the place where the child was. When they saw the star they rejoiced exceedingly. They entered the house, saw the baby with his mother Mary and fell down to pay him homage. Then they opened their treasures and presented to him gifts of gold, frankincense, and myrrh. Being warned in a dream not to return to Herod, they departed for their own country by another way.

13 When they were gone, an angel of God appeared to Joseph in a dream, saying, "Arise! Take your child and his mother, flee to Egypt, and remain there until I tell you, for Herod is ready to demand the child to destroy him." Then Joseph rose up, took the infant boy and his mother in the night, and escaped to Egypt. They remained there until the death of Herod so that it might be fulfilled what was spoken by God through the prophet, saying, *"1 When Israel was a child, then I loved him and called my son out of Egypt."*15 When Herod saw that he had been tricked by the wise men, he was infuriated. He sent soldiers to kill all the boys in Bethlehem and its suburbs who were two years of age and under, according to the time that he had learned from the wise men. Then it was fulfilled what was spoken by the prophet Jeremiah, *"5 A voice is heard in Ramah, lamentation and bitter weeping. Rachel is weeping for her children and refused to be comforted because they are not."*16

19 When King Herod died, the angel of God appeared in a dream to Joseph in Egypt. The angel said, "Arise, take your infant boy and his mother, and go to the land of Israel for those who are seeking the young boy's life are dead." So Joseph rose up, took the infant boy and his mother, and returned to the land of Israel. He was afraid to go to the region of Judea when he heard that Archelaus was ruling there in place of his

father Herod the Great and it was revealed in a dream to go to the region of Galilee. They came to live in a city called Nazareth[17] so that what was spoken through the prophet might be fulfilled, "He will be called a Nazarene."[18]

Matthew 3:1–17

1 In those days John the Baptist came preaching in the wilderness of Judea, saying, "Repent, for the kin-dom of heaven[19] is at hand." He was spoken of by the prophet Isaiah, saying, *"1 Comfort, yes comfort My people!" says your God. "Speak tenderly to the heart of Jerusalem. Cry out to her that her warfare is ended and penalty is paid for she has received from Me double for all her sins." The voice of one cries out in the wilderness, "Prepare the way of our God; make directly in the desert a highway for our God."*[20] John's garment was woven from camel's hair and he wore a leather girdle around his waist. His food was locusts and wild honey.[21] The people from Jerusalem, all over Judea, and the region around the Jordan River went out to him. Those who confessed their sins were baptized by him in the water of the Jordan River.

7 When he saw many Pharisees and Sadducees[22] coming to be baptized, he said, "Oh generation of scorpions![23] Who warned you to flee from the wrath to come? Bring forth fruits which are worthy of repentance and don't even think to say within yourselves, 'We have Abraham as our ancestor!' For I say to you that God is able to raise up children to Abraham from these stones. Even now the ax is already placed at the root of some trees. So every tree which does not bear good fruit will be cut down and cast into the fire.

11 I am baptizing you in water to show a change of heart but there comes one after me who is superior to me and I am not worthy to carry his sandals. He will baptize you with the Holy Spirit and with fire.[24] He will thoroughly purge his threshing floor with his pitchfork, gather his wheat into the granary, and burn up the chaff with an unquenchable fire." Jesus came from Galilee to be baptized by John in the Jordan River. John tried to prevent this, saying, "I need to be baptized of thee and yet you come to me!" Jesus answered, **"Permit it to be so now, it is good to be replete with as many merits as possible."**[25] Then he consented. When Jesus was baptized, he went straightway out of the water and he saw the Spirit

of God descending like a dove and alighting upon him.26 A voice spoke from heaven, *"This is My beloved Son, in whom I am well pleased."*27

Matthew 4:1–25

1 Then Jesus was carried away by the Holy Spirit into the wilderness to be tried out by the devil.28 He fasted for forty days and forty nights but now he was very hungry. The tempter drew near Jesus, saying, "If you are the Son of God,29 command that these stones be made into bread!" He answered, **"It is written, *'People shall not live by bread alone but are nourished by every word that proceeds from the mouth of God'"*30** Then the devil took him up into the holy city of Jerusalem, set him on the pinnacle of the Temple, and said, "If you are the Son of God, throw yourself down, for it is written *'11 God will give angels over you to keep you in all your ways! They will bear you up in their hands so you will not strike your foot against a stone.'"*31 Jesus replied, **"It is written again, *'Do not involve the Eternal your God in a foolish test!'*32"** Then the devil took him up on a very high mountain and showed him all the empires of the world with their glory and he said, "I will give thee all these, if only you will fall down and worship me." Then Jesus said, **"Get away from me Satan! For it is written, *'You shall worship the Eternal your God and God only you shall serve.'*33"** Then the devil left him alone and angels came and cared for him.34

12 Now when Jesus heard that John had been imprisoned, he left Judea to return to Galilee. Leaving Nazareth, he came to settle in Capernaum by the sea in the territory of Zebulun and Naphtali. So that what was spoken by the prophet Isaiah might be fulfilled, *"1 There will be no gloom for those who were in anguish. In the former time God brought contempt and judgment into the land of Zebulun and the land of Naphtali. In the latter time he will make glorious the way of the sea, the land beyond the Jordan, and the Galilee of the Gentiles. The people who walked in darkness have seen a great light. This light will shine on those who dwelt in the land of the shadow of death."*35

17 From that time on Jesus began to preach, saying, **"Repent, for the kin-dom of heaven is at hand!"** While he was walking by the Sea of Galilee, he saw two brothers: Simon who was called Peter and Andrew. They were fishing people who were casting their nets by the sea. Jesus

told them, **"Follow me and I will have you fish for people."** So they immediately left their nets and followed him. When he departed, he saw two other brothers, James the son of Zebedee and his brother John, in a boat with their father Zebedee, who were repairing their nets when he called them. They immediately left the boat and their father to follow him. He traveled throughout Galilee, teaching in the synagogues, preaching the Good News of the kin-dom of God, and healing every disease and disability among the people. His fame spread throughout Syria and they brought him all the sick, those afflicted with various diseases and pains, the insane, epileptics, and the paralyzed. He cured them all and great crowds from Galilee, Decapolis, Jerusalem, Judea, and beyond the Jordan River followed him.

Matthew 5:1–48

1 When Jesus saw the multitudes, he went up to the mountain where he sat down and his disciples came near to him. He broke the silence and began to teach them, saying: **"Blessed are the poor in pride,[36] for theirs is the kin-dom of heaven. Blessed are those who mourn, for they shall be comforted. Blessed are the meek, for they shall inherit the earth. Blessed are those who hunger and thirst for justice, for they shall be filled.[37] Blessed are the merciful, for they shall obtain mercy. Blessed are the pure in heart, for they shall see God. Blessed are the peacemakers, for they shall be called the children of God. Blessed are those who are persecuted for the sake of justice, for theirs is the kin-dom of heaven. Blessed are you when people abuse you, persecute you, and say all manner of evil against you for my sake. Rejoice and be exceedingly glad, for great is your reward in heaven, for in the same way they persecuted the prophets who came before you.[38]**

13 You are the salt of our land but if salt becomes foul, how can one salt things with it?[39] It is then good for nothing but to be thrown outside and trampled under people's feet? You are the light of the world. A city that is set on a hill cannot be hidden.[40] People light a candle, not to put it under a basket but to set it on a candlestick so it gives light to all who live in that house. Let your light shine before others so that they can see your good works grow and glorify your heavenly Divine Parent.[41]

17 Think not that I have come to weaken the Torah[42] or the prophets for I have not come to weaken but to fulfill them. For truly I say to you, until heaven and earth pass away, neither a iota[43] nor a particle of it will pass from the law until all is accomplished. Whoever tries to weaken one of the least of these commandments and teaches others to do the same, they will be called least in the kin-dom of heaven. Whoever observes the law and teaches others to do the same will be called great in the kin-dom of heaven. For I say to you, that unless your righteousness exceeds that of the scribes[44] of the Pharisees, you will not enter the kin-dom of heaven.

21 You have heard that it was said to those in ancient times, *'Thou shall not murder'*[45] and whoever murders will be liable to judgment but I say to you, that whoever becomes angry with their brother without cause, will be liable to judgment. Whoever says to their brother, 'Raca!'[46] will be liable before the court and whoever says to their brother, 'You are a fool!' will be in danger of a living hell. Therefore when you are presenting your offering at the altar and there you remember that your sister has any animosity against you: leave your gift there before the altar. First go and be reconciled to your sister, then come back and present your offering.

25 Be reconciled with your opponent quickly before you come together with them about a legal decision or your adversary[47] might hand you over to the judge. The judge might commit you to the jailer and you will be thrown into prison. Truly I tell you,[48] you will not come out of there until you have paid the last penny.[49] You have heard that it was said by those of old, *'Thou shall not commit adultery.'*[50] but I tell you, that whoever looks on another person to lust after them has already committed adultery with them in their heart. If your right eye offends you, pluck it out and throw it away. [*Stop envying!*][51] It is better for you to lose one of your members than for your whole body to be thrown into a living hell. If your right hand offends you, cut it off and throw it away. [*Stop stealing!*][52] It is better for you to lose one of your members than for your whole body to go into a living hell.

31 It has been said that whoever divorces their spouse must give them their divorce papers[53] but I tell you that whoever divorces

their spouse, except for sexual immorality,[54] causes them to commit adultery and whoever marries a spouse who is separated but not divorced, commits adultery.[55]

33 Again, you have heard that it was said by those in ancient times, 'Thou shall perform your oaths to God but shall not swear falsely.'[56] But I tell you, never swear: neither by heaven, for it is God's throne; nor by the earth, for it is God's footstool:[57] nor by Jerusalem; for it is the city where God is great. Don't swear by your head because you cannot make one hair black or white but simply let your 'Yes be Yes,' or 'No be No,' for anything which adds to these is a deception.

38 You have heard that it was said, 'An eye for an eye and a tooth for a tooth.'[58] but I tell you not to resist injustice![59] Whoever will strike you on your right cheek, turn the other to them also.[60] If someone wishes to sue you in court to take away your shirt, let them have your coat too! Whoever compels you to carry a burden a mile: go with them for two miles. Give to everyone who begs from you and do not refuse anyone who wants to borrow from you.

43 You have heard that it was said, *'Thou shall love thy neighbor and hate your enemies who hate your God.'*[61] but I tell you to love your enemies, bless those who curse you, do good to those who hate you, and pray for those who carry you away by force and persecute you, so that you may be the children of your heavenly Divine Parent Who makes the sun to shine on the good and the evil and Who pours down rain on the just and the unjust. If you love only those who love you, what reward will you have? For even the tax collectors love those who love them. If you greet your brothers and sisters only, what have you done more than others? Do not even the Gentiles do the same thing. Therefore become perfect,[62] even as your heavenly Divine Parent is perfect.

Matthew 6:1–34

1 Take heed that you do not do your alms[63] to be seen in the presence of other people; otherwise you will have no reward from your heavenly Divine Parent. Therefore, when you give alms, do not blow a trumpet before you as the hypocrites do in the synagogues[64] and in the market

places[65] so that they may be glorified by people. Truly I tell you, they have already received their reward. When you give alms, don't let your left hand know what your right hand is doing.[66] So while your kind deed may be in secret, your Divine Parent Who sees in secret, will reward you openly.

5 When you pray, do not be as the hypocrites for they love to stand and pray in the synagogues and at the street corners that they may be seen of people. Truly I tell you, they already have their reward. So when you pray, enter into your closet[67] and when you have shut your door; pray to thy Divine Parent, Who is there in secret.[68] Then your Divine Parent Who sees in secret, will reward you openly. When you pray, do not use vain repetitions as the Gentiles[69] do for they think that they will be heard for their many words. Do not be like them for your Divine Parent knows what you have need of before you ask. Therefore pray in this way: Our heavenly Divine Parent,[70] hallowed be Thy name. Thy kin-dom come, Thy will be done, on earth as it is in heaven. Give us our bread day by day,[71] and forgive us our offenses as we forgive our offenders.[72] Leave us not in temptation but deliver us from injustice.[73]

14 If you forgive other people their offenses, your heavenly Divine Parent will also forgive you but if you do not forgive other people their offenses, neither will your Divine Parent forgive your offenses. When you fast, do not be like the hypocrites for they disfigure their faces so that they may appear to other people to be fasting. Truly I tell you, they have their reward. Comb your hair and wash your face when you fast so that your fasting will not be seen by others but your Divine Parent Who sees in secret will reward you openly.[74]

19 Do not lay up for yourselves treasures buried in the earth where moth or weevil consumes[75] and where thieves break through and steal. Lay up for yourself treasures in heaven where neither moth nor weevil consumes and where thieves do not break through and steal, for where your treasure is, there your heart will be also. The lamp of the body is the eye. If therefore your eye is generous, your whole body will be full of light but if your eye be grudging, your whole body will be full of darkness. If the light in you be darkness, how great is that darkness![76]

24 No one can serve two masters; for either you will hate the one and love the other, or else you will endure the one and despise the other. You cannot serve God and mammon.[77] Therefore I say to you, don't worry about your life, what you will eat or what you will drink, nor about what you will put on your body. Isn't life more than food and the body more than clothes? Observe the birds of the air: they neither sow nor do they reap and gather into barns and yet your heavenly Divine Parent feeds them. Are they of more value than you?

27 Which of you by worrying can add a single hour to your life span or add a foot to your height? Why do you worry about clothing? Consider how the lilies of the field grow; they do not work, become tired, or spin and yet I tell you that Solomon in all his glory was not clothed as beautifully as one of these. Now if God clothes in such fashion the grass, which is alive in the field today and will be cooked in the oven tomorrow, will not God be much more mindful of you, ye of little faith? Therefore do not worry, saying, 'What will we eat?' or 'What will we drink?' or 'What will we wear?'[78] for the worldly people[79] seek after all these things and your heavenly Divine Parent knows that you need them all. Seek first the kin-dom of heaven and its righteousness, then all these things will come to you. Therefore do not worry about tomorrow for tomorrow will worry about its own things. Sufficient for each day are the troubles found therein.

Matthew 7:1–29

1 Judge not, that you may not be judged. For with the same judgment you judge, you will be judged and with what measure you use to measure, it will be used to measured you. Why do you behold the speck of sawdust that is in your sister's[80] eye but do not feel the log that is in your own eye? How can you say to your sister, 'Let me pull out the speck from your eye!' when behold, a log is in your own eye? Oh hypocrites, first take out the log from your eye and then you will see clearly to remove the speck of sawdust from your sister's eye.[81]

6 Do not give what is holy to the dogs or cast your pearls[82] before swine,[83] least they trample them under their feet and turn again to maul you.[84] Ask and it will be given to you; seek and you will find;[85] knock and it will be opened to you. For everyone who asks, they will

receive; for everyone who seeks, they will find; and for everyone who knocks, the door will be opened to them. What parent is there among you who, when your child asks for bread, will you give them a stone? If your child asks for a fish, will you give them a snake? If you then, who are evil acting, know how to give good gifts to your children; how much more will your heavenly Divine Parent give good things to those who ask? Therefore in all things, do unto others as you would have them do unto you, for this is the meaning of the law and the prophets.[86]

13 Enter through the narrow gate for wide is the gate and easy is the way that leads to destruction and there are many who travel that way.[87] How narrow is the gate and how hard is the way which leads to life and few are those who find it.[88] Beware of false prophets who come to you in lamb's clothing but inwardly they are ravenous wolves. You will know them by their fruits. Do people gather grapes from thorn bushes or figs from thistles? Even so, every good tree produces good fruit but a bad tree produces bad fruit. A good tree cannot yield bad fruit, nor can a bad tree yield good fruit. Every tree which does not yield good fruit[89] is cut down and thrown into the fire. Therefore you will know them by the fruits they produce.

21 Not everyone who says to me, 'My Saviour, My Saviour,'[90] will enter into the kin-dom of heaven but you who do the will of my heavenly Divine Parent. Many will say to me on their last day, 'My Saviour, my Saviour, did we not prophesy[91] in your name, cast out devils in your name, and accomplished many mighty works in your name?' Then I will declare: 'I never knew you, depart from me, ye who work iniquity!'

24 Therefore whoever hears these sayings of mine and does them, they are like a wise person who built their house on rock. The rains descended, the floods came, the winds blew and beat on that house, but it did not fall because its foundations were built with rock. Whoever hears these sayings of mine but doesn't act on them are like the foolish person who built their house on sand. When the rains descended, the floods came, the winds blew and beat on that house so that it fell and great was the fall of it!" When Jesus had finished these

sayings the people were astonished at his teaching, for he taught them as one having authority and not as their own scribes.

Matthew 8:1–34

1 Great multitudes followed when he came down the mountain. Behold, a leper[92] came, knelt before him, and said, "My Saviour! You can make me clean if you are willing!" Jesus put out his hand and touched him, saying, **"I am willing; be cleansed!"** Immediately his leprosy was cleansed. He then asked him, **"See that you tell no one but go and show yourself to the priests and present an offering as Moses has commanded for a testimonial to them."**

5 When Jesus entered Capernaum, a centurion[93] approached him and appealed to him, saying, "Sir, my boy is lying at home paralyzed in dreadful pain." Jesus told him, **"I will come and heal him."** The centurion answered and said, "Sir [*Saviour*], I am not worthy for you to come under the shadow of my roof but only speak a word and my son will be healed. I am also a man in authority and soldiers are under my command. When I order this one, 'Go!' then he goes; then I order another, 'Come!' then he comes; or I tell my servant, 'Do this!' then he does it."

10 When Jesus heard it, he marveled and said to those who followed, **"Truly I tell you, that not even in Israel have I found such great faith in me as this! Many will come from the east and the west to sit down with Abraham, Isaac and Jacob[94] in the kin-dom of heaven but many heirs of those in the kin-dom will be cast out into the darkness of the dungeon[95] where there will be weeping and gnashing of teeth."[96]** Then Jesus said to the soldier, **"Go thy way! Let it be done to you according to your belief."** Immediately his boy was healed.

14 When Jesus entered Simon Peter's home, he saw his mother-in-law lying in bed sick with a fever. He touched her hand, the fever left, she got up, and began to serve them. That evening they brought him many who were possessed with demons[97] and he cured them just by a word. He healed all who were badly afflicted, so that what was spoken by the prophet Isaiah might be fulfilled, saying, "*4 It was our grief that he bore and our sorrows that weighted him down. We considered him stricken, afflicted, and struck down by God for his own sins. He was stricken that we*

might be healed, afflicted that we might have peace, and struck down for our transgressions; the punishment that made us whole.[98] Jesus saw the crowds about him and told his disciples to depart for the other shore. A certain scribe came and said, "Oh my Teacher, I will follow you wherever you go." Jesus said, **"Foxes have holes and birds of the air have nests but the Son of humanity**[99] **has nowhere to lay his head."** Then another disciple said, "My Saviour, let me first go and bury my father."[100] but Jesus said, **"Follow me and let the town bury their own dead."**[101]

23 His disciples followed him when he got in the boat. When Jesus was asleep, a great storm arose on the sea so that the boat was covered with waves. They came near and awoke him saying, "Our Saviour, save us, we are perishing!" Jesus said to them; **"Why are you so fearful? Oh ye of little faith!"** Then he arose, rebuked the winds and the sea so there was a great calm. They marveled saying, "What kind of person is this, that even the winds and the sea obey him?"

28 When they came to the port on the other side in the country of the Gerasenes, he met two men possessed by demons who came out of the tombs. They were exceedingly vicious so that no one could travel that way. They cried out, saying, "What do you want with us, Jesus, Son of God? Have you come to bind us before our time?" Now in the distance was a large herd of swine who were feeding. The demons said, "If you would heal the men, let us attack the herd of swine." Jesus said to them, **"Go!"** Immediately they left, attacked the swine and the whole herd rushed down the steep bank into the sea[102] and were overwhelmed by the waves.[103] The swineherds ran away, went to the city, and reported everything that happened when they told about the men who were possessed by demons. Behold, the entire city came out to meet Jesus and when they saw him they urged him to leave their neighborhood.

Matthew 9:1–38

1 He crossed over in a boat and came to his own town. There they brought him a paralyzed man lying on a quilt[104] and when Jesus saw their faith, he said, **"Take heart, my son, thy sins are forgiven thee."** Then behold, some of the scribes said to themselves, "This man blasphemes!" Jesus knew their thoughts, saying, **"Why do you think evil in your hearts? For which is easier to say, 'Thy sins are forgiven thee!' or to say, 'Arise and**

walk?' So that you may know that the Son of humanity has authority on earth to forgive sins," he said to the paralytic one, "Arise, take up your quilt and go to your home." He arose and went home. When the crowds saw it they were filled with awe and they glorified God Who had given such power to people.

9 As Jesus was walking along, he saw a man named Matthew sitting at the tax office, and said, "Follow me!" So Matthew got up to follow him. While they were guests in the house, many tax collectors[105] and sinners[106] came and reclined at the dinner table with Jesus and his disciples. When some Pharisees saw it, they said to his disciples, "Why does your teacher eat with tax collectors and sinners?" When Jesus heard that, he said, "Those who are seriously sick need a physician but not those who are healthy. Go and learn what this means, 'I desire mercy and not sacrifice.'[107] For I have come to call sinners to repentance, not the righteous."

14 Some disciples of John the Baptist said, "Why do we and the Pharisees fast often but your disciples do not fast?" Jesus answered, "Can the guests at the wedding fast as long as the bridegroom is with them? The days will come when the bridegroom will be taken from them and then they will fast. No one puts a piece of new cloth on an old garment or else the patch tears away from the garment and a worse tear is made. People do not pour new wine into old wineskins[108] or else the wineskin bursts, the wine runs out, and the wineskin is ruined. They pour new wine into new wineskins and both are well preserved."[109]

18 While he spoke, a leader in a local synagogue came and knelt before him. When he finished, this man said, "My daughter has just died but if you come and lay a hand on her, she will live!" Jesus and his disciples rose to follow him. Then suddenly a woman, who had suffered from hemorrhages for twelve years, came up behind him and touched the hem of his garment. She said within herself, "If I may only touch his garment, I will be healed!" Jesus turned and saw her, "Have courage, my daughter, thy faith has made thee whole." Immediately the woman was made whole. Jesus arrived at the house of the synagogue leader and saw the flute players who accompanied the wailing professional mourners and the noisy crowd. He said to them, "That is enough for the girl is

not dead but sleeping." They laughed at him, but when he put the noisy crowd outside, he went in, he held her by the hand, and the little girl got up. The news of this miracle spread all over that district.

27 When Jesus departed from there, two blind people followed him, crying out, "Have mercy on us, Oh son of David!" When he had entered a house, the blind men came up to him and Jesus said, **"Do you believe that I am able to do this?"** They said, "Yes Saviour!" Then he touched their eyes, saying, **"According to your faith, be it done to you."** When their eyes were opened he told them, **"See that no one knows it."** They left but spread the news all over that part of the country. As Jesus went out they brought him a man who was mute because of a demon and when the demon was cast out the man spoke and the crowds were amazed, saying, "Nothing like this has ever been seen in Israel!" Then some Pharisees charged, "He casts out demons with the help of the ruler of demons!"

35 Jesus traveled in all the cities and villages, teaching in their synagogues, preaching the Good News of the kin-dom, and healing every kind of disease and disability among the people. When he saw the multitudes he was moved with compassion because they were listless and adrift, like sheep without a shepherd. Then he said to his disciples, **"The harvest truly is plentiful but the laborers are few. Pray therefore that the One in charge of the harvest sends out more laborers into the harvest."**

Matthew 10:1–42

1 Then he called his twelve disciples to him and gave them power over unclean spirits, to cast them out and to heal every kind of disease and sickness. These are the names of the twelve apostles: first, Simon whose name is Peter and his brother Andrew; James the son of Zebedee and his brother John; Philip and Bartholomew; Thomas and Matthew the tax collector; James the son of Alphaeus; Lebbaeus whose surname is Thaddaeus; Simon the Cananaean;[110] and Judas Iscariot, the one who betrayed him. Jesus sent these twelve out, commanding them: **"Keep away from the way of the Gentiles,[111] and do not enter into any city of the Samaritans but go rather to the lost sheep of the house of Israel.[112] As you go, preach and say, 'The kin-dom of heaven is at hand!' Heal the sick, cleanse the leapers, raise the dead, cast out devils, and give as freely as you have received.[113] Do not accumulate**

gold, silver, copper, or brass in your belts. Carry neither a purse for your journey nor two shirts and sandals, nor a staff, for the laborer is worthy of their food.[114]

11 When you enter a city or town, inquire who is trustworthy, and stay there until you leave. When you enter into a house, salute the family![115] If the family is trustworthy, let your peace come upon them but let your peace return to you if they do not welcome you. For those who will not welcome you and will not listen to your words, shake off the dust[116] from your feet[117] when you depart out of that house or village. Truly I tell you, it will be more tolerable in the cities of Sodom and Gomorrah in their day of judgment than for that house. Behold! I am sending you out like lambs in the midst of wolves, therefore be wise as serpents and innocent as doves.[118] Beware of men, for they will deliver you up to their councils and whip you in their prisons. They will bring you before governors and other rulers[119] for my sake, as a testimony to them and to the Gentiles. When they deliver you up, do not worry how or what ye will speak, for it will be given to you in that very hour what you are to speak. It is not you who will be speaking but the Holy Spirit of your Sacred Father[120] Who speaks through you.

21 Now the brother will deliver up his own brother to death and the father his son. Children will rise up against their parents and put them to death. Many will hate you because of my name but those who hope to the end will be saved.[121] When they persecute you in one city, flee to another, for truly I tell you that you will not have gone through the cities of Israel before this Son of humanity returns. No disciple is more important than their teacher and no servant is more important than their employer. It is enough for the disciple to be like their teacher and the servant be like their employer. If then, they have called the head of the house, Beelzebul,[122] how much more will they malign those of his household?

26 Therefore do not fear them for whatever is concealed will be revealed and every secret will be made known.[123] What I tell you in the darkness, tell it in the daylight; what you hear whispered in your ear, preach it from the housetops. Do not fear those who can kill

the body but cannot kill the soul. Rather, fear one[124] who is able to destroy both body and soul in a living hell.[125] Are not two sparrows sold for a penny? Yet, not one of them will fall to the ground outside your Divine Parent's will. So far as you are concerned, every hair on your head is accounted for. Therefore, fear not for you are much more important than many sparrows.

32 Everyone who will acknowledge me before people, I will acknowledge them before my heavenly Divine Parent, but whoever will deny me before people, I will also deny them before my heavenly Divine Parent. Do you think that I have come to bring peace on earth? I have not came to bring peace but a sword.[126] I have come to '*set a son against his father, a daughter against her mother, a daughter-in-law against her mother-in-law, and a person's foes will be members of their own household.*'[127] Whoever loves your mother or father more than me is not worthy of me, whoever loves your son or daughter more than me is not worthy of me, and whoever will not take up their cross[128] and follow me is not worthy of me.[129] You who are concerned about your life will lose it and you who lose your life for my sake will find it.

40 Whoever welcomes you welcomes me and whoever welcomes me welcomes God Who sent me. Whoever welcomes a prophet in the name of a prophet will receive a prophet's reward and whoever welcomes a righteous person in the name of a righteous person will receive the reward of the righteous. Whoever gives a drink to one of these little ones,[130] even if only a cup of cold water in the name of a disciple; truly I tell you, that person will not lose their reward."

Matthew 11:1–30

1 When Jesus finished instructing his disciples he departed from that place to teach and to preach in their cities. When John the Baptist heard in prison of the works of Christ, he sent word by his disciples, who asked him, "Are you the one who is coming or do we look for another?" Jesus answered, **"Go and describe to John the things which you hear and see; the blind see, the lame walk, the leapers are cleansed, the deaf hear, the dead are raised up, and the poor are given hope.[131] Blessed are ye who have no trouble accepting me."**

7 As they departed, Jesus spoke to the multitudes concerning John: **"What did you go out into the wilderness to see? One frenzied by a spirit?**[132] **If not, what did you go out to see? Someone dressed in fancy clothes? Behold! Those who wear expensive clothes live in palaces.**[133] **Why then what did you go out? To see a prophet? Truly, I tell you, much more than a prophet for this is the one of whom it is written,** *'Behold! I send My messenger before your face to prepare the way before you.'*[134] **Truly I tell you, that among those who are born of a woman, there has never risen one greater than John the Baptist but one who is least in the kin-dom of heaven is greater than he.**[135] **From the days of John the Baptist until now, the Torah has suffered violation and the violators take it by force.**[136] **For all the prophets and the law prophesied until John and if you are willing to accept this idea, he is Elijah who is to come.**[137] **Whoever has ears to hear, will understand!**[138]

16 To what will I compare this generation? It is like children sitting in the marketplace and calling to their friends, saying, 'We played the flute for you but you would not dance; we have wailed to you but you would not mourn.' For John came neither eating nor drinking and they say, 'He is crazy!' The Son of humanity came eating and drinking and they say, 'Behold, a glutton and an alcoholic, a friend of tax collectors and sinners.'[139] **Wisdom is known by Her children"**[140]

20 Then Jesus began to reproach the cities where he showed many mighty works because they did not repent. He said, **"Woe to you, Chorazin! Woe to you, Bethsaida! For if the works which were done in you had been done in Tyre and Sidon, they would have repented long ago in sackcloth and ashes, but I tell you that it will be more tolerable for Tyre and Sidon in their day of judgment than for you. As for you, Capernaum, will you be exalted to heaven? No, you will be brought down to a living hell for if the works which were done in you had been done in Sodom, it would be standing to this day. I tell you that it was more tolerable for the city of Sodom in their day of judgment than it will be for you."**

25 Then Jesus declared, **"I thank Thee, Oh my Divine Parent, Ruler of heaven and earth because You have revealed these things to young**

children, while You hide the truth from the wise and the prudent.[141] **Oh yes, my Divine Parent, for this choice is your great pleasure. All things have been delivered to me by my Divine Parent and no one knows the Son except the Divine Parent. No one knows the Divine Parent but the Son and those to whom the Son wishes to reveal the Divine Parent.**[142] **Come to me, all you who labor and carry burdens for I will give you rest.**[143] **Take my yoke upon you and learn from me for I am meek**[144] **and humble**[145] **in my heart. You will find rest for your souls for my yoke is easy**[146] **and my burden is light."**[147]

Matthew 12:1–50

1 Then Jesus walked through the grain fields on the Sabbath,[148] and his disciples became hungry so they began to pluck heads of the grain to eat them. When some Pharisees saw it, they said, "Behold! Your disciples are doing what is unlawful to do on the Sabbath." Jesus taught them, **"Have ye not read what David did when he and those who were with him were hungry? How he entered the house of God and ate the bread of the Presence,**[149] **which was not lawful for him or his companions to eat but only for the priests and their families.**[150] **Or have you not read in the Torah that the priests in the Temple disregard the Sabbath and yet are blameless?**[151] **I tell you that someone greater than the Temple is here and if you had only known what this means,** *'I desire mercy, not sacrifice and the knowledge of God rather than burnt offerings!'*[152] **you would not have condemned the innocent. The Son of humanity is ruler even of the Sabbath."**

9 He left the field and entered their synagogue where there was a man whose hand was withered so that he could not work with it anymore. They questioned him so that they might accuse him, saying, "Is it lawful to heal on the Sabbath?" He answered, **"If one of you has only one sheep who falls into a pit on the Sabbath, will you lay hold of it and lift it out? How much more important is a person than a sheep? Therefore it is lawful to do good on the Sabbath."** Then he said to the man with the withered hand, **"Stretch out your hand!"** When he stretched out his hand, it was restored whole like the other. Then those Pharisees went out and conspired against him, how they might destroy him. When Jesus knew of this, he withdrew from there, and great multitudes followed so Jesus healed them all.

---

16 He charged them not to tell others about him, so that what was said by the prophet Isaiah might be fulfilled: *"1 Behold, My servant, whom I uphold! My chosen in whom My Soul delights. I have put My Spirit[153] upon him; he will bring forth justice to all peoples. He will not quarrel or cry out; nor will anyone hear his voice in the streets. He will not break a bruised reed nor quench a smoldering wick; he will faithfully bring forth justice.[154] He will not fail nor be discouraged until he has set justice in the earth: in his name will the Gentiles hope."[155]*

22 Then they brought to him one possessed who was blind and mute. He healed him so that this blind and mute man could see and speak. All the people were amazed, saying, "Can this be the Son of David?" Now when some Pharisees heard of it, they said, "This fellow casts out demons only by Beelzebul, the prince of devils." Jesus knew their thoughts and taught, **"Every nation divided against itself is brought to ruin and no city or house divided against itself will survive. If Satan casts out Satan then he is divided against himself. How then will his domain endure? If I cast out devils through Beelzebul, then by whom do your exorcists cast them out? Therefore they will be your judges but if I cast out devils by the Spirit of God, then the kin-dom of God has come to you. How else can one enter into a strong person's house and plunder their valued goods? They first bind that strong person and then they will plunder their house. Whoever is not with me is against me and whoever does not gather with me will scatter.[156]**

31 Therefore I tell you, that all sin[157] and blasphemy[158] will be forgiven to people but the blasphemy against the Holy Spirit will not be forgiven to people.[159] Whoever speaks a word against the Son of humanity will be forgiven; but whoever blasphemes against the Holy Spirit will not be forgiven in this world or your world to come.[160] Either produce like a good tree with good fruits or produce like a bad tree with bad fruits for a tree is known by its fruits. Oh generation of scorpions,[161] how can you speak of good things out of your evil filled heart? The mouth speaks from the fullness of the heart, for the good acting person brings forth good things from good treasures in their heart, while the evil acting person brings forth evil things from their evil treasures. I tell you that for any idle word[162] that people speak, they will have to answer for it on their day of judgment;[163]

for by your own words you will be justified or by your own words you will be found guilty!"

38 Then some of the scribes of the Pharisees[164] demanded, "Teacher, we would like to see a sign from you!" Jesus answered them, **"The evil and adulterous acting people in this generation seek for a sign[165] and no sign will be given to them, except the sign of the prophet Jonah. For as Jonah was in the belly of a large fish for three days and three nights, so the Son of humanity will be in the heart of the earth three days and three nights.[166] The men of Nineveh will rise up in the judgment with this generation and condemn them because they repented through the preaching of Jonah and behold, a greater than Jonah is here. The Queen of the South[167] will rise up in the judgment with this generation and condemn them for she came from the far ends of the earth to hear the wisdom of Solomon and behold, a greater than Solomon is here.**

43 **When an unclean spirit[168] goes out of a person, it roams around the ruins[169] seeking rest while finding none. Then it says, 'I will return to the same abode where I came from.' So the demon returns to find it the person vacant, warm, and desirable.[170] Then it goes away and brings with it seven other spirits more evil than itself. They enter in to dwell there and the last state of this person becomes worse than the first. Even so, that is the way it will be for the evil acting** [*or the addicted*][171] **people in every generation."**

46 While Jesus was teaching the people, his mother and his brothers came, and stood outside wanting to speak with him. Someone told him, "Behold, your mother and your brothers are standing outside asking to speak to you!" He answered, **"Who is my mother and who are my brothers?"** He pointed his hand toward his disciples and said, **"Behold, here is my mother and my brothers for whoever does the will of my heavenly Divine Parent is my brother and sister and mother** [*and father*]**."[172]**

Matthew 13:1–58

1 That same day Jesus went out of the house and sat by the sea. Great multitudes gathered around him so that he had to go and sit in a boat

while all the people stood on the shore. Jesus spoke of many things to the multitudes in parables,173 saying, **"Behold, a sower went out to sow and when he sowed, some seed fell on the pathway where the birds came and devoured them. Other seed fell on rocky ground where there was little soil and they quickly withered away because the ground was not deep enough for when the sun shone they were scorched because they had no root. Other seed fell among thorns and the thorns sprang up and choked them. Other seeds fell on good soil and yielded fruit, some a hundred fold, some sixty fold, and some thirty fold. Whoever has ears to hear, will understand."174**

10 His disciples drew near to him and asked, "Why do you speak to them in parables?" Jesus answered, **"Because to you it is given to know the mysteries of the kin-dom of heaven but to them it is not granted. For those who have, more will be given and they will have an abundance but for those who do not have, even that which they have will be taken away from them.175 Therefore I speak to them in parables because they see but do not perceive and they hear but they neither listen nor do they understand.**

14 In them is fulfilled the prophecy of Isaiah, which says: '8 *Also, I heard the voice of God, saying, "'Whom will I send and Who will go for Us."176 Then I said, "Here I am; send me!" God said to me, "'Go and tell this people, ""You listen carefully but you will not understand; you look intently but you will not perceive."'" For the heart of this people is hardened, their ears are closed, and their eyes are shut; so that they may not look with their eyes, listen with their ears, understand with their heart, turn to Me, and be healed.'"* 177 Blessed are your eyes for they see and your ears for they hear. For truly I tell you that many prophets and righteous people have desired to see what you see but did not see it and hear what you hear but did not hear it.

18 Therefore hear the parable of the sower. Whoever hears the words of the kin-dom and does not understand it, Satan comes and snatches away the word that has been sown in their heart. This is the seed which was sown on the pathway. That which was sown upon rocky ground is whoever hears the word and immediately welcomes it with joy. Yet, they have no root in themselves and hope only for a while. They quickly fall

away when trial and suffering arises because of the word. That which was sown among the thorns is whoever hears the word but the cares of this world and the deceitfulness of riches choke the word and it yields no fruit. That which is sown upon good soil is whoever listens to the word and understands it so they bear fruit and yield in one case a hundred fold, in another sixty fold, and in another thirty fold."

24 Jesus told them another parable: "The kin-dom of heaven is like a person who sowed good seed in their field. Then while everyone slept, an enemy came, sowed tares among the wheat, and went away. When the plants grew and bore fruit, then the tares also appeared. So the servants of the household came and said to him, 'Sir, where are the tares from if you sowed good seed in your field?' He answered them, 'An enemy has done this.' The servants asked, 'Do you want us to go and pull them up now?' The owner replied, 'No, then you might uproot the wheat while you gather up the tares! Let both grow together until the harvest and at the time of the harvest I will say to the reapers, "First gather the tares and bind them into bundles to be burned. Then gather the wheat into my barns."'"

31 Jesus told them another parable: "The kin-dom of heaven is like a grain of mustard seed,[178] which a man took and sowed in his field. It is one of the smallest of all seeds but when it is grown, it is larger than all the herbs and it becomes a bush, so that the birds of the air come and nest in its branches." He told them another parable: "The kin-dom of heaven is like the yeast which a woman took and inserted in three measures of flour[179] until the whole dough was leavened." Jesus spoke all these things to the people in parables and said nothing to them without parables. This was to fulfill what was spoken by the prophet: *"1 Give ear, Oh my people, to my teaching; incline your ears to the words of my mouth. I will open my mouth in parables; I will utter proverbs of old which we have heard and known, that our ancestors have told us. We will not hide them from their children; telling to the coming generation: the praises of God, the strength of God, and the wonderful works that God has done."*[180]

36 Then he left the multitudes and went into the house. His disciples approached him saying, "Explain to us the parable of the tares in the field." He answered, **"The one who sows the good seed is the Son of**

humanity, the field is the world, the good seeds are the children of the kin-dom, but the tares are the children of the evil one. The enemy who sowed them is the devil, the harvest is the end of your world,[181] and the reapers are the angels. Therefore as the tares are picked out and burned in the fire, so will it be at the end of your world. The Son of humanity will send forth angels and they will pick out of the kin-dom all those who cause others to stumble and those who work iniquity. They will be thrown into the furnace or fire and there will be wailing and gnashing of teeth![182] Then the righteous will shine forth as the sun in the kin-dom of their Divine Parent. Whoever has ears to hear, will understand!

44 The kin-dom of heaven is like treasure hidden in a field which a man discovered and hid again. Then in his excitement he went and sold all that he had and bought the field. Again, the kin-dom of heaven is like a merchant seeking fine pearls, who, when he[183] had found one pearl of great value,[184] he went and sold everything he had to buy it. Again, the kin-dom of heaven is like a net that was cast into the sea and caught fish of every kind. When it was full, the people hauled the net to the shore, sat down, sorted the edible fish into bags, and threw the others back into the sea.[185] So will it be at the end of your world. The angels will come forth to separate those who work iniquity from the righteous and throw them into a furnace of fire where there will be wailing and gnashing of teeth." Jesus said, "Have you understood all these things?" They replied, "Yes!" He said to them, "Therefore every scribe[186] who is converted to the kin-dom of heaven is like the householder who brings things out from their treasures what is new and what is old."

53 Jesus finished these parables and moved on from there. When he came to his hometown of Nazareth, he taught them in their synagogue so that they were astonished, saying, "Where is the source of all this wisdom and all these miracles? Isn't this the builder's son?" "Isn't his mother called Mary?" "Aren't his brothers James, Joseph, Simon, and Judas?" "Aren't all his sisters here with us?" "Where then did he get all this?" They made light of him but Jesus taught them, "A prophet is not without honor except in their own country and in their own home." Now he performed few miracles there because they didn't believe in him.

Matthew 14:1–36

1 Then Herod the tetrarch[187] heard the news about Jesus and said to his servants, "This is John the Baptist; he has risen from the dead, and this is why great miracles are wrought by him." For Herod Antipas had arrested John, bound him, and put him in prison because of Herodias, his brother Philip's wife. John had been telling him, "It is not lawful for you to have her as your wife."[188] So Herod wanted to kill him but he was afraid of the people who accepted him as a prophet.

6 When Herod's birthday came, the daughter of Herodias[189] danced before the guests and she pleased Herod. He therefore swore to her with oaths that he would give her anything that she would ask. Prompted by her mother, she asked, "Give me the head of John the Baptist here on a silver platter!" Herod was grieved but because of his oath before his guests, he commanded that it be given to her. So he had John beheaded in prison, his head was brought in on a silver platter, it was given to her, and she brought it to her mother. His disciples came, took the body, and buried it. Then they came and informed Jesus.

13 When Jesus heard this, he left by boat to a deserted place to be alone. The crowds heard of it and followed him on foot from the towns. When Jesus went out, he saw a great multitude, he was moved to compassion for them, and healed their sick. When it was evening his disciples came to him, saying, "This is a deserted place and the hour is already late. Send the people away so they may go into the villages and buy food for themselves." Jesus said, **"They don't need to go away. You give them something to eat!"** They said, "We only have five loaves of bread and two fish."[190] He told them, **"Bring them here to me!"** He asked the people to sit down on the grass, took the five loaves and two fish, looked up to heaven, blessed them, broke them, gave them to his disciples, and the disciples placed them before the people. They all ate and were satisfied. They filled up twelve baskets when they took up the morsels of bread[191] which were left over and those who had eaten were more than five thousand men, women, and children!

22 Immediately he urged his disciples to get into a boat and cross to the other side before him while he dismissed the people. He took leave of the crowds and he went up the mountain by himself to pray so he was there

alone when evening came. The boat was many miles from the land and tossed by the waves for the wind was blowing against it. In the fourth watch of the night[192] Jesus came to them walking on the sea. When the disciples saw someone walking on the sea, they were frightened, saying, "It's a spirit!" and they cried out in fear! Immediately he spoke to them, **"Be of good cheer! I AM,[193] do not be afraid."** Peter answered, "Saviour, if it is you, command me to come to you on the water." Jesus said, **"Come!"** So Peter went down out of the boat and he walked on the water to go to him. When he felt a strong wind, he was afraid and began to sink, saying, "Jesus, save me!"[194] Immediately he stretched out his hand and caught Peter, saying, **"Oh ye of little faith, why did you doubt?"** The wind ceased when they got in the boat. The people in the boat knelt down before him, saying, "Truly you are the Son of God."

34 When the disciples rowed over to the land at Gennesaret, the people there recognized him, sent word to all the villages around them, and brought to him all who were seriously sick. They begged him that they might touch only the hem of his robe and those who touched it were completely healed.

Matthew 15:1–39

1 Then the scribes of the Pharisees from Jerusalem came to Jesus, saying, "Why do your disciples disregard the tradition of the elders[195] for they do not wash their hands when they eat?" Jesus answered, **"Why do you also disregard the commandment of God because of your tradition? God said, *'Honor your father and your mother that your days may be long upon the land which your God gives you[196] and whoever curses your father or your mother may be put to death.'[197]* Then you say, 'Whoever says to their father or mother, '"Whatever support you might have received from me is an offering to God;"'[198] and they do not need to honor their mother or father.' Thus by your tradition, you have made the word of God to have no effect. Oh ye hypocrites! Isaiah was right to prophesy concerning you, saying, *'These people draw near to Me with their mouths, honor Me with their lips, but have removed their hearts far from Me. They worship Me in vain by teaching the precepts and doctrines of people.'[199]"***

10 Then he called the multitudes and taught them, **"Listen and understand! It is not what enters into the mouth that defiles a person**

but what comes out of the mouth that defiles a person." His disciples told him, "Those Pharisees were offended when they heard this saying." He answered, **"Every plant200 that my heavenly Divine Parent did not plant will be uprooted. Leave them alone: they are blind guides of the blind and if the blind lead the blind, both will fall into the ditch."** Simon Peter asked him, "Explain this parable to us." He replied, **"Are you also still without understanding? Don't you know that whatever enters into the mouth goes into the stomach and then is eliminated through the intestines but what comes out of the mouth comes from the heart and this defiles a person. For from the heart come evil thoughts, murder, adultery, sexual immorality,201 thefts, false witness, and slander. These are what defile a person but eating with unwashed hands does not defile a person."**

21 Jesus departed to the region of Tyre and Sidon, and behold a Canaanite woman came from that region and cried out to him, saying, "Sir, Oh Son of David! My daughter is severely tormented by a demon." He said nothing but his disciples said, "Send her away for she cries after us." He replied, **"I am sent only to the lost sheep of the house of Israel."** She came and knelt before him, saying, "Saviour, help me!" Jesus answered, **"It's not right to take the children's bread and throw it to the dogs."**202 She replied, "Yes, Saviour; yet even the puppies eat the crumbs that fall from the table where the children eat." **"Oh woman, great is thy faith! Let it be unto thee as you desire."** Her daughter was healed instantly.

29 Jesus departed from there, walked along the shores of the Sea of Galilee, went up on a mountain, and sat down there. Many people came to him who brought the lame, the maimed, the blind, the mute with many others, and they laid them down at the feet of Jesus and he healed them. The crowds marveled when they observed the lame walking, the maimed healed, the blind seeing, the mute speaking, and they praised the God of Israel. Jesus called his disciples to him, saying, **"I have compassion on the multitude; they have remained with me for three days and have nothing to eat. I do not wish to dismiss them fasting for they might faint on the way."** His disciples asked, "Where can we get enough bread in this desolate place to feed all these people?" Jesus said, **"How many loaves of bread do you have?"** They replied, "Seven and a few small fish." Jesus told the people to sit down

on the ground. Then he took the seven loaves of bread and the fish, gave thanks, broke them up, and gave them to his disciples who gave them to the multitudes. All the people ate and were satisfied. They filled up seven baskets when they took up the morsels of bread which were left over and those who had eaten were more than four thousand women, men, and children. After taking leave of the multitude, he boarded the boat, and came to the region of Magadan.

Matthew 16:1–28

1 Then the Pharisees and Sadducees came to test him and they asked him to show them a sign from heaven. Jesus answered, **"When it is evening you say, 'It will be fair weather for the sky is red.' In the morning you say, 'It will be stormy today for the sky is red with low dark clouds.' Oh ye hypocrites! You know how to discern the face of the sky but you are not able to interpret the signs of the present time. The evil and adulterous acting people of this generation seek for a sign and the sign given to you is the sign of the prophet Jonah."** He left them and departed.

5 When his disciples reached the other shore, they had forgotten to bring any bread. Jesus said to them, **"Take heed and beware of the leaven of the Pharisees and the Sadducees!"** They reasoned among themselves, saying, "Is it because we forgot to bring bread?" Jesus perceived this and said, **"Oh ye of little faith, why do you reason among yourselves because you have not brought bread? Do you not yet understand? Don't you remember the five loaves of bread for the five thousand people and how many baskets you took up, or the seven loaves of bread for the four thousand people and how many baskets you took up? How is it you don't understand that I do not speak to you concerning bread but to beware of the leaven of the Pharisees and of the Sadducees!"** Then they understood that he did not say to beware the leaven of the bread but to beware of the teaching of the Pharisees and of the Sadducees.

13 When Jesus came into the country of Caesurae Philippi, he asked his disciples, saying, **"Who do people say that I, the Son of humanity, am?"**[203] They said, "Some say John the Baptist, some say Elijah, others say Jeremiah or one of the prophets." **"Who do you say that I am?"**

Simon Peter answered, "You are the Christ, the Son of the Living God."204 **"Blessed are you, Simon son of Jonah, for flesh and blood has not revealed this to you but my heavenly Divine Parent. I also say that you are Peter and on this stone205 I will build my [*spiritual*] church and the gates of a living hell will not prevail against it. I will give you the keys206 to the kin-dom of heaven and whatever you bind on earth will be bound in heaven, and whatever you release on earth will be released in heaven."** Then he sternly ordered his disciples to tell no one that he was the Christ.

21 From that time on, Jesus began make known to them that he must go to Jerusalem and suffer many things of the elders, the chief priests, and the scribes. He would be killed and be raised on the third day. So Peter protested to him and began to rebuke him, saying, "God forbid, Saviour! This will not happen to you!" Then he turned to Peter and said, **"Get away from me, Satan! You are a stumbling block to me for you savor not the things that be of God but those that be of men."207**

24 He said to his disciples, **"Whoever wishes to come with me must deny yourself, take up your cross,208 and follow me. For those who wish to save their life will loose it and those who lose their life for my sake, will find it. What will it benefit a person if they will gain the whole world but loose their own soul, or what will a person give in exchange for their soul?209 For the Son of humanity will come with his angels in the glory of his Divine Parent and then he will reward everyone according to what they have done.210 Truly I tell you, there are some standing here now who will not taste of death211 until they see the Son of humanity coming in his kin-dom."**

Matthew 17:1–27

1 Six days later Jesus took Peter, James, and his brother John up to a high mountain alone where he was transfigured212 before them, his face shone like the sun and his garments became a dazzling white. Behold, Moses and Elijah appeared to them as they were talking with him. Then Peter said to Jesus, "My Saviour, it is good that we are here and if you wish we will make three tents here; one for you, one for Moses, and one for Elijah. While he was speaking, a bright cloud rested upon them and a Voice came out of the cloud, saying, "You are My beloved Son in whom

my Soul delights! Listen to him!"213 When the disciples heard this, they fell to the ground overcome with fear. Jesus came near and touched them, saying, **"Arise. Do not be afraid."** When they looked up, only Jesus was with them. As they were going down from the mountain, Jesus instructed them, **"Do not speak of this vision in the presence of anyone until the Son of humanity has risen from the dead."**

10 His disciples asked, "Why then do the scribes say that Elijah must come first?" He replied, **"[*People say that,*]214 'Elijah will come first and restore all things.'215 but I tell you that Elijah has come already, they did not know him and they did to him whatever they pleased. Likewise the Son of humanity is also about to suffer at their hands."** Then the disciples understood that what he had told them was about John the Baptist.

14 When they came to the multitude, a man approached him, fell on his knees, and said, "My Saviour, have mercy on my son for he is an epileptic and has become worse; he often falls into the fire216 or into the water! I brought him to your disciples but they were not able to heal him!" Jesus answered, **"Oh faithless and corrupt people of this generation, how long will I be with you and how long will I preach to you? Bring him here to me."** He rebuked the demon out of him and the boy was healed instantly. Then the disciples came up to him privately and said, "Why couldn't we heal him?" He replied, **"Because of your unbelief, for truly I tell you, if you have faith even as a grain of mustard seed, you will say to this mountain, 'Move from here to there!' and it will move away and nothing will be impossible for you!"217** But this kind does not come out except by prayer and fasting.

22 While they were traveling through Galilee, Jesus said, **"The Son of humanity will be delivered into the hands of men, they will kill him, and he will be raised again on the third day."** His disciples were greatly distressed.

24 When they came to Capernaum, the collectors of the half-shekel Temple tax came to Peter, asking, "Does your Teacher pay the Temple tax?" He replied, "Yes! He does." When he came into the house, Jesus anticipated him, saying, **"What do you think, Simon? From whom do**

the rulers of the earth collect custom duties and head taxes, from their own children or from strangers?" When he replied, "From strangers." Jesus said, "**Then the children are free. However, so as not to be caught and arrested, go to the sea, cast in a hook, and take the first fish that comes up. You will find a shekel in the mouth of the fish,**[218] **take it and give it to them for me and for you.**"

Matthew 18:1–35

1 Then his disciples came to him, saying, "Who is the greatest in the kin-dom of heaven?" So Jesus called over a little child who stood in the midst of them while he taught, "**Truly I tell you, that unless you change and become like little children, you will not enter into the kin-dom of heaven. Whoever will humble themselves like this little child will be the greatest in the kin-dom of heaven. Whoever welcomes one little child like this in my name, welcomes me but whoever causes one of these little ones who believe in me to stumble,**[219] **it will be better for them if a great millstone were hung around their neck and they were drowned in the depth of the sea. Woe to the worldly because of offenses! Although offenses are bound to come, woe to that one by whose hand the offense comes!**

8 **If your hand or foot offends you, cut it off, and cast it away from you.** [*Stop stealing! Stop trespassing!*][220] **It is better for you to enter life maimed or lame, rather than having two hands for stealing or two feet for trespassing, and be thrown into a living hell. If your eye offends you, remove it, and cast it away from you.** [*Stop envying!*][221] **It is better for you to enter life with one eye rather than having two eyes for envying and be thrown into a living hell. Take heed that you do not despise**[222] **one of these little ones for I tell you that their angels always see the face of my heavenly Divine Parent.**

11 **The Son of humanity has come to save those who are lost. What do you think? If a person has a hundred sheep and one of them goes astray, they will leave the ninety-nine on the mountain and go to seek the one who went astray. If they will find it, truly I tell you, they will rejoice more over that sheep than over the ninety-nine who did not go astray. Even so, it is not the will of your heavenly Divine Parent that one of these little ones would be lost.**[223]

15 Moreover, if a friend[224] is at fault against you, tell them their fault between you, and them alone. If they hear you, you have gained your friend but if they will not hear you, take one or two other people with you so that *on the testimony of two or three witnesses every word may be established.*[225] If they refuse to hear them, tell it to the church[226] but if they refuse even to hear the church, let them be to you as a pagan[227] and a tax collector. Truly I tell you, whatever you will bind on earth will be bound in heaven and whatever you release on earth will be released in heaven. Again, I tell you that if two of you will agree concerning anything that you ask for, it will be done for you by my heavenly Divine Parent for where two or three are gathered in my name, I am there in the midst of them!"

21 Then Peter came and said, "Teacher, how often do I forgive my brother if he is at fault against me? As many as seven times?" Jesus replied, "**I tell you, up to seventy times seven! Therefore the kin-dom of heaven is like a certain ruler who wanted to settle accounts with his servants. When he began to settle accounts, one was brought who owed him ten thousand talents[228] but as he was not able to pay, this ruler commanded that he would be sold, together with his wife, his children, and all that he had to pay the debt. The servant therefore fell on his knees and begged him, saying, 'Sir, have patience with me and I will pay you everything!' Then the ruler of that servant had pity on him, released him, and forgave him his debt.**

28 **So that servant went out and found one of his servants who owed him a hundred denarii,[229] so he laid his hands on him and took him by the throat, saying, 'Pay me what you owe!' His servant fell down and begged him, saying, 'Have patience with me and I will pay you!' He refused, so he went and had him put in prison until he would pay off his debt. When his other servants saw what had been done, they were very sad, and went to tell this ruler what had just happened. The ruler called him in and said, 'You wicked servant! I forgave you all your debt because you begged me. Couldn't you show mercy to your servant just as I showed mercy to you.' The ruler was angry and delivered him to the jailers until he pays off all of his debt. So will my heavenly Divine Parent do to you unless you forgive your sister and brother from the love in your heart.**"

Matthew 19:1–30

1 When Jesus had finished these sayings, he departed from Galilee, and entered the region of Judea beyond the Jordan. Great multitudes followed him and he healed them there. Some Pharisees also came up to test him, asking, "Is it lawful for a man to divorce his wife for just any fault?" He answered, **"Didn't you read that in the beginning God created** *them* *male and female.*[230] *For this reason a person will leave their parents, be joined to their spouse and the two will become one flesh,*[231] **so they are no longer two but one flesh. Therefore, don't let people put asunder what God has joined together."** They said, "Why then did Moses command one to give a certificate of divorce and separate from their spouse?[232] He replied, **"Moses, considering of the hardness of your hearts, allowed you to divorce your spouse but it was not so from the beginning and I say to you that whoever leaves their spouse without a charge of adultery and marries another commits adultery, and one who marries a spouse thus separated commits adultery."**[233]

10 His disciples asked him, "If there is so much difficulty between man and woman, is it then worthwhile not to marry?" Jesus told them, **"This saying does not apply to every person but only those for whom it is given. For while there are some people incapable of marriage**[234] **who have been so from birth or who were made that way by people and there are other people who do not marry for the sake of the kin-dom of heaven. Let those who can accept this saying receive it."**[235] Then little children were brought to him so he might lay his hands on them and pray but the disciples turned them away. Jesus said, **"Allow the little children to come to me and do not stop them for the kin-dom of heaven is for such as these."** So he laid his hand on the children and then departed from there.

16 Then a man approached him, saying, "Good Teacher, what good deed must I do to have eternal life?" He said, **"Why do you ask me about what is good? There is only One Who is good. If you wish to enter into life, keep the commandments."** He said, "Which ones?" Jesus replied, *"Thou shall not murder. Thou shall not commit adultery. Thou shall not steal. Thou shall not bear false witness.*[236] *Honor thy father and thy mother.*[237] *Love your neighbor as yourself."*[238] The young man replied, "All these things have I kept from my youth. What do I still lack?" Jesus

answered, "**If you wish to be perfect;**[239] **go, sell your possessions and share**[240] **them with the poor so that you will have treasure in heaven; then come and follow me.**" When the young man heard this saying, he went away sorrowful for he had great possessions.

23 Jesus said to his disciples, "**Truly I tell you it's difficult for one who has an abundance of things**[241] **to enter into the kin-dom of heaven. Again I tell you, it's easier for a rope**[242] **to go through the eye of a needle**[243] **than one who has an abundance of things**[244] **to enter into the kin-dom of God.**" His disciples were astonished when they heard, saying, "Who then can be saved?" Jesus looked at them and replied, "**For people this is impossible but with God all things are possible.**"

27 Peter asked him, "Behold, we have left everything and followed you! What will we get out of it?" Jesus answered, "**Truly I tell you, at the spiritual renewal of all things,**[245] **when the Son of humanity will sit on the throne**[246] **of his glory; you who have followed me will sit on twelve smaller thrones and judge the twelve tribes of Israel.**[247] **Then everyone who leaves houses or sisters or brothers or wife or husband or children or fields for my name's sake, will receive a hundred fold and inherit eternal life. Many who are first will be last and many who are last will be first.**

Matthew 20:1–34

1 The kin-dom of heaven is like a landowner who went out early in the morning to hire laborers for his vineyard. He bargained with the laborers for a denarius a day and sent them into the vineyard. He went out about nine o'clock and saw others standing idle in the marketplace. He told them, 'Go into the vineyard and I will give you whatever is right.' So they went. He went out about noon and again at three o'clock and did the same. About five o'clock he went out to find others still standing there. He talked with them, saying; 'Why have you been standing here idle all day?' They replied, 'Because no one hired us.' The owner said, 'You go into my vineyard too.' So when evening came, the owner of the vineyard told his steward, 'Call the laborers and give them their wages, beginning from the last to the first.' When those who were hired about five o'clock came, they each received a denarius.

10 So when the first came they each received a denarius but they thought that they would receive more. When they received it, they grumbled against the owner, saying; "The last laborers worked only on hour and you made them equal to us who have borne a hard day's work in the scorching sun! He answered one and said, 'Friend, I did you no injustice. You agreed to work for a denarius, so take what is yours, and go your way. I wish to give to this last person hired the same as to you. Is it not lawful for me to do what I will with what is mine? Are you jealous of my generosity?' Even so, the last will be first and the first will be last. Many are called for work but only a few collect fully for work done."[248]

17 Jesus was going up to Jerusalem and on the way he took his twelve disciples aside privately and said, "Behold, we go up to Jerusalem and the Son of humanity will be delivered to the chief priests and the scribes who will condemn him to death. Then they will hand him over to the Gentiles to mock, scourge, and crucify him and on the third day he will rise again."

20 Then the mother[249] of the sons of Zebedee came up to him with her sons and knelt before him to request something of him. He asked her, "What do you wish?" She said, "Grant that these two sons of mine may sit, one at your right hand and the other at your left hand in your kin-dom." Jesus answered, "You do not know what you ask. Are you able to drink the cup that I am about to drink and be baptized with the baptism that I am to be baptized with?" They relied, "Yes, we can!" Jesus said, "You will indeed drink from my cup and be baptized with the baptism that I am baptized with but to sit on my right hand or on my left hand is not mine to give.[250] This will be given to those for whom it is prepared by my Divine Parent." When the other ten heard this, they became angry at the two brothers. Jesus called them and said, "You know the rulers of the Gentiles have power over them and their great men exercise authority over them. This will not be so with you for whoever wishes to be great among you, let them be a minister to you and whoever wishes to be first among you, let them be a servant to you. Just as the Son of humanity came not to be ministered to but to minister and to give his life as a salvation for the sake of many."

29 A great multitude followed him as he left Jericho. Behold, two blind people were sitting by the roadside and when they heard that Jesus was passing by, they cried out, "Have mercy on us, Oh Saviour, Son of David!" The people rebuked them, telling them to keep quiet but they only cried louder, "Have mercy on us, Oh Saviour, Son of David." So Jesus stood still and called them, saying, **"What do you wish me to do for you?"** "Saviour, that our eyes be opened!" Moved with compassion, Jesus touched their eyes and immediately they received their sight and followed him.

Matthew 21:1–46

1 When he drew near to Jerusalem, he came to Bethphage on the side of the Mount of Olives and sent two disciples, saying, **"Go into the village which is in front of you and right away you will find an ass tied up with a colt alongside her. Untie them, bring them to me, and if anyone says something to you, tell them; 'Our Saviour has need for them!' Immediately, they will send them here."** This event fulfills the words spoken by the prophet: *9 Rejoice greatly Oh daughter Zion! Shout aloud, Oh daughter Jerusalem! Behold, your ruler [king] is coming to you. He is just and having salvation. Lowly and riding on a colt, the foal of an ass. I will disarm all peoples of the earth, including My people in Israel. The battle bow will be broken and he shall bring peace among the nations. His realm shall stretch from sea to sea, from the river to the ends of the earth.*[251]

6 The disciples went and did what Jesus had commanded them and they brought the ass and the colt, put their garments on the colt, and Jesus rode on it.[252] A great multitude spread their garments on the road and others cut down branches from the trees and laid them on the road. Then the multitudes who went before and those who followed him all cheered and cried out, "Hosanna[253] to the Son of David! *Blessed is the one who comes in the name of God!'*[254] Hosanna in the highest heaven!" When he came into Jerusalem, all the city was moved, saying, "Who is this man?" So people were saying, "This is the prophet Jesus from Nazareth in Galilee."

12 Then Jesus entered into the Temple of God and drove out all those who were buying and selling in the Temple and he overturned the trays of the money changers and the stands of those who sold doves. He told

them, **"It is written, *'My house will be called a private prayer place,*** [255] **but you have made it a *'den of thieves'.***[256]**"** Now in the Temple, they brought to him the blind and the disabled and he healed them. When the chief priests and scribes saw the wonderful things that he did and heard the children crying out in the Temple, "Hosanna to the Son of David!" they were indignant. They asked Jesus, "Do you hear what these children are saying?" He answered, **"Yes, have ye never read, *'Out of the mouths of babes and nursing infants You have established Your Glory in their perfect praise because of Your foes. May their example silence the enemy and the avenger.'"***[257] He left them, went outside the city to Bethany, and camped there.

18 Now in the morning as he returned to the city he was hungry. When he saw a fig tree by the road, he came to it and finding only leaves on it, said, **"Let no fruit grow on you ever again!"** At once[258] the fig tree withered and when the disciples saw it, they marveled, saying, "How did the fig tree wither away at once?" He answered, **"Truly, I tell you, if you have faith in God and do not doubt, you will not only do what was done to this fig tree but also if you say to this mountain,**[259] **'Be removed and fall into the sea,' it will be done. You will receive everything you ask for in prayer, if you have faith."**

23 Jesus was teaching in the Temple when the chief priests and elders of the people[260] confronted him, "By what authority do you do these things and who gave you this authority?" He replied, **"I also will ask you one question. If you answer me, then I will likewise tell you by what authority I do these things. Did the baptism of John come from heaven of was it of human origin?"** They reasoned with themselves, saying, "If we would say, 'From heaven,' then he will say to us, 'Then why didn't you believe him.' If we would say, 'Of human origin,' we are afraid of the people for all of them regard John as a prophet." So they answered, "We don't know." Jesus told them, **"Neither will I tell you by what authority I do these things.**

28 **What do you think? A man had two sons and he came to the first and said, 'My son, go work today in my vineyard!' 'I will not,' he answered but later he regretted saying that and went. Then he approached his other son with the same request and he answered, 'I**

will go, sir,' but he did not go. Which of these two did the will of his father?" They said, "The first!" Jesus told them, **"Truly I tell you that the tax-collectors and prostitutes**261 **will enter the kin-dom of God before you. For John came to you advocating justice in the way of righteousness and you did not believe him but the tax-collectors and prostitutes believed him. Even when you saw this, you did not repent later and believe him.**

33 Hear another parable: there was a certain landowner who planted a vineyard, put a fence around it, dug a winepress in it, built a tower, leased it to tenants, and then he went into a far country. When the fruit season drew near, he sent his servants to the tenants to collect the fruits of his vineyard. The tenants took his servants, beat some, stoned some, and killed others. Again, he sent more servants than the first time but they did likewise to this group. Then last of all, he sent his son to them, saying, 'They will respect my son,' but when the tenants saw the son, they said among themselves, 'This is the heir, come let us kill him, and retain his inheritance!' So they caught him, took him out of the vineyard, and killed him. What will the owner of this vineyard do to those tenants when he comes?" They said, "He will savagely destroy them and lease the vineyard out to other tenants262 who will give him the fruits in their seasons."263

42 Jesus said, "Have ye never read in the scripture, '*The stone which the builders rejected*264 *has become the chief cornerstone. This was God's doing, and it is marvelous in our eyes?*265 Therefore I tell you, the kin-dom of God will be taken from you, and given to the people bringing forth the fruits thereof. Whoever falls on this stone will be broken to pieces but it will crush whoever it falls upon."266 Now the chief priests and some Pharisees knew that he was speaking against them when they heard his parables but while they wanted to arrest him, they feared the multitudes who regarded Jesus as a prophet.

Matthew 22:1–46

1 He answered them again by parables, saying, **"The kin-dom of heaven is like a ruler who gave a wedding banquet for his son and sent out his servants to call those who were invited to the wedding but they would not come. Again he sent out other servants to tell those who were**

invited, 'Behold, I have prepared my dinner, my oxen and fat calves are killed, and all things are ready! Please come to the marriage feast!' They made light of it and went their ways; one to his farm; another to his business, while the rest seized his servants, treated them shamefully, and with blows. When the ruler heard of this, he was furious. So he sent forth his armies who destroyed those evildoers and burned their city.

8 Then he said to his servants, 'The marriage feast is ready but those who were invited are not worthy. Therefore, go out to the main roads and invite to the wedding as many as you find there!' So the servants went out to the main roads and gathered all whom they found, both good and bad. The banquet hall was filled with guests and when the ruler came in to see the guests, he saw a man who didn't have on a wedding garment. He said, 'My friend, how did you get in here without a wedding garment?' The man was speechless and then the ruler said to his servants, 'Bind his hands and his feet, take him away and put him into the darkness of the dungeon[267] where he will weep and gnash his teeth.' For many are called but few are chosen."

15 The Pharisees left and took counsel about how they might entangle him in his words. Then they sent their disciples to him along with the Herodians,[268] saying, "Teacher, we know that you are sincere, you teach the way of God truthfully, and you show deference to no one for you don't regard their status. Therefore tell us what you think. Is it lawful to pay taxes to Caesar, or not?" Jesus perceived their malice and said, **"Why do you test me, Oh ye hypocrites? Show me the tax money!"** So they brought him a denarius and he asked, "Whose image and inscription is this?" They said, "Caesar's!" He said, **"Therefore pay to Caesar what is due to Caesar and give to God the things that belong to God."**[269] They marveled at hearing these words, left him, and went their way.

23 That day the Sadducees[270] who say there is no resurrection of the dead, asked him, "Teacher, Moses says that if a man dies with no children, then let the man's brother marry his wife and raise children for his brother.[271] Now there were seven brothers among us and the first died with no children, leaving his wife to marry his brother. The second died also and the third up to the seventh died. The woman died last of

all. So, in the resurrection, whose wife, of the seven brothers she married, will she be for they all married her?" Jesus answered, **"You are in error because you neither understand the scriptures nor the power of God. For at the resurrection of the dead, they neither marry nor are given in marriage but are like the heavenly angels of God. As touching the resurrection of the dead, have ye not read what was spoken to you by God?** *I am the God of your father, the God of Abraham, the God of Isaac and the God of Jacob.*[272] **God is the God of the living, not of the dead."**[273] The people were amazed at his teaching when they heard it.

34 The Pharisees gathered when they heard that he had silenced the Sadducees. One of them who knew the law tested him with a question, "Teacher, what is the greatest commandment in the law?" Jesus said, " *'You shall love the Eternal your God with all your heart, with all your soul and with all your mind.'*[274] **This is the first and great commandment and the second has the same importance as the first:** *Love your neighbor as yourself.*[275] **All the law and the prophets depend on these two commandments."** Jesus asked the Pharisees who came together, **"What do you think of the Christ?**[276] **Whose son is he?"** They said, "The Son of David!" He said, **"How does David, inspired by the Spirit, call him 'lord'** [*the Christ*],[277] **saying,** *'God said to my lord, "'Sit at my right hand*[278] *until I make your enemies your footstool?'"* [279] **If David calls him 'lord'** [*the Christ*], **how can he be his son?"** No one was able to answer him and from that day no one dared to question him.

Matthew 23:1–39

1 Jesus spoke to the multitudes, including his disciples, saying, **"The scribes of the Pharisees**[280] **sit on Moses' seat. Therefore, whatever they tell you, that observe and practice but do not according to their works for they say and do not. They bind heavy burdens and lay them on people's shoulders but they themselves will not even touch them with one of their fingers.**

5 **They do all their works to be seen by people as they widen the fringes on their robes and lengthen the ends of their robes. They love the upper rooms at feasts, the best seats in the synagogues, greetings in public places, and to be called by people, 'Rabbi'**[281] **but you, are not to be called 'Rabbi,' for one is your teacher, the Christ,**[282] **and**

you are all brothers and sisters. Do not call any person on earth your Divine Parent for you have one heavenly Divine Parent. Do not be called 'leader' for one is your leader, the Christ. Those who are greatest among you will be your servants, for whoever exalts yourself will be humbled and whoever humbles yourself will be exalted.

13 Woe to you, scribes of the Pharisees, hypocrites, for you shut up the kin-dom of heaven against people! You do not go in yourselves and you hinder those who are entering to go in.[283] Woe to you, scribes of the Pharisees, hypocrites, for you embezzle the property of widows, and for a show you make long prayers! Therefore you will receive a greater judgment. Woe to you, scribes of the Pharisees, hypocrites, for you travel over sea and land to make one new convert and when they are converted, you make them twice as much a child of hell[284] as yourselves!

16 Woe to you, ye blind guides who say, 'Whoever swears by the Temple; it does no harm, but whoever swears by the gold which is in the Temple is bound by their oath.' Oh ye blind fools, for which is greater, the gold or the Temple that sanctifies the gold? Also, you say, 'Whoever swears by the altar is not bound by their oath but whoever swears by the offering that is on it, they are bound by their oath.' Oh ye blind fools, for which is greater, the offering or the altar that sanctifies the offering? Therefore, whoever swears an oath by the altar, swears by it and everything on it, and whoever swears by the Temple, swears by it and by the One Who dwells there. Whoever swears by heaven, swears by the throne of God and by the One Who sits upon it. Woe to you, scribes of the Pharisees, hypocrites, for you take tithes[285] of mint, dill, and cumin but ye have abandoned the more precious matters of the Torah: justice, mercy, and honesty![286] These are necessary for you to have done without neglecting the others. Oh ye blind guides, who strain out a gnat but swallow a camel!

25 Woe to you, scribes of the Pharisees, hypocrites, for you clean the outside of the cup and of the plate but inside you are full of extortion and self-indulgence! Blind Pharisees, first clean the inside of the cup and of the plate so that the outside may also be clean. Woe to you,

scribes of the Pharisees, hypocrites, for you are like whitewashed tombs which indeed appear beautiful on the outside but inside are full of dead people's bones and all kinds of corruption! Even so, you appear righteous to people on the outside but within you are full of hypocrisy and iniquity. Woe to you, scribes of the Pharisees, hypocrites, for you build the tombs of the prophets and decorate the monuments of the righteous! You claim, 'If we had lived in the days of our ancestors, we would not have joined them in shedding the blood of the prophets.' Therefore you bear witness against yourselves, that you are the children of those who murdered the prophets. Fill up, then, the measure of your ancestors.[287]

33 Oh ye serpents and offspring of scorpions! How can you escape the judgment of a living hell? Behold, I send to you prophets, sages, and scribes: some of them you will murder and crucify while others you will whip in your prisons and persecute from city to city. So that all the righteous blood shed upon the earth may come upon you; from the blood of righteous Abel to the blood of Zachariah, son of Jehoiada, whom you murdered between the Temple and the altar.[288] Truly I tell you, all these things will come down upon this generation.[289]

37 Oh Jerusalem, Jerusalem, the city that murders the prophets and stones those who are sent to her! How often I wanted to gather your children the way a hen gathers her chicks under her wings but you are unwilling. Behold, your house will be left to you desolate for I tell you that you will not see me again until you say, *'Blessed is the one who comes in the name of God!'*[290]

Matthew 24:1–51

1 As Jesus departed from the Temple to go away, his disciples came up to him and showed him the buildings of the Temple. Then he asked, **"Behold, do you see all these buildings? Truly I tell you, that not one stone will be left upon another: all will be thrown down."** While he sat on the Mount of Olives, his disciples came to him privately, saying, "Tell us when these things will happen. What is the sign of your coming and of the end of the world?"[291] He answered, **"Take heed that no one deceives you for many will come in my name saying, 'I am Christ!'**

and they will deceive many. You will hear of revolutions and rumors of wars, so watch out but do not be troubled. All these things must happen but your end has not yet come.

7 For nation will rise up against nation and empire[292] against empire. There will be famines, plagues, and earthquakes in all countries. All these things are like the first pains of childbirth. They will deliver you over to be oppressed, they will murder you, and you will be hated in all nations because of my name! Then many will stumble, hate one another, and betray one another. Many false prophets will rise up to deceive a great number of people and the love of many will grow cold because iniquity will abound but whoever hopes to the very end will be saved.[293] This Good News of the kin-dom will be preached throughout your world as a testimony to all peoples and then your end will come.

15 Therefore when you see the *abomination of desolation*[294] as was spoken of by Daniel the prophet, standing in a holy place, (let the reader understand)[295] then those who are in Judea must flee to the mountains. She who is on the housetop must not come down to remove anything out of her house and he who is in the field better not return to get his coat. Woe to those who are pregnant and to those who are nursing mothers in those days![296] Pray that your flight may not be in the winter or on the Sabbath for then there will be great tribulation such as has not been since the beginning of the world until this time and never will be. These days will be shortened for the sake of the chosen ones or no flesh would be saved.

23 Then if anyone says to you, 'Behold, here is the Christ,' or 'There is the Christ,' do not believe it. For false Christ's and lying prophets will rise and show great signs and wonders to deceive, if possible, even the chosen ones. See, I have told you in advance, so if they say to you, 'Look, Christ is in the wilderness,' do not go out; if they advise, 'Look, Christ is in the inner rooms,' do not believe it![297] For as the lightning comes from the east and flashes to the west, so also will be the coming of the Son of humanity. The vultures will gather wherever there is a carcass.[298]

29 Immediately after the suffering of those days; the sun will be darkened, the moon will not give her light, the stars will fall from heaven, and the constellations of heaven will be shaken.[299] Then the sign of the Son of humanity will appear in the sky and the tribes of the earth will mourn and they will see the Son of humanity coming in the clouds of the sky with power and great glory. He will send out his angels with a loud trumpet call and they will gather his chosen ones from the four winds; from one end of the earth to the other.

32 Now learn this parable of the fig tree. When its branches become tender they bursts into leaves and you know that summer is near at hand. So when you see these things, you know that I am near, even at the door. Truly I tell you, this generation will not pass until all these things take place. Heaven and earth will pass away but my words will not pass away.[300] No one knows concerning that day and hour, neither the angels of heaven, nor the Son but only my Divine Parent.

37 Just as in the days of Noah, so also will be the coming of the Son of humanity. For as in the days before the flood people were eating, drinking, marrying and giving in marriage, until the day when Noah entered the ark. They knew nothing until the flood came and took them all away, so will be the coming of the Son of humanity. Then two men will be in the field; one will be taken and the other left. Two women will be grinding at the hand mill; one will be taken and the other left.[301] Watch, therefore, for you don't know what hour your Saviour will come to you. You know that if the homeowner had known what hour the thief would come, they would have watched and not allowed anyone to break into their house. Therefore you also must be ready for the Son of humanity is coming at an hour you do not expect.[302]

45 Who then is that faithful and wise servant whose employer has made them manager over his household, to provide them food[303] at the proper time? Blessed is that servant whose employer comes back and finds them working. Truly I tell you, that this employer will make that worker a manager over his entire operation. However, if the servant thinks evil in their heart, 'My boss will be delayed,' and

begins to oppress his coworkers and to party with drunks, then his employer will come on a day when he is not expecting him at an hour that is unknown. He will punish him, give him a portion like that of the hypocrites, and there will be weeping and gnashing of teeth.[304]

Matthew 25:1–46

1 Then the kin-dom of heaven will be like ten bridesmaids who each took their lamp and went out to meet the bridegroom and the bride. Five of them were wise while five were foolish. Now those who were foolish took their lamps but brought no extra oil with them. The wise ones took vessels of oil with their lamps. When the bridegroom was delayed, they all slumbered and slept.

6 At midnight a cry is heard, 'Behold! The bridegroom is coming! Go out to greet him!' Then all the bridesmaids arose and prepared their lamps. The foolish ones said to the wise ones, 'Give us some of your oil for our lamps are going out!' Then the wise bridesmaids answered, 'No! There is not enough for both of us. Go to the merchants who sell oil and buy some for yourselves.' The bridegroom arrived while they went to buy oil and those who were ready entered with him into the wedding banquet and the door was locked shut. Afterward the foolish bridesmaids came also, each saying, 'Lord, lord, open up the door for us!' Then he answered, 'Truly I say that I don't know you.' Watch therefore for you know neither the day nor the hour when the Son of humanity is coming.

14 The kin-dom of heaven is just like a person who went on a journey, called in his employees and entrusted his property to them. He gave five talents[305] to one person, two talents to another, and one talent to a third; to each one according to their abilities. Immediately this person went on a journey. The one who had received five talents went and traded with them and earned five more talents. Likewise, the one with two talents; gained two more but the one who received only one talent went out, dug a hole in the earth and hid his employer's money.

19 After a long time the employer came back and began to settle accounts with them. The one who had received five talents brought ten back, saying, 'Sir, you delivered five talents to me; look, I have

gained five more besides them.' The employer said, 'Well done, my good and reliable servant! You have been fruitful over a little so I will have you manage many things. Enter into the merrymaking of your employer!'306 The one who had received two talents came and said, 'Sir, you delivered two talents to me; look, I have earned two more.' This employer said, 'Well done! My good and faithful servant! You have been fruitful with a few things so I will appoint you over much more. Enter into the merrymaking of your employer!'

24 The third person who had received one talent came and said, 'Sir, I know you are a hard man; reaping where you have not sown and gathering where you have not scattered seed. I was so afraid that I went and hid your talent in the ground and here is the one you gave me.' His employer answered, 'Oh you incompetent lazy servant, you knew that I reap where I have not sown and gather where I have not scattered seed. Therefore you ought to have deposited my money with the bankers so when I returned I would have received back my capital with usury. Take the talent from him and give it to the one with ten talents. To everyone who has, more will be given and they will have an abundance but for those who don't have; even that which they have will be taken away. Throw this useless servant into the darkness of the dungeon where he will weep and gnash his teeth.'

31 When the Son of humanity comes into his glory with all the holy angels, then will he sit on the [*spiritual*] throne of his glory.307 Before him will be gathered people of all nations and he will separate them one from another, just as a shepherd divides the sheep from the goats. He will set the sheep on his right and the goats on his left. Then the kin to all people308 will say to those at his right, 'Come, ye blessed of my Divine Parent, inherit the kin-dom which has been prepared for you from the foundation of the world. For I was hungry and you gave me food, I was thirsty and you gave me drink, I was a stranger and you took me in, I was naked and you clothed me, I was sick and you visited me, I was in prison and you came to me.'

37 Then the righteous will ask, 'Saviour, when did we see thee hungry and feed thee, or thirsty and give thee drink? When did we see thee as a stranger and welcome thee, or find thee naked and clothe thee?

When did we see thee sick or in prison and come to thee?' The kin to all people will answer them, 'Truly I tell you, whatever you did to one of the least of these in my spiritual family, you did it to me.' Then he will say to those on his left, 'Depart from me, ye cursed, into a living hell prepared for the devil and his angels for I was hungry and you did not give me food, I was thirsty and you did not give me a drink, I was a stranger and you did not take me in, I was naked and you did not clothe me, I was sick and you did not visit me, I was in prison and you did not come to me.' Then they will answer him, 'Sir, when did we see thee hungry, or thirsty, or a stranger, or naked, or sick, or in prison and did not minister to thee?' Then he will answer them, 'Truly I tell you, that when you did not do it to one of the least of these in my spiritual family, you also did not do it to me.' So these will go away into everlasting torment [*a living hell*] and the righteous into eternal life."

Matthew 26:1–75

1 When Jesus had finished all these sayings, he told his disciples, **"You know that after two days is the Passover**[309] **and the Son of humanity will be handed over to be crucified."** The chief priests, the scribes, and the elders of the people assembled in the courtyard of the high priest who is called Caiaphas.[310] They took counsel together to arrest Jesus by treachery and have him killed but they added, "Not during the festival or it may cause a riot among the people."

6 While he was in Bethany at the house of Simon the leper, a woman came up to him with an alabaster jar of very precious ointment and poured it on his head as he reclined at the table to eat. When his disciples saw it, they became indignant with her, saying, "Why this waste? This could have been sold for a small fortune to be given to the poor!" When Jesus understood this, he said, **"Why do you trouble this woman? She has accomplished a beautiful thing to me, for you have the poor with you always but you won't always have me. She poured this perfume on my body to prepare me for my burial. Truly I tell you that wherever this Good News is preached in the whole world, what she has done will be told as a memorial to her."**

14 Then one of the twelve named Judas Iscariot, approached some chief priests, saying, "What are you willing to give me if I deliver Jesus to you?"

They paid him thirty pieces of silver[311] and from that time on he sought an opportunity to betray him.

17 On the first day of Passover, some disciples came to Jesus, "Where do you want us to prepare the Passover for you to eat?" He said, **"Go into the city to a certain man and say, 'Our Teacher says, "'My time is at hand and I will keep the Passover with my disciples at your house.'"'"** They did as he told them and prepared the Passover. When evening came he reclined at the table in that house with the twelve disciples.[312] While they were eating, he said, **"Truly I tell you that one of you will betray me!"** They became very upset and one by one each said, "Saviour, is it I?" He answered them, **"He who dips their hand with me in the dish will betray me. The Son of humanity goes as it is written of him but woe to the man by whom the Son of humanity is betrayed! It would have been better for him if he had not been born."** Judas, who betrayed him asked, "Teacher, is it I?" He replied, **"You have said it!"**

26 While they were eating, Jesus took some bread, blessed it, broke it, and gave it to his disciples, saying, **"Take, eat, this is my body!"** He took a cup of wine, gave thanks, and gave it to them, saying, **"Take, drink of it, all of you, for this is my blood of the covenant which is shed for many for the remission[313] of sins. I tell you, henceforth, I will not drink from the fruit of the vine until that day when I drink it again with you in my Divine Parent's kin-dom."** When they had sung a hymn of praise, they went over to the Mount of Olives.

31 Jesus said to them, **"All of you will desert me this night, for it is written, *I will strike the shepherd and his sheep will be scattered.*[314] Then after I am raised up, I will go to Galilee before you."** Peter said, "Even if everyone will desert you, I will never desert you." Jesus said to him, **"Truly I tell you that tonight you will deny me three times before the rooster crows!"** Peter replied, "Even if I must die with thee, I will never deny you!" All the disciples said this.

36 Then Jesus went with them to a place called Gethsemane and he said to his disciples, **"Sit down here while I go to pray."** He took Peter and the two sons of Zebedee with him and he became greatly distressed and

troubled. He told them, **"My soul is sorrowful as I come close to death. Wait for me here and watch with me."** He went a little farther and laid down on his face and prayed, **"Oh my Divine Parent! If it is possible, let this cup**[315] **pass from me. Nevertheless, let it be as Thy will, not as I will"** He came back to his disciples, found them sleeping, and said to Peter, **"Wake up! Couldn't you watch with me for just one hour? Watch and pray that you will not fail in the test!**[316] **The spirit indeed is willing but the body is weak."**

42 Again, for a second time, he went away and prayed, **"Oh my Divine Parent! If this cup will not pass unless I drink it, Thy will be done."**[317] He came again and found them sleeping for their eyes were heavy. He went away for a third time to pray and said the same words. Then he came to his disciples and said, **"You are sleeping too much and you are resting too long!**[318] **Behold, the time has come and the Son of humanity will be delivered into the hands of sinners. Rise, let us be going, behold, my betrayer is close at hand!"**

47 While he was speaking, Judas, one of the twelve arrived with a large crowd, armed with swords and clubs, sent by the chief priests and the elders of the people. Judas had given them a sign, saying, "Arrest the man I will greet with a kiss" He came up to Jesus at once and said, "Peace, Teacher!" and kissed him. Jesus said, **"Friend, do that for which you have come."** Then they came near, seized him, and arrested him. Suddenly, one of those with him drew his sword, struck it at the servant[319] of the high priest and cut off his ear. Jesus told him, **"Put your sword in its place! All those who take up the sword will perish by the sword. Don't you think that I can appeal to my Divine Parent Who will immediately send me more than twelve legions of angels? As the scriptures**[320] **have to be fulfilled, so this must be."**

55 Jesus spoke to the crowd, **"Why have you come out to take me with swords and clubs to arrest me like a bandit?**[321] **I sat daily with many of you teaching in the Temple and you did not arrest me. All this has happened so that the scriptures**[322] **of the prophets may be fulfilled."** Then all of his disciples deserted him and fled. Those who had Jesus arrested brought him before Caiaphas the high priest in whose house the scribes and elders were assembled. Peter followed him at a distance

as far as the courtyard of the high priest. He went inside and sat with the soldiers to see how it would turn out.

59 Now the chief priests, the elders and the whole council[323] were seeking witnesses against Jesus so they might condemn him but found none, even though many false witnesses came forward. Finally two came and said, "This fellow said, 'I am able to tear down the Temple of God and rebuild it in three days.'" The high priest arose and said, "What is it that these two men testify against you? Why don't you answer them?" Jesus remained silent. Caiaphas said, "I put you under oath before the Living God, tell us if you are the Christ, the Son of God."

64 Jesus told him, **"You have said so but I tell you that from now on you will see the Son of humanity sitting at the right hand of Power and coming upon the clouds of heaven!"**[324] The high priest then tore his clothes, saying, "He has spoken blasphemy![325] Why do we still need witnesses? You have all heard his blasphemy. What is your judgment?" They answered, "He deserves to die!" Then they spat on his face, struck him on the head while others slapped him, saying, "Prophesy to us, Oh Christ! Who struck you?"

69 Peter was sitting in the courtyard when a maidservant came up to him and said, "You were also with Jesus the Galilean!" He denied it before everyone, saying, "I don't know what you're talking about!" When he went out to the porch, another girl saw him and she said to those around her, "This fellow was also there with Jesus of Nazareth!" Again he denied it, saying,[326] "I don't know that man!" After a while those who stood by came up and told Peter, "Surely you are one of them for your own accent betrays you!" Then he began to curse and swear, "I don't know the man!" Immediately a rooster crowed, and Peter remembered the words that Jesus said, **"Before the rooster crows, you will deny me three times!"** He went outside and wept bitterly.

Matthew 27:1–66

1 When morning came, all the chief priests and the elders of the people took counsel against Jesus to put him to death.[327] So they bound him, led him away, and delivered him to Pilate, the Roman governor. When Judas, the traitor, saw that Jesus was condemned; he repented, went away,

and brought back the thirty pieces of silver to the chief priests and the elders, saying, "I have sinned by betraying innocent blood" They said, "What is it to us what you see for yourself?" He laid down the thirty coins in the Temple, departed, went, and hanged himself. The chief priests picked up the coins, saying, "The money are not lawful to put in the house of offerings[328] because it is blood money." They took counsel and used it to buy the potter's field to bury strangers in. For this reason that field has been called the Field of Blood to this day. Then what was spoken by the prophet Zechariah[329] was fulfilled, saying, "They took the thirty pieces of silver, the price of him on whom a price had been set by some of the children of Israel and they gave them for the potter's field, as God directed me."[330]

11 Now Jesus stood before the governor who questioned him, "Are you the king of the Jews?" Jesus replied, **"You say so!"**[331] He didn't answer any of the accusations by the chief priests and the elders. Pilate asked, "Don't you hear how many things they testify against you?" The governor was greatly surprised that he didn't answer, not even a word to a single charge. During the festival it was the custom of the governor to release one prisoner chosen by the crowd. They had a well-known prisoner named Jesus Barabbas[332] who was bound. When they had gathered, Pilate asked them, "Whom do you want me to release to you; Jesus Barabbas or Jesus who is called the Christ?" Pilate realized that they had delivered him because of angry zeal.[333] While he was sitting on his judgment seat, his wife sent word to him, "Have nothing to do with this righteous man for I felt apprehension much of today through my dream about him."

20 The chief priests and elders urged their crowd to free Barabbas and condemn Jesus. The governor asked this crowd,[334] "Which of these two do you want me to release to you?" They said, "Barabbas!" He said, "Then what shall I do with Jesus who is called the Christ?" They all said, "Let him be crucified!" Pilate said, "Why, what has he done wrong?" but they only shouted more, "Let him be crucified!" When Pilate saw that he was gaining nothing and that a riot was developing, he took water and washed his hands[335] before the crowd, saying,[336] "I am innocent of this righteous man's blood, do as you please." Then the Jewish authorities answered,[337] "Let his blood be on us and our children." Then he

released Barabbas to them, had Jesus scourged,[338] and delivered him to be crucified. The governor's soldiers took Jesus to the Praetorium[339] where the whole company gathered around him.

28 They stripped him and dressed him in a crimson cloak.[340] They wove a crown of thorns, placed it on his head, put a reed in his right hand, fell on their knees before him, and mocked him, saying, "Hail! King of the Jews!" They spit in his face, took the reed, and struck him on the head. After the they had mocked him, they stripped him of the robe, put on his own clothes, and led him away to be crucified. When they came out they found an African from Cyrene named Simon and compelled him to carry his cross. They came to a place called Golgotha (which means Skull Hill) and gave him wine mixed with gall to drink: he tasted it but would not drink it.[341]

35 Then they crucified him and divided his garments by casting lots that it might be fulfilled what was spoken by the prophet: *They divided my garments among them and for my clothing they cast lots.*[342] They were sitting there watching him and they placed a sign above his head with the reason for his death in writing: This is Jesus, the King of the Jews. Two bandits were crucified with Jesus, one on his right and one on his left. People passing by hurled insults at him and shook their heads, saying, "Oh you who can tear down the Temple and build it in three days, deliver yourself if you are the Son of God and come down from the cross." The chief priests, the scribes, and the elders likewise mocked him, saying, "He saved others but he can't save himself. If he is the king of Israel, let him come down from the cross now and we will believe him. He trusted in God, let God deliver him[343] now if God is pleased with him for he said, 'I am the Son of God.'" The bandits who were crucified with him also taunted him in the same way.

45 Now from noon there was a great dark storm all over the land until three o'clock. About three o'clock, Jesus cried out in a loud voice, *"Eli, Eli, lama sabach-thani?"* that is, *"My God, my God, why have you forsaken me?"*[344] When some of the people who were standing by heard it, they said, "This man is calling Elijah." Immediately one of them ran, took a sponge, filled it with vinegar, put it on a reed, and gave it to him to drink. Then the others said, "Wait, let's see whether Elijah will come

and save him." Another took a spear, pierced his side and out came water and blood.

50 Then Jesus again cried out in a loud voice and he gave up his spirit. Immediately, the curtain at the door of the Temple[345] were torn in two, from top to bottom; the earth quaked, rocks split, tombs were opened, and the bodies of many saints who were sleeping in death rose up. They left their graves after his resurrection, entered into the holy city, and appeared to many people. When the centurion and those who were watching Jesus with him saw the earthquake and all that had happened, they were filled with awe, saying, "Truly this man was the Son of God."

55 Many women, who had followed him from Galilee and provided for him, were also there looking on from afar. These included Mary Magdalene,[346] Mary the mother of James and Joseph, and the mother of the sons of Zebedee. When it was evening, Joseph, a wealthy man from Arimathaea who was a disciple of Jesus, went to Pilate and asked for the body of Jesus. Pilate commanded the body to be given to him and Joseph took the body, wrapped it in a shroud of new fine linen, laid it in a his own new tomb which had been hewn out of rock, rolled a large stone against the door of the tomb, and departed. Mary Magdalene and the other Mary were there sitting opposite the tomb.

62 On Saturday, the next day after the day of Preparation, the chief priests and Pharisees gathered before Pilate, saying, "Sir, we just remembered that when this deceiver was alive, he used to say, **'After three days I[347] will raise again!'** Therefore, order that the tomb be made secure for three more days to prevent his disciples from coming by at night, stealing his body away, and telling all the people, 'He has risen from the dead.' This last deception would be worse than the first." Pilate told them, "Go your way and make it as secure as you know how with your Temple guard!" So they went to make the tomb secure by sealing the stone and posting a guard.

Matthew 28:1–20

1 Now after the Sabbath as the first day of the week began to dawn, Mary Magdalene and the other Mary came to see the tomb. Behold, a great earthquake took place, for an angel of God descended from heaven,

went up to the stone, rolled it back, and sat on it. His appearance was like lightning and his clothes were as white as snow. The guards who were watching shook with fear and became like dead men. Then the angel spoke to the women, "Do not be afraid, for I know you are seeking Jesus who was crucified. He is not here for he has risen, just like he said. Come and see where he was laid, go quickly, and tell his disciples that he has risen from the dead. Behold, he will go to Galilee before you[348] and you will see him there. Lo,[349] I have told you."

8 Quickly, they left the tomb with fear and great joy as they ran to tell the other disciples and behold, Jesus met them on their way, saying, **"Peace be with you!"** So they came over to him, held him by the feet and paid him homage. He said to them, **"Do not be afraid but go and tell my disciples to leave for Galilee and there they will see me."** While they were going, some of the guards came into the city and told the chief priests everything that had happened. So they gathered with the elders, took counsel, gave a large sum of money to the guards, and told them, "Say that his disciples came at night and stole him while you were sleeping. If this would be heard by the governor, we will appeal to him, and declare that you are blameless." So they took the money, did as they were directed, and this story has been passed around among the Jewish authorities to this day.[350]

16 Now his disciples went to Galilee to a mountain where Jesus had arranged to meet them and when they saw him, they fell down before him[351] but some were doubtful. Then Jesus came up and spoke with them, saying, **"All authority has been given to me in heaven and on earth. Just as my Divine Parent has sent me, I am also sending you. Go therefore, make disciples in all nations, and baptize them in the name of the Sacred Father and in the name of the Christ in Every Child[352] and in the name of the Holy Spirit. Teach them to observe all that I have commanded you and lo, I am with you always, even to the end of your world!"[353]** Amen.[354]

The Gospel According to Mark

Mark 1:1–45

The beginning of the gospel of Jesus the Christ, the Son of God.1 As it is written in the prophets: *"Behold, I will send My messenger and he shall prepare the way before Me."*2 *"The voice of one is crying out in the wilderness; 'Prepare the way of our God, make directly in the desert a highway for our God!'"*3 John the Baptist appeared in the wilderness proclaiming the baptism of repentance for the forgiveness of sins. People from Jerusalem and all over Judea traveled out to him confessing their sins and he baptized them in the Jordan River. He was dressed in camel hair, wore a leather belt around his waist, and ate locusts and wild honey.4

7 He preached, "There comes one after me who is mightier than I am! I am not worthy even to bend down and loosen the straps of his sandals. I have baptized you with water but he will baptize you with the Holy Spirit!" Now it happened in those days that Jesus came from Nazareth in Galilee and was baptized by John in the Jordan River. Immediately, as he came out of the water, he saw the heavens torn open and the Holy Spirit descending upon him like a dove. A voice came from heaven, *"You are My beloved Son, in you I am well pleased!"*5 Immediately the Holy Spirit drove him out into the wilderness. Jesus was in the wilderness among the wild animals for forty days, tested by Satan and ministered to by angels.

14 Now after John the Baptist was arrested, Jesus returned to Galilee preaching the Good News of the kin-dom of God, saying, **"The time**

is fulfilled, the kin-dom of God[6] is at hand, repent, and believe in the Good News!" As he walked beside the Sea of Galilee, he saw Simon and his brother Andrew throwing their nets into the lake for they were fishing people.[7] Then Jesus said to them, "Follow me and I will have you fish for people." Immediately, they left their nets and followed him. When he went a little further, he saw James and his brother John, the sons of Zebedee, while they were mending their nets in the boat. He called them and at once they left their father Zebedee with the hired help and followed him.

21 When they entered into Capernaum he taught in their synagogues on the Sabbaths and they were astonished at his teaching for he taught as one having authority and not as their scribes. Now there was a man in their synagogue with some unclean spirits[8] who cried out, "Leave us alone Jesus of Nazareth, what do we have in common with you? Have you come to destroy us? We know you are the Holy One of God!" Jesus rebuked them, saying, "Be quiet and come out of that person!" The unclean spirits convulsed the man and screamed on their way out. They were all amazed and kept asking one another, "What does this mean? What new teaching is this? With authority he commands even the unclean spirits and they obey him." At once his fame spread throughout the surrounding region of Galilee.

29 After leaving the synagogue they entered the home of Simon and Andrew together with James and John. The mother of Simon's wife lay sick in bed with a fever so they spoke to Jesus about her. He went over, took her by the hand, lifted her up, and immediately the fever left her so that she began serving them. In the evening towards sunset, they brought him all who were sick or possessed with demons. The whole city was gathered by the door. He healed many who were seriously sick with various diseases and restored many who were possessed but he wouldn't permit the demons to speak because they knew him.

35 Now in the morning he rose up before daylight and went out to a solitary place where he prayed. Simon and his companions searched for him and when they found him, they said, "Everyone is seeking you!" Jesus replied, "Let's walk to the neighboring towns and cities so I may preach there also for this is what I have come to do." So he went

throughout the province of Galilee, preaching in all the synagogues, and casting out demons. Now a leper[9] came over, knelt down at his feet, and begged him, "If you are willing you can make me clean!" Then Jesus, becoming angry,[10] reached out his hand and touched him, saying, **"I am willing; be cleansed!"** When he spoke the leprosy departed and he was made clean. He sent him away at once, saying, **"See that you say nothing to anyone but go and show yourself to the priests and offer for your cleansing those things which Moses commanded, as a testimony to them."** However, when he went out, he spread the word and told everyone, so that Jesus could no longer enter the city openly but stayed out in the country and people came to him from every direction.

Mark 2:1–28

1 Again, Jesus entered Capernaum for a few days and when they heard he was in a certain house, a great number came together so that it was impossible to hold them back even in front of the door and he preached the word to them. Four men carried a paralyzed man to him but they were unable to come near him because of the crowd. So they went up to the roof, uncovered it over the place where Jesus was, and lowered the quilt in which the paralyzed man lay. When Jesus saw their faith, he said to this paralytic, **"My son, thy sins are forgiven thee!"**

6 Now some of the scribes[11] were sitting there and they reasoned in their hearts; "Why does this fellow speak blasphemy like this? Who can forgive sins except God only?" When Jesus perceived in his spirit their reasoning among themselves, he said, **"Why do you reason these things in your hearts? Which is easier to say to the paralytic; 'Thy sins are forgiven thee!' or, 'Arise, take thy quilt, and walk?' So that you may know that the Son of humanity has authority on earth to forgive sins,"** he said to the paralytic, **"I tell you, arise, take up your quilt, and walk!"** Immediately he arose, took up his quilt, and went out before all of them. They were all amazed and glorified God, saying, "We have never seen anything like it!"

13 He went out by the seaside and taught the multitude who kept coming to him. Passing by the tax office he saw Levi, the son of Alphaeus, sitting at the custom house and said, **"Follow me!"** He arose and followed him. It happened that while he was reclining at dinner in his house, many

tax-collectors[12] and sinners were also guests with Jesus and his disciples for there were many who followed him. Now when the scribes of the Pharisees saw him eating with tax collectors and sinners, they asked his disciples, "Why does he eat and drink with tax collectors and sinners?" When Jesus heard it, he told them, **"Those who are seriously sick need a physician but not those who are healthy. I came to call sinners to repentance but not the righteous."**

18 Both the disciples of John the Baptist and of the Pharisees were fasting when they came to him and said, "Why do we fast but your disciples do not fast?" Jesus taught them, **"Can the friends of the bridegroom fast while the bridegroom is with them? So long as the they are with him, they can't fast but the days will come when the bridegroom will be taken away from them and then they will fast in those days. No one sews a piece of new cloth on an old garment or else the new piece that fills it tears away from the old and the tear becomes worse than before. Nobody pours new wine into old wineskins for new wine will burst the old skins, the wine will run out, and the skins will be ruined. New wine is poured into fresh wineskins."**

23 While Jesus went through the grain fields of the Sabbath day,[13] his disciples began to pluck the heads of grain. Some Pharisees said, "Behold, why are they doing what is unlawful on the Sabbath day?" He asked them, **"Have you never read what David did when he and his companions were hungry and in need of food; how he entered into the house of God when Ahimelech[14] was the high priest and ate of the bread of the Presence,[15] which only the priests were permitted to eat? David also shared this bread with his companions."[16]** He said to them, **"The Sabbath was made for people and not people for the Sabbath. Therefore, this Son of humanity is ruler also of the Sabbath."**

Mark 3:1–35

1 Jesus entered the synagogue on the Sabbath and there was a man with a withered hand. They watched him closely so they might accuse him of healing on the Sabbath. He told the man with the withered hand, **"Arise in the midst of us!"** Then he asked the Pharisees, **"Is it permitted to do good or to do harm on the Sabbath day; to save life or destroy life?"** They held their peace and he looked at them with anger but sad because

of the hardness of their hearts. He said to this man, **"Stretch out your hand!"** So he stretched out his hand and it was restored as whole as the other. Then these Pharisees went out and immediately held counsel with the Herodians against him concerning how to destroy him.17

7 So Jesus went to the sea with his disciples and a great multitude from Galilee followed him. Also, from Judea, Jerusalem, Idumea, beyond the Jordan River, and the region around Tyre and Sidon; a great multitude heard about what great things he was doing and came to him. He told his disciples to have a boat ready for him because of the multitude, so they wouldn't crush him, for he was healing so many that others pushed toward him to touch him. When those who were afflicted with unclean spirits saw him, they fell down before him, and cried out, saying, "You are indeed the Son of God!" He cautioned them earnestly not to make him known.

13 Jesus went up on the mountain, called those he wanted, and they came to him. He chose twelve to be with him so that he might send them out to proclaim the message and to have authority to cast out demons. Their names are: Simon, whom he surnamed Peter; James and John, the sons of Zebedee whom he surnamed Boanerges which means sons of thunder; Andrew; Philip; Bartholomew; Matthew; Thomas; James the son of Alphaeus; Thaddaeus; Simon the Cananaean; and Judas of Iscariot who betrayed him. Then they went into a house and the multitude came together again so that they could not even eat bread. When his family heard it, they went out to take him home for they were saying, "He has gone out of his mind!"

22 The scribes who came down from Jerusalem said, "Beelzebul is with him and he casts out demons by the ruler of the demons!" Jesus called them and spoke to them in parables: **"How can Satan cast out Satan? If a kingdom**18 **is divided against itself, that kingdom cannot stand. If a household is divided against itself, that household will not be able to stand. If Satan has risen up against himself and is divided, he cannot stand for his end has come. No one can break into a strong person's house and steal their goods, unless they first tie up that strong person; then they will ransack the house. Truly, I tell you that all manner of sin and blasphemy which people are guilty of will be forgiven them, but one who blasphemes against the Holy Spirit will**

never be forgiven but is subject to everlasting judgment."[19] For they had said, "He has an unclean spirit![20]"

31 Then his mother and his brothers came by, stood outside, and sent for him, calling him. A crowd was sitting around him and they said, "Behold, your mother and your brothers and sisters are outside, asking for you."[21] He answered, **"Who are my mother and my brothers and my sisters?"** He looked at those seated near him and said, **"Behold, here are my mother and my brothers and my sisters! For whoever does the will of God is my sister and my brother and my mother** [*and my father*]."

Mark 4:1–41

1 Again he began to teach by the seaside and the multitudes gathered around him so that he went out to sit in a boat on the sea and all the people stood on the land by the sea. He taught them many things by parables and said in his teaching, **"Listen! A sower went out to sow and when he had sowed, some seed fell on the path and the birds came and ate it up. Other seed fell on rocky ground where there wasn't much soil and immediately it withered away because the ground wasn't deep enough. In the sunshine they were scorched and dried up because they had no root. Some fell among thistles where the thistles grew up with them and choked them so that they yielded no fruit. Other seed fell on good soil and the plants sprouted, grew up, and bore fruit that yielded thirty, sixty, and a hundred fold."** He said, **"Whoever have ears to hear, will understand!"**

10 Apart from the crowds, those who were with him together with the twelve asked him about the parable. Jesus said, **"To you it has been given to know the secret[22] of the kin-dom of God but to outsiders everything has to be explained in parables** *so that they may not look with their eyes, hear with their ears, understand with their heart, turn to Me, and be healed.*"[23]

13 He said to them, **"If you don't understand this parable, how are you going to understand other parables? The sower sows the word. Those on the path are the ones in whom the word is sown and when they have heard it, Satan comes immediately to take away the word that was sown in their hearts. Likewise, those on the rocky ground where the word**

is sown are the ones who when they hear the message, immediately welcome it with joy but they have no root in themselves and only hope for a while. Then, when trouble or persecution arises because of the word, they quickly stumble and fall away. Those among the thorns where the word was sown are the ones who have heard the word but the cares of the world, the deceitfulness of riches, and the desire for superfluous luxuries[24] enter in to choke the word and they bear no fruit. Those on the good soil where the seed is sown are those who receive it and bear fruit: some thirty, some sixty, and some a hundredfold."

21 Jesus asked them, "Is a lamp brought in to be put under a bushel basket or under a kneading trough?[25] Is it not put on a lamp stand? There is nothing hidden which will not be revealed and nothing secret that will not become known.[26] If anyone has ears to hear, they will understand!" He told them, "Take heed of what you hear! The same measure that you use on others will be measured to you again and will increase, especially to those who listen. To the one who has, more will be given but from the one who doesn't have, even what they have will be taken away."[27]

26 He said, "The kin-dom of God is as one who plants seeds in the ground; then sleeps and rises up, night and day. The seeds will sprout and grow while one does not know how for the earth produces fruit of herself; first the blade of grass, then the ear, and last the full grain in the ear. When the crop is ready, immediately comes the sickle because the harvest is ripe."

30 He asked, "To what will we compare the kin-dom of God? With what parable can we picture it? It is just like a grain of mustard seed,[28] which, when it is sown in the earth is one of the smallest of all the seeds on earth. Yet when the seed is grown, it becomes greater than all the herbs and puts forth large branches so that the birds can settle under their shadow." Jesus taught them with parables as they were able to understand and he did not speak to them without parables but he explained everything to his disciples privately.

35 In the evening on that day he said to his disciples, "**Let's cross over to the other side!**" They left the people and took him away with them

in the boat. Also there were other boats with them. A great storm of wind arose and the waves kept beating into the boat so that the boat was almost swamped. Jesus was sleeping on a blanket in the stern of the boat when they came to him and woke him up saying, "Teacher! Don't you care that we are going to perish?" He got up, rebuked the wind and said to the sea, **"Peace, be still!"** The wind quieted down and there was a great calm. He asked his disciples, **"Why are you so fearful? Don't you have any faith?"** They were filled with great fear, saying to each other, "Oh, who is this that even the wind and the sea obey him?"

Mark 5:1–43

1 Then they came to the other shore in the country of the Gerasenes. When he came out of the boat he was met by a man from the cemetery who had an unclean spirit. He lived in the cemetery and no one could bind him in chains because whenever he was bound with shackles and chains, he broke the chains and cut the shackles so no one was strong enough to control him. Night and day, he was in the mountains or the cemetery, crying out, and cutting himself on the rocks.

6 When he saw Jesus from afar, he ran to him, bowed down before him, and shouted at him with a loud voice, "What do I have in common with thee, Jesus, Son of the Most High God? For God's sake, don't torture me!" as he had said to him, **"Get out of that man, oh you unclean spirit!"** Jesus asked, **"What is your name?"** The reply was, "Our name is legion[29] because we are many." They begged him eagerly that he would not drive them away out of their territory. Now a large herd of swine was feeding there on the hillside and the demons begged him, "Send us to the swine so that we may attack them." He permitted them so the demons went out and attacked the swine.[30] The herd of about two thousand ran to the steep rocks where they fell into the sea and were overwhelmed by the waves.[31]

14 The swineherds fled and reported the incident in the city and throughout the countryside and people came out to see what had happened. They came to Jesus and saw that the man, who was possessed by the Legion, was clothed, well behaved, and sitting down quietly. They were seized with fear. Those who saw it told them just what happened to the man and to the swine, so they urged him to leave their neighborhood.

As he was getting into the boat, the man who had been possessed with demons begged Jesus that he might be with him. He refused, saying, **"Go home to your friends, tell them what I have done for you and what compassion I have shown you."** He departed and began to proclaim in the Decapolis[32] about what great things Jesus had done for him, so that they were all astonished.[33]

21 Jesus crossed over in a boat to the other side and a great multitude gathered around him while he was by the sea. One of the leaders of the synagogue whose name was Jairus came over and when he saw Jesus in a crowd, he fell at his feet to plead with him earnestly, "My daughter is at the point of death! Come and lay your hands on her so that she will be healed and live." So Jesus went with him and a large multitude followed them and pressed about him. Now there was a women who had been sick from hemorrhages for twelve years. She suffered much at the hands of many physicians, had spent all her money, and was not helped at all but rather grew worse. When she heard about Jesus, she came up behind him in the dense crowd and touched his garment, for she said, "If only I may touch his garment, I will be healed!" The fountain of her blood dried up instantly and she felt in her body that she was healed of her disease.

30 Immediately, Jesus knew in himself that power[34] had gone out of him. Turning around in the crowd, he said, **"Who touched my garments?"** His disciples questioned him, "You see the multitude pressing in on you and yet you ask, **"Who touched me?"** He was looking around to see who had done this when the woman, frightened and trembling because she knew what had happened to her, came to him, fell down before him, and told him the whole truth. He told her, **"My daughter, thy faith has made thee whole. Go in peace and be healed of your disease."**

35 While he was still talking, some men came from the house of the leader of the synagogue, saying. "Your daughter is dead. Why trouble the Teacher any longer?" Jesus overheard the words which they spoke and he said to the leader of the synagogue, **"Do not be afraid, only believe!"** He did not permit any one to go with him except Simon Peter, James, and his brother John. When they came to the house of the leader of the synagogue, Jesus saw a great commotion with people weeping and wailing. So he entered and asked, **"Why are you all excited and weeping? The little girl is not**

dead but asleep." They ridiculed him but he put everyone outside and took the little girl's father, her mother, and those who were with him. He entered where the little girl was laid, took her by the hand, and said, **"Talitha koomi!"** which is translated, **"Little girl, rise up!"** Immediately she got up and walked (she was twelve years old) and they were overcome with great amazement. He gave them strict orders not to tell any one of this and told them to give her something to eat.

Mark 6:1–56

1 Jesus departed from there, came to his own town, and his disciples followed him. When the Sabbath came, he began to teach in the synagogue and many who heard him were astonished, saying, "Where does this fellow get these things?" "What is the source of all this wisdom that allows him to perform such miracles?" "Isn't this the builder, the son of Mary[35] and the brother of James, Joses, Judas, and Simon?" "Aren't his sisters here with us?" They were offended by him, so Jesus told them, **"A prophet is not without honor except in their own hometown, among their own kin, and in their own home."**[36] He was unable to perform even a single miracle there except to lay hands on a few sick people and heal them. He wondered at their lack of faith so he traveled in the villages teaching.

7 Then he called his twelve to him, began to send them out two by two, and gave the power to cast out unclean spirits. He commanded them to take nothing with them except a staff only; no bread, no bag, and no coins under their belts but wear sandals under their feet and not two tunics.[37] He told them, **"Whatever house you enter, stay there until you leave that place for whoever will not welcome you or listen to you, shake off their dust from under your feet as a testimony against them when you leave there. Truly, I tell you, it will be easier for Sodom and Gomorrah in their day of judgement than for that city."** So they went out and preached that all people must repent. They cast out many demons and anointed many with oil who were sick and they were healed.

14 Now King Herod Antipas heard about Jesus for his name was known to him and said, "John the Baptist has risen from the dead and this is why miracles are performed by him." Others said, "He is Elijah." and "He is a prophet, just like one of the prophets of old." Then when Herod Antipas

heard it, he said, "It is John, whom I beheaded; he has risen from the dead." For Herod Antipas had sent out and arrested John, to cast him into prison because of Herodias, the wife of his half-brother Philip,38 whom he had married. John had said to Herod Antipas, "It is not lawful for you to marry your brother's wife." Herodias was bitter toward him and would have killed him but she could not for Herod Antipas was afraid of John because he knew that he was a righteous and holy man, so he kept him safe. When he heard him he was greatly perplexed, yet he gladly listened to him. Then an opportunity came when Herod Antipas gave a banquet on his birthday for his officials, military officers, and the chiefs of the districts.39

22 When the daughter of Herodias entered and danced, she pleased Herod Antipas and the guests who were with him. The king said to the girl, "Ask me whatever you wish and I will give it to you." He swore to her, "Whatever you ask me, I will give it to you; as much as half of my kingdom!" She went out and said to her mother, 'What shall I ask him?" She replied, "The head of John the Baptist." Immediately she rushed back to the king, saying, "I want you to give me at once the head of John the Baptist on a platter." The king was exceedingly sorry but because of his oaths and for the guests, he did not want to refuse her. So the king sent a soldier of the guard with orders to bring the head of John. He went, beheaded John in the prison, brought the head on a platter, gave it to the girl, and the girl gave it to her mother. When his disciples heard of it, they came, took his body, and buried it in a grave.

30 The apostles returned to Jesus and told him what they had done and taught. He said to them, **"Come away all by yourselves to a deserted place and rest a while."** For many were coming and going and they had no chance even to eat. So they went away in a boat to a deserted place by themselves. The multitudes saw them when they were leaving, hurried by land from all the towns, and reached the place ahead of them. Jesus came ashore deeply moved with compassion for the multitude because they were like sheep without a shepherd, so he began to teach them many things.

35 When it was getting late, his disciples came up to him and said, "This is a deserted place and the hour is late. Send these people away so they can go to the farms and villages around here to buy themselves

something to eat." Jesus answered, **"You give them something to eat!"** They replied, "Shall we go to buy two hundred denarii worth of bread and give it to them to eat?" He said to them, **"Go and see how many loaves of bread you have here."** They found out and said, "Five loaves and two fish." He commanded them to make everyone sit down in groups on the green grass. So they sat down in groups of hundreds and fifties. He took the five loaves of bread and the two fish, looked up to heaven, blessed and broke the loaves of bread, gave them to his disciples to place before them, and he divided the two fish among them all. They all ate and were satisfied. They gathered up twelve baskets of morsels from the bread and fish. Those who ate bread were over five thousand people.

45 Immediately he urged his disciples to embark on a boat and go before him to the port of Bethsaida while he was dismissing the crowd. He went up to the mountain to pray after he dismissed them. When evening came the boat was out on the sea and he was alone on the shore. He saw his disciples struggling to row against the wind. About three in the morning Jesus came to them walking on[40] the sea. He wanted to pass by them but when they saw him walking on the sea, they thought he was a ghost. They all saw him and were terrified so immediately he spoke to them saying, **"Be of good cheer! I AM! Don't be afraid."** He climbed into the boat with them and the wind quieted down. They were completely astounded and wondered for they did not understand the miracle of the bread because their hearts were hardened.

53 When they had crossed over, they landed at the port of Generate, moored to the shore, and climbed out of the boat. Immediately the people recognized him, ran around the surrounding country, and began to bring those who were seriously sick; carrying them in their quilts to places where they heard he was. Wherever he entered in villages, cities, or the countryside; they laid the sick in the market places and begged him that they might even touch the edge of his garment. All who touched it were healed.

Mark 7:1–37

1 Now when the Pharisees gathered around him, some of their scribes who had come from Jerusalem saw his disciples eating bread with unwashed hands, so they reproached them. For the Pharisees and many

of the Jewish people,[41] do not eat at all except they wash their hands carefully because they strictly observed the tradition of the elders.[42] When they come from the market place they do not eat anything from the market unless they purify themselves and they do not eat anything from the market unless they purify it. There are many other things which they have traditionally observed such as the washing of cups, pots, copper utensils, bronze kettles, dining couches, and the bedding of the dead.

5 So the scribes of the Pharisees asked Jesus, "Why don't your disciples walk according to the tradition of the elders but eat bread with their hands unwashed?" He answered them, saying, **"Isaiah accurately prophesied of you hypocrites when he wrote:** *'God*[43] *said, "'These people draw near to Me with their mouths and honor Me with their lips, but they have removed their hearts far from Me. In vain do they worship Me by teaching the precepts and doctrines of people.'"* [44] **You have ignored the commandments of God to cling to human traditions."** He continued, **"You have a fine way of rejecting God's commandments to uphold your own tradition. For Moses said,** *'Honor your father and your mother that your days may be long upon the land which your God gives you.'*[45] and *'Whoever curses your father or your mother may be put to death.'*[46] **Yet you say, 'A person may say to their father or mother, "'What you would have gained from me is Korban** (that is, an offering to God).'" **Then you no longer permit them to do anything for their father or mother. So you dishonor the word of God for the sake of the tradition which you have established and you do many other things like this."**

14 He summoned the multitude to come closer and said, **"Listen to me everyone and understand: there is nothing outside a person that goes into them which can defile them but the things that come out of that person are what defiles them. Whoever has ears to hear, will understand!"** When he entered a house to leave the people, his disciples asked him concerning the parable. He said, **"Are you so far from comprehending? Don't you realize that whatever goes into a person does not defile that person because it enters not into their heart but into their stomach and passed out through the intestines, thereby purifying the food."**[47] He said, **"It is what goes out of a person that defiles that person. From out of the human heart come evil thoughts, murder,**[48] **theft, adultery,**[49] **sexual immorality,**[50] **extortion, slander,**

deceit,[51] wickedness,[52] **greed, coveting, envy, licentiousness,**[53] **false pride, and folly. All of these evils come from within and they defile the person.**"[54]

24 From there he arose, went to the region of Tyre and Sidon, entered into a house, and didn't want anyone to know it. Yet he could not hide himself for immediately a woman, whose daughter had an unclean spirit, heard about him so she came and fell at his feet. Now this woman was a Gentile, from Phoenicia of Syria and begged him cast the demon out of her daughter. Jesus said, **"Let the children**[55] **first be fed, since it's not right to take the children's bread and throw it to the dogs."**[56] She answered, "Yes Saviour, but even the puppies eat the children's crumbs under the tables." He said, **"For this saying you may go your way, the demon has gone out of your daughter."** She went home to find her child lying on the bed and the demon gone.

31 Then he returned from the region of Tyre and went through Sidon towards the Sea of Galilee in the region of Decapolis. They brought a man to him who was a deaf man with a speech impediment and asked Jesus to lay his hand on him. He drew him apart from the multitude in private and put his fingers in the man's ears, then he spat and touched his tongue. While he looked to heaven he sighed and said to him, **"Ethpathah!"** which means **"Be opened!"**[57] Immediately his ears were opened, his speech impediment was removed, and he spoke plainly. He warned them to tell no one but the more he warned them, the more zealously they proclaimed it. They were astonished beyond measure, saying, "He does everything so well! He makes the deaf hear and the mute speak!"

Mark 8:1–38

1 In those days when a great multitude had gathered who had nothing to eat, he called his disciples aside and said, **"I have compassion for the multitude because they have remained with me for three days and have nothing to eat! If I send them away hungry to their homes, they will faint on the way for some of them have come a great distance."** His disciples said, "How can anyone feed these people with bread out here in this deserted place?" Jesus asked, **"How many loaves do you have?"** They replied, "Seven." So he commanded the people to sit on the ground, took the seven loaves of bread, blessed them, broke them up, and

gave them to his disciples who set them before the multitude. There were a few small fish which he also blessed and ordered them to be set before the people. So they ate and were satisfied. They took up seven baskets of the morsels which were left over. The people who had eaten were about four thousand and he dismissed them.

10 Immediately he entered a boat with his disciples and came to the district of Dalmanutha.58 Some Pharisees came out, began to argue with him and to test him, and asked for a sign from heaven. He sighed deeply in his spirit, saying, **"Why does this generation seek after a sigh? Truly I tell you, no sign will be given to this generation."** He left them, got back into the boat, and departed for the other side.

14 Now his disciples had forgotten to bring bread and they had only one loaf with them in the boat. He cautioned them, saying, **"Take heed, beware of the leaven of the Pharisees and the leaven of Herod!"** They discussed with one another, saying, "Is it because we brought no bread." Aware of this, Jesus said, **"Why do you reason this way because you have brought no bread? Don't you perceive nor understand yet? Are your hearts so hardened? Having eyes, do you not see? Having ears, do you not hear? Don't you even remember? When I broke up five loaves for the five thousand, how many full baskets of morsels did you pick up?"** They replied, "Twelve." He said, **"When I broke up the seven loaves for the four thousand, how many baskets of morsels did you collect?"** They replied softly, "Seven." He asked again, **"Do you still not understand?"**59

22 When they arrived at Bethsaida some people brought him a blind man and begged him to touch him. He took the blind man by the hand, bought him outside of the village, spat on his eyes, put his hands on him, and asked, **"Can you see anything?"** He looked up and replied, "I see people that look like trees walking!" Again he put his hands on his eyes; he looked intently so he was restored and saw everything clearly. He sent him home, saying, **"Don't even go into the village or tell anyone in the village!"**

27 Jesus went out with his disciples to the towns of Caesarea and Philippi and on the road he asked his disciples, **"Who do people say that I am?"**60 They answered, "John the Baptist" but some said, "Elijah," and yet others

replied, "One of the prophets." He asked them, **"Who do you say that I am?"** Peter answered, "You are the Christ." He warned them not to tell anyone about him. He began to teach them that the Son of humanity must suffer many things, be rejected by the elders, the chief priests and the scribes, be killed, and rise again on the third day. He spoke this saying openly, so Peter took him aside and began to rebuke him but he turned around, looked on his disciples, and rebuked Peter, saying, **"Get behind me, Satan! For you do not savor the things that be of God but the things that be of men."**

34 Jesus called the people together with his disciples, saying, **"Whoever wants to come after me must deny yourself, take up your cross, and follow me. For whoever desires to save your life will lose it and whoever loses your life for my sake and for the sake of the Good News, will save it. What will it benefit a person if they gain the whole world and lose their own soul?**61 **What will a person give in exchange for their soul? For whoever is ashamed of me and my words from the adulterous and sinful people of this generation, of them the Son of humanity also will be ashamed when he comes in the glory of his Divine Parent with the holy angels."**

Mark 9:1–50

1 He said to them, **"Truly I tell you, there are some standing here who will not taste death before they see the kin-dom of God has come with power."**62 Six days later, Jesus took Peter, James, and John and brought them alone up to a high mountain where he was transfigured before their eyes. His clothes shone and became dazzling white like snow in such a manner as no one on earth could bleach them. There appeared to them Moses and Elijah, talking with Jesus and Peter said to him, "Teacher, it is good for us to be here. So let us make three tabernacles, one for you, one for Moses, and one for Elijah." for he did not know what he was saying as they were afraid. There was a cloud overshadowing them and a Voice out of the cloud said, "This is my beloved Son. Listen to him!"63 Suddenly, when the disciples looked around, they saw no one except Jesus alone with them. As they came down from the mountain, he commanded them to tell no one what they had seen until the Son of humanity has risen from the dead. So they kept the matter to themselves but they wanted to know what "rising from the dead" meant.

11 They asked him, "Why do the scribes say that Elijah must come first?" He answered, **"Elijah does comes first and restores all things.**[64] **It is written concerning the Son of humanity that he will suffer many things and be despised and rejected by men**[65] **but I tell you that Elijah has come and they did to him whatever they pleased, as it is written concerning him."** When he came to his disciples, he saw a great multitude around them with some scribes debating with them. Immediately all the people saw him, were greatly amazed, ran up to him, and greeted him. He asked the scribes, **"What are you debating with them?"** One of multitude answered, "Teacher, I brought you my son for he has a mute spirit and whenever it seizes him and throws him down; he foams at the mouth, grinds his teeth, and becomes rigid. I asked your disciples to cast it out but they could not."

19 Jesus replied to them, **"Oh the faithless of this generation, how long shall I be with you? How long shall I preach to you? Bring him to me!"** They brought the child to him and when the spirit saw him, immediately it convulsed the boy and he fell on the ground; rolling about, gasping, and foaming at the mouth. Jesus asked his father, **"How long has he been like this?"** He replied, "From childhood and many times it has thrown him into the fire[66] and into the water to destroy him but if you can do anything, have mercy on us, and help us!"

23 Jesus said, **"If you can believe, faith is the power of God. All things are possible for one who believes."** The father cried out immediately, weeping and said, "I do believe! Help my little faith!" When Jesus saw that people were running and gathering about him, he rebuked the foul spirit, saying, **"Oh deaf and mute spirit, I command you, come out of him and never enter him again!"** After crying out and convulsing him terribly, the spirit came out so the boy was like a corpse, so many said, "He is dead!" Jesus took him by the hand, lifted him up, and he arose. When Jesus entered the house, his disciples asked him privately, "Why couldn't we cast it out?" He said, **"This kind can come out only by prayer."**

30 They went from there and passed through Galilee. He taught them, **"The Son of humanity will be delivered into the hands of men, they will kill him, and after he is killed he will rise on the third day."** They

didn't understand the saying and were afraid to ask him. They came to Capernaum and when they entered the house, he asked, **"What were you reasoning about on the way?"** They kept silent for on the way they had been arguing with one another who was the greatest of them. Jesus sat down, called the twelve, and taught them, **"If anyone wishes to be first, they must be the last of all, and the servant of all."** He took a little child and placed her in the midst of them, then he took her in his arms, saying, **"Whoever receives a little child like this in my name, they receive me, and whoever receives me does not receive me but God Who sent me."**

38 John said, "Teacher, we saw a person casting out demons in your name and we forbad him because he didn't follow us." Jesus said, **"Do not forbid him for no one who performs a miracle in my name is likely to speak evil of me for whoever is not against us is for us. Whoever gives you even a cup of water to drink in my name because you are followers of me, truly I tell you, they will not lose their reward. Whoever will cause one of these little ones who believe in me to stumble, it would be better for them to have a great millstone hung around their neck and thrown into the sea!**

43 **If your hand offends you, cut it off!** [*Stop stealing!*]67 **It is better for you to enter life maimed than with two hands and go into a living hell,** *where your worms do not die and the fire is not quenched.*68 **If your foot offends you, cut it off!** [*Stop trespassing!*]69 **It is better for you to enter life lame than with two feet and be thrown into a living hell,** *where your worms do not die and the fire is not quenched.* **If your eye offends you, pluck it out.** [*Stop envying!*]70 **It is better for you to enter the kin-dom of God with one eye than with two eyes and be thrown into a living hell,** *where the worms do not die and the fire is not quenched.* **Everyone will be salted with fire and every sacrifice will be salted with salt. Salt is a good thing but if the salt has lost its savor,**71 **how can you season with it? Have salt in yourselves**72 **and make peace with one another."**

Mark 10:1–52

1 He left there, came to the region of Judea beyond the Jordan, and many people went to him there. He taught them as he was accustomed to do,

and some Pharisees came to tempt him by asking, "Is it lawful for a man to divorce his wife?" He said, **"What did Moses command you?"** They said, "Moses gave us permission to write a letter of separation and then to divorce." He answered, **"It was because of the hardness of your heart that he wrote for you this particular law. From the beginning God** *made them female and male.*[73] *For this reason a person will leave their mother and father and be united with their spouse. Both will become one flesh; henceforth they are not two, but one flesh.*[74] **Therefore, what God has joined together, let no person separate."** Then in the house the disciples asked him about this matter and he said to them, **"Whoever divorces his wife and marries another commits adultery against her and if a woman divorces her husband and marries another, she commit adultery."**[75]

13 They brought little children to him that he might touch them but his disciples rebuked those who brought them. When Jesus saw it he became indignant, saying, **"Let the little children come to me! Do not hinder them for the kin-dom of God belongs to such as these little ones. Truly I tell you, whoever does not receive the kin-dom of God like a little child will never enter in."**[76] Jesus took them up in his arms, laid his hands on them, and blessed them.

17 As he was leaving on a journey, a young man came running up, knelt before him, and asked, "Good Teacher! What must I do to inherit eternal life?" Jesus replied, **"Why do you call me good? No one is good but God alone! Do you know the commandments?** *Do not commit adultery. Do not murder. Do not steal. Do not bear false witness.* **Do not defraud.** *Honor thy mother and thy father."*[77] He answered, "Teacher, I have observed all these things since I was a child." Jesus looked at him, loved him, and said, **"You lack one thing; go your way, sell whatever you own, give it to the poor, and you will have treasure in heaven. Then come, take up your cross, and follow me!"** He became sad at this saying and went away grieving for he had great possessions.

23 Jesus looked around and told his disciples, **" How difficult it will be for those who have an abundance of things**[78] **to enter into the kin-dom of God!"** His disciples were perplexed at his words and Jesus said, **" Children, how hard it is for those who trust in riches**[79] **to enter**

the kin-dom of God! It is easier for a rope to pass through the eye of a needle than for a person who has an abundance of things to enter into the kin-dom of God." They were greatly astonished and said to one another, "Who then can be saved?" Jesus looked at them, saying, "With people this is impossible but not with God for all things are possible with God."

28 Peter told him, "Look, we have left everything and followed you!" So Jesus explained, "Truly, I tell you there is no one who leaves houses or brothers or sisters or father or mother or husband or wife or children or lands for my sake and for the Good News; who will not receive a hundred fold now in this time, houses and sisters and brothers and children and lands by following me,[80] and eternal life in your world to come. Many who are first will be last and the last first."[81]

32 Jesus was ahead of the disciples while they were on the road going up to Jerusalem and they were amazed while those who followed behind were afraid. He took the twelve aside and began to tell them what was going to happen to him, saying, "Behold, we are going up to Jerusalem, the Son of humanity will be delivered to the chief priests and the scribes who will condemn him to death[82] and deliver him to the Gentiles. They will mock him, scourge him, spit on him, kill him, and on the third day he will rise again."

35 James and John, the sons[83] of Zebedee came up to him, saying, "Teacher, we wish you would do whatever we ask of thee." Jesus answered, "What do you want me to do for you?" They replied, "In your glory, let one of us sit on thy left hand and let the other sit on thy right hand." Jesus told them, "You don't know what you are asking! Can you drink the cup which I drink and be baptized with the baptism with which I am to be baptized?" They said, "Yes, we can!" So Jesus said, "You will indeed drink the cup that I will drink and you will also be baptized with the baptism with which I am baptized but to sit at my right hand or at my left hand is not my choice to give but will be given to those for whom it has been prepared."

41 When the ten heard of it, they became angry with James and John. Then Jesus called them closer to him, explaining, "You know that those

who consider themselves to be rulers over the Gentiles have power over them and their great people exercise authority over them. This will not be so with you but whoever wishes to be great among you, let them be a minister to you and whoever wishes to be first among you, let them be a servant to all. For the Son of humanity did not come to be ministered to but to minister and to give his life as a salvation for the sake of many."

46 They came to Jericho and as he was leaving Jericho with his disciples and a great multitude; Bartimaeus, a blind man, the son of Timaeus, sat by the roadside begging. When he heard that it was Jesus of Nazareth, he began the cry aloud, "Jesus, Oh Son of David, have mercy on me!" Many disapproved and told him to be quiet but he cried out even more, saying, "Oh Son of David, have mercy on me!" Jesus stood still, saying, **"Call him!"** So they called the blind man, "Have courage, rise, he is calling you." The blind man threw off his robe, got up, and went to Jesus. Then Jesus asked him, **"What do you wish me to do for you?"** Bartimaeus told him, "Rabbouni,[84] I want to receive my sight!" Jesus said, **"Go thy way! Thy faith has made thee whole."** Immediately, he received his sight and followed him on the way.

Mark 11:1–33

1 When he came near to Jerusalem, towards Bethhage and Bethany at the Mount of Olives, he sent two of his disciples; instructing them, **"Go into the village across the way and after you enter it, you will find a colt tied up that has never been ridden. Untie it, bring it, and if anyone questions you, 'Why are you untying that colt?' tell them, 'Our Saviour needs it and immediately they will send it here.'"** So they went and found the colt tied by the door outside in the street. When they were untying it, some of the people standing there said, "What are you are doing, untying the colt?" They answered them as Jesus had instructed and they let them take it. They brought the colt to Jesus after spreading their garments on it and he rode on it. Many spread their garments on the road while others cut down leafy branches from the fields and spread them on the road.

9 Then all who went ahead and those who followed cried out together: "Hosanna! *Blessed is the one who comes in the name of God!*[85] Blessed

is the coming kin-dom of our father David! Hosanna in the highest heaven!" Jesus entered Jerusalem, went into the Temple, looked around at everything, and went out to Bethany with the twelve when evening came. He was hungry when they left Bethany the next day and when he spotted a fig tree in the distance with leaves on it, he went up to the tree to see if he could find anything on it but when he came to the tree, he found nothing on it except leaves for it was not yet time for the figs. He reacted by saying, **"May no one ever eat fruit from you again!"** and his disciples heard it.

15 They came to Jerusalem where Jesus entered into the Temple of God and began to chase out those who were buying and selling in the Temple, overturned the tables of the money changers, pushed over the stands of the dove merchants, and allowed no one to carry merchandise through the Temple area. He taught them, **"It is written, *'My house will be called a private prayer place for all peoples!'*[86] but you have turned it into a *den of thieves!'*[87]** The chief priests and the scribes[88] who heard this sought a way to get rid of him but they were afraid of him because all the people there were astonished by his teachings. They left the city when evening came.[89]

20 In the morning as they passed by, they saw the fig tree dried up from the roots. Peter remembered and said, "Teacher, behold the fig tree you cursed has withered away! Jesus answered them, **"If you have faith in God,[90] truly I tell you that whoever will say to this mountain; 'Be moved from your place and fall into the sea!' and does not doubt in their heart but believes that what they say will come to pass, then it will be done for them.[91] Therefore I tell you that whatever you ask for in prayer, believe that you will receive it and it will be yours. When you stand to pray, if you are holding anything against anyone forgive them, so that your heavenly Divine Parent may forgive you your offenses but if you do not forgive, neither will your heavenly Divine Parent forgive you your offenses."**

27 Again they went to Jerusalem and while he was walking in the Temple, the chief priests, the scribes, and the elders came and asked him, "By what authority are you doing these things? Who gave you the authority to do them?" Jesus answered, **"I also have a question for you! If you**

answer me then I will tell you by what authority I do these things. Was the baptism of John from heaven or from people? Answer me!" They reasoned among themselves, "If we say, 'From heaven,' then he will reply, 'Why then didn't you believe John?' If we say, 'From people,' then we must fear the people for they all consider John to be a true prophet!" So they answered, "We don't know!" Jesus said, **"Neither will I tell you by what authority I do these things."**

Mark 12:1–44

1 He began to speak to them in parables: **"A man planted a vineyard, put a fence around it, dug a pit in it for a winepress, built a tower on it, leased it to tenant farmers, and went on a journey to a far country. In due season he sent his servant to the tenant farmers to receive some of the fruits of the vineyard but they beat him and sent him away empty. Again he sent another servant but they stoned him, wounded him, and sent him away in disgrace. Again he sent another but they killed him so he sent many other servants; some of them they beat and some they killed. Finally, he still had one other, a beloved son, and he sent him to them, saying, 'They will respect my son.' Then the tenant farmers said among themselves, 'This is the heir; come, let us kill him, and the inheritance will be ours.' So they took him, killed him, and threw him outside of the vineyard. What then will the owner of the vineyard do?"** [*The Jewish authorities replied,*] "He will come, destroy those tenant farmers, and lease the vineyard to others." [*Jesus asked,*] **"Haven't you read this scripture, *'The stone which the builders rejected has become the chief cornerstone?*[92] *This was God's doing; it is marvelous in our eyes.*[93]"**

12 They [*The Jewish authorities*] wanted to arrest him when they realized that he had told this parable against them[94] but they feared the multitudes. So they left him and went on their way. Then they sent some of the Pharisees and some of the Herodians to catch him in his words. They came and asked, "Teacher, we know that you are sincere and impartial as you seek no one's favor. You truly teach the way of God. Is it lawful to pay taxes to Caesar or not? Should we pay them or not pay them?" He knew their hypocrisy and said, **"Why do you test me? Bring me a denarius and let me see it!"** So they gave the coin to him and he said, **"Whose is this image and inscription?"** They

replied, "Caesar's!" Jesus told them, **"Pay to Caesar what belongs to Caesar, and give to God what belongs to God."**95 and they were amazed at him.

18 Then some Sadducees, who say there is no resurrection, came to him asking, "Teacher, Moses wrote for our benefit that if a man's brother dies and leaves a wife but no children; his brother may take this widow as his wife and raise up offspring for his brother.96 The first of seven brothers married a woman but left no offspring when he died. Another brother married her but they still had no children when he died and a third brother did likewise. All seven had married her and left no children. Last of all the woman also died. So, at the resurrection whose spouse will this woman be, for all seven had married her?"

24 Jesus answered, **"Isn't this why you are in error, because you neither understand the scriptures nor the power of God? For when they rise from the dead, they neither marry nor are given in marriage but are like the angels in heaven. Now concerning the dead being raised, haven't you read in the book of Moses where God spoke to him from the burning bush, saying, *'I am the God of your father, the God of Abraham, the God of Isaac, and the God of Jacob!'*97 God is not the God of the dead but of the living. Therefore you make a great error!"**

28 One of the scribes came near, heard them reasoning, and understood how skillfully Jesus had answered them. He asked him, "Which commandment is the first? He replied, **"The first is: *'Hear Oh Israel, the Eternal is our God, the Eternal is One. You shall love the Eternal your God with all your heart, with all your soul, with all your mind, and with all your strength.*98 The second is this, *'You shall love your neighbor as yourself.'*99 There is no other commandment greater than these."** The scribe said, "You have said the truth, Teacher, that God is One and there is no other God; and to love God with all the heart, with all the understanding, with all the soul, and with all the strength and to love one's neighbor as oneself. This is more important than all the whole burnt offerings and sacrifices." Jesus saw that he had spoken wisely, saying, **"You are not far from the kin-dom of God."** After that, no one dared to ask him any questions.

35 Jesus taught in the Temple, **"How can the scribes claim that the Christ is the son of David? David himself, inspired by the Holy Spirit, declared,** *'God said to my lord, "'Sit at my right hand*[100] *until I make your enemies your footstool.'"* **'**[101] **Now if David calls him 'lord'** [*the Christ*]**, how can he be his son?"** The common people heard his sayings with delight. In his teaching he said, **"Beware of scribes who desire to go around in long robes, love to be saluted in the marketplaces, have the best seats in their synagogues, take the honored places at feasts,**[102] **and embezzle the property entrusted to them by widows**[103] **under pretense of making long prayers. They will receive the greater condemnation."**

41 He sat opposite the treasury observing how people put alms into the treasury and many rich men were giving large sums. A poor widow came and put in two small coins worth only a penny. He called his disciples close to him, saying, **"Truly I tell you that this poor widow has put more into the treasury than all the men who contributed. For they all contributed out of their abundance but this woman out of her poverty put in everything, all that she had to live on."**

Mark 13:1–37

1 When Jesus went out of the Temple, one disciple remarked, "Teacher, behold the massive stones and beautiful buildings!" He told him, **"Take a good look at these great buildings! No stone will be left upon another for all will be thrown down."** Now as Jesus sat on the Mount of Olives opposite the Temple; Peter, James, John, and Andrew asked him privately, "Tell us when these things will take place. What will be the sign when all these things will be fulfilled?"

5 He began his answer, **"Be careful that no one deceives you, for many will come in my name, saying, 'I AM!' and lead many astray. When you hear of wars and rumors of revolutions, don't be afraid for these things are inevitable but your end is not yet. For nation will rise against nation and empire against empire. There will be earthquakes in all countries and there will be famines and uprisings. These are the beginnings of the birth pangs of sorrows. Watch out for yourselves for they will deliver you up to the judges, you will be beaten in their prisons, and you will stand before rulers and monarchs for my**

sake, to give testimony against them. **The Good News must first be preached among all peoples. When they deliver you up, don't worry or premeditate on what you will speak. Say whatever is given to you at the moment for it is not you who speak but the Holy Spirit.**

12 Now the brother will betray his brother to death, a father will betray his son, and the children will rise up against their parents and put them to death. You will be hated by many because of my name but whoever hopes until the end will be saved. So when you see the *abomination of desolation,*[104] **spoken of by Daniel the prophet, set where it ought not to be,** (let you who reads understand)[105] **then let those who are in Judea flee to the mountain. She who on the roof must not go down to take anything out of the house. He who is in the field must not go back again to take up his garment. Woe to those women who are pregnant or nursing babies in those days. Pray that you won't need to flee in winter for in those days there will be great tribulation such as has not occurred since God created the world until this time and never will be. For the sake of the elect,**[106] **whom God chose, God will shorten those days or no flesh would be saved.**

21 Then, if someone tells you, 'Behold, here is the Christ!' or 'Look, there is the Christ!' don't believe them for false Christs and phony prophets will arise and show signs and wonders to seduce even the chosen ones if possible.[107] **Be careful, I have told you about these things in advance but in those days, after that tribulation, the sun will be darkened, the moon will not give its light, and the constellations of heaven will be shaken! Then you will see the Son of humanity coming in clouds with great power and glory. He will send out the angels to gather his elect from the four winds, from the ends of the earth to the uttermost parts of heaven.**

28 Learn this parable of the fig tree; when its branches become tender and brings forth leaves, you know that summer is near. So also, when you see these things happening; know that the Christ is near, at the very doors! Truly I tell you, this generation will not pass away before all these things take place. Your heaven and earth will pass away but my words will remain. No person knows concerning the day or the hour, neither the angels in heaven nor the Son, but only the Divine

Parent. Beware, watch and pray for you don't know when your time will come! It is like a man going on a journey who leaves home and gives authority to his employees, each with their own work, and commands the doorkeeper to keep watch. Therefore watch for you never know when the owner of the house will return: in the evening, at midnight, when the rooster crows, or early morning. He may come back suddenly and find you sleeping. I tell everyone what I say to you 'Watch!'"

Mark 14:1–72

1 It was two days before the Passover[108] and the Feast of the Unleavened Bread. The chief priests and the scribes were seeking how to arrest him secretly and have him killed. They said, "Not during the feast for it may cause a riot of the people." When he was in the house of Simon the leper at Bethany, reclining at a table, a woman came in carrying an alabaster jar of pure nard, of good quality and very expensive.[109] Then she opened the jar and poured it on the head of Jesus. There were some men of the disciples who were indeed vexed,[110] and said among themselves, "Why was this ointment wasted like this? It could have sold it for more than three hundred denarii and the money given to the poor." So they scolded her. Jesus said, **"Leave her alone! Why do you trouble her? She has done a beautiful thing to me. You always have the poor with you and whenever you wish, you can do good to them but you will not always have me. She has done all that was in her power to do by anointing my body beforehand for burial. Truly I tell you, wherever the Good News is preached in the whole world, what this woman has done will also be told as a memorial to her."**

10 Judas Iscariot, one of the twelve, went to the chief priests to deliver Jesus to them. They were delighted when they heard it and promised to give him money, so he began to look for an opportunity to betray him.

12 On the first day of the Feast of the Unleavened Bread when the Passover lamb is sacrificed, his disciples asked, "Where do you want us to go and make preparations to eat the Passover meal? He sent two disciples, saying, **"Go into the city where you will meet a man carrying a pitcher of water; follow him and wherever he enters, say to the owner of the house, 'The Teacher asks, "'Where is the guest room where I may**

observe the Passover with my disciples?'"111' He will show you an upper room, furnished and ready. Make preparations for us there." His disciples went to the city, found the upper room just as he said, and prepared the Passover.

17 In the evening he came with his twelve disciples and as they were reclined at the table and eating, Jesus said, "Truly I tell you, one of you eating with me will betray me." They became distressed and said to him one after another, "Am I the one?" He answered, "It is one of the twelve disciples who is dipping bread with me in the same bowl. The Son of humanity will go as it is written but woe to the man by whom the Son of humanity will be betrayed. It would be better for that one if they had not been born." While they were eating, Jesus took bread, blessed it, broke it in pieces, and gave it to them, saying, "Take it, this is my body!"112 Then he took a cup, gave it to them after giving thanks, and all of them drank from it. He told them, "This is the blood113 of the new covenant,114 which is shed for the sake of many. Truly I tell you, I will not drink of the fruit of the vine115 until that day when I drink it new in the kin-dom of God." When they had sung a hymn, they went out to the Mount of Olives.

27 Then Jesus said, "You will all be offended because of me this night, for it is written, *'I will strike the shepherd that his sheep may be scattered.'*116 Then after I am risen, I will go to Galilee before you." Peter insisted, "Although all will be offended, I won't!" Jesus informed him, "Truly I tell you, this day, even this very night before the rooster crows twice, you will deny me three times." Then he protested vehemently, "Even if I have to die with you, I will never deny you!" All the rest said the same.

32 They came to a place named Gethsemane and he told his disciples, "Sit down here while I go to pray." He took Peter, James, and John with him but he became greatly distressed and agitated. He said, "My soul is deeply troubled even to death! Stay here and watch!" He walked a little farther, fell on the ground, and prayed that if it were possible, this hour might pass from him. He said, "Abba,117 Sacred Father, all things are possible for Thee, take this cup away from me; yet not according to my will but Thy will!" He returned to find them sleeping and woke

Peter, saying, **"Simon, are you sleeping? Couldn't you watch for just one hour? Watch and pray that you will not fail in the test. The spirit is indeed ready and willing but the body is weak."** Again he went away and prayed the same words. He returned to find them sleeping again because their eyes were heavy and they didn't know what to say. He came back a third time and said, **"You are sleeping too much and you are resting too long!**[118] **The end and the hour are pressing. Behold, the Son of humanity is betrayed into the hands of sinners! Rise up! Let us go! Behold, my betrayer is near!"**

43 While he was speaking, Judas, one of the twelve, came in a crowd with swords and clubs from the chief priests, the scribes, and the elders. The betrayer gave them a sign, saying, "Carefully seize the one I shall kiss and take him away securely." When he came, he went up to him immediately and said, "My Teacher!" and he kissed him. They laid hands on him and arrested him but one of those standing nearby drew his sword, struck the servant of the high priest and cut off his ear. Jesus answered them, **"Have you come to arrest me with swords and clubs as against a bandit? I was with you every day teaching in the Temple and you didn't arrest me but this has happened so that the scriptures might be fulfilled."** *"7 He was oppressed and he was afflicted but never opened his mouth; like a lamb led to the slaughter and like a sheep silent before its shearers. So he did not open his mouth."*[119] Then his disciples deserted him and fled. They seized a young man following him with only a linen cloth around his naked body but he left the linen cloth and fled naked.

53 They took Jesus away to the high priest where the chief priests, the scribes, and the elders were assembled. Peter had followed him at a distance right into the courtyard of the high priest where he was sitting with the guards, warming himself by the fire. Now the chief priests and the whole council[120] were looking for testimony against Jesus that they might put him to death but found none. Many gave false testimony against him but their testimony didn't agree. Then some men who were false witnesses stood up against him, saying, "We heard him say, 'I will destroy this Temple which is made by hands and in three days I will build another which is not made with hands.'[121]" Even on this point their testimony did not agree.

60 Then the high priest stood up in the midst and asked Jesus, "Have you nothing to answer why these people are testifying against you? He remained silent and made no answer. The high priest asked him, "Are you the Christ, Son of the Blessed One?" Jesus said, **"I am and you will see the Son of humanity sitting at the right hand of the Power**[122] **coming upon the clouds of the sky."** The high priest then tore his clothes, saying, "Why do we still need witnesses! Behold, you have heard this insolence[123] from his own mouth, what do you think?" They adjudged him worthy of the death penalty.[124] Some began to spit on him, to cover his face, and struck him on the head, saying. "Prophesy!" The guards also beat him up with the palms of their hands.

66 Now while Peter was below in the courtyard, a maid of the high priest came over, and saw Peter warming himself by the fire. She looked at him and said, "You also were with Jesus of Nazareth!" He denied it, saying, "I don't know or understand what you mean." Then he went out into the forecourt and the rooster crowed. The maid saw him again and told the bystanders, "This man is one of them," but again he denied it. A little later, the bystanders told Peter, "Truly you are one of them, since you are also a Galilean and even your speech is like theirs." He began to curse at them and to swear, "I don't know the man of whom you speak!" Immediately the rooster crowed again and Peter remembered Jesus' words, **"Before the rooster crows twice, you will deny me three times."** Then he broke down and wept.

Mark 15:1–47

1 First thing in the morning the high priest took counsel together with the chief priests, the scribes, the elders, and his whole council. Then they bound Jesus, led him away, and delivered him to Pilate, the governor. Pilate asked him, "Are you the King of the Jews?" He answered, **"You say so."** The chief priests accused him of many things but he answered nothing. Then Pilate asked again, "Have you no answer? See how many are testifying against you." Jesus gave no answer so that Pilate was amazed.

6 Now it was the custom on every feast to release one prisoner whom they asked for. A man called Barabbas was then in prison with the rebels who had committed murder during the insurrection. So the crowd[125] came up and began to ask Pilate to do for them according to his custom.

He answered, " Are you willing that I release to you the King of the Jews?" Pilate knew that the chief priests had delivered him because of angry zeal.126 Then the chief priests stirred up their crowd to have him release Barabbas to them. Pilate said, "What then do you wish me to do with the man whom you call the King of the Jews?" They shouted back, "Crucify him!" Then Pilate asked, "Why, what has he done wrong?" Then they shouted all the more, "Crucify him!" Now Pilate, willing to satisfy the crowd, released Bababbas to them and delivered Jesus, when he had scourged him, to be crucified.

16 Then the soldiers took him to the inner courtyard of the palace, which is the Praetorium and called their whole company together. They dressed him in a purple cloak, twisted a crown of thorns, put it on him, and began to salute him, "Hail! King of the Jews!" They struck him on the head with a reed, spat in his face, and knelt down in homage to him. When they had mocked him, they stripped him of the purple cloak, put on his own clothes, and took him out to crucify him. Simon from Cyrene,127 the father of Alexander and Rufus was coming in from the country and passing by so they compelled him to carry his cross.

22 They brought Jesus to Golgotha which means the "Skull Place" and gave him wine mixed with myrrh128 to drink but he would not take it. When they had crucified him, they divided his clothes, and cast lots on them to see what each man would take. It was nine in the morning when they crucified him. The inscription stating the charge against him read, The King of the Jews. They crucified two bandits with him, one on his right and one on his left. The scripture was fulfilled which said, *"12 Therefore I will divide him a portion with the great and he will divide the spoil with the strong because he poured out his soul unto death. He bore the sins of many and made intercession for the transgressors so he was numbered with the transgressors."*129 Those who passed by derided him, nodding their heads, saying, 'Aha, you who would destroy the Temple and build it up in three days, save yourself and come down from the cross." The chief priests with the scribes mocked him among themselves, saying, "He saved others but he cannot save himself. Let Christ, the king of Israel, descend from the cross, so we may see and believe in him." Even those who were crucified with him, also insulted him.

33 At midday a darkness fell all over the land which lasted until three. At three in the afternoon Jesus cried out in a loud voice, *"Eloi! Eloi! Lama sabachthani?"* which is translated, *"My God, my God, why have you forsaken me?"*[130] Some of the bystanders who heard this, said, "Behold, he is calling for Elijah. One ran, filled a sponge full of vinegar, tied it on a reed to give him a drink, and said, "Hush, let us see whether Elijah will come to take him down." Then Jesus gave out a loud cry and took his last breath. The curtain[131] at the door of the Temple were torn in two, from the top to the bottom. When the centurion, who stood facing him, saw that he cried out in this manner and died, he said, "Truly this man was the Son of God!" There were also women who were looking on from afar and among these were Mary Magdalene and Mary, the mother of James the younger and of Josses, and Salome, who had all followed him when he was in Galilee and ministered to him. Many other women who came up with him to Jerusalem were also there.

42 When it was already evening, since it was the day of Preparation, that is, the day before the Sabbath,[132] Joseph of Arimathea, a respected member of the council[133] who was also waiting for the kin-dom of God, took courage and went to Pilate to ask for the body of Jesus. Pilate marveled that he was already dead, so he summoned the centurion and asked him if he had already died. When he learned from the centurion that he was dead, Pilate released his body to Joseph. He brought linen, took him down, wrapped him in it, placed him in tomb which had been hewn out of rock, and rolled a stone against the door of the tomb. Mary Magdalene and Mary, the mother of Josses saw where he was laid.

Mark 16:1–20

1 When the Sabbath had past; Mary Magdalene, Salome, and Mary, the mother of James bought spices so that they might come and anoint him. Just as the sun rose on Sunday morning, they came to the tomb. They said among themselves, "Who will roll away the stone from the door of the tomb for us." They looked and saw that the stone had been rolled away for it was very large. They entered the tomb and saw a young man sitting on the right side, wearing a long white robe and they were frightened. He spoke to them, "Do not be afraid, you seek Jesus of Nazareth who was crucified. Behold, there is the place where they laid him but he is not here, he has risen! Go tell his other disciples and Peter that he will go to

Galilee before you;[134] there you will see him, just as he told you." When they heard this, they went out, and fled from the tomb for amazement and trembling came upon them; and they said nothing to anyone for they were afraid.

[[[135] 9 Now when he rose early on the first day of the week, he appeared first to Mary Magdalene from whom he had cast out seven demons.[136] She went out and brought glad tidings[137] to those who had been with him as they mourned and wept. When they heard that he was alive and had been with her, they didn't believe her.[138] Later that day he appeared in another form to two of them as they were walking along in the country. They returned and told the rest but they didn't believe them either. Afterward he appeared to the eleven who were reclining at a meal and he upbraided them for their lack of faith and hardness of heart because they didn't believe those who had seen him after he had risen.

15 Then he taught them, **"Go into all the world and preach the Good News[139] to the whole creation! Whoever believes and is baptized will be saved and whoever does not believe is condemned already.[140] These wonders will accompany those who have believed: in my name they will cast out demons; they will speak with new tongues;[141] they will handle snakes;[142] if they drink any deadly thing, it will not harm them;[143] and they will lay hands on the sick and they will be healed."** Then after the Saviour had spoken to them, he was taken up into heaven and sat down at the right hand of God. They walked forth and preached everywhere while the Saviour worked with them and confirmed their words by the miracles which they performed.]] Amen.

THE GOSPEL ACCORDING TO LUKE

Luke 1:1–80

1 Since many have desired to have in writing the story of those works with which we are familiar, according to what was handed down to us by those who were eyewitnesses and ministers of the word from the very beginning. It seemed good to me also, having considered them all very carefully for a long time to write an account for you in sequence, most honorable Theopilus,1 so that you may have assurance about the words in which you have been instructed.

5 There was in the days of Herod, king of Judea, a priest of the order of Abijah whose name was Zechariah, and he had a wife Elizabeth of the daughters of Aaron. They were both righteous before God and walked in all the commandments and requirements of God without blame but they had no son because Elizabeth was infertile and they were both on in years. Now while he was serving as a priest in his order before God, he was chosen by lot according to the custom of the priesthood, so he entered the Temple of God to burn incense.

10 All the people prayed outside at the time of incense and an angel of God appeared to Zechariah, standing on the right side of the altar of incense. Zachariah was troubled when he saw the angel and fear came over him but the angel said to him, "Do not be afraid, Zechariah for your prayer has been heard and your wife Elizabeth will bear you a son and you will call his name John. You will have joy and gladness for many will rejoice at

his birth. He will be great in the sight of God. He will not drink wine or liquor and he will be filled with the Holy Spirit even while he is still in the womb of his mother. He will cause many children of Israel to turn back to their God and he will go before them with the spirit and the power of Elijah. '*He will turn the hearts of the parents back to their children and the hearts of the children back to their parents,*'[2] to bring the unbelievers back to the wisdom of the just and to restore to God a people about to be lost."[3]

18 Zechariah said to the angel, "How will I know this? For I am an old man and my wife is advanced in years." The angel answered, "I am Gabriel who stands in the Presence of God; I am sent to speak to you and bring you these glad tidings but now, because you did not believe my words which will be fulfilled in their time, you will become unable to speak until the day when these things happen." Now the people stood waiting for Zechariah and wondered why he remained for so long in the Temple. When Zechariah came out they realized that he had seen a vision in the Temple from the signs he made to them but he remained unable to speak. He went home when the days of his service were finished. Elizabeth, after her longed-for pregnancy had come to pass, adorned herself (daily) for five months, to make known and to glory in her pregnancy, saying, "Thus has God done for me for the days that God has looked upon me, to remove my reproach from among men."[4]

26 Now in the sixth month the angel Gabriel was sent from God to a city called Nazareth in Galilee, to a young woman named Mary who was acquired for a dowry by a man named Joseph of the house of David. The angel went in and said, "Peace be to you, Oh favored one, God is with you, blessed are you among women." When she saw him, she was disturbed at his word and wondered what kind of greeting this might be. The angel said, "Do not be afraid, Mary, for you have found favor with God. Behold, you will conceive and give birth to a son and you will call his name Jesus. He will be a Teacher,[5] he will be called a divine being,[6] and God will give him the throne of his ancestor David. He will rule over the house of Jacob forever and there will be no limit to his dominion." Then Mary said to the angel, "How can this be for no man has known me." The angel answered her, "The Holy Spirit will come and the power of the Most High shall rest upon you,[7] therefore the child to be born will be holy and he will be called a divine being.[8]

36 Behold, your kinswoman, Elizabeth in her old age has also conceived a son and yet, this is the sixth month for her who was called infertile for with God all things are possible." Mary said, "Here I am, the servant of God, let it be to me according to your word." Then the angel departed from her. In those days, Mary went with concern to a Judean town in the hill country. She entered the house of Zachariah and saluted Elizabeth. When Elizabeth heard the salutation of Mary, the baby leaped in her womb and Elizabeth was filled with the Holy Spirit and exclaimed to Mary in a loud voice, "Blessed are you among women and blessed is the fruit of your womb. How does it happen that the mother of my Saviour[9] would come to me? Behold, when the voice of your salutation reached my ears, the baby in my womb leaped with great joy. Blessed is she who believed for there will be a fulfillment of the words which were spoken to her from God."

46 Mary said, "My soul magnifies my God and my spirit rejoices in God, my Savior, for You have regarded the meekness of Your servant; behold from henceforth all generations will call me blessed, for the Mighty One has done great things for me and holy is Your name. Your mercy is for centuries and generations upon those who worship You. You have brought victory with Your arm for You have scattered the proud with the imagination in their heart. You have put down the mighty from their seats and You have lifted up the meek. You have filled the hungry with good things and sent the rich away empty. You have helped Your servant Israel and You remembered Your mercy, just as You spoke with our ancestors, with Abraham and with his descendants forever!"[10] Mary stayed with her about three months and then returned to her own home.

57 Now the time came for Elizabeth's child to be delivered and she gave birth to a son. When her neighbors and relatives heard that God had shown great mercy to her, they rejoiced with her. It happened on the eighth day that they came to circumcise the boy and they would have named the boy after his father but his mother told them, "No! He is to be called John." They said to her, "There is no man in your family who is called by this name." Then they made signs to his father to find out what name he wanted to give him. He asked for a writing tablet and wrote, "John is his name." Everyone was surprised. Immediately, his mouth and

tongue were opened; he spoke and praised God. Fear came on all their neighbors and these things were talked about throughout the hill country of Judea. All who heard it reasoned in their hearts, saying, "What then will this child become?" for the hand of God was with him.

67 Then his father Zechariah was filled with the Holy Spirit and prophesied, saying, "Blessed is the God of Israel for You have visited and redeemed Your people. You have raised up a horn of salvation[11] for us in the house of Your servant David as You spoke through the mouth of Your holy prophets[12] which have been since the world began. You have saved us from our enemies and from the hand of all who hate us. You have shown the mercy shown to all our ancestors and You have remembered Your holy covenants and the oaths You swore to ancestor Abraham, to grant to us that we may be saved from the hand of our enemies and serve before God without fear, in justice and righteousness all the days of our lives. You, child, will be called the prophet of the Most High for you will go up before the face of God to prepare the way, to give knowledge of salvation to God's people by the forgiveness of their sins.[13] Through the tender mercy of our God, when the Messiah[14] will visit us from on high to give light to those who sit in darkness and in the shadow of death, to guide our feet into the way of peace." The child grew and became strong in spirit and he was in the wilderness until the day of his appearance to Israel.

Luke 2:1–52

1 It happened in those days that there went out a decree from Caesar Augusts to take a census of all the people in his empire. This first census took place before[15] Quirinius was governor of Syria and everyone went to be registered in their own home town. Joseph also went up from the town of Nazareth, in Galilee to the city of David called Bethlehem in Judea, because he was of the house and family of David.[16] He went to be registered with his purchased bride,[17] Mary, who was with child and while they were there the time came to deliver her child. She gave birth to her firstborn son, wrapped him in swaddling clothes, and laid him in a manger because there was no room for them in the inn.

8 In that region there were shepherds living in the fields keeping watch over their flocks at night. Behold, an angel of God came to them, the

glory of God shone on them, and they were in great fear. The angel told them, "Do not be afraid for behold, I bring you glad tidings of great joy which will come to all the people. There is born to you this day in the city of David, a Saviour, who is Christ of God, and this will be a sign for you: you will find a baby wrapped in swaddling clothes and lying in a manger." Suddenly, a heavenly host appeared with the angel, praising God, saying, "Glory to God in the highest, peace on earth among people of goodwill!"

15 When the angels departed from them and went to heaven, the shepherds spoke to one another, "Let's go to Bethlehem and see what has happened that the angel has made known to us." So they went with haste and found Mary and Joseph with the baby laid in the manger. When they saw this, they made known the saying which had been told them concerning the child, and all who heard them were amazed at what the shepherds told them. Mary treasured all these things and pondered them in her heart. The shepherds returned, glorifying God and speaking about the things they had seen and heard as it had been told to them.

21 He was circumcised at the end of eight days[18] and his name was called Jesus for he was named by the angel before he was conceived in the womb. When their time came for their purification offering at the Temple according to the law of Moses,[19] they brought him up to Jerusalem to present him to God (as is written in the law of God, *"1 Then God spoke to Moses, 'Consecrate to me every first-born who opens the womb among the Israelites, both of human beings and animals, for they are Mine.'"*[20]) and to offer a sacrifice according to what is said in the law of God, *"If she can not afford to bring a lamb, then she may bring two turtledoves or two young pigeons, one as a burnt offering and the other as a sin offering, so the priest will make atonement for her and she will be clean."*[21]

25 Now there was a man in Jerusalem whose name was Simeon. This man was pious and righteous, waiting for the consolation of Israel, and the Holy Spirit was upon him. It was revealed to him by the Holy Spirit that he would not see death before he had seen the Christ[22] of God. He was led by the Spirit to the Temple and when the parents brought in the child Jesus, to do for him according to the custom of the law,[23] he received him in his arms and blessed God, saying, "Oh my God, now let

Your servant depart in peace, according to Your promise for my eyes have already seen Your mercies which You have prepared in the presence of all people, a light to shine upon the Gentiles and the glory of Your people Israel." Jesus father and mother marveled about these things which were spoken concerning him. Simeon blessed them and said to Mary his mother, "Behold, this child is set for the downfall and uprising of many in Israel and for a sign to be disputed. A sword will pierce through your own soul, so that the thoughts out of the hearts of many may be revealed."

36 There was a prophet, Hanna, the daughter of Phanuel of the tribe of Asher, who was of a great age, having lived with her husband for seven years and then as a widow until the age of eighty-four. She never left the Temple but worshipped there with fasting and prayer, night and day. At that moment she came, began to praise God, and spoke about the child to all who were looking forward to the salvation of Jerusalem. When they had performed everything according to the law of God, they returned into Galilee to their own city of Nazareth. Jesus increased and grew in spirit, filled with wisdom and the grace of God was upon him.

41 His parents went to Jerusalem every year for the festival of the Passover. He was twelve years old when they went up to the festival as they were accustomed. When the festival was over they returned while the boy Jesus stayed behind in Jerusalem but his parents didn't know it. They assumed he was with the children of their party as they traveled for a day and then they searched for him among their relatives and friends. When they didn't find him they returned to Jerusalem. After three days they found him in the Temple area, sitting in the midst of a group of teachers, listening to them, and asking questions. All who heard him were amazed at his understanding and his answers.

48 When they saw him there they were astonished and his mother said, "My son, why have you treated us like this? Behold, your father and I were looking for you with great anxiety!" He answered, **"Why were you looking for me. Didn't you know that I must be about my Divine Parent's business?"** They did not understand the words that he said to them. He was obedient to them, went down with them, came to

Nazareth, and his mother treasured all these sayings in her heart. Jesus grew in stature, in wisdom and in favor with God and people.

Luke 3:1–38

1 Now in the fifteenth year of the reign of Tiberius Caesar, Pontius Pilate was governor of Judaea, Herod Antipas was tetrarch of Galilee, his brother Philip ruled over Iturea and Trachonitis, and Lysanias was tetrarch of Abilene. During the high priesthood of Annas and Caiaphas, the word of God came to John, the son of Zechariah and Elizabeth, in the wilderness and he went throughout the country around the Jordan to preach the baptism of repentance for the forgiveness of sins. As it is written in the book of the words of the prophet Isaiah: *"1 Comfort, yes comfort My people!" says your God. "Speak tenderly to the heart of Jerusalem. Cry out to her: that her warfare is ended; that her penalty is paid and that she has received from Me double for all her sins." The voice of one crying in the wilderness, "Prepare the way of our God! Make directly in the desert a highway for our God. Every valley will be filled up,24 every mountain and hill will be leveled,25 the crooked ways will be made straight,26 and the rough places smooth." Then the glory of our God will be revealed and all people will see it27 together for the mouth of God has spoken.28*

7 Then he said to the multitudes who came to be baptized by him, "Oh offspring of scorpions!29 Who warned you to escape from the coming wrath? Therefore produce fruits which are worthy of repentance and don't say within yourselves, 'We have Abraham as our ancestor,' for I tell you, God is able from these stones to raise up children for Abraham. Even now the ax is placed at the root of the trees and every tree that does not produce good fruit will be cut down and thrown into the fire."

10 When the people asked him, "What shall we do?" John answered, "Whoever has two coats must share with one who has none and whoever has food let them do likewise!" Even tax collectors came there to be baptized, saying, "Teacher, what shall we do?" He answered, "Collect no more than the amount authorized for you." Soldiers also asked, "What shall we do?" and he told them, "Do not extort money from people by using threats and false accusations and be satisfied with the wages you agreed to."

15 While people were placing their hope in John, all of them in their hearts wanted to know if John was the Christ. John answered, "I baptize you with water, but one mightier is coming and I am not worthy to loose the thong of his sandals. He will baptize you with the Holy Spirit and with fire. His winnowing fork is in his hand to thoroughly purge his threshing floor, gather the wheat into his barn, and burn the straw in an unquenchable fire." John urged the people in many ways as he taught and preached to the people. Now Herod Antipas, the tetrarch of Galilee, who had been criticized by John in the affair with Herodias, the wife of his stepbrother Philip and other evil acts Herod Antipas was doing, added to them all by putting John in prison.

21 Now when all the people were baptized, it happened that Jesus was also baptized. While he prayed, the heaven opened, the Holy Spirit descended upon him in bodily form like a dove, and a voice from heaven said, "You are My Son, today I have begotten[30] you!"[31]

23 Jesus was about thirty years old when he began his ministry. He was the son of Joseph (as was supposed), who was the son of Hedi, who was the son of Matthat, who was the son of Levi, who was the son of Melchi, who was the son of Jannai, who was the son of Joseph, who was the son of Mattathias, who was the son of Amos, who was the son of Nahum, who was the son of Esli, who was the son of Naggai, who was the son of Maath, who was the son of Mattathias, who was the son of Semein, who was the son of Josech, who was the son of Joda, who was the son of Joanan, who was the son of Rhesa, who was the son of Zerubbable, who was the son of Shealtiel, who was the son of Neri, who was the son of Melchi, who was the son of Addi, who was the son of Cosam, who was the son of Elmadam, who was the son of Er, who was the son of Joshua, who was the son of Eliezer, who was the son of Jorim, who was the son of Matthat, who was the son of Levi, who was the son of Simeon, who was the son of Judah, who was the son of Joseph, who was the son of Jonam, who was the son of Eliakim, who was the son of Melea, who was the son of Menna, who was the son of Mattatha, who was the son of Nathan, who was the son of David, who was the son of Jesse, who was the son of Obed, who was the son of Boaz, who was the son of Salmon,[32] who was the son of Nahshon, who was the son of Amminadab, who was the son of Admin, who was the son of Arni, who was the son of Hezron, who was

the son of Perez, who was the son of Judah, who was the son of Jacob, who was the son of Isaac, who was the son of Abraham, who was the son of Terah, who was the son of Nahor, who was the son of Serug, who was the son of Reu, who was the son of Peleg, who was the son of Eber, who was the son of Shelah, who was the son of Cainan, who was the son of Arphaxad, who was the son of Shem, who was the son of Noah, who was the son of Lamech, who was the son of Methuselah, who was the son of Enoch, who was the son of Jared, who was the son of Mahalaleel, who was the son of Cainan, who was the son of Enos, who was the son of Seth, who was the son of Adam, who was the Son of God.

Luke 4:1–44

1 Now Jesus was full of the Holy Spirit and returned from the Jordan when the Spirit led him away into the wilderness for forty days where he was tempted by the devil. He didn't eat anything in those days and when they were over he was famished. The devil tempted him, saying, "If you are the Son of God, command this stone become a loaf of bread!" Jesus answered him, **"It is written, *'People do not live by bread alone but are nourished by every word that proceeds from the mouth of God'*33"** Then the devil took him up high and showed him in an instant all the empires of the world, and told him, "I will give you all this power and glory which are entrusted to me and I can give it to anyone I please. It will all be yours if you will only worship me!" Jesus replied, **"Get away from me Satan for it is written, *'You shall worship the Eternal your God and God only you shall serve.'"*34** Then he brought him to Jerusalem and set him on the pinnacle of the Temple, saying, "If you are the Son of God, jump down from here! For it is written, *'11 God shall provide angels over to you, to protect you in all your ways. With their hands they will lift you up, least you strike your foot against a stone."*35 Jesus responded, **"It has been said, *'Do not involve the Eternal your God in a foolish test.'"*36** After the devil had finished every temptation, he departed from him for a more opportune time.

14 Then Jesus returned in the power of the Spirit into Galilee and a report concerning him went out all around the surrounding country. He taught in their synagogues and was praised by everyone. He came to Nazareth where he had been brought up and went into the synagogue on the Sabbath, as was his custom. He stood up to do the reading and was

handed the book of the prophet Isaiah. He opened the book and found the place where it was written: **"The Spirit of God is upon me because God**[37] **has anointed me to bring Good News**[38] **to the poor. God has sent me to heal the brokenhearted, to proclaim release to the captives and recovery of sight to the blind, to set at liberty those who are oppressed, to proclaim the year of God's favor.**[39]**"**[40]

20 After rolling up the scroll, he returned it to the attendant, and sat down. With the attention of everyone fixed on him, Jesus told them, **"Today this scripture is fulfilled as you listen."** All spoke well of him and marveled at the gracious words which he delivered, but some added, "Isn't this man Joseph's son?"[41] He responded, **"No doubt you will quote me the proverb: 'Physician, heal yourself!' Then you will say, 'Do here in your hometown what we heard you did in Capernaum and elsewhere!'"** Then he said, **"Truly I tell you, no prophet is accepted in their own hometown**[42] **but in truth, there were many widows in Israel during the time of Elijah, when three years and six months of poor rainfall led to severe famine throughout the land. Then Elijah was sent to none of them but to a single mother who was a widow in Zarephath, in the region of Sidon.**[43] **There were many lepers in Israel in the time of Elisha the prophet and none of them were cleansed but Naaman the Syrian"**[44] Those who heard these sayings were all filled with anger and they rose up to put him out of the city. They led him to the edge of a hill on which the city was built so that they might throw him down from the cliff but he passed through the midst of them and went on his way.

31 He was teaching on the Sabbath in the synagogue at Capernaum, a city in Galilee, and they were astonished at his teaching for his words had authority. There was a man in the synagogue who had an unclean demonic spirit and he cried out with a loud voice, "Leave us alone, what have you to do with us, Jesus of Nazareth? Have you come to destroy us? I know you are the Holy One of God!" He rebuked him saying, **"Be silent and come out of him!"** and the demon threw him down in the midst of them but came out without hurting him. They were all amazed and said to one another, "What kind of word is this that he commands unclean spirits with power and authority and they come out?" His fame spread throughout the surrounding region.

38 He left the synagogue and entered the home of Simon where Simon's mother-in-law was suffering from a high fever and they asked Jesus to help her. At her bedside he bent over and commanded the fever to depart. It left her and immediately she rose up and began to serve them. When the sun was setting, all those with loved ones who were sick with various diseases brought them to him. He laid hands on each one and healed them. The demons came out of many,45 screaming, "You are the Christ, the Son of God!" He stopped them from speaking so that people would not know that he was the Christ. In the morning he departed for a desert place but people sought him, came to him, and tried to prevent him from leaving them, so he said; **"I must preach the Good News of the kin-dom of God to other towns also because I was sent for this purpose."** He continued preaching in the synagogues of Galilee.

Luke 5:1–39

1 It happened that Jesus was standing on the shore of the Lake of Gennesaret while people were pressing upon him to hear the word of God. He saw two boats by the shore but the fishers had gone out of them and were washing their nets. Jesus entered into the boat that belonged to Simon Peter and he asked him to shove off a little way from the shore where he sat down and taught the people out of the boat.

4 When he finished speaking, he told Simon, **"Launch out into the deep water and let down your nets for a catch!"** Simon answered, "We have toiled all night and caught nothing but because of your word I will let down the net. When they did this, they enclosed many fish and their net was breaking. So they signaled for their partners in the other boat to come and help them and when they came, they filled both of the boats until they were almost sinking. When Simon Peter saw this, he fell at the knees of Jesus, saying, "Depart from me, my Teacher, for I am a sinful man!" For he and everyone with him were astonished at the catch of fish they had taken. So also were James and John, sons of Zebedee, who were partners with Simon but Jesus spoke to Peter, **"Do not be afraid! From now on you will be catching people!"** When they had brought their boats on shore, they left everything and followed him.

12 When Jesus was in one of the cities, a man came who was covered with leprosy, fell on his face when he saw Jesus, and besought him. "My

Saviour, if you are willing, you can make me clean!" He reached out his hand and touched him, saying, **"I am willing, be cleansed!"** Immediately the leprosy left him and he ordered him not to tell anyone, saying, **"Go and show yourself to the priests, make an offering for your cleansing as Moses commanded for a testimony to them."** Now more than ever the fame concerning him spread abroad, so great multitudes gathered to hear him and to be healed of their diseases. He withdrew to the wilderness and prayed.

17 It happened on one of the days as Jesus was teaching that there were teachers of the law of[46] the Pharisees sitting by, who had come from every village of Galilee, Judea, and Jerusalem. The power of God was present with him to heal them. Some people brought a paralyzed man on a quilt who they wanted to bring in and lay before him. When they couldn't find a way to bring him in because of the multitude, they went up on the roof to let him down on his quilt through the tiles into the midst of them before Jesus. When he saw their faith, he said to the man, **"Friend, thy sins are forgiven thee!"** The scribes of the Pharisees began to reason, "Why! This fellow blasphemes![47] Who can forgive sins but God alone?"

22 When Jesus perceived their thoughts, he answered them; **"Why do you reason in your hearts? Which is easier to say: 'Thy sins are forgiven thee!' or, 'Arise and walk!' So that you may know that the Son of humanity has authority on earth to forgive sins,"** he told this paralyzed man, **"Arise, take up your quilt and go home!"** He immediately stood up, rolled up his quilt and went home, praising God! Amazement seized everyone, they praised God and were filled with awe, saying; "We have seen marvelous things today!"

27 After this he went out, saw a tax collector named Levi sitting in the tax office, and said to him, **"Follow me!"** He rose up, left everything there, and followed him. Then Levi held a great banquet for him in his home. There was a large gathering of tax collectors and others reclining at the table with them. The scribes of the Pharisees murmured to his disciples, saying, "Why do you eat and drink with tax collectors and sinners?" Jesus answered, **"Those who are sick need a physician[48] not those who are well. I have come to call sinners to repentance, not**

the righteous!" They asked, "Why do the disciples of John the Baptist and those of the Pharisees frequently fast and offer prayers but yours eat and drink?" Jesus replied, "**Can you expect the wedding guests to fast while the bridegroom is still with them? The days will come when the bridegroom will be taken away from them and then they will fast in those days.**"

36 He told them a parable, "**No one tears a piece from a new garment to put on an old garment otherwise the new piece will make a tear and the new piece will not blend with the old material. Nobody pours fresh wine into old wineskins because the new wine will burst the aged skin so that the wine pours out and the skins will be ruined. New wine must be put into fresh wineskins so both are preserved. No one after drinking old wine immediately desires new wine for they say, 'The old wine is better!'**"49

Luke 6:1–49

1 Then on the Sabbath as Jesus walked through the grain fields, his disciples plucked some heads of grain, rubbed the husks off in their hands, and ate them.50 Some Pharisees asked, "Why are you doing what is unlawful to do on the Sabbath?" Jesus answered, "**Have you never read what David did when he and his companions were hungry? He entered into the house of God, took the bread of the Presence, and ate that which is lawful only for the priests to eat. He also gave some to those with him.**"51 He added, "**The Son of humanity is also ruler over the Sabbath!**"52

6 On another Sabbath when he entered the synagogue and taught, there was a man whose right hand was withered. The scribes of the Pharisees watched him closely to see if he would heal on the Sabbath so they might have an accusation against him. He knew their thoughts and asked the man with the withered hand, "**Rise up and stand in the midst.**"53 When he arose and stood there, Jesus said, "**Is it lawful on the Sabbath to do good or to do harm, to save life or to destroy it?**" He looked around at all of them and said to the man, "**Stretch out your hand!**" He did so and his hand was restored whole like the other one. They were filled with bitterness54 and discussed with one another what they might do with Jesus.

12 Now it happened in those days that he went out to a mountain to pray and spent the night in prayer to God. When it was day, he called his disciples and chose twelve of them whom he called apostles: Simon who is called Peter; Andrew, his brother; James; John; Philip; Bartholomew; Matthew; Thomas; James son of Alphaeus; Simon, who is called the Zealot; Judas son[55] of James; and Judas Iscariot who became a traitor. Jesus went down with them and stood up in the plain with a large group of his disciples and a great multitude of people from all over Judea, from Jerusalem, and from the seacoast of Tyre and Sidon; who came to hear him and be healed of their diseases. Those troubled with unclean spirits were cured and everyone was trying to touch him for power came out from him and healed them all.

20 He lifted up his eyes on his disciples saying: **"Blessed are you poor for yours is the kin-dom of God. Blessed are you who hunger now for you will be satisfied. Blessed are you who weep now for you will laugh. Blessed are you when people hate you, discriminate against you, reproach you, and slander your name as evil for the sake of the Son of humanity. Rejoice in that day and leap for joy, for behold, your reward is great in heaven for their parents treated their prophets in the same way. Woe to you who are rich! You have gotten your delights.[56] Woe to you who are full for you will know hunger! Woe to you who laugh now for you too, will mourn and weep. Woe to you when everyone speaks well of you for so did their parents to the false prophets.**

27 I say to you who understand, love your enemies and do good to those who hate you. Bless those who curse you and pray for those who spitefully abuse you. When someone strikes you on your cheek, offer them the other. If someone takes away your coat, allow them to take your shirt also. Give to everyone who would borrow from you and from someone who takes what belongs to you, do not demand it back again.[57] Do to others as you would have them do to you. If you love those who love you, what is your blessing? For sinners also love those who love them. If you do good only to those who do good to you, what is your blessing? For sinners also do the same. If you lend only to those from whom you expect to be paid back, what is your blessing? For sinners also lend to sinners to receive as much again.

35 Love your enemies, do good, and lend to other people without hoping for anything in return so your reward will be great for then you will be children of the Most High, Who is kind to the ungrateful and the selfish. Therefore be merciful as your Divine Parent is also merciful. Do not judge and you will not be judged, do not condemn and you will not be condemned, forgive and you will be forgiven, give and it will be given to you; good measure, pressed down, shaken together, and running over they will pour into your bosom.58 Whatever measure you apply will be the measure applied to you."

39 He also taught them in parables: "**Can a blind person lead another blind person? Surely they will both fall into a ditch!**59 **A disciple is not above their teacher but everyone who learns may be as their teacher.**60 **Why do you see the speck of sawdust in your sister's eye**61 **but do not notice the log in your own eye? Then how do you say to your sister, "My sister, let me remove the speck from your eye," when you yourself do not even see the log that is in your own eye? Oh hypocrite, first get that log out of your own eye and then you can see clearly to remove the speck from your sister's eye!**

43 **A good tree doesn't produce bad fruit, nor does a bad tree produce good fruit. Each tree is known by the quality of its own fruit. Figs are not gathered from thistles, nor are grapes gathered from bramble bushes. The good acting person out of the good treasure of their heart produces good and the evil acting person out of evil treasure of their heart produces evil, for out of the abundance of the heart their mouth speaks! So why do you call to me, saying; 'My Saviour, My Saviour' and will not do what I tell you? I will show you what someone is like who comes to me, hears my words, and does them. This one is like a person building a house who dug deep and laid its foundation on rock. When the floodwaters arose, the stream slammed against that house but could not shake it for its foundation was laid upon rock. The one who hears my words but does not do them is like a person who built their house on the earth without a foundation**62 **so when the river slammed against it, the house fell immediately and the ruin of that house was great."**

Luke 7:1–50

1 When he had finished all his sayings in the hearing of the people, he went into Capernaum. The servant of a centurion, one who was very dear to him, was seriously sick and near death. When this centurion heard of Jesus, he sent some Jewish elders who asked him to come and heal his servant. When they came to Jesus they pleaded earnestly, saying, "He is worthy to have this done for him for he loves our people and even built a synagogue for us!" Jesus came back with them but just before they arrived at the house the centurion sent some of his friends to him to say to him, "Sir [*Saviour*], do not trouble yourself for I am not worthy to have you under my roof. That is why I didn't consider myself worthy to come to you but just say a word and my servant will be healed. I also am a man who has authority under the governor and I have soldiers under my command. I say to one, 'Go!' and he goes; I tell another 'Come!' and he comes and to my servant, 'Do this!' and he does it." When Jesus heard this, he admired the man and turning to the multitude who were following him, he said, **"I tell you not even in Israel have I found such great faith."** When those who had been sent returned to the house, they found the servant in good health.

11 Then on the next day he was going to a city called Nain with his disciples and a large crowd. When they came near the gate of the city, he saw a dead man being carried out who was the only son of a widowed mother. Many people from the city came with her. When Jesus saw her, he had compassion on her and said; **'Don't cry!'** He went up and touched the bier[63] while the bearers who carried it stood still. He said, **"Young man, I tell you, arise!"** The dead man sat up, began to speak and Jesus gave him back to his mother. All the people were seized with fear and they praised God, saying; "A great prophet has risen among us," and "God has visited the people of God." This report concerning him spread through the whole of Judea and all the country around them.

18 The disciples of John the Baptist told him all these things. So John called two of his disciples and sent them to Jesus to ask, "Are you the one who is to come or are we to expect another?" They came to him and said, "John the Baptist sent us to ask, 'Are you the one who is to come or are we to expect another?'" Immediately he proceeded to heal[64] many

people of their diseases, plagues, and evil spirits and to give sight to many who were blind. He answered, **"Go report to John everything you have seen and heard; the blind see, the disabled walk, lepers are cleansed, the deaf hear, the dead are raised up, and the poor are given hope.**[65] **Blessed is the one who takes no offense at me."**

24 When John's disciples left, he began to speak to the people concerning John: **"What did you go out in to the wilderness to see? One frenzied by the spirit?**[66] **What then did you go out to see? Someone all dressed up in fancy clothes? Behold! Those who wear expensive clothes and live delicately are found in palaces. What really drew you all the way out into the desert to look at? A prophet? Yes, and I say that you have found much more than a prophet! This is the one of whom it was written:** *'Behold, I am sending My messenger who will prepare the way before Me'*[67] **For I say to you, among those born to women, there is none greater than John the Baptist. Yet one who was just born anew into the kin-dom of God is greater than he."** All the people, including the tax collectors, who heard John preach, justified themselves before God for they were baptized by the mikvah[68] of John. The lawyers of the Pharisees[69] suppressed the will of God in themselves because they were not baptized by him.

31 The Saviour said, **"To what shall I compare the people of this generation? What are they like? They are like children sitting in the marketplace and calling to their friends, 'We played the flute for you and you would not dance! We have wailed to you and you would not weep!' John came neither eating bread nor drinking wine and you say, 'He must be crazy!'**[70] **The Son of humanity came eating and drinking so you say, 'Behold a glutton and an alcoholic, a friend of tax collectors and sinners.' Wisdom is justified by all Her children."**[71]

36 Then one of the Pharisees asked him to eat with him so he entered the house of that Pharisee and reclined at the table as a guest. Now in that city there was a woman who was a sinner and she brought an alabaster jar of perfume when she knew that he was a guest in the Pharisee's house. She stood behind him at his feet, weeping and began to wash his feet with her tears, wipe them with the hair on her head, kiss his feet, and anoint them with perfume. When the Pharisee who invited him saw

this, he reasoned in himself, "If this man were a prophet he would know who she is and her reputation for the woman who has touched him is a sinner." Jesus answered him, **"Simon, I have something to tell you!"** He replied, "What is it, Teacher?" **"There was a certain creditor had two debtors; one owed five hundred denarii and the other fifty. When they had nothing to pay, he frankly forgave them both. Tell me which one will love him more!"** Simon answered, "I suppose the one with the bigger debt." Jesus replied, **"You're right!"**

44 Then he turned to this woman and said to Simon, **"Do you see this woman? When I entered into your house, you provided no water to wash my feet but she has washed my feet with her tears and wiped them with the hairs of her head. You gave me no kiss but this woman has not ceased to kiss my feet since the time she came in. You didn't anoint my head with olive oil but this woman has anointed my feet with perfume.**72 **Therefore I tell you that her sins, which are many, are forgiven for she has shown great love but one to whom little is forgiven, they show little love."** He said to her, **"Your sins are forgiven!"** Those he ate with began to say within themselves, "Who is this who even forgives sins?" Jesus continued talking with the woman, **"Thy faith has saved thee, go in peace!"**

Luke 8:1–56

1 Soon afterward he was traveling through cities and villages, preaching and giving the Good News of the kin-dom of God. The twelve were with him and many women who were healed of unclean spirits and diseases; Mary, called Magdalene, from whom seven demons had gone out; Joanna, the wife of Herod's steward Chuza; Susanna; and many other women who ministered to them out of their own resources. When a great multitude who were coming to him from all the cities had gathered, he said in a parable: **"A sower went out to sow their seed and as they sowed, some fell on the path where it was trampled and the birds of the air devoured it. Some fell on rocks where it withered away because it has no moisture. Other seed fell among thorns and the thorns grew up with it and choked it. Other seed fell on good ground, grew up, and yielded a hundred fold."** Having said this, he cried out, **"Whoever has ears to hear, will understand!"**

9 When his disciples asked him what the parable meant, he said, **"To you it is given to know the mystery of the kin-dom of God but to those outside it comes by means of parables so that;** *'You listen carefully but you will not understand; you look intently but you will not perceive.'*[73] **This is what the parable means: the seed is the word of God. The ones on the path are those who hear the word but the devil comes and takes away the word from their hearts so that they may not believe and be saved. The ones on the rocks are those who when they have heard, receive the word with joy and believe for a while but fall away in time of temptation because they have no root. That which fell among the thorns are those who hear the word but go out and choke themselves with worries of this world, the deceitfulness of riches,**[74] **and the superfluous things**[75] **of life so their fruit remains unripe. The ones in good soil are those who understand the word, hold it in an honest and fertile heart, and produce ripe fruit with patience.**

16 **No one lights a candle and covers it with a kneading trough**[76] **or puts it under a bushel but they put it on a candlestick so whoever enters may see the light. Nothing is hidden that will not be disclosed nor is anything secret that will not come to light and become known.**[77] **Pay attention to how you are instructed for more will be given to one who has**[78] **and for one who has not, even that which they think they have will be taken away."**[79] Then his mother and his brothers came to see him but could not reach him because of the crowd. He was told, "Your mother and your brothers are standing outside and they want to see you." He answered, **"My mother and my brothers** [*and my sisters and my father*] **are those who hear the word of God and do it!"**[80]

22 One day he went up in the boat with his disciples and said to them, **"Let us cross over to the other side of the lake!"** So they set out and while they were sailing he fell asleep. When a windstorm came down on the lake and they were in grave danger because the boat was near sinking, they awoke him saying, "Teacher, Teacher, we are perishing!" He woke up and rebuked the wind with the raging waves. They quieted down and there was a calm, but he asked them, **"Where is your faith?"** They were afraid and wondered, saying one to another,"Who is this man, that he commands even the wind and the water so they obey him?

26 They sailed to the region of Gerasenes which is on the shore opposite Galilee. As he stepped on the land he was met by a man from the city who was possessed by demons and for a long time wore no clothes. He didn't live in a house but among the graves in the cemetery.[81] When he saw Jesus he cried out, fell down before him, and shouted, "Jesus, Son of the Most High God, I beg thee not to bind me!" for he had commanded the unclean spirit to come out of the man. (He was kept under guard and bound with chains and shackles but he would break these bonds and was driven by the demons into the wild.) Jesus asked him, **"What is your name?"** He said, "Legion," because many demons had entered into him.[82] They begged him not to command them to go down into the abyss.[83] A herd of swine was feeding there on the hillside and they begged Jesus to permit them to attack the swine, so he gave them permission. The demons went out of the man and attacked the swine. The whole herd rushed down the steep bank into the lake and were overwhelmed by the waves.[84]

34 When the swineherds saw what happened, they fled to spread the news in the city and in the country. Then people went out to see what happened and found the man from whom the demons had gone out, sitting at the feet of Jesus, fully dressed, and well behaved. They became afraid and those who had seen it told them how the possessed man had been healed. Then all the people of the region of Gerasenes asked him to leave because they were seized with great fear, so Jesus went into the boat and returned. Now the possessed man begged to remain with him but Jesus sent him away, saying, **"Return to your own home and declare how much God has done for you."** He went away to proclaim throughout the whole city how much Jesus had done for him.

40 When Jesus returned, a large multitude welcomed him for they were all expecting him. A man named Jairus, a leader in the synagogue, came and fell at Jesus feet to beg him to come to his home for he had an only daughter, about twelve years old, who was dying. As Jesus went with him, a large crowd pressed against him. A woman had been suffering from hemorrhages for the last twelve years and spent all she had on physicians who could not heal her. When she came up behind Jesus and touched the fringe of his garment, her bleeding stopped immediately. He said, **"Who touched me?"** When all of them denied it, Peter and those who

were with him, said, "Teacher, the multitudes surround you, press upon you, and yet you say, **"Who touched me?"** He said, **"Somebody has touched me for I know that power has gone out of me!"** When the woman realized that she could not remain hidden, she came trembling, fell down before him, and explained in the presence of all the people why she had touched him and how she was immediately healed. He told her, **"My daughter, be of good comfort; thy faith has made thee whole; go in peace!"**

49 While they were still talking, a man who came from the home of the leader of the synagogue told Jairus, "Your daughter has died, do not trouble the Teacher!" Jesus heard this and said to the father of the girl, **"Do not be afraid but only believe and she will be restored to life!"** Jesus came to the house and would not allow anyone to enter with him except Peter, James, John, and the father and mother of the girl. All of them were weeping and mourning over her but Jesus said, **"Do not weep for she is not dead but sleeping."** They laughed at him, knowing that she was dead. Then he put them outside, took her by the hand, and called to her, **"Little girl, arise!"** Her spirit returned, she got up immediately, and he directed them to give her something to eat. Her parents were ecstatic but Jesus told them not to tell anyone what happened.

Luke 9:1–62

1 He called his twelve disciples together to give them power and authority over all the demons and the ability to heal disease. He sent them to preach the kin-dom of God and heal the sick. He told them, **"Take nothing for your journey; no staff, no backpack, no food, no money, and not even an extra coat.**[85] **Whatever house you enter, stay there and depart from there. Whoever will not welcome you, shake the dust off your feet as you leave that city for a testimony against them."** They departed and traveled through village and town preaching the Good News and healing people everywhere.

7 Now Herod the tetrarch heard all that was done and he was perplexed because some people said that John has risen from the dead, some that Elijah has appeared, and others that an ancient prophet has arisen. Herod said, "I beheaded John, so who is this I hear all these things about?" and he tried to see him.

10 When they returned, the apostles told Jesus everything they had done. He took them and withdrew privately to the ruins[86] belonging to the city of Bethsaida. When the people found out, they followed him, and he welcomed them. He spoke to them concerning the kin-dom of God and healed those in need of healing. His disciples came up to him when the day began to close and said, "Send the people away so they can find food and shelter in the farms and villages around us for we are in a deserted place." Jesus said, **"You give them something to eat!"** They replied, "We have no more than five loaves of bread and two fish, unless we go and buy food for all the people." There were over five thousand people and Jesus said, **"Have them sit down in groups of fifty!"** The disciples did this, making them all sit down. He took the five loaves and the two fish, looked up to heaven, and broke them into pieces for his disciples to distribute to the hungry multitude. They all ate and were satisfied. Then they collected the morsels of bread that were left over into twelve baskets.

18 Once when Jesus was praying by himself with only some disciples near him, he asked them, **"Who do the people say that I am?"** They answered, "John the Baptist," but others say, "Elijah" while others believe that one of the ancient prophets has arisen. He said, **"Who do you say that I am?"** Peter answered, "The Christ of God"[87] He cautioned them and warned them not to tell anyone about this. He said, **"The Son of humanity must suffer many things; he will be rejected by the elders, the chief priests, and the scribes; he will be killed; and he will rise on the third day."**

23 Then he said in the presence of everyone, **"If anyone will be my follower, you must deny yourself,[88] take up your cross, and follow me. Whoever will save their life will lose it but whoever loses your life for my sake, will save it. What benefit is there for a person to gain the whole world but lose their own soul or even weaken it?[89] Whoever is ashamed of me and of my words, the Son of humanity will be ashamed of them when he come in his own glory and the glory of the Divine Parent and the holy angels. I tell you the truth, there are some standing here who will not taste death before they see the kin-dom of God."[90]**

28 It happened about eight days after these sayings that he took Peter, John, and James with him, and went up on a mountain to pray. While he prayed, his face changed in appearance and his clothes became a dazzling lightning white. Behold, two men were speaking with him; Moses and Elijah, who appeared in glory and spoke concerning his departure to be accomplished in Jerusalem. Peter and those who were with him were heavy with sleep but when they awoke they saw his glory and the two men who stood with him. When they began to leave, Peter said to Jesus, "Teacher, it is better for us to remain here and let us make three tabernacles;91 one for you, one for Moses, and one for Elijah but he did not know what he was saying. When he had said these things, a cloud came and rested upon them. They were frightened when they saw Moses and Elijah enter into the cloud and a Voice came out of the cloud, saying, "This is My Son whom I have chosen, hear him!"92 When the voice was heard, they found Jesus alone. In those days they did not tell any person what they saw, they kept silent.

37 On the next day a great multitude met them as they came down from the mountain. Just then a man from the crowd cried out, "Oh Teacher! I beg you to have mercy on me. I have an only son and a spirit seizes him so that he suddenly shrieks. It convulses him until he foams at the mouth, it bruises him, and it hardly leaves him after tormenting him. I begged your disciples to cast it out but they could not." Jesus said in reply **"Oh crooked and faithless people in this generation how long will I be with you and preach to you? Bring your son to me!"** On the way there, the demon attacked and threw him into convulsions. He rebuked the unclean spirit, healed the boy, and gave him back to his father. They were all astonished at the majesty of God. While everyone wondered at everything that Jesus did, he said to his disciples, **"Let these sayings sink down into your ears, for the Son of humanity will be delivered into the hands of men."** They did not yet understand this saying because it was hidden from them so that they might not know it and they were afraid to ask about it.

46 An argument arose among them over which one will be the greatest. When Jesus perceived the thoughts in their hearts he brought a little child, put him by his side, and said, **"Whoever welcomes this little child**

in my name, welcomes me and whoever welcomes me welcomes God who sent me for whoever is least among all of you is the greatest."[93] John answered, "Teacher, we saw someone casting out demons in thy name and we tried to forbid him because he did not follow with us." Jesus said, **"Do not forbid him, for whoever is not against us is for us!"**

51 When the days drew near for him to be taken up, he set his face to go to Jerusalem. So he sent messengers ahead of him and they went away and entered into a Samaritan village to prepare for him. They did not welcome him because his face was set to go straight to Jerusalem. When his disciples, James and John, saw this, they said, "Saviour, would you be willing that we command fire from heaven to kill them!" He turned and rebuked them, **"You don't know how bad tempered you are**[94] **for the Son of humanity did not come to destroy people's lives but to save them."** So they went on to another village.

57 As they were going along the road, a man said, "Teacher, I will follow you wherever you go." Jesus said, **"Foxes have holes and the birds of the air have nests but the Son of humanity has nowhere to lay his head."** He told another, **"Follow me!"** but he replied, "Saviour, let me first go and take care of my father until he dies."[95] Jesus said, **"Let the town bury their own dead but you go and preach the kin-dom of God!"**[96] Another said, "I will follow you, my Saviour but let me first entrust my household to someone and then come." Jesus answered, **"No one who puts their hand on the plow handle and looks back is ripe for the kin-dom of God."**

Luke 10:1–42

1 After this the Saviour selected seventy-two people from his disciples and sent them before him, two by two, into every town and place where he was to go. Jesus said, **"The harvest is truly great but the workers are few; pray that the Owner of the harvest will send out more laborers into the harvest. Walk forth, behold I send you out as lambs in the midst of wolves. Carry no purse, no backpack, no sandals, and salute no one on the road. When you enter someone's home, first say, 'Peace be to this house!' If a kindred spirit is there then your peace can rest on them; otherwise, it will return to you. Remain in the same home and avoid going from house to house. Eat and drink from what they**

provide for the worker is worthy of their wages. **Whenever you visit a town and they welcome you; eat from what is set before you, heal the sick, and say to them, 'Now the kin-dom of God is near to you.' Whenever you enter a town and they do not welcome you; go out into the streets and say, 'Know that the kin-dom of God has come near to you but to protest against you, we wipe off even the very dust of your town which clings to our feet!'**[97]

12 I tell you, it will be easier for Sodom on their day than for that town. Woe unto you, Chorazin! Woe unto you, Bethsaida! If the miracles which were accomplished in you had been done in Tyre or Sidon; they would have repented long ago, sitting in sackcloth and ashes. It will be more tolerable for Tyre and Sidon at their judgment day than for you! As for Capernaum, who has exalted yourself up to heaven, you will be brought down into a living hell. Whoever welcomes you welcomes me, whoever oppresses[98] **you oppresses me, and whoever oppresses me oppresses the One Who sent me."**

17 Then, the seventy-two disciples returned with great joy, reporting, "Our Saviour, even the demons submit to us in your name." Jesus said, **"I watched Satan falling from heaven like lightning. Behold, I have given you the authority to walk upon snakes and scorpions and to overcome the power of your enemies. Nothing will harm you but rejoice because your names are written in heaven and not because the demons submit to you!"**

21 Then Jesus rejoiced in the Holy Spirit, saying, **"I thank Thee, Oh my Divine Parent, Creator of heaven and earth, because You have revealed these things to young children but hid them from the wise and prudent. Oh yes, my Divine Parent for so it was pleasing in Thy Presence!"** Turning to his disciples he said, **"All things have been entrusted to me by my Divine Parent. No one knows who is the Son except the Divine Parent and Who is the Divine Parent except the Son and anyone to whom the Son wishes to reveal the Divine Parent."** He turned to his disciples and told them privately, **"Blessed are the eyes which see what you see for I tell you that many prophets and rulers have desired to see what you see but did not see it and to hear what you hear but did not hear it."**

25 Behold, a certain lawyer stood up to test him, saying, "Teacher, what must I do to inherit eternal life?" Jesus answered, **"How do you read what in written in the Torah?"** He answered, *"You shall love the Eternal your God with all your heart, with all your soul, with all your strength, and with all your mind*[99] *and love your neighbor as yourself."*[100] He replied, **"You speak the truth, do this, and you will live."**

29 As he wanted to accumulate more merits,[101] he asked, "Who is my neighbor?" Jesus explained; **"There was a man who traveled down from Jerusalem to Jericho, when he fell among bandits. They attacked him, striped him of his clothes, beat him, and left him half dead. Now, by chance a priest was going down the road and when he saw him, he walked by on the other side. Likewise a Levite came to this place, saw him, and passed by on the other side. Then a Samaritan while traveling, stopped by this place and when he saw him, he felt compassion for him. He went to him, poured wine and oil on his wounds, bandaged them, set him on his animal, and brought him to an inn where he took care of him. On the next day he took out two denarii, gave them to the innkeeper, and said, 'Please take care of him and if you spend more, I will repay you when I return.' Which of these three do you think acted as a neighbor to this man who fell into the hands of bandits?"** The lawyer replied, "The one who showed mercy on him." Then Jesus said, **"Go and do likewise!"**

38 It happened while they were traveling that he entered a village where a woman named Martha welcomed him into her home. She had a sister called Mary, who came and sat at Jesus' feet and listened to his teaching. Martha was busy with many household cares so she went over to him and said, "Saviour, you don't seem to care that my sister has left me to serve alone. Tell her to come and help me!" Jesus answered, **'Martha, Martha, you are worried and troubled about many things but Mary is seeking the one thing needed and she has chosen the good portion**[102] **which will not be taken away from her."**

Luke 11:1–54

1 Jesus was praying in a certain place and when he finished one of his disciples asked, "Saviour, teach us to pray just as John taught his disciples!" He said, **"When you pray, say, 'Our Sacred Father, hallowed**

be Thy name. Thy Holy Spirit come upon us and cleanse us. Give us our bread day by day, and forgive us our offenses for we also forgive everyone who has offended us. Leave us not in temptation but deliver us from error.'103"

5 He said to them, "Who is there among you who has a friend and if you would go to them at midnight to ask, 'My friend, please lend me three loaves of bread! A friend has come to visit me in their travels and I have nothing to set before them.' The friend will answer from inside, 'Don't bother me! My children are in bed with me and the door is locked. So I can't get up and give you bread.' I tell you that if he will not rise and give to him anything because he is his friend, yet because of his persistence, he will rise and give him whatever he needs.

9 So I tell you, ask and it will be given to you; seek, and you will find; knock, and the door will be opened to you for everyone who asks, receives; for everyone who seeks, finds; and for everyone who knocks, the door will open. Is there anyone among you who, if your child would ask for bread, will give them a stone? If your child asks for a fish, will you give them a snake instead of a fish? If your child asks for an egg, will you give them a scorpion? Then if you, who are evil acting, know how to give good gifts to your children, how much more will your heavenly Sacred Father give the Holy Spirit to those who ask?"

14 While he was casting out a demon from a mute man, it happened that the demon went out, the man spoke, and the people marveled. Some of them said, "This man casts out demons through Beelzebul,104 the chief of the devils." Others asked him for a sign from heaven to test him. Jesus knew their thoughts and said, "Every nation divided against itself will be destroyed and a house divided against itself will fall. If Satan is also divided against himself, how can his domain endure for you say that I cast out demons by Beelzebul? If you say I expel by Satan, then how do you cast him out? If you do cast him out, those actions themselves expose you to judgment.105 If I cast out devils by the finger of God,106 then no doubt the kin-dom of heaven has come to you. When a fully armed strong man keeps watch over his courtyard,

his property is secure. Then, if one who is stronger comes, they will attack him, overcome him, take away his armor in which he trusted, and divide up the spoil. Whoever is not with me is against me and whoever does not gather with me will scatter.[107]

24 When an unclean spirit goes out a person, it roams around the ruins seeking rest while finding none, it says, 'I will return to my abode where I came from.' When it returns it finds the person vacant, warm, and desirable.[108] Then it goes away and brings with it seven other spirits more evil than itself. They enter in to dwell there and the last state of that person is worse than in the first."[109] As he was speaking, a woman in the crowd called out, "Blessed is the womb that carried you and the breasts which nursed you." Jesus informed her, **"Rather, blessed are those who hear the word of God and keep it."**[110]

29 When the crowds were increased around him, he began to say, **"The evil acting people of this generation seek a sign but no sign will be given to them except the sign of the prophet Jonah. Just as Jonah was a sign to the Ninevites, so also will the Son of humanity be a sign to this generation. The queen of the South**[111] **will rise up in the judgment with this generation and condemn them for she came from the far ends of the earth to hear the wisdom of Solomon and behold, a greater than Solomon is here. The people of Nineveh will rise up in the judgment with this generation and condemn them for they repented at the preaching of Jonah and behold, a greater than Jonah is here.**

33 **No one lights a lamp and puts it in a secret place**[112] **or under a bushel basket but on a lamp stand so that those who enter may see its light. The lamp of your body is your eye. If your eye is generous then your whole body will be full of light but if your eye is grudging then your whole body is full of darkness.**[113] **Take heed, therefore, whether the light within you is not darkness. If your whole body is filled with light and there is no part that is dark then the whole of it will be bright just like a lamp gives you light."**

37 While he spoke a Pharisee invited him to dine with him, so he went in and reclined at the table to eat. The Pharisee was astonished when

he saw that he had not washed before dinner. Jesus said, **"Now you Pharisees clean the outside of the cup and the dish but within you are full of impurity and foulness.**[114] **You fools! The One Who made the outside also make the inside. So give for alms those things which are from within and behold, everything will be clean for you. Woe unto you Pharisees! For you take tithes**[115] **of mint and dill and every kind of vegetable**[116] **but you neglected justice and duty towards God. These are the precious things, the ethical elements inherent in the law.**[117] **Woe unto you Pharisees! For you love the best seats in the synagogues and salutations in the marketplaces. Woe unto you, scribes of the Pharisees, hypocrites! For you are like unmarked graves which people walk over without realizing it."**

45 One of the lawyers answered, saying, "Teacher, when you say these things, you insult us too!" He replied, **"Woe unto you also, you lawyers! For you lay heavy burdens on people while you yourselves will not even touch these burdens with one of your fingers. Woe unto you for you help build the tombs of the prophets whom your ancestors killed. Truly you bear witness that you approve the works of your ancestors for they killed them and you finance their tombs. Therefore the Wisdom of God said, 'Behold, I will send them prophets and apostles, some of whom they will kill and persecute,' so that this generation may be charged with the blood of all the prophets shed since the foundation of the world, from the blood of Able to the blood of Zechariah who perished between the altar and the sanctuary.**[118] **Yes, I tell you, it will be charged against this generation. Woe unto you lawyers! For you have closed the doors of knowledge; you did not enter in yourselves, and hindered those who were entering."** When he had said these things to them, the scribes of the Pharisees began a furious attack on him to provoke him to speak of many things. They plotted against him in many ways, seeking to catch something out of his mouth so they might be able to accuse him.

Luke 12:1–59

1 Meanwhile, when so many thousands of the multitude had gathered that they trampled one another, Jesus began to speak to his disciples, **"Again, beware of the leaven of the Pharisees, which is hypocrisy. Everything that is covered up will be revealed and all secrets will become known.**[119]

Therefore, whatever you have spoken in the dark will be heard in the light and whatever you have spoken in private rooms will be proclaimed upon the housetops. I tell you my friends, do not fear those who kill the body but after that they can do no more, but I will warn you whom to fear: fear one who, after they have killed, have the power to cast your body into Gehenna.[120] Yes, I tell you, fear that one! Five sparrows are sold for a few assarions[121] and God has remembered each one of them. Even the hairs of your head are all numbered, so don't be afraid for you are of more value than many sparrows.

8 I tell you that I will acknowledge before the angels of God every one who acknowledges me before people but I will deny before the angels of God every one who denies me before people. Whoever speaks a word against the Son of humanity will be forgiven but whoever blasphemes against the Holy Spirit will not be forgiven.[122] When they bring you before the rulers and authorities in the synagogues, do not worry how you will answer or what you will say for the Holy Spirit will teach you in that very hour the right words to say."

13 Then one of the men from the crowd said, "Teacher, tell my brother to divide the family inheritance with me!" He replied, "Friend, who made me a judge or arbitrator over you?" Then he said to his disciples, "Beware of covetousness because a person's life does not depend on an abundance of possessions." Then he told them a parable. "The ground of a wealthy farmer produced great harvests. So he thought within himself, 'What will I do? I have no room to gather my crops.' He decided, 'I know what to do! I will have my barns pulled down and then have larger ones built to store all my grain and my goods.' Then I will say to my soul, 'Soul, you have plenty stored away for many years, so take it easy; eat, drink, and be merry!' but God said, 'Oh you fool, your soul will be required of you this very night and then who will receive all these things that you have prepared?' Such is one who lays up treasures for themselves but is not rich in the things of God."[123]

22 He taught his disciples, "Therefore I tell you, don't worry about your nourishment, what you will eat, or about your body, what you will wear for living is more than food and the body is more than clothes. Consider the ravens: they neither plant nor harvest, they

have neither storehouse nor barn, and yet God feeds them. You are much more valuable than birds! Do you think that by worrying you can add one cubit[124] to your stature or a day to your span of life? If you then are unable to do that which is least, why worry about the rest? Consider how the lilies grow, they neither spin nor weave and yet, I tell you that Solomon in all his glory was not dressed as fine as these. If God dresses in such fashion the grass which is alive today and tomorrow is thrown into the oven, how much more will God dress you? Oh ye of little faith!

29 Don't worry about what you will eat or what you will drink and don't let your mind be disturbed by these things. Most people seek after all these things and your Divine Parent knows that that ye also have need of these things. Seek the kin-dom of God and all these things will be added to you. Fear little this decree for your Divine Parent has chosen you to give you the kin-dom.[125] Sell your possessions and give alms.[126] Provide yourselves with purses that do not grow old and treasure in Spirit that does not fail, where no thief approaches and no moth corrupts, for where your treasure is, your heart will be there also.[127]

35 Be dressed for action and have your lamps lit! Be like servants who are waiting for the return of their employer from a wedding feast, so that they will open the door immediately when he comes and knocks. Blessed are those servants who are found ready when their employer returns. Truly I tell you, he will dress himself to serve, have them sit down to eat, come over, and serve them. If he would arrive at midnight or just before dawn and finds them ready, blessed are those servants. If a homeowner knows at what hour the thief will come; they will be ready and prevent their house from being plundered. You also must be ready for the Son of humanity will come at the very hour you do not expect."[128]

41 Peter asked him, "Teacher, are you relating this parable to just us, or to everyone?" Jesus continued, "Who is the steward of a household? He is faithful and wise, whom his employer set up over the household to give out their ration at the appointed time? Fortunate is the steward whom the employer of the house finds doing his

work conscientiously, for the employer will appoint him all his possessions.[129] However, if this servant says in their heart, 'My employer is delayed in coming!' and begins to beat the other male and female servants and to eat, drink, and get drunk. The employer of that servant will arrive on a day when he does not expect him and in an hour he does not know, punish him severely, and put him with those who are not trustworthy. The servant who knew their employer's wishes and didn't make ready or prepare according to those wishes will receive a severe punishment. The one who did not know and did what deserved punishment will receive a light punishment. Much is demanded from whom much is given and more is asked from whom more has been entrusted.

49 I came to light a fire on the land[130] and how I wish it were already kindled. I have a cleansing to make[131] and how impatient am I until it is completed.[132] Do you think I have come to bring you peace on earth? No, I tell you, but rather division for from henceforth there will be five in a house who will be divided, three against two, and two against three. The father will be divided against his son and *the son against his father; the mother against her daughter and the daughter against her mother; the mother-in-law against her daughter-in-law and the daughter-in-law against her mother-in-law.*"[133]

54 Then he said to the multitudes, "**When you see a cloud rising out of the West, you immediately say, 'A shower is coming!' and so it is. When you see the south wind blow, you say, 'There will be hot weather,' and so it is. Oh ye hypocrites! You know how to interpret the appearance of the sky and the earth so why don't you know how to interpret this present time?[134] Why don't you judge for yourselves what justice is? When you go with your opponent-at-law to the magistrate for a legal ruling, give into the complaint, otherwise they may drag you over to the judge, the judge will deliver you to the officer, and the officer will throw you into prison.[135] I tell you, you will not be released until you have paid the very last penny.**"

Luke 13:1–35

1 Then some men came and told him about the Galileans whose blood Pilate had mingled with their sacrifices.[136] Jesus answered them, "**Do**

you think that these Galileans suffered in this way because they were greater sinners than all other Galileans because they suffered this way? I tell you, 'No,' but unless you repent, all of you will perish in the same way! Do you think that those eighteen people killed when the tower of Siloam fell on them were greater sinners than all other people who lived in Jerusalem? I tell you, 'No,' but unless you repent, all of you will perish like them."

6 He told this parable: "A certain farmer had a fig tree planted in his vineyard and he came seeking fruit on it but did not find any. He said to the gardener, 'Behold, for three years now I have been seeking fruit on this fig tree and found none. Cut it down. Why waste this ground?' The gardener explained, 'Sir, let it remain for one more year while I dig around it and put on manure. If it bear fruit, that will be good! If not, you can cut it down.'"[137]

10 Jesus was teaching in one of the synagogues on the Sabbath. There was a woman who had been afflicted with rheumatism for eighteen years; she was bent down and could never stand up straight. Jesus called her over when he saw her and said, **"Woman, you are now free from your ailment!"** She immediately straightened up when he laid his hand on her and praised God. The leader in the synagogue was angry because Jesus had healed on the Sabbath and said to the people, "There are six days in which people may be healed, so come on those days and not on the Sabbath!" Jesus answered, **"Oh hypocrites! Doesn't each of you on the Sabbath untie their ass or their ox from the manger and go with it to give it a drink? This woman is a daughter of Abraham whom Satan bound for eighteen years, so isn't it necessary for her to be set free of this bondage on the Sabbath?"** When he said these things, all who opposed him were ashamed and all the people rejoiced over every glorious thing that he did.

18 Then he said, **"What is the kin-dom of God like? What can I compare it to? It is like a grain of mustard seed which a man took and planted in his garden. It grew to become a great bush and the birds of the air made nests in its branches."** Again he said, **"To what can I compare the kin-dom of God? It is like yeast which a woman took and inserted in three measures[138] of flour until all of it was leavened"**

———

22 He taught in the cities and villages on his way to Jerusalem. Someone asked, "Sir, will only a few people be saved?" Jesus replied, **"Struggle to enter in through the narrow door for I tell you that many will seek to enter in but will not be able. After the head of the house rises up and locks the door; you will be standing outside and knocking on the door, saying, 'Sir, Sir, open up for us!' and he will answer, 'I do not know where you are from.' Then you will say, 'We ate and drank in your presence and you taught in our streets!' Then he will reply, 'I tell you, I do not know where you are from! Depart from me, Oh ye workers of iniquity!' There will be weeping and gnashing of teeth when you see Abraham, Isaac, Jacob, and all the prophets in the kin-dom of God while you are thrown out.**[139] **People will come from the east, from the west, from the north, and from the south to sit down in the kin-dom of God. Behold, there are some who are last who will be first and there are some who are first who will be last."**[140]

31 On the same day some Pharisees drew near, saying, "Go away from here for Herod wants to kill you!" Jesus said, **"Go and tell that fox,**[141] **'Behold I cast out demons and I perform cures today and tomorrow and after a short time I will be resurrected.'**[142] **Nevertheless, today and tomorrow I must do my work,**[143] **then one day soon pass on**[144] **because it is impossible that a prophet perish outside of Jerusalem. Oh Jerusalem, Jerusalem, who kills the prophets and stones those who are sent to thee. How often have I desired to gather your children as a hen gathers her brood under her wings but you were not willing. Behold, your house is left desolate unto you and I tell you that you will not see me until you say, *'Blessed is the one who comes in the name of God.'*"**[145]

Luke 14:1–35

1 One Sabbath day Jesus entered the house of one of the leading Pharisees to dine and they were watching him closely. Behold here was a man before him who had dropsy[146] and Jesus spoke to the lawyers of the Pharisees, saying, **"Is it lawful to heal on the Sabbath, or not?"** They held their peace while he took the man, healed him, and let him go. Then he asked them, **"Which of you, if your son**[147] **or your ox has fallen into a well on the Sabbath, will not immediately pull them out?"** They could not reply to this so when he noticed how the guests

chose the places of honor, he told them a parable. **"When you are invited by someone to a wedding feast, don't sit down at the place of honor in case someone more distinguished than you has been invited by your host. Then the host who invited you both may come and say to you, 'Give up your place to this guest.' Then you will be embarrassed when you get up and sit in a lower seat. When you are invited, go and sit in the lowest place so that when your host who invited you comes over, they will say, 'Dear friend, please come up front.' Then you will be honored in the presence of all who sit with you. Whoever exalts yourself will be humbled and whoever humbles yourself will be exalted.**[148]

12 He also said to the one who invited him, saying, 'When you give a luncheon or a dinner party, do not invite your friends, your sisters, your brothers, your relatives, or your wealthy neighbors for they may invite you in return so you will be repaid. When you give a banquet; invite the destitute, the afflicted, the disabled, and the blind, so you will be truly blessed because they have nothing to repay. You will be rewarded at the resurrection of the just.'"[149]

15 When one of the guests at the table heard these sayings, he said, "Blessed is the one who will eat bread in the kin-dom of God!" Jesus responded, **"A man gave a great banquet and invited many guests. At the time for the banquet, he sent a servant out to those who were invited, saying, 'Come now for everything is ready!' Then they all together began to make excuses. The first one said, 'I have just bought a field and I must go to check it out, so please excuse me.' Another said, 'I recently bought five pair of oxen and I am just going to examine them so please excuse me.' A third person told the servant, "I have just been married and that is why I cannot come." The servant returned and reported all this to his employer. The owner of the house became very angry and told his servant, 'Go quickly into the streets and lanes of the city to bring in the destitute, the afflicted, the disabled, and the blind to come for dinner.' The servant said, 'Sir, what you have ordered has been done but there is still room.' The employer said to his servant, 'Go out on the country roads and walks to urge**[150] **people to come in so my home may be filled. For I tell you, none of those people who were invited will taste my banquet.'"**

25 Now great multitudes accompanied him when he turned to them, saying, **"If anyone comes to me and does not put aside**[151] **your father, your mother, your brothers, your sisters, your spouse, your children, and even your own life; they cannot be my disciple. Whoever does not bear their cross and follow me cannot be my disciple. Which of you, intending to build a tower, does not sit down first and count the cost, to see whether you have enough to finish it? Otherwise, after you have laid the foundation but you are not able to finish it, all who see this will begin to mock you, saying, 'This person began to build but was not able to finish.'**

31 Or which ruler, going out to wage war against another ruler equal to him, would not at first reason whether he is able with ten-thousand to oppose one who comes against him with twenty-thousand? If not, he will send envoys and seek peace while the other ruler is still far away. So therefore, whoever is willing to leave all their possessions[152] **can be my disciple. Salt is good but if the salt has lost its savor, how can it be used for seasoning? It is neither fit for the ground nor for the manure pile so people throw it out. Whoever has ears to hear, will understand!"**

Luke 15:1–32

1 Now the tax collectors and sinners came close to hear Jesus, and the scribes of the Pharisees complained, "This man welcomes sinners and even eats with them!" So he told them this parable, **"Which of you, who has a hundred sheep and loses one of them, will not leave ninety-nine where they were grazing to go after the lost one until he finds it? When he has found it, he places it on his shoulders, brings it home, and when he arrives, he calls together his friends and neighbors to tell them, 'Rejoice with me for I have found my sheep which was lost!' Likewise, I tell you there will be more joy in heaven over one sinner who repents than over ninety-nine just people who do not need to repent.**[153]

8 Or what woman having ten silver coins[154] **and losing one, does not light a lamp, turn the house upside down,**[155] **and search diligently until she finds it? When she has found it, she calls together her friends and neighbors, saying, 'Rejoice with me for I have found my**

coin which was lost!' Likewise, I tell you there is joy among the angels of God over one sinner who repents."

11 He said, "There was a man who had two sons. The younger son asked him, 'My father, give me the share of your estate which is coming to me.' So he divided his possessions between them. After a few days the younger son gathered all he had and traveled to a distant country where he squandered his wealth in prodigal living.[156] When he had spent everything, there was a great famine in that country and he began to be in need. So he went to work with one of the citizens of that country who sent him in the field to feed the pigs. There he would gladly fill his belly on the pods[157] that the pigs were eating and no one gave him anything. When he came to himself he said, 'How many hired workers are now in my father's house who have plenty of bread but I perish here with hunger. I will rise, go to my father and say, '"My father, I have sinned against heaven and before you. I am no longer worthy to be called your son, just treat me like one of your hired servants."'

20 He rose up and came to his father but while he was still at a distance his father saw him, had compassion on him, ran to him, embraced him, and kissed him. He said, 'My father, I have sinned against heaven and before you. I am no longer worthy to be called your son, just treat me like one of your hired servants!' His father said to his servants, 'Quickly bring the finest robe, put it on him, put a ring on his hand, put shoes on his feet, bring the fatted calf, kill it, and then let's eat and celebrate for this, my son, was dead and is alive again; he was lost and now he is found!' So they began to celebrate!

25 Now his elder son was in the field and as he came and approached the house, he heard music and dancing. He called one of the servants and asked what was going on. He said, 'Your brother has come and your father has killed the fatted calf because he received him safe and sound.' He became angry and refused to go in so his father came out, began to plead with him, and he answered his father, 'Lo, all these years I have worked hard for you, I never disobeyed your orders, and yet, you have never given me even a young goat so I could celebrate with my friends. Now when this son of yours came back after he

devoured your wealth in an expensive lifestyle,[158] you killed the fatted calf for him.' Then the father said, 'My son, you are always with me and all that is mine is yours but it was right to celebrate and rejoice because this brother of yours was dead and he is alive;[159] he was lost and now he is found.'[160]"

Luke 16:1–31

1 He spoke a parable to his disciples, "**There was a certain rich man who employed a steward accused of wasting his wealth. So he called him in, saying, 'What's this I hear about you? Give me an accounting of your stewardship for you may no longer be my manager.' Then he thought within himself, 'What will I do? For my boss is taking away my position! I am not strong enough to dig and I am ashamed to beg. Now I know what to do so people will receive me into their houses when I am dismissed as steward.' So one by one, he called in his employer's debtors and asked the first, 'How much do you owe my employer?' She replied, 'A hundred jugs of olive oil.' So he told her, 'Take your papers, sit and in discharge of the debt, write fifty.'[161] He said to another, 'How much do you owe?' He replied, 'One hundred bushels of wheat.' He said, 'Take your papers, sit and in discharge of the debt, write eighty.' The employer commended this dishonest steward because he acted shrewdly, for the children of the worldly are more shrewd in dealing with their own generation than the children of light. I also ask you, if you use this earthly wealth, however acquired, to make friends so that when it is gone and they receive you, will you have everlasting habitation?[162]**

10 Whoever is faithful with very little is also faithful with much and whoever is dishonest with very little is also dishonest with much. Therefore if you have not been faithful with the wealth of iniquity, who will trust you with the true riches? If you have been found dishonest with that which is another person's, who will give you that which is your own? No servant can serve two authorities for either they will hate the one and love the other or you will honor the one and despise the other. You cannot serve God and mammon!"[163]

14 When some of the Pharisees, who were covetous,[164] also heard these things, they ridiculed him. Jesus told them, "**You are those who justify**

yourselves before people, but God knows your hearts for what is highly esteemed among men is detestable in the sight of God. The Torah and the prophets were until John and now the Good News of the kin-dom of God has been preached and everyone oppresses it.[165] It is still easier for heaven and earth to pass away than for one letter of the Torah to pass away.[166] Whoever divorces their spouse and marries another commits adultery and whoever marries the spouse who is illegally separated commits adultery.[167]

19 There was a rich man who dressed in purple and fine linen and feasted sumptuously every day. At his door lay a poor man named Lazarus who was afflicted with boils. He longed to be fed with the crumbs that fell from the rich man's table. Dogs even used to come and lick his sores. The poor man died and was carried by the angels to the bosom of Abraham. The rich man also died and was buried. While he was tormented in hell, he looked up to see Abraham far off in the distance with Lazarus in his bosom. He cried, 'Father Abraham, have mercy on me and send Lazarus to dip the tip of his finger in water to cool my tongue for I am tormented in this flame!'

25 Abraham said, 'My son, remember that you received your pleasures while you were living and Lazarus received his hardships. Behold, now he is comforted here and you are suffering. Besides this, there is a great chasm fixed between us and you, so that even those who want to pass from here to you, cannot and no one can cross from there to us.' He said, 'Oh my father, I beg you that you will send him to my father's house where I have five brothers and warn them so that they may not also come to this place of torment.' Abraham said, 'They have Moses and the prophets, let them listen to them.' He replied, 'Oh no, father Abraham but if someone goes to them from the dead, they will repent.' Abraham answered, 'If they do not listen to Moses and the prophets, neither will they be convinced even if someone arose from the dead.'"

Luke 17:1–37

1 He taught his disciples, "It cannot be avoided that offenses will come but woe to anyone by whom they come. It would be better for them if a millstone were tied around their neck and they were thrown into the sea than for them to despise one of these little ones! Pay attention

even among yourselves! If your brother[168] offends you, tell him about it and if he repents, forgive him. Even if he wrongs you seven times in a day and turns to you, saying, "I repent!" you must forgive him."

5 His apostles said to their Saviour, "Increase our faith!" He said, **"If you have faith the size of a grain of mustard seed, you could tell this mulberry tree; 'Be uprooted and planted in the sea!' and it would obey you. Who among you will say to your servant who has just come in from plowing or tending the sheep in the field, 'Go and sit down to eat.'? Rather you will say, 'Prepare supper for me, put on your apron, serve me while I eat and drink and then you can eat and drink.' Do you thank the servant for doing what they were told to do? I don't think so. So likewise, when you have done all those things you have been told to do, say, 'We are idle[169] servants, we have done what was our duty to do.'"**

11 Then it happened on his journey to Jerusalem that he was passing through Galilee and Samaria. When he entered a village, he was met by ten people with leprosy who were unclean. They lifted up their voices, crying, "Oh Jesus, Teacher, have mercy on us!" When he saw them, he said, **"Go and show yourselves to the priests!"** and as they went, they were made clean. Then one of them realized that she had been healed and returned, praising God in a loud voice. She fell down on her face at his feet,[170] thanking him and she was a Samaritan. He answered, **"If there were ten made clean, where are the other nine? Could none be found to return and give praise to God, except this Samaritan."** He told her, **"Arise and go, thy faith has made thee whole."**[171]

20 When some of the Pharisees asked Jesus when the kin-dom of God would come, he answered, **"The kin-dom of God does not come by observation. Neither will they say, 'Behold, it is here!' or 'Behold, it is there!' because the kin-dom of God is within you."**[172] Then he said to his disciples, **"The time will come when you will desire to see one of the days of the Son of humanity and you won't see one. If they will say to you, 'Behold, he is here!' or 'Behold, he is there!' Don't go after them or follow them for as the lightning flashes and lights up everything under the sky, so will the Son of humanity be in his day. First he will suffer many things and be rejected by this generation.**

26 Just as the world was in the days of Noah, so will it be in the days of the Son of humanity. They were eating, drinking, marrying, and being given in marriage right until the day when Noah entered the ark, the floods came, and destroyed them all. Again, just as it was in the days of Lot; they were eating, drinking, buying, selling, planting, and building; but the same day when Lot left Sodom, fire and brimstone rained down and destroyed them all. So will it will be on the day when the Son of humanity is revealed to you. In that day she who is on the roof with her goods in the house, must not come down to take them away and he who is in the field, must not turn back.

32 Remember Lot's wife.[173] Whoever will seek to save their life will lose it and whoever will lose their life will save it. I tell you that on that night there will be two men in one bed; one will be taken and the other left. Two women will be grinding grain together; one will be taken and the other left. Two men will be in the field; one will be taken and the other left." They answered and said to him, "Where, Saviour?" Jesus replied, "The vultures will gather wherever there is a carcass."[174]

Luke 18:1–43

1 He told them a parable about their need to always pray and never to lose heart: "In a certain city there was a judge who neither feared God nor respected people. In that city there was a widow who kept coming to him, saying, 'Get justice for me against my adversary!' He refused for a while but later he said within himself, 'I neither fear God nor respect people, yet because this widow troubles me, I will take on her case so that she will not keep coming and annoying me.'" Then the Saviour said, "Listen to what this unjust judge said. 'Will not God execute justice for God's chosen ones who call to God day and night and stir the Spirit of God on their account?' I tell you, 'God will execute justice for them at once but when the Son of humanity comes, will he find persistence on the earth?'"[175]

9 He told this parable against some who took pride in themselves that they were righteous and despised other people: "Two people went up to the Temple to pray: one a Pharisee and the other a tax collector. The Pharisee stood and prayed in himself, 'God, I thank Thee that

I am not like other people; unjust, extortioners, adulterers, or even like that tax collector. I fast twice a week and I pay tithes on all that I earn!' The tax collector, who stood far away, would not look up to heaven and beat on his breast praying, 'Oh God, be merciful to me a sinner!' I tell you that this person went to his home justified rather than the other for everyone who exalts themselves will be humbled and everyone who humbles themselves will be exalted."**

15 Now parents were bringing even their babies to him that he might touch them until his disciples saw them and yelled at them. Then Jesus called them over, saying, **"Permit the little children to come to me and do not hinder them for the kin-dom of heaven belongs to little ones like these. Truly I tell you, whoever will not receive the kin-dom of God like a little child will never enter in."**

18 A certain ruler asked him, "Good Teacher! What must I do to inherit eternal life?" Jesus said, **"Why do you call me good? No one is good but God alone. You know the commandments:** *Do not commit adultery; Do not murder; Do not steal; Do not bear false witness and Honor your father and your mother.*"[176] He replied, "I have observed all these things since I was a child." When Jesus heard this, he said, **"You lack one more thing. Go and sell everything you have, distribute the money to the poor, and you will have treasure in heaven, then come and follow me!"** He was very rich and felt sad when he heard this saying.

24 Jesus observed his sorrow and said to him, **"How difficult for those who have an abundance of things to enter the kin-dom of God. It is easier for a rope to go through the eye of a needle than for one who has an abundance of things to enter the kin-dom of God."** Many who heard this asked, "Who then, can be saved?" He answered, **"What is impossible for people becomes possible with God."** Peter said, "Lo, we have left everything to follow you!" So, he said, **"Truly I tell you that there is no one who has left home, parents, brothers, sisters, spouse, or children for the sake of the kin-dom of God, who will not receive many times more in this present time and eternal life in your world to come."**

31 He took the twelve in private, saying, **"Behold, we are going to Jerusalem and all things that are written by the prophets concerning**

the Son of humanity will be fulfilled. For he will be delivered up to the Gentiles and they will mock him, shamefully treat him, spit in his face, scourge him, curse him, kill him, and on the third day he will rise again." This saying was hidden from them; they didn't understand these things or grasp what was said.

35 It happened as he drew near Jericho that a blind man sat begging by the side of the road. Hearing a multitude pass by, he asked what was happening. They told him, "Jesus of Nazareth is passing by." So he cried out, "Oh Jesus, son of David, have mercy on me!" Those who were in the front yelled at him to shut up but he shouted even louder, "Oh Son of David, have mercy on me!" Jesus stood still and commanded them to bring the man to him and when he came near, he asked, **"What do you want me to do for you?"** He replied, "My Saviour, let me receive my sight!" Jesus said, **"Receive thy sight, thy faith has made thee whole!"** He saw immediately and followed him, praising God. All the people who saw this, praised God.

Luke 19:1–48

1 Jesus entered Jericho and passed through. There was a very wealthy man named Zacchaeus who was a chief tax collector and he tried to see who Jesus was but he could not because he was too short to see over the crowds. So he ran ahead and climbed into a wild fig tree to meet him when he passed that way. When Jesus came to that place, he looked up and said, **"Zacchaeus! Make haste and come down for I must stay in your house today!"** He came down in a hurry and welcomed him with joy. Now when they saw it, they all grumbled, "He is going to be the guest with a man who is a sinner!" Zacchaeus stood and said to Jesus, "Behold, My Saviour, I will give half of my wealth to the poor and I will pay fourfold[177] to everyone whom I have extorted." Jesus said, **"Today salvation has come to this house since he is also a son of Abraham for the Son of humanity have come to seek and to save the lost!"**

11 While they were listening to this, he continued by relating a parable because he was near Jerusalem and they expected the kin-dom of God would appear immediately, he said, **"An aristocrat went to distant country to welcome the royal presence[178] for himself and then return. He called ten of his servants, gave them ten minas,[179] and said to**

them, 'Transact business until I come back.' Now, the people of his city hated him and sent a delegation after him, saying, 'We do not want him to rule over us!' When he returned, having received royal power, he ordered the servants, to whom he gave the money, to be summoned so he might find out what they had gained in business.

16 The first one came and said, 'My lord, your mina has earned ten more minas!' He replied, 'Well done, good servant, because you have been faithful with a small amount, you will have charge over ten talents.'[180] **The second one came and said, "My lord, your mina has gained five more minas!' Likewise he replied, 'You will have charge over five talents!' Then another came and said, 'My lord, here is your mina which I kept laid away in a napkin**[181] **for I was afraid of you because you are a harsh man who takes what you did not deposit and reaps where you did not sow.' He replied, 'You incompetent servant, I will judge you from your own mouth. You knew I was a harsh man who takes what I did not deposit and reaps where I did not sow. Why didn't you put my money in the bank, so when I returned I could demand it back with usury?' He said to those who stood by, 'Take away the mina from him and give it to him who has ten minas!' (They told him, 'Lord, he has ten minas!') He said, 'To everyone who has, more will be given and from one who has not, even that which they have will be taken away from them. Bring over my enemies who were not willing to have me reign over them and slay [lay] them before me.'"**

28 After Jesus had said these things, he went on ahead up to Jerusalem. When he came near to Bethphage and Bethany, at the Mount of Olives he sent two disciples, saying, **"Go into the next village and as you enter it, you will find a colt**[182] **tied up, which has never been ridden. Untie it and bring it here. If anyone asks, 'Why are you untying this colt?' tell them this, 'Our Saviour needs it.'"** Those who were sent, went away and found it just as he had told them. When they were untying the colt, the owners said, "Why are you untying the colt?" They replied, "Our Saviour needs it!" They brought the colt to him, threw some of their clothes on it, and set Jesus down on it. People spread their garments on the path as he rode. When he came near the path down from the Mount of Olives, the whole multitude of his disciples began rejoicing and praising God with loud voices for all the marvelous miracles which

they had seen, saying, "Blessed is the one who comes in the name of God! Peace in heaven and glory in the Highest!" Some Pharisees in the multitude told him. "Teacher, rebuke[183] your disciples!" He answered, **"I tell you that if they would hold their peace,[184] the stones will immediately cry out."**

41 When he drew near to Jerusalem and saw the city, he wept over it, saying, **"If you had only known, especially on this your day, all that belongs to your peace but for now is hidden from your eyes. The days will come when your enemies will set up ramparts around you, surround you, press in on you from every side; they will lay you even with the ground, you and your children within you. They will not leave one stone upon another in you because you didn't know the time of your visitation."** Then he entered the Temple and began to drive out those who were buying and selling in there, saying, "It is written, *"My house will be called a private prayer place for all people[185]* **but you have turned it into a *den of thieves."*[186]** He taught daily in the Temple. The chief priests, scribes, and elders of the people tried to get rid of him but they didn't find anything they could do for all the people gathered around, listening to every word.

Luke 20:1–47

1 One day, while he was teaching the people in the Temple and preaching the Good News, the chief priests and the scribes with the elders rose up against him, saying, "Tell us by what authority you do these things and who gave you this authority?" He answered, **"I also will ask you a question; now tell me, was the baptism of John from heaven or from people?"** They reasoned among themselves, saying, "If we say, 'From heaven,' he will ask, 'Why we didn't believe him.' Then if we say, 'From people,' all the people will stone us because they are convinced that John was a prophet." So they answered that they didn't know where it came from. Jesus said, **"Neither will I tell you by what authority I do these things."**

9 He began to tell the people this parable, **"A man planted a vineyard, leased it to tenant farmers, and went to a far country for a long time. When the season came, he sent a servant to the tenant farmers to give him some of the fruit of the vineyard but the tenant farmers beat him and sent him away empty-handed. He sent another servant**

but they beat him also, treated him shamefully, and sent him back empty-handed. He sent yet a third and this one they wounded and threw him outside. Then the owner of the vineyard asked himself, 'Now, what am I to do?' He answered, 'I will send my beloved son and perhaps they will see him and respect him!' When the tenant farmers saw him, they reasoned among themselves, saying, 'This is the heir! Come, let's kill him and the inheritance will be ours.' They threw him out of the vineyard and killed him. Therefore, what will the owner of the vineyard do to them?" [*The Jewish authorities replied,*] "He will come, destroy those tenant farmers, and lease the vineyard to others." When the people heard this they cried, "God forbid!" He looked at the people and said, **"It is written, *'The stone which the builders rejected has become the chief cornerstone.'*187 Whoever falls on that stone will be broken but on whomever the stone falls will be destroyed."188**

19 The scribes and the chief priests realized that he had spoken this parable against them and sought to lay hands on him that very moment but they were afraid of the people. They watched him and sent spies who pretended to be sincere to entangle him by what he said to deliver him up to the authority and jurisdiction of the governor.189 So they asked him, "Teacher, we know that you speak and teach truthfully and show deference to no one but teach the way of God justly. Is it lawful for us to pay taxes to Caesar or not?" He saw through their craftiness and replied, **"Why do you tempt me? Show me a coin!190 Whose image and inscription are on it?"** They answered, "Caesar's" He told them, **"Therefore, pay to Caesar what belongs to Caesar and give to God what belongs to God."191** They were not able to catch him by what he said in the presence of the people but they were amazed at his answer and became silent.

27 Some of the Sadducees, who deny there is a resurrection, came over and asked him, "Teacher, Moses wrote to us that if a man's brother dies with a wife but no children, he will marry her and raise children for his brother. Now there were seven brothers; the first married and died without children. The second brother married her and died without children. Then the third married her and likewise all seven left no children when they died. Finally, the woman also died. Whose wife will this woman be in the resurrection for all seven were married to her?"

34 Jesus answered them, **"The children of this world marry and are given in marriage but those who are judged worthy of the other world and the resurrection from the dead, neither marry nor are given in marriage. They are equal to the angels for they cannot die again and they are the children of God because they are the children of the resurrection. Even Moses showed that the dead are raised in the story about the bush when,** *God said further, 'I am the God of your father, the God of Abraham, the God of Isaac and the God of Jacob.'*192 **For God is not the God of the dead but of the living for all live in God."** Then some of the scribes told him, "Teacher, you have answered well." After this, they stopped their questions.

41 So he asked them, **"How can you say that Christ is the son of David? David wrote in the Book of Psalms:** *'God said to my lord, "Sit at My right hand until I make your enemies into your footstool.'*193 **If David calls him 'lord'** [*the Christ*], **how can he be his son?"** While all the people were listening, he said to his disciples, **"Beware of the scribes who desire to walk around in long robes, who love to be greeted with respect in the marketplaces, who want the best seats in the synagogues and the place of honor at feasts, who embezzle the property of widows, and for a show they say long prayers. They will receive the greater condemnation!"**

Luke 21:1–38

1 He looked up and observed wealthy people putting their gifts into the treasury.194 Then he saw this poor widow put in two small copper coins.195 So he said, **"Truly, I tell you, that this poor widow has given more than all the rest combined for out of their abundance have they made offerings but this woman out of her poverty has offered all that she has."**

5 Some disciples were talking about the Temple, adorned with beautiful and heavy stones.196 Jesus said, **"As for the things you see here, the days will come when not one stone will be left upon another, that will not be knocked down."** They asked him, "Teacher, when will these things happen? What will the sign be when this is about to take place?" He replied, **"Take heed so you are not deceived for many will come in my name, saying, 'I AM!' and 'The time has come!' but do not follow**

them. When you hear about wars and revolutions, do not be afraid for these things must happen but the end will not follow immediately."

10 He taught them, "**Nation will rise against nation and trade group against trade group. There will be great earthquakes and famines and plagues in various places. There will be alarming sights, great signs will appear from heaven, and the winters will be severe.**[197] **Before all this, they will lay hands on you, pursue you, deliver you to the synagogues and the prisons, and bring you before rulers and governors for the sake of my name. This will be an opportunity for you to testify! Treasure it in your hearts and do not meditate beforehand how to answer for I will give you a mouth full of wisdom which none of your adversaries will be able to withstand. You will be betrayed by your parents, brothers, sisters, kinfolks, and friends and they will put some of you to death. You will be hated by all because of my name but not a hair on your head will perish. Prepare your lives in hope.**[198]

20 **When you see Jerusalem surrounded by armies, know that it's destruction is near. Then those in Judea must flee to the mountains, those inside the city must leave it, and those in the fields must not enter it. These are the days of vengeance so that all things which are written must be fulfilled.**[199] **Alas, for pregnant women and nursing mothers there will be great distress in the land and wrath against this people who will fall by the edge of the sword or taken away captive to every country. Jerusalem will be trampled on by the Gentiles until the time of the Gentiles is fulfilled. There will be signs in the sun, the moon, and the stars. On the earth there will be distress among the nations and bewilderment from the roaring of the surging sea. People will have heart attacks because of fear and foreboding of what is coming upon the world, and the powers of the heavens will be shaken. Then they will see the Son of humanity coming in the clouds with power and great glory! Have courage when all these things begin to happen to you and lift up your heads because your salvation draws near.**"

29 He told him a parable, 'See the **differences between the fig tree and all other trees.**[200] **When they sprout leaves, you see and know of your own selves that summer is near. So, also when you see what's**

happening, then you know that the kin-dom of God is near. Truly **I tell you, this generation will not pass away until all these things happen. Heaven and earth will pass away but my words will not pass away.**[201] **Watch out for yourselves so that your hearts may not become heavy by extravagance, drunkenness, and worries of the world for when that day comes suddenly upon you for like a downpour, it will entrap**[202] **all who dwell on the face of all the earth. Therefore, watch at all times! Pray that you will have the strength to escape the things which will take place and to stand before the Son of humanity."** He taught in the Temple during the day but at night he went out to lodge on the Mount of Olives. The multitudes gathered early in the morning to listen to him in the Temple.

Luke 22:1–71

1 The Festival of Unleavened Bread, which begins the Passover celebration, drew near and the chief priests and the scribes were seeking a way to kill him but they were afraid of the people. Then Satan entered Judas Iscariot who was one of the twelve. So he went and spoke with the chief priests and officers of the Temple guard on how to deliver him to them. They were delighted and promised to give him money. He gave them his word and he looked for a way to deliver him apart from the multitudes.

7 The day of the Unleavened Bread arrived when the Passover lamb was sacrificed. So Jesus sent Peter and John ahead, saying, **"Go and make preparations for us to eat the Passover."** They asked, "Where will you have us make the preparations?" He explained, **"Behold when you have entered the city, a man carrying a pitcher of water will meet you. Follow him and wherever he enters, say to this owner of the house, 'Our Teacher asks you where is the guest room where I may eat the Passover with my disciples?' Then he will take you upstairs and show you an upper room already furnished, so make the preparations there."**

13 They left for Jerusalem, found the situation just as he described and prepared the Passover. When it was time, Jesus reclined to eat and the apostles with him. He said to them, **"I have eagerly looked forward to eating this Passover with you before my suffering begins for I tell you that I will never eat it again until it comes to fulfillment in the**

kin-dom of God." Then he took his cup and when he had given thanks, he said. **"Take this and share it among yourselves, for I tell you, I will not drink of the fruit of the vine again, until the kin-dom of God comes."** Then he took a loaf of bread, gave thanks, broke it, and gave it to them saying, **"This is my body."**[203] **Behold, the hand of him who will betray me is on the table for the Son of humanity will go just as he has been destined but woe to the one who betrays me."** They began to question one another, which of them would do this.

24 Now there arose a dispute among them over which one of them was to be considered the greatest. Jesus spoke to them, **"The rulers in this world exercise authority over people and yet they are called 'benefactors'**[204] **It will not be like this for you; let the greatest among you become as the youngest and let the leader be as one who serves. Who is greater: the guest who reclines at the table, or one who serves? Isn't it the guest who reclines at the table? Yet, I am among you as one who serves. You are those who have remained with me throughout my ordeals and I give you a kin-dom just as my Divine Parent has given one to me. So that in my kin-dom you may eat and drink at my table and you will sit on seats and judge the twelve tribes of Israel."**

31 Jesus said to Simon Peter, **"Simon, behold, Satan has desired to have you that he may sift you like wheat**[205] **but I have prayed for you that your faith will not weaken and in time even you will repent and strengthen your brothers and sisters!"** Simon said, "My Saviour, I am ready to follow even for prison and for death!" He answered, **"I tell you, Peter, you will deny three times that you know me before the rooster crows in the morning."**

35 He asked his disciples, **"Did you lack anything when I sent you without money, bag, and sandals?"** They answered, "Not a thing." He said, **"Now, one who has a purse, take it and likewise your bag. Whoever has no sword, sell your robe and buy one.**[206] **I tell you that which is written must be fulfilled in me. *Therefore, I will divide him a portion with the great and he will divide the spoil with the strong because he poured out his soul unto death. He bore the sins of many and made intercession for the transgressors so he was numbered with the transgressors.*[207] for the end is near."** They said, "Our Saviour, behold,

here are two swords!" He replied, **"That is futile."**208 As it was his custom he came out and went away to the Mount of Olives and his disciples followed him.

40 When they arrived he said to them, **"Let us not fail the test."**209 He withdrew the distance about a stone's throw, knelt down, and prayed, **"Oh Divine Parent, remove this cup from me if it is in Thy will. Nevertheless, not my will but Thy will be done."** [[210 There appeared to him an angel from heaven to strengthen him. Being in agony,211 he prayed more earnestly and his sweat was like great drops of water falling down upon the ground.212]] When he arose up from prayer and came to his disciples, he found them sleeping without a care.213 He asked, **"Why are you sleeping? Rise up and let us not fail the test."**

47 While he was speaking, behold a crowd came and a man called Judas, one of the twelve, was leading them. He drew near to Jesus and kissed him for this was the sign he had given them, "He who I kiss is the one!" Jesus asked, **"Judas, do you betray the Son of humanity with a kiss?"** When the others realized what was happening, they said, "Teacher, shall we strike with the sword?" One of them struck the servant of the high priest and cut off his right ear. Jesus answered, **"It is enough for the present!"** He touched the ear of the one who was wounded and healed it. Then he said to the chief priests, the elders, and the officials of the Temple guard who came out to arrest him, **"Have you come out with swords and clubs like I was a revolutionary. You never tried to lay a hand on me when I was with you daily in the Temple but this is your hour, the time for the power of darkness."**

54 After arresting him, they brought him to the house of, the high priest,214 while Peter followed at a safe distance. They kindled a fire in midst of the courtyard, sat around it, and Peter sat among them. A young woman saw him sitting by the fire, she looked at him and said, "That man was also with him!" He denied him, saying, "Woman, I do not know him!" Later, another saw him and said, "You are also one of them!" Peter replied, "Man, I am not!" An hour later another argued and said, "Truly, this man was also with him for he is also a Galilean." Peter said, "Man, I don't know what you're talking about!" Immediately, a rooster crowed while he was still speaking. The Saviour turned and

looked over at Peter who remembered the words the Saviour had said to him, **"You will deny three times that you know me before the rooster crows in the morning."** Peter went out and wept bitterly.

63 Now the Temple guards holding Jesus mocked him and beat him. They also blindfolding him, hit his face, and asked him, "Prophesy!" "Who struck you?" They kept heaping terrible insults upon him. When daybreak came the elders, the chief priests, and the scribes gathered and brought him up to their council.[215] They said, "Tell us if you are the Christ!" He replied, **"You won't believe me if I tell you. If I ask you, you will not answer me or release me but from this time the Son of humanity will be seated at the right hand of the power of God."**[216] Then they all asked, "Are you the Son of God?" Jesus replied, **"You say that I am."** Then they said, "Why do we need witnesses for we ourselves have heard it from his own lips."

Luke 23:1–56

1 Then the whole company of them rose up to bring him before Pilate and they began to accuse him, saying, "We found this man misleading our people, forbidding us to pay the head tax to Caesar, and saying about himself that he is Christ, a king.[217] Pilate asked him, "Are you the king of the Jews?" Jesus answered, **"You say so."** Pilate spoke to the chief priests and the crowd, "I find no case against this person." So they were yelling, "He stirs up our people teaching throughout Judea, beginning from Galilee even up to this place." When Pilate heard the name Galilee[218] he asked if the man was a Galilean. When he confirmed that he was under Herod's jurisdiction, he sent him to Herod who was in Jerusalem then.

8 Herod was delighted to see Jesus for he had wanted to see him for a long time because he has heard about him and he was hoping to see some miracle done by him. So he questioned him at great length but Jesus gave him no answer. The chief priests and the scribes stood and vehemently accused him. Herod with his men of war treated him with contempt, mocked him, dressed him in a gorgeous robe, and sent him back to Pilate. On that very day Pilate and Herod became friends with each other for they were enemies before. Then Pilate called together the chief priests and leaders of the people and said to them, "You brought

me this man as one who was misleading the people and after examining him before you, I find this man innocent of all charges against him. Neither did Herod for I sent him to him and behold, he has done nothing worthy of death. Therefore I will have him flogged[219] and release him." There was a custom for him to release one prisoner to the people at the festival.

18 They all cried out in a loud voice, "Away with this man and release Barabbas to us." He was a man who was thrown into prison because an insurrection and for murder. Pilate was willing to release Jesus and spoke to them but they cried out, "Crucify him, crucify him!" Then he spoke to them a third time, "Why, what has he done wrong? I found no reason to sentence him to death. Therefore, I will have him flogged and let him go." They persisted with loud voices and asked to crucify him and their voices and those of the chief priests prevailed.[220] Then Pilate commanded to have their demand granted. He released the man who they asked for, the one who was thrown into prison because an insurrection and murder, and delivered Jesus up to their will.[221]

26 While they took Jesus away they seized Simon from Cyrene who was coming in from the country and they placed the end of the cross on him, to carry it with him.[222] A multitude of people followed him and the women mourned and wailed over him but Jesus turned to them, saying, **"Daughters of Jerusalem, don't weep for me but for yourselves and your children. Behold the days are coming when they will say, 'Blessed are the women whose wombs never gave birth and whose breasts never nursed babies!'**[223] **Then they will say to the mountains, 'Fall on us!' and to the hills, 'Cover us!'**[224] **If they do these things when the wood is green what will be done when the wood is dry?"**[225]

32 Two others who were criminals were led to be put to death with him. When they came to a place called Calvary,[226] they crucified him with the criminals; one on the right and one on the left. [[227 He said, **'Oh Divine Parent, forgive them for they know not what they do!'**]] They cast lots to divide his garments. The people stood by watching but the rulers with them mocked him, saying, "He saved others, let him save himself if he is the Christ of God, the Chosen One!" The soldiers mocked him as they came near him and offering him vinegar, saying, "If

you are the King of the Jews, save yourself." There was also an inscription which was written over him, "This is the King of the Jews."

39 One of the criminals who was crucified with him derided him, saying, "If you are the Christ, save yourself and save us too!" The other one rebuked him, saying. "Don't you fear God since you are also under the same judgment? Ours is just for we are receiving what we deserve for our deeds but this man is innocent!" Then he asked, "Jesus, remember me when you come into your kin-dom!" Jesus replied, **"Truly I say to you, today you will be with me in Paradise!"**[228]

44 Now it was about noon and darkness fell upon the whole land until three in the afternoon while the sun was darkened and the curtain[229] at the Most Holy Place in the Temple was torn in two. Jesus died about three in the afternoon after he cried out in a loud voice, *"1 In Thee Oh God, I put my trust; let me never be put to shame; deliver me in Thy justice. Incline Your ear to me, rescue me speedily. Be my rock of refuge for me and a fortress of defense to save me. For You are my rock and my fortress; therefore for Thy name's sake lead me and guide me. Pull me out of the net which they have secretly laid for me for You are my strength. Into Thy hands I commit my spirit; You have redeemed me, Oh God of truth."*[230] When a centurion saw what had happened, he praised God, saying, "Certainly this man was innocent!" All the multitudes who had assembled to see this sight returned home beating their breasts when they saw what happened. All his friends, including many women who had followed him from Galilee, stood at a distance and watched these things.

50 There was a good and righteous man named Joseph from the town of Arimathea in Judea. He was a member of the council[231] but disagreed with their wishes and their actions and he was looking for the kin-dom of God. He went to Pilate, asked for the body of Jesus, took it down, wrapped it in fine linen, and laid it in a tomb hewn out rock where no one had ever been laid. This was a Friday and the Sabbath was approaching. The women who had come with him from Galilee were near, saw the tomb, and observed how the body was placed. They returned to prepare spices and fragrant oils but on the Sabbath they rested as the Torah commands.[232]

Luke 24:1–53

1 On the first day of the week at early dawn, they came to the tomb bringing spices which they had prepared and there were other women with them.233 They found the stone rolled away from the tomb and when they went in they did not find the body of Jesus. While they were confused about this, suddenly, two men stood by them in dazzling garments. The women were afraid, bowed their faces to the ground and the men asked them, "Why do you seek the living among the dead? Jesus is not here but has risen! Remember how he spoke to you while he was in Galilee, saying that the Son of humanity must be delivered into the hands of sinners, be crucified, and rise again on the third day. They remembered his words. Then they returned from the tomb and told all these things to the eleven and everyone else. They were Mary Magdalene, Joanna, Mary the mother of James and the rest with them; who told these things to the apostles. They did not believe them for their words seemed like an idle tale.234 [[235 Peter rose up, ran to the tomb, stooped down, looked in, saw the linen cloths by themselves, and then he went home wondering what had happened.]]

13 On the same day two of them were traveling to a village called Emmaus, about seven miles from Jerusalem. They were talking with each other about everything that had happened. While they were talking and discussing together, Jesus joined them and walked with them. A spell came over their eyes, they failed to recognize him, and he said, **"What is this conversation you are holding with each other while you walk?"** They stood still and looked sad. Then one of them named Cleopas answered, "You must be the only person in Jerusalem who doesn't know the events which have happened in these days"

19 He asked, **"What things?"** They replied, "Concerning Jesus of Nazareth who was a prophet, mighty in word and deed before God and everybody, how the chief priests and our rulers delivered him up to be condemned to death, and he was crucified. We were hoping that he was going to redeem Israel and behold, this is the third day since these things happened. Also, some of the women in our group amazed us for they went to the tomb early in the morning and when his body was not found they came and told us, "We saw angels there and they said that he is alive." Some of our men also went to the tomb and found it

just like the women had said but they did not see him." Jesus said, **"Oh foolish people, so slow of heart to believe all that the prophets have spoken! It was necessary for Christ to suffer all these things to enter his glory."** He explained for them all the things concerning him in the scriptures, beginning with Moses and all the prophets.

28 As they approached the village where they were going, he made them think he was going further, but they urged him, saying, "Stay with us, the day is nearly over, and it is almost evening!" He entered in to stay with them and then as he reclined at the table with them he took the bread, blessed it, broke it, and gave it to them. Immediately their eyes were opened and they recognized him but then he disappeared from their sight. They told each other, "Our hearts burned within us when he talked with us and while he explained the scriptures to us." Then they rose up and returned to Jerusalem where they found the eleven and those with them were gathered, saying, "Truly our Saviour has risen indeed and has appeared to Simon." Then they reported what had happened to them on the road and how they knew him as he broke bread.

36 Now while they were talking about these things, Jesus stood in the midst of them and said to them, **"Peace be with you, I AM, do not be afraid"**[236] They were startled, frightened, and thought they were seeing a ghost. He asked them, **"Why are you troubled? Why do doubts arise in your hearts? Behold my hands and feet, see that it is I, myself. Feel me and understand for a spirit doesn't have flesh and bones as you see that I have."** He showed them his hands and his feet when he said this. While in their joy, they still did not believe and wondered, so he asked, **"Have you anything here to eat?"** They gave him a piece of broiled fish and some honeycomb, he took it and ate before them.

44 Then he said, **"Remember these words which I spoke to you when I was with you that all things will be fulfilled which are written in the law of Moses, the prophets, and the Psalms concerning me."** Then he opened their minds to understand the scriptures. He taught, **"Thus it is written, that Christ would suffer and rise from the dead on the third day and that repentance for the forgiveness[237] of sins will be preached in his name to all peoples[238] beginning at Jerusalem. You are witnesses of all these things and behold, I will send the Promise[239] of**

my Sacred Father upon you but remain in the city of Jerusalem until you are clothed with power from on high!" He led them out as far as Bethany where he lifted up his hands and blessed them. It happened that while he blessed them, he parted from them,[240] and[241] they returned to Jerusalem with great joy where they were continually in the Temple praising God. Amen.

The Gospel According to John

John 1:1–51

1 In the beginning was the Word,[1] the Word was with God, and the Word was God. The Word[2] was in the beginning with God. All things came into being through the Word and nothing came into being without the Word.[3] In the Word is eternal life and this life is the light for all people. The light shines in the darkness but the darkness does not overcome it.

6 A man named John was sent by God to bear witness to the Light so that all might believe through him. He was not the Light but sent to bear witness to the Light. This was the true Light who gives light to everyone coming into the world. He[4] was in the world, the world was under his hand and yet, the worldly did not know him.[5] He came into his own domain but most of his own people did not receive him. To those who received him, who believed in his name, were given the right to become children of God. They are born not of blood, nor the will of the flesh, nor the will of people but of God. The Word became flesh[6] and lived among us. We see his glory, a glory as the unique Son[7] of the Divine Parent[8] full of grace and truth. John testified about him, crying out, "This is the one of whom I said, 'There comes one after me who is superior[9] to me because he was before me.'" From his fullness we have all received, grace upon grace. The Law[10] was given through Moses but grace and truth come by Jesus the Christ. No one has seen God at any time but the unique Son[11] who is in the bosom of the Divine Parent and he has made God known.[12]

19 This is the testimony of John when the scribes of the Pharisees sent priests and Levites from Jerusalem to question him, "Who are you?" He confessed without delay, "I am not the Christ!" They said to him, "Well then, are you Elijah?"[13] He replied, "I am not." They inquired, "Are you a prophet?" He answered, "No." They repeated, "Who are you? Tell us so that we can report to those who sent us! What do you say about yourself?" John spoke from Isaiah, *I am the voice of one crying in the wilderness: 'Prepare the way of our God. Make directly in the desert a highway for our God.'"*[14]

24 Those questioning John were from the Pharisees. They asked, "Why do you baptize if you are not the Christ, Elijah, or a prophet?" John answered, "I baptize with water but one stands among you whom you don't know. This is the one coming after me, the one who I am not even worthy to loosen the strap of his sandal." This happened in Bethany beyond the Jordan River where John was baptizing. The next day he saw Jesus coming and said, "Behold the Lamb of God[15] who takes away the sins of the worldly! This is the one of whom I said, 'There comes one after me who is superior to me because he was before me.' I didn't know him but for this I came to baptize with water so that he might be revealed to Israel." John gave witness, saying, "I saw the Spirit descending from heaven like a dove and remain upon him. Yet I didn't know him myself but the One who sent me to baptize with water, said, 'The one upon whom you see the Spirit descend and remain is the one who will baptize with the Holy Spirit.' I myself have seen and testified that this is God's Chosen One."

35 Again, the next day John stood with two of his disciples and looked at Jesus as he walked, saying, "Behold the Lamb of God![16] The two disciples heard him speak and followed Jesus. Then Jesus turned to see them following and asked. **"What do you seek?"** They replied, "Rabbi," (which is to say, when translated, Teacher) "where are you staying?" He said, **"Come and see!"** About four o'clock in the afternoon these two came and saw where he was staying and remained with him the rest of the day. One of the two was Andrew who went to find his brother Simon to say, "We have found the Messiah" (which is translated, Christ).[17] He brought him to Jesus who looked at him, saying, **"You are Simon the son of John. You will be called Cephas"** (which is translated, Peter, a Stone).[18]

43 The next day Jesus was ready to go to Galilee when he found Philip and told him, **"Follow me!"** Now Philip was from Andrew and Peter's hometown of Bethsaida. Philip found Nathanael and told him, "We found the one Moses wrote about in the Torah and of whom the prophets also wrote, Jesus of Nazareth, the son of Joseph." Nathanael replied, "Can anything good ever come out of Nazareth!"[19] Philip answered, "Come and see for yourself!" As they approached Jesus said, **"Now here comes a true Israelite who is an honest man!"** "Where do you know me from?" asked Nathanael. Jesus replied, **"I saw you under the fig tree before Philip called you."** Nathanael responded, "Teacher, you are the Son of God, you are the king of Israel!" Jesus said, **"Do you believe this just because I told you I saw you under the fig tree? You will see far greater things than this. Very truly, I tell all of you, you will see heaven opened and the angels of God ascending and descending[20] on the Son of humanity."**

John 2:1–25

1 On the third day there was a marriage in the village of Cana in Galilee and the mother of Jesus was there. Jesus and his disciples were also invited to the wedding. When the wine ran out, his mother told him, "They have no more wine!" He answered, **"Mother, what concern is that to you and to me? They invited me and not my sign!"**[21] Mary spoke to the servants, "Whatever he tells you to do, please do it!" They set six stone water pots used in Jewish ceremonial purification rituals[22] with each holding twenty to thirty gallons. Jesus told them, **"Fill the jars with water!"** So they filled them to the brim. He said, **"Now draw some out and take it to the master of ceremonies."** So they brought it out. The master of ceremonies tasted the water that had become wine and called the bridegroom. He did not know where it came from but the servants who drew the water knew. He told him, "Every one brings out the best wine first and then the inferior wine when the guests have already become drunk but you have kept the best wine for now!" This is the first of the signs[23] that Jesus performed at Cana in Galilee and revealed his glory so his disciples believed in him. After the wedding he went down to Capennaum with his mother, his brothers, and his disciples where they remained for a few days.

13 Jesus went up to Jerusalem just before the Jewish Passover. In the Temple he found merchants who sold oxen, sheep, and doves while

moneychangers sat at tables. He made a whip of chords and drove them all out of the Temple, including the sheep, the oxen, and the moneychangers. He cast out the coins of the moneychangers and overturned their tables. He told the dove merchants, **"Take these away from here: do not make my Divine Parent's house into a house of business!"** His disciples remembered the words of the Psalm, *"It is zeal for Your house that has given me courage."*[24] The Jewish authorities[25] asked Jesus, "What sign can you show to us, since do these things? He answered, **"Destroy this Temple and I will raise it up in three days!"** They said, "It has taken forty-six years to build this Temple and will you raise it up in three days?" but he was speaking of the temple of his body.[26] Later when Jesus was risen from the dead, his disciples remembered that he said this so they believed the Scripture and the words which Jesus had spoken.

23 Now when he was in Jerusalem in the Passover week, many believed in his name when they saw the sign which he did.[27] Jesus did not remain with them because he knew all men and he needed no one to testify about himself for he knew the fate in store for him.[28]

John 3:1–36

1 Nicodemus was a Pharisee and a leader among the Jews. He approached Jesus at night saying, "Teacher, we all know that you are sent from God to teach us because no one could perform the signs that you have unless God is with them." Jesus replied, **"Very truly, I tell you that unless a person be born anew,[29] they cannot see the kin-dom of God."** Nicodemus asked, "How can a man be born when he is old? Can he enter into his mother's womb and be born a second time? Jesus answered, **"Very truly, I tell you, If a person is not born in the likeness of the Spirit[30] they cannot enter the kin-dom of God. That which is born of the person is human but that which is born of Spirit is spirit. Don't be surprised that I told you that, 'You must be born anew!' The wind blows where it wishes and you hear the sound of it but you can't tell from whence it comes or whither it goes. So is everyone who is born of the Spirit!"[31]**

9 Nicodemus asked, "How can this be? Jesus answered, **"You are a teacher of Israel and do not understand this? Very truly, I tell you, we speak only what we know and testify only what we have seen but**

you will not accept our testimony. If you don't believe when I speak of earthly things, how will you believe when I tell you of heavenly things? No one has ascended to heaven but this Son of humanity who has come down from heaven. Just as Moses took away the serpent in the wilderness, so will the Son of humanity be taken away that whoever believes in him will not perish but have eternal life.[32]

16 God so loved the world that God's unique Son[33] was given that everyone who believes in him shall not perish but have eternal life. For God sent the Son of God into the world, not to condemn the world but that the worldly will be saved through him. Whoever believes in him will not be judged but whoever[34] does not believe is judged already for not believing in the name of the unique Son[35] of God. This is the judgment; that light has come into the world and yet people loved darkness rather than light because their deeds were evil, for everyone who does evil hates the light and avoids the light where their deeds will be exposed. The person who lives by the truth comes to the light so that it may be clearly seen that God is in all they do."

22 After these things, Jesus and his disciples went into the land of Judea and he remained with them and baptized. John was baptizing at the spring of Aenon near Salim because there was plenty of water there and people came and were baptized for John was not yet cast into prison. Now it happened that a discussion arose between a Judean and some of John's disciples about the ceremony of purification. So they came to John and told him, "Rabbi, he who was with you beyond the Jordan, whom you testified about, behold he is baptizing and all are going to him."

27 John answered, "No one can receive anything of their own will except what is given them from God. You yourselves bear witness that I said, 'I am not the Christ.' but only a messenger to go before him. He who has a bride is the bridegroom and the best man of the bridegroom stands up, listens to him, and rejoices greatly because of the bridegroom's voice, so this joy of mine is now complete. He must become greater and I must become lesser. The one who has come from above is above all and the one who is of the earth belongs to the earth and speaks of earthly things. The one who comes from heaven is above all and testifies of what he has seen and heard, even if his testimony is not accepted. Those who accept

his testimony confirm thereby that God is true. The one whom God has sent speaks with the fullness of God for God does not give the Spirit by measure. The Divine Parent loves the Son and has placed everything in his hands. Those who believe in the Son have eternal life and those who do not obey the Son will not see real life but the judgement of God remains upon them."36

John 4:1–54

1 Now Jesus knew that the Pharisees had heard that he made many disciples who were baptizing more people than John. (His disciples baptized although Jesus himself did not baptize.37) He left Judea to go to Galilee but on the way he had to go through Samaria. In the Samaritan city of Sychar near the field that Jacob gave to his son Joseph, was Jacob's well. Tired from his long journey, Jesus sat down by the well at around noon. A woman of Samaria came to draw water from the well. He said, **"Please give me a drink."** His disciples had gone to town to buy food for themselves. She asked, "How is it that you are a Jew and yet you ask me, who is a Samaritan woman, for a drink? For Jews do not associate with Samaritans."

10 Jesus answered her, **"If you knew the gift God has for you and who is saying to you, 'Please give me a drink,' you could have asked me for a drink and I would have given you living water."**38 The woman said, "Sir, the well is deep and you have no leather bucket or a rope to draw up the water. Where will you get this living water? Are you greater than our ancestor Jacob who gave us this well and drank from it himself with his sons and daughters, and his livestock?" Jesus answered, **"Whoever drinks of this water will thirst again, but whoever drinks the water that I give you will never thirst for the living water that I give you will be in you a fountain of water springing up into eternal life."** She asked, "Sir, give me this water so I will neither thirst nor have to come here to draw more water."

16 He told her, **"Go! Call your husband and come back here."** She said, "I have no husband!" Jesus added, **"You are right in saying, 'I have no husband' for you have had five husbands and the one with you now is not your husband; you said this truly."** She said, "Sir, I perceive that you are a prophet. My ancestors worshiped on this mountain39 but you say that the Temple in Jerusalem is the place to worship." He taught her,

"Woman, believe me, the hour will come when you will worship our Divine Parent neither on this mountain nor in Jerusalem. You worship what you do not know. We worship what we do know for salvation is from the Jews.[40] **The time is coming and now is here when the true worshipers worship the Divine Parent in spirit and in truth for the Divine Parent desires worshipers such as these. God is Spirit and those who worship God must worship in spirit and truth."**

25 The woman said, "I know that the Messiah is coming (who is called the Christ) and when he comes, he will teach us all things." Jesus said, **"I AM, the one who speaking to you now!"**[41] Just then his disciples returned and were astonished to see him talking with a married women but held back their questions like, "What do you want with her?" or "Why are you talking with her?" The woman left her water jar, went into the city and told the people, "Come and see a man who told me everything that I have done! Could he be the Christ?" So they left the city and came to him.

31 Meanwhile his disciples urged him to eat, saying, "Teacher, eat something!" He explained, **"I have food to eat of which you do not know of."** The disciples asked one another, "What? Who else brought him food?" Jesus said, **"My food**[42] **is to do the will of the One Who sent me and complete this work. You have been saying, 'After four more months comes the harvest.' Behold, I tell you to lift up your eyes and look at the fields for they are already ripe for harvesting. The one who reaps receives wages and gathers fruit for eternal life so those who sow and those who reap may rejoice together. That saying is true in this harvest, 'One sows and another reaps.' I send you to reap that for which you have not labored. Others labored and you have joined in their work."**

39 Many Samaritans from that city believed on him because of the word of the woman who testified, "He told me everything that I have done." So when the Samaritans came to him, they asked him to stay and he stayed there two days. Many more believed in him because of his own word and they said to the woman, "Now we believe not only because of what you said but we have heard him ourselves and we know that he is indeed the Christ, the Saviour of the worldly."

43 He departed after two days and went to Galilee. Jesus himself testified that a prophet has no honor in their own country. Then when he came to Galilee, the Galileans welcomed him for they had been to the feast in Jerusalem and saw what wonders Jesus had done there. Jesus returned to Cana of Galilee where he had turned the water into wine. There was a certain royal official whose son lay sick at Capernaum. When he heard that he was back from Judea to Galilee, he went and begged him to come down and heal his son who was near death. Jesus said, **"Unless you see signs and wonders you will not believe."** The official answered, "Sir, come down before my child dies!" Jesus told him, **"Go, your son will live!"** The man believed Jesus word and went on his way. On returning his servants met him and brought him good news, saying, "Your son is healed!" He asked his servants what hour he got well and they replied, "The fever left him yesterday afternoon at one. The father knew that this was the same hour at which Jesus said, **"Your son will live!"** and he and his whole household believed. This was a second sign Jesus did after returning to Galilee from Judea.

John 5:1–47

1 After these things there was a Jewish festival and Jesus went up to Jerusalem. In Jerusalem near Sheep's Gate there was a double mikvah[43] pool which were called in Hebrew, Bethesda. They were surrounded by four porticoes[44] and a fifth portico between the pools. On these lay a great multitude of sick, blind, disabled, and paralyzed [[[45] waiting for a stirring of the water, for an angel of God goes down at a certain time to the mikvah pools and stirs the water. The first person to step in after the stirring of the water was healed from whatever disease they had.]] A man was there who had been sick for thirty-eight years. Jesus saw the man lying down and knew he had been waiting for a long time. He asked him, **"Do you wish to be healed?"** The sick man answered, "Yes Sir, but I have no one to put me in the pool when the water is stirred up. While I am coming down, another one goes in before me." Jesus told him, **"Rise, take up your quilt, and walk!"** The man was healed immediately, got up, took his quilt, and walked. This happened on the Sabbath.

10 So the Jewish authorities[46] said to the man who was healed, "It is not lawful for you to carry your quilt on the Sabbath." He answered them,

"The man who healed me told me, **'Take up your quilt and walk.'**" They asked him, "Who said, **'Take up your quilt and walk.'**" The man who was healed didn't know for Jesus had disappeared into the multitude in that place. After a while Jesus found him in the Temple and said, **"Behold, now you are healed, sin no more for something worse may happen to you."** So the man went away to the Jewish authorities to report that it was Jesus who had healed him. Therefore, the Jewish authorities started persecuting Jesus and wanted to kill him because he was doing these things on the Sabbath. Jesus answered them, **"My Divine Parent is still working so I am working too."** For this the authorities wanted all the more to kill him, not only because he was weakening the Sabbath but also because he said that God was his own Divine Parent, making himself equal to God.[47]

19 Jesus answered them, **"Truly I tell you, the Son can do nothing of his own accord but what he sees the Divine Parent doing for whatever the Divine Parent does, the Son does likewise. The Divine Parent loves the Son and shows him everything that the Divine Parent does and will show him greater works than these so that you may marvel. For as the Divine Parent raises the dead and gives them life, so the Son gives life to whom he will. The Divine Parent does not judge any one but has entrusted judgment to the Son. Everyone shall honor the Son just as they honor the Divine Parent. Those who do not honor the Son do not honor the Divine Parent Who sent him. Truly I tell you, whoever hears my word and believes in the One Who sent me has eternal life. They do not come before the judgment but have passed from death to life.**[48]

25 Truly I tell you, the hour is coming and now is already here when the dead[49] will hear the voice of the Son of God and those who listen will live. For as the Divine Parent is a source of life in God-self, so the Son has also been given to be a source of life in himself. The Son has also been given authority to execute judgment for he is the Son of humanity. Do not wonder at this for the time is coming when all who are in your graves[50] will hear my voice, and come out. Those who have done good works will go to the resurrection of life and those who have done evil works will go to fulfill judgment.**

30 I can do nothing on my own. As I hear, I judge and my judgment is just because I do not seek my own will but the will of the Divine Parent Who sent me. If I bear witness concerning myself, my witness is not valid as testimony.[51] **There is Another Who bears witness concerning me and I know that the witness which God witnesses of me is true. You sent messengers to John and he testified concerning the truth. I do not depend on any testimony from people but I tell you these things so you may be saved. John was a lamp which burns to gives light and you were willing to rejoice in his light for a time. I have a witness greater than the witness of John. I do the works which my Divine Parent has given me to accomplish. These works testify concerning me that my Divine Parent has sent me. The Divine Parent Who sent me has also testified concerning me. You have neither heard God's voice nor seen God's image, so God's word does not abide in you since you don't believe the one God has sent.**

39 Search the scriptures in which you think you have eternal life. Those are the scriptures bearing witness of me, and yet, you will not come to me so that you may have life. I am not interested in praise from people but I know you well, that you do not have the love of God in you. I have come in the name of my Divine Parent but you don't receive me. If another comes in their own name you will receive them. How can you believe when you receive honor one from another but do not seek the honor that comes from the One Who is God alone? What, do not think that I will accuse you before our Divine Parent? Moses, in whom you trust is the one who accuses you.

46 You would have believed in me if you really believed in Moses for he wrote of me," *"15 Your God will raise up for you a prophet like me from the midst of your people. Listen to him! Just as you asked of God at Horeb the day of the assembly, 'If I hear the voice of my God anymore or ever again see this great fire, I will die!' Then God replied to me, 'They are right in what they have spoken. I will raise up for them a prophet like you from among their own people and will put My words in the mouth of that prophet who will speak to them everything that I command him. I will hold accountable anyone who does not heed the words that prophet will speak in My name.'"*[52] **"If you do not believe his written word, how can you believe my words."**

John 6:1–71

1 After these events Jesus crossed over the Sea of Galilee which is the Sea of Tiberias. Many people followed him because they saw the signs which he performed on sick people. So Jesus climbed the hillside and sat there with his disciples. The Jewish festival of the Passover was at hand. Jesus lifted up his eyes and saw the multitudes coming up the hillside and asked Philip, **"Where can we buy food for all these people to eat?"** He said this merely to test him for he knew what he was going to do. Philip said, "Two hundred denarii worth of bread would not be sufficient for them to each take more than a bite." One of his disciples, Andrew the brother of Simon Peter, said, "There is a boy here who has five barley loaves and two fish but what are they among so many?"

10 Jesus said, **"Have all the people sit down."** There was a large area of grass and more than five thousand people sat down. He took the bread and when he had given thanks, he distributed it to those who were sitting down; likewise the fish also, as much as they wanted. When they were filled, he said to his disciples, **"Gather up the remaining morsels so that nothing is lost."** They gathered them up and filled twelve baskets of morsels left over by the those who had eaten. Then the people who experienced the sign which Jesus performed said, "Truly, this is a prophet who has come into the world!" Jesus knew that they were ready to take him by force to make him a king so he withdrew to a mountain by himself alone.

16 When evening came his disciples went down to the shore, entered into a boat, and started going to the port of Capernaum. Now it was dark and Jesus had not come to them. Then the sea became rough because a strong wind was blowing. When they had rowed about three or four miles they saw Jesus walking on[53] the sea. They became frightened as he walked towards their boat but he said to them, **"I AM! Do not be afraid."** Then they wanted to receive him into the boat but soon the boat reached the shore where they were heading.

22 The next day, the multitude which stood waiting on the shore saw no other boat there, except the boat which the disciples had entered. Jesus had not entered the boat with his disciples but other boats had come from Tiberias, near the place where they ate the bread and fish after

Jesus had given thanks. The people had entered their boats and came to Capernaum looking for him when they saw that Jesus and his disciples were not there. When they found him there, they asked, "Teacher, when did you come here?" Jesus answered, **"Truly, I tell you that you seek me just because you ate the food and were filled and not because you saw the signs. Don't labor for the food that is consumed but for that nourishment of faith into eternal life which the Son of humanity will give you. For this one God the Divine Parent has confirmed."**[54]

28 They said, "What shall we do to labor for the works of God?" Jesus answered, **"A work of God is to believe on him whom God has sent."** They asked him, "What sign will you perform that we may see and believe in you? What work will you perform? Our ancestors ate manna in the wilderness: as it is written, 'Moses gave them bread from heaven to eat.'"[55] Jesus said, **"Truly I tell you, It was not Moses who gave you bread from heaven but my Divine Parent gives you the true bread from heaven. The bread of God is one who comes down from heaven and gives life to the world."** They said, "Sir, give us this bread always!"

35 Jesus taught them, **"I AM the bread of life;**[56] **whoever comes to me will never hunger and whoever believes in me will never thirst. I have said to you that you have seen me but still refuse to believe. Everyone that my Divine Parent gives me will come to me and I will never reject anyone who comes to me. For I have come down from heaven to do the will of the One Who sent me and not to do my own will. The will of my Divine Parent Who sent me is that I will not lose even one of those given to me but raise them up in their last day. This is the will of my Divine Parent Who sent me, that whoever sees the Son and believes in him will have eternal life and I will raise them up on their last day."**

41 Some of the Jewish people began to murmur against him because he said, **"I AM the bread of life which came down from heaven."** They said, "Isn't this Jesus, the son of Joseph, whose mother and father we know? How can he say, 'I have come down from heaven.'" He answered, **"Do not murmur among yourselves. No one can come to me unless drawn by the Divine Parent Who sent me and I will raise them up on their last day. It is written in the prophets, '13 All your children**

shall learn from God and great will be the peace of your children. In righteousness will you be established. You will be far from oppression for you will not fear. You will be far from terror for it will not come near you. If anyone stirs up strife, it is not because of Me. Whoever stirs up strife with you will fall because of you. 57 **Everyone who hears and has learned from the Divine Parent will come to me.**

46 No one has seen the Divine Parent except one who is from God, they have seen the Divine Parent. 58 **Truly I tell you, whoever believes in me has eternal life. I AM the bread of life. Your ancestors ate manna in the wilderness and yet they died. This is the bread which came down from heaven, that a person may eat of it and not die. I AM the living bread because I came down from heaven and if anyone eats of this bread, they will live forever. The bread which I will give for the life of the world is my body."**

52 Some of the Jewish people argued among themselves saying, "How can this man give us his body to eat?" Jesus said, **"Truly I tell you, unless you eat the body of the Son of humanity and drink his blood, you have no life in yourselves.**59 **Whoever eats my body and drinks my blood has eternal life and I will raise them up on their last day. For my body truly is the food and my blood truly is the drink. Whoever eats my body and drinks my blood abides with me and I with them. Just as the living Divine Parent sent me and I am living because of the Divine Parent, so whoever eats of me will live because of me. This is the bread which came down from heaven. It is not like the manna which your ancestors ate and died for whoever eats of this bread will live forever."** He said these words while teaching in the synagogue at Capernaum.

60 Many of his disciples who heard it said, "This is a hard saying! Who can understand it?" Jesus knew in himself that his disciples were murmuring about this, so he said, **"Does this saying offend you? What then if you will see the Son of humanity ascend to where he was before? It is the Spirit that gives life; the body will not help you. The words that I have spoken to you, they are spirit and they are life. Yet there are some of you who do not believe."** Jesus knew for a long time who did not believe and who was to betray him. He said, **"Therefore I**

have told you that no one can come to me unless it is given to them by my Divine Parent."

66 Many of his disciples turned away and did not follow him just because of this saying. Then Jesus asked the twelve, **"Do you also want to go away?"** Simon Peter answered, "Saviour, to whom will we go? You have the words of eternal life. We believe them and know that you are the Holy One of God!" Jesus said, **"Did I not choose you twelve and yet one of you is Satan?"**[60] He spoke of Judas, the son of Simon Iscariot for he was the one of the twelve who was going to betray him.

John 7:1–53

1 After this Jesus traveled in Galilee for he did not wish to travel in Judea because the Jewish authorities wanted to kill him. Now the Jewish festival of Tabernacles[61] was at hand. His brothers said, "Depart from here and go to Judea so your disciples may see the deeds that you do. For no one does anything in secret and yet wants it to become known. Show what you are doing to the world." Not even his brothers believed in him yet. Jesus said, **"Your time is fixed by the calendar to go regularly to the feasts. My time is not ordered that way.**[62] **The world cannot hate you but it hates me because I testify against it, that many of its works are evil. You go up to the feast. I am not going to the feast just now for my time has not yet come."**

9 He remained in Galilee after saying these things. After his brothers left, he also went to the feast, not openly but in private. The Judean authorities were looking for him at the feast saying, "Where is he?" There was much discussion about him among the people. Some said, "He is a good man!" and others replied, "No! He just deceives the people." However, nobody spoke openly about him for fear of the Jewish authorities.

14 Now about the middle of the feast, Jesus went up to the Temple and taught. Some Jewish people marveled, saying, "How does this man know so much when he has not been instructed." Jesus answered them, **"My teaching is not mine but from God who sent me. Anyone determined to do the will of God can understand if my teaching is from God or I am speaking on my own authority. Whoever speaks on your own authority seeks their own glory but whoever seeks the glory of the**

one who sent them is true and there is no deception in their heart. Didn't Moses give you the law? Yet, not one of you obeys the law. Why do you want to kill me?" The crowd answered, "You are crazy! Who is seeking to kill you?" Jesus replied, **"I did one work and you all marvel. Moses gave you circumcision, which came not from Moses but from your ancestors and yet you circumcise on the Sabbath. So if a man is circumcised on the Sabbath that the law of Moses may not be broken; why are you angry with me because I made a man whole on the Sabbath? Do not judge by appearances but judge according to what is just."**

25 Some of them from Jerusalem said, "Is this not the man whom they seek to kill? Behold he speaks openly and they say nothing to him. Have the authorities found out that he is the Christ? Yet we know where he comes from but when the Christ appears, no one will know where the Christ comes from." Jesus then lifted up his voice and taught in the Temple, **"You know me and you know where I come from. I have not come on my own accord but the Divine Parent Who sent me is true, Whom you don't know. I know the Divine Parent for I am from the One Who sent me."** So they wanted to seize him but no man laid a hand on him because his time to be taken had not yet come. Many of the people believed in him, saying, "When the Christ comes, will the Christ do greater signs than this man does?"

32 Some Pharisees heard the people talking about him, so they and the chief priests sent some Temple guards to arrest him. Jesus said, **"I shall remain with you a little while longer and then I am going to the One Who sent me. You will seek me but you will not find me for where I AM, you cannot come."** Then some Jewish people said among themselves, "Where is he going that we can't find him? Is he planning to go to countries of the Gentiles to teach the pagans? What do the words mean, when he said, **'You will seek me but you will not find me for where I AM, you cannot come.'?"**

37 Now on the greatest day which is the last day of the feast, Jesus stood up and cried out, **"If anyone is thirsty, let them come to me and drink!**[63] **Whoever believes in me, just as the scriptures have said, the rivers of living water will flow from your innermost being."**[64] He

said this concerning the Spirit which those who believed in him were to receive, for the Holy Spirit was not yet given because Jesus was not yet glorified.

40 Many of the people who heard his words were saying, "This man truly is a prophet!" Some were saying, "He is the Christ." but others said, "Is it possible that the Christ will come from Galilee? Do not the scriptures say that Christ will come from the seed of David and from Bethlehem, the town of David?"65 So the people were divided because of him and there were some men among them who wanted to arrest him but no one laid hands on him.

45 The Temple guards returned to the chief priests and the Pharisees who asked them, "Why didn't you bring him?" The guards answered them, "No man ever spoke as this man speaks!" These Pharisees said, "What? Have you also been deceived? Have any of the rulers66 or the Pharisees believed in him? This crowd who do not know the law are accursed?"67 Nicodemus, one of them who had came to Jesus at night, said to them, "Our law does not convict a person unless it first hears from them and knows what they have done." They answered, "What? Are you also from Galilee? Search the scriptures for yourself and see that no prophet has ever come from Galilee!"68 [[69 So everyone returned to their own home.

John 8:1–59

1 Then Jesus went to the mount of Olives. In the morning he came again into the Temple where all the people came to him. He sat down and began to teach them. Then the scribes of the Pharisees brought a woman who was caught in adultery. They made her stand in the midst of the people and said to him, "Teacher, this woman was caught openly in the very act of adultery. Moses, in the Law,70 commanded us that such people be stoned but what do you say?" They were testing him so they might have a cause to accuse him. Jesus bent down and wrote on the ground with his finger. So when they were through questioning him, he straightened himself up and said, **"Whoever is without sin among you can throw the first stone!"** Again he bent down and wrote on the ground. When the people heard this saying they left one by one, beginning with the oldest. The woman was left alone standing before him. When Jesus

straightened up and said to her, **"Where are your accusers? Has no one condemned you?"** She answered, "Not one, Saviour!" Jesus said, **"Neither do I condemn you. Go now and sin no more."]]**

12 Later Jesus spoke to the people again, **"I AM the light of the world. Whoever follows me shall not walk in darkness**[71] **but shall find in yourselves the light of life."**[72] Some Pharisees said, "You testify concerning yourself so your testimony is not valid." Jesus answered, **"Even though I testify concerning myself, my testimony is true because I know from whence I came from and whither I go but you don't know where I came from or where I am going. You judge in a human fashion; I do not judge as a man.**[73] **When I do judge, my judgment is true for I am not alone. My Divine Parent Who sent me is with me now. It is written in the law that the testimony of two people is true.**[74] **I am one who testifies concerning myself and my Divine Parent testifies concerning me."** They asked, "Where is your Divine Parent?" Jesus answered, **"You know neither me nor my Divine Parent. If you knew me, you would also know my Divine Parent."** These words he spoke in the treasury while he taught in the Temple but no one arrested him for his time had not yet come.

21 Jesus again said to them, **"I am going away and you will seek me. You will die in your sins but where I am going you can't come."** So the Pharisees said, "Is he planning suicide? What does he mean when he says, 'Where I am going you can't come.'" He said, **"You are from below and I am from above.**[75] **You are of this world but I am not of this world. I told you that you would die in your sins for if you do not believe that I AM, you will die in your sins."** Then they asked, "Who are you?" Jesus replied, **"What I have told you from the beginning. I have many things to say and judge concerning you but the Divine Parent Who sent me is true. I speak to the world those things which I have heard from the One Who sent me."** They didn't understand that he spoke to them concerning the Divine Parent. Again Jesus said, **"When I will be taken away from you then you will realize I AM. I do nothing of my own accord but I speak as my Divine Parent has taught me. The One Who sent me is with me. My Divine Parent has never left me alone because I always do what is pleasing to the Divine Parent."**

30 As he was speaking these words, many believed in him. Jesus addressed those Jewish leaders[76] who believed in him, **"If you continue in my word then you are my disciples indeed. You will know the truth and the truth will make you free."** They answered him, "We are Abraham's seed and we were never in bondage to anyone. How can you say, **'You will be made free.'?"** Jesus answered them, **"Very truly, I say to you, whoever commits sin is the servant of sin. The servant never stays in the house; but the Son abides always.**[77] **You will be free indeed if the Son will make you free. I know you are the descendants of Abraham but still some of you want to kill me because you have no room in you for my words. I speak of what I have seen with my Divine Parent and you do what you have seen from your parent."**

39 They [*The Jewish leaders*] answered, "Abraham is our father." Jesus said, **"If you were the children of Abraham, you would be doing the works of Abraham. Behold, now you want to kill me, even a man who has told you the truth which I heard from God. Abraham didn't do this. You do the deeds of your father."** They replied, "We are not the children of immorality: we have one Divine Parent, God." Jesus said, **"If God were your Divine Parent, you would love me for I came forth from God. I did not come of my own accord but God sent me. Perhaps you do not understand my teaching because you can't bear to listen to my discourse. You are of your father the devil and you will pursue your father's desires. He was a destroyer from the beginning. He is not concerned with the truth and will not stand by the truth because the truth is not in him. When he tells a lie, he expresses his own nature for he is a fraud and the producer of it.**[78] **You do not believe me because I speak the truth. Which one of you can accuse me of sin? Why don't you believe me if I speak the truth? Whoever is of God will hear God's words. The reason you do not hear them is because you are not of God."**

48 The Jewish leaders answered, "Aren't we right in saying that you are a Samaritan and have a demon?'" Jesus responded, **"I am not crazy but I honor my Divine Parent and you curse me. I do not seek my own glory but there is One Who seeks it and judges. Truly, I tell you, whoever keeps my word will never see death."**[79] They replied, "Now we are sure that you are insane. Abraham and the prophets have died;

yet, you say, 'Whoever keeps my word will never see death.' What? Are you greater than our father Abraham, who died and the prophets, who died? Who do you claim to be?" Jesus said, **"If I honor myself, my honor is nothing but it is my Divine Parent Who honors me, the One you say is our God. Yet you have not known God; I know God. If I said I do not know God, I would be a liar like yourselves but I do know God and I keep God's word. Your father Abraham rejoices to see my day, he saw it and he was glad."** Then they said, "You are not even fifty years old and you have seen Abraham? Jesus answered, **"Very truly, I tell you, before Abraham lived, I AM."**[80] So they picked up stones to throw at him but he hid himself and went out of the Temple; he passed by through the midst of them and went away.

John 9:1–41

1 As he was leaving, he saw a man who was blind from his mother's womb. His disciples asked him, "Teacher, who sinned that he was born blind; this man or his parents?" Jesus answered, **"It was not that this man sinned or his parents but that the works of God might be made manifest in him. I must do the works of God Who sent me while it is day for the night is coming when no one can work. I AM the light of the world as long as I in the world."** When he said these words, he spat on the ground and made clay with his saliva. He applied this to the eyes of the blind man, saying, **"Go and wash in the pool of Siloam."** (The name means "sent.") He went, washed his eyes, and came back able to see.

8 His neighbors and those who had seen him begging before, said, "Is this the one who used to sit and beg?" Some agreed, "He is the one!" Others were saying, "No, but he resembles him." He insisted, "I am he." Then they asked, "How were your eyes opened?" He answered, "A man named Jesus made clay and placed it on my eyes, saying, **'Go and wash in the pool of Siloam.'** So I went and washed and received my sight." They said, "Where is he?" He replied, "I don't know."

13 They brought the man who had been blind from birth to the Pharisee leaders. Now it was the Sabbath day when Jesus had made the clay and opened his eyes. The Pharisees asked him, "How did you receive your sight?" He answered, "He placed clay on my eyes, I washed them and

I see." Some of the Pharisees said, "This man is not from God because he does not observe the Sabbath." Others said, "How can a man who is a sinner do such miracles? So there was a division among them. They questioned the man who had been blind, "What do you say of him who has opened your eyes?" He answered, "I say he is a prophet!"

18 The Pharisees did not believe concerning him, that he had been blind and had received his sight, so they called in the parents of the man who had received his sight, and they asked them, "Is this your son who you say was born blind? How then does he now see?" His parents answered, "We know that he is our son and that he was born blind, but we don't know how he sees or who opened his eyes. He is an adult, ask him and he will speak for himself. His parents said this because they were afraid of the Pharisee leaders who had already decided that if anyone would confess that he was the Christ, they would be put out the synagogue.[81] For this reason his parents said, "He is an adult, ask him."

24 So they called the man who had been blind for a second time, saying, "Confess before God for we know this man to be a sinner." He answered, "I do not know if he is a sinner but one thing I do know; once I was blind and now I see!" They asked him again, "What did he do to you? How did he open your eyes?" He replied, "I told you already but you did not listen; do you want to hear it again? Perhaps you should be taught by him!" Then they cursed him, saying, "You are his disciple but we are disciples of Moses. We know that God spoke with Moses but as for this fellow, we don't know where he is from. The man answered, "This is marvelous! You don't know where he is from and yet he opened my eyes. We know that God doesn't hear the voice of sinners but listens to one who worships God and does God's will. Never since the world began has it been heard of that anyone opened the eyes of someone born blind. He couldn't do this if he were not from God." They answered, "You were born entirely in sin and yet, you try to teach us!" Then they threw him out.

35 Jesus heard that they had thrown him out and he found the man and said, **"Do you believe in the Son of humanity?"** The one who was healed answered, "Who is he, sir, so that I may believe in him?" Jesus said, **"You have already seen him and he is speaking with you now."** He said, "Saviour, I do believe!" and bowed down before him. Then Jesus said, **"I**

have come for the judgment of this world, so that those who can't see may see and those who see may become blind."[82] When some of the Pharisees who were with him heard these words, they said, "What, are we also blind?" Jesus replied, **"If you were really blind, you would not have guilt but you say, 'We see.' Therefore your guilt remains.**

John 10:1–42

1 **Truly I tell you, anyone who does not enter by the gate into the sheepfold but climbs from another place is a thief and a robber. The one who enters by the gate is the shepherd of the sheep. The gatekeeper opens the gate for him, the sheep hear his voice and he calls his own sheep by name and leads them out. After he has brought out his own, he goes before them and the sheep follow for they know his voice. They will not follow a stranger but will turn from them because they don't know the voice of strangers."**

6 Jesus spoke this parable to them but they did not understand what he meant, so he explained, **"Truly I tell you, I AM the gatekeeper of the sheep. All who came before me were thieves and robbers but the sheep did not listen to them. I AM the gatekeeper of the sheep. If anyone enters by me, they will be saved and will go in or out to find pasture. A thief does not come except to steal, kill, and destroy. I have come that they might have life and have it more abundantly.**

11 **I AM the good shepherd.**[83] **The good shepherd risks their life for the sake of the sheep. The hired person who is not the shepherd and not the owner of the sheep will leave the sheep and flee when they see the wolf come. Then the wolf snatches them and scatters them. The hired person runs away because that person works for money and does not care for the sheep. I AM the good shepherd for I know my own and my own know me, just as my Divine Parent knows me and I know my Divine Parent. I will lay down my life for the sake of the sheep. Also, I have other sheep which are not of this fold and I must bring them too. They will hear my voice and all the sheepfolds will become one flock with one shepherd.**

17 **This is why my Divine Parent loves me because I will lay down my life so that I may take it up again. No one takes it away from me but**

I lay it down of my own will. Therefore I have the power to lay down my life and I have the power to take my life up again. I received this command from my Divine Parent." There was again a division among the Jewish people because of these sayings. Many said, "He is demon possessed and insane, why do you listen to him?" Others said, "These are not the words of someone who is possessed by a demon. Can a crazy person open up the eyes of a blind man?"

22 It was the Festival of the Rededication of the Temple[84] at Jerusalem. It was winter and Jesus was walking in the portico of Solomon in the Temple. Then the Jewish leaders surrounded him, saying, "How long are you going to keep us in suspense? Tell us openly if you are the Christ!" Jesus answered, **"I have told you but you do not believe me. The works that I do in the name of my Divine Parent testify of me. You don't believe me because you are not my sheep. My own sheep hear my voice, I know them, and they follow me. I give them eternal life, they will never perish, and no one will snatch them from my hands. My Divine Parent Who gave them to me is greater than all and no one is able to snatch them from my Divine Parent's hand. My Divine Parent and I are one."**[85]

31 Then the Jewish leaders took up stones again to stone him. Jesus said, **"I have shown you many good works from my Divine Parent, for which one of them do you stone me?"** They answered, "We don't stone you for your good works but because you blaspheme, for while you are only a person, you make yourself into a God. Jesus replied, **"It is written in the law, *'1 God stands in the congregation of the mighty: God judges among the gods. How long will you judge unjustly, and show favor to the evil acting people? Selah! Defend the weak and the orphan; do justice to the afflicted and destitute. Deliver the poor and the needy; free them from the hands of evil acting people. These don't know or understand for they walk about in darkness. All the foundations of the earth are unstable, changing. I said, "'You are gods!*[86] *All of you are children of the Most High but you will die like other people, and fall like one of these rulers.'" Arise! Oh God! Judge the earth; for You will inherit all people.*[87]**

35 God called them gods because the word of God was with them and the scripture cannot be broken. Can you say to the one whom the

Divine Parent has sanctified and sent into the world, 'You blaspheme,' just because I told you, 'I am the Son of God?'[88] **Do not believe me if I am not doing the works of my Divine Parent. Even though you do not believe in me, believe in the works that I am doing so that you may know and understand that my Divine Parent is in me and I am in my Divine Parent."**

39 They tried to seize him again but he escaped from their hands. He went away across the Jordan River to the place where John first baptized and remained there. Then many came to him and said, "John did not perform a single sign but everything which he told us about this man is true." Many people believed on Jesus there.

John 11:1–57

1 Now there was a man who was seriously ill, Lazarus of Bethany, the village of Mary and her sister Martha. This was the Mary who anointed Jesus with ointment and wiped his feet with her hair. Lazarus, who was sick, was her brother, so his sisters sent for Jesus, saying, "Our Saviour, behold the one whom you love is sick." Jesus received the news, saying, **"This is not a sickness unto death but for the sake of the glory of God, that the Son of God may be glorified on his account."** Now he loved Martha, Mary, and Lazarus but when he heard he was sick he remained where he was for two more days. After that he told his disciples, "Come, let us go again to Judea." His disciples replied, "Teacher, not long ago some of the Jewish authorities wanted to stone you and yet you are going there again."

9 Jesus replied, **"There are twelve hours in the day. If a person walks in the daytime, they will not stumble because they see the light of this world but if a person travels at nighttime, they will stumble because there is no light in them."** He said these things and then he said, **"Our friend Lazarus is asleep but I go that I may awaken him out of sleep."** His disciples responded, "Our Saviour, if he is sleeping, he will get well." Jesus was speaking of his death but they thought that what he said was he was sleeping in bed. Then Jesus told them plainly, **"Lazarus is dead and for your sakes I am glad I was not there, so that you may believe. Let us walk there to him!"** Then Thomas, who is called, the Twin[89] said to the other disciples, "Let us go that we may accompany him."[90]

17 When Jesus arrived, he found Lazarus had already been in the tomb four days. Now Bethany was about two miles from Jerusalem and many Judeans had joined the women around Martha and Mary to comfort their hearts concerning their brother. Martha went out to meet Jesus when she heard that he had come but Mary sat in the house. Martha said to Jesus, "My Saviour, if you had been here my brother would not have died but even now I know that whatever you ask of God, God will give you." Jesus said to her, **"Your brother will rise again."** Martha replied, "I know that he will rise up in the resurrection on the last day." He said, **"I AM the resurrection and the life. Whoever believes in me even though they die, they will live. Whoever is alive and believes in me shall never die.[91] Do you believe this?"** She replied, "Yes, my Saviour, I do believe that you are the Christ, the Son of God who was to come into the world.

28 At this time she went to call on her sister Mary, telling her privately, "Our Teacher has come and is asking for you." Mary rose up quickly and went to him when she heard this. Jesus had not yet come to the village as he was still at the same place where Martha met him. Those friends who were in the house to comfort her, saw her get up and go out quickly. They followed her for they thought that she was going to the tomb to weep. When Mary arrived where Jesus was and saw him, she threw herself at his feet,[92] saying, "My Saviour, if you had been here then my brother would not have died!" When Jesus saw her weeping and the Judeans who had come with her were also weeping, he groaned deeply in spirit[93] and was greatly disturbed.[94] He asked, **"Where is he buried?"** They answered, "Sir, come and see." and Jesus wept too. The Judeans said, "See how much he loved him!" Some of them said, "Couldn't this man who opened the eyes of that blind man, have also kept Lazarus from dying?"

38 As he came to the tomb Jesus was disturbed in himself because of them. The tomb was in a cave with a stone placed at the entrance. Jesus said, **"Take away the stone!"** Martha said, "My Saviour, his body already stinks for he has been dead four days." He told her, **"I said to you that if you believe, you will see the glory of God."** They took away the stone and Jesus looked upward, saying, **"Oh Divine Parent, I thank Thee for having heard me. I know that You always hear me but I say these things so the people who stand around may believe that You**

have sent me." After saying this, he cried in a loud voice, **"Lazarus! Come out!"** The dead man came out with his hands and feet bound with strips of linen and his face wrapped with a burial cloth. Jesus told them, **"Unbind him and let him go!"**

45 Many of the Judeans who had come with Mary, believed in him when they saw what Jesus had done. Some of them went to the Pharisees and told them everything Jesus had done. So the high priest, the chief priests and the Pharisees gathered and said, "What shall we do? This man performs many signs. If we allow him to continue like this, everybody will believe in him and the Romans will come and take over our land and people." One of them, called Caiaphas who was high priest for that year, said, "You know nothing! Don't you realize that it is better for you to have one person die for the people than for the whole nation to perish." He did not say this on his own but being high priest for that year, he prophesied that Jesus had to die for the sake of the people and he would die not only for the nation but to gather in unity the children of God scattered around the world. From that very day they[95] planned to put him to death.

54 Therefore Jesus did not walk openly among the Judeans but withdrew to a region close to the wilderness in the ruins of a city called Ephriam where he stayed with his disciples. Now the Passover of the Jews was at hand and many went up from the towns to Jerusalem, before the feast, to purify themselves in the mikvah pools there. They were looking for Jesus and at the Temple they kept saying to one another, "What do you think? Surely he will not come to the festival, will he?" The chief priests and the Pharisees had already commanded that if anyone would know where he was, they were to let the authorities know so they might arrest him.

John 12:1–50

1 Six days before the Passover, Jesus arrived in Bethany at the home of Lazarus whom he had raises from the dead. They gave him a banquet there where Martha served and Lazarus was one of the guests at the table with him. Then Mary took a pound of expensive perfume made from pure nard,[96] anointed the feet of Jesus, and wiped his feet with her hair. The house was filled with the fragrance of the perfume. Judas Iscariot, the disciple who was about to betray him, said, "Why wasn't this

perfume sold for three hundred denarii to give to the poor?" He said this because he was a thief and not because he cared for the poor. He kept the common purse with him and used to steal from the money put in there. Jesus said, **"Leave her alone! She has kept this for the day of my burial. You will always have the poor with you but you will not always have me."**

9 Many of the Jewish people heard that Jesus was there, so they came not only because of Jesus but also came to see Lazarus whom he had raised from the dead. The chief priests planned to put Lazarus to death as well because on his account many Judaens were leaving and believing in Jesus. On the next day, the large crowd which had come to the feast heard that Jesus was going to Jerusalem, so they took branches from palm trees, went out to greet him, and cried out: *"Hosanna! Blessed is the one who comes in the name of God,*[97] even the ruler of Israel!" Then Jesus found a young donkey and sat on it, as it is written, *9 Rejoice greatly, Oh daughter of Zion! Shout, Oh daughter of Jerusalem! Behold, your ruler [king] comes to you. He is just and having salvation. Lowly and riding on a donkey; upon a colt, the foal of an ass. I will disarm all peoples of the earth, including My people in Israel. The battle bow will be broken and he shall bring peace among the nations. His realm shall stretch from sea to sea, from the river to the ends of the earth.*[98]

16 His disciples didn't understand these things then. When Jesus was glorified, then they remembered what was written of him and those things that happened to him. The people who were with him testified that he had called Lazarus from the tomb and raised him from the dead. It was on this account that large crowds went out to meet him for they heard that he had performed this sign. The Pharisees said to one another, "You see, we have not been able to do anything. Behold, all the people have gone after him!"

20 Now there were some Gentiles[99] among those who came to worship in the Passover. They came and approached Philip of Bethsaida from Galilee, saying, "Sir, we would like to see Jesus." Philip came and told Andrew, then Andrew and Philip told Jesus. Jesus answered them, **"The hour has come that the Son of humanity will be glorified. Truly I tell you that unless a grain of wheat falling to the ground dies, it remains**

as one; but if it dies, it bears much fruit.[100] **Whoever loves their life will lose it but whoever has no concern for their life[101] in this world will keep it for eternal life.[102] If any one will serve me, let them follow me and where I am, there my servant will be also. My Divine Parent will honor anyone who serves me.**

27 Now my soul is disturbed and what shall I say? Oh my Divine Parent, deliver me from this hour but for this cause I have come to this very hour. Oh Divine Parent, glorify Thy name!" Then a Voice was heard from heaven, "I am glorified and I will again be glorified!" The people who stood by heard it, saying, "It was thunder!" others said, "An angel spoke to him." Jesus explained, **"The Voice was not on my account but for your sake. Now is the judgment of this world; the ruler[103] of the worldly will be driven away and I, when I disappear[104] from the world, will draw all people to myself."** He said this to show what kind of death he was going to die. The people said, "We have been taught from the law that the Christ will remain forever.[105] So how can you say that the Son of humanity will disappear?" "Who is this Son of humanity?" Jesus said, **"The light is in you for a little while longer. Walk while you have the light so that the darkness may not overcome you. Whoever walks in darkness doesn't know where they are going. While you have the light, believe in the light so that you may become children of the light."** After Jesus said this, he departed, and hid himself from them.

37 They still did not believe in him even though he had performed all these signs before them. Thus was fulfilled the words that Isaiah spoke; *"1 Who has believed our report? To whom is the power of God revealed? He grew up before God as an infant like a tender green shoot sprouting from a root in the dry ground. He was not attractive in our eyes so we denied him. We despised and rejected him; a man of sorrows and acquainted with grief. We turned away from him as he came by us. He was despised and we didn't care. It was our grief that he bore and our sorrows that weighed him down. We considered him stricken, afflicted, and struck down by God for his own sins. He was stricken that we might be healed, afflicted that we might have peace, and struck down for our transgressions; the punishment that made us whole.*

6 We are all like sheep who have strayed; each going our own way. So God laid the sins of all of us on him. He was oppressed and afflicted but never opened his mouth. He was as a lamb led to the slaughter and like a ewe before her shearers he remained silent. By a perversion of justice he was taken from prison to suffer punishment for their transgressions. He was cut off from the land of the living and beat up by some men of my own people. He was buried as a criminal but in a rich man's grave, although he had done no violence and there was no deceit in his mouth.

*10 Yet it pleased God to afflict him, put him to grief, and lay down his life as an offering for sin so that posterity will see him, his days will be prolonged, and the pleasure of God shall prosper in his hand. Out of anguish he will see light and he will find satisfaction through his knowledge. As the servant of many, he will make them righteous for he will bear their iniquities. Therefore, I will divide him a portion with the great and he will divide the spoil with the strong because he poured out his soul unto death. He bore the sins of many and made intercession for the transgressors so he was numbered with the transgressors."*106

39 For this reason they could not believe because Isaiah also said; *"8 Also, I heard the voice of God, saying, 'Whom will I send and who will go for Us?' Then I said, 'Here I am; send me!' God said to me, 'Go and tell this people, '"You listen carefully but you will not understand; you look intently but you will not perceive.'" For the heart of this people is hardened, their ears are closed, and their eyes are shut; so that they may not look with their eyes, hear with their ears, understand with their heart, turn to Me, and be healed.'"*107 Isaiah said this when he saw his glory and spoke concerning him. Nevertheless many, even some of the authorities, believed in him but because of the Pharisees they would not confess it for fear they would be put out of their synagogue.108 They loved the honor of people more than the glory of God.

44 Jesus cried out, **"Whoever believes in me, believes not in me but in the One Who sent me. Whoever sees me has already seen the One Who sent me. I have come as a light into the world, so that whoever believes in me may not remain in darkness. If anyone hears my words and does not keep them; I will not judge you as a person for I have not come to judge the world**109 **but to save the worldly. Whoever oppresses me and will not receive my sayings has a judge; the words that I have spoken will judge them on their last day. I do not speak on**

my own authority but my Divine Parent Who sent me has commanded me to say what I speak. I know that God's commandment is eternal life, therefore, I speak exactly what my Divine Parent told me to say."

John 13:1–38

1 Now before the feast of the Passover was over, Jesus knew the hour had come to depart from this world and return to his Divine Parent. He loved his own who were in this world and he loved them to the end. During supper, Satan had already entered the heart of Judas Iscariot, Simon's son, to betray him. Jesus knew that his Divine Parent had given everything into his hands and that he came from God and was returning to God. He got up after supper, took off his outer clothing, put it aside, and wrapped a towel around his waist. Then he poured water into a basin, began to wash the feet of his disciples, and wipe them with the towel that was wrapped around him.

6 When he came to Simon Peter, Peter said, "My Saviour, are you going to wash my feet?" Jesus answered, **"Right now you don't understand what I am doing but later on you will."** Peter protested, You shall never wash my feet!" Jesus replied, **"If I do not wash your feet, you will have no part with me."** Peter said, "My Saviour, then wash not only my feet but my hands and my head!" Jesus said, **"Whoever is bathed does not need to wash, except for their feet for they are already clean. You are clean but not all of you."** He knew who was to betray him and therefore he said, **'You are not all clean."**

12 When he had washed their feet, he put on his clothes, sat down and asked, **"Do you know what I have done to you? You call me, Teacher and Saviour, and you're right for that is who I am. If I then, your Saviour and Teacher has washed your feet, you ought to wash one another's feet. I have given this to you as an example so that you will do to others just as I have done to you. Truly I tell you, there is no disciple who is greater than their teacher**[110] **and no one who is sent is greater than the one who sent them. If you know these things, blessed are you who do them. I do not speak this to all of you for I know whom I have chosen so that the scripture may be fulfilled,** *'Even my own familiar friend in whom I*

*trusted, who ate my bread, has lifted up his heal against me.'*111 **I tell you this now before it happens, so that when it happens you may believe that I AM. Truly I tell you, whoever welcomes the person that I send welcomes me and whoever welcomes me welcomes the One Who sent me."**

21 When Jesus said these words, he was moved and disturbed in spirit, testifying, **"Very truly, I tell you that one of you will betray me!"** The disciples then looked at one another because they were uncertain of whom he spoke. Now one of his disciples, whom Jesus loved, was reclining on Jesus bosom,112 when Peter beckoned to her113 to ask Jesus of whom he spoke. So that disciple leaned herself on the breast of Jesus saying, "Saviour, who is it?" Jesus answered, **"The one to whom I hand this morsel of bread after I have dipped it."** So he dipped the morsel and gave it to Judas Iscariot, the son of Simon. After he received the morsel, Satan took possession of him. So Jesus told him, **"What you are going to do, do it quickly!"** None of those reclining at the table realized why he said this to him. Since Judas kept the money purse, some of them thought he asked him to buy what was needed for the feast or to give something to the poor. He took the morsel, went out immediately and it was night.

31 When he had gone out, Jesus said, **"Now the Son of humanity is glorified and God is glorified in him. If God is glorified in him, God will also glorify him in God-self and will glorify him at once. My little children, I will be with you yet a little longer. You will seek me and just as I said to some other Jewish people**114 **so I now say to you, 'Where I go, you can't come.' A new commandment I give you, that you love one another just as I have loved you, that you also love one another. By this everyone will know that you are my disciples, if you have love one for another."**115

36 Peter asked, "My Saviour, where are you going?" Jesus answered, **"Where I go you cannot follow me now but you will follow later."** He said, "My Saviour, why can't I follow you now? I will even lay down my life for you!" Jesus said, **"Will you lay down your life for me? Very truly I tell you, the rooster will not crow until you have denied me three times.**

John 14:1–31

1 Do not let your heart be troubled; you believe in God, believe also in me. In my Divine Parent's home are many mansions.[116] If this were not so I would have told you for I go to prepare a place for you. If I go and prepare a place for you, I will come again and take you to myself, so that where I am you may be also. You know where I am going and you know the way." Thomas asked, "Saviour, we don't know where you are going so how can we know the way?"[117] Jesus answered, "I AM the way, the truth, and the life. No one comes to my Divine Parent except by me.[118] If you had known me, you would have also known my Divine Parent. From this moment on, you know God and have seen God."

8 Philip said, "My Saviour, show us the Divine Parent and we will be satisfied." Jesus taught, "All this time I have been with you and you do not know me, Philip? Whoever sees me has seen the Divine Parent. How can you say, 'Show us the Divine Parent?' Don't you believe that I am in my Divine Parent and my Divine Parent is in me? The words that I say, I do not speak of myself but my Divine Parent, Who abides in me, does these works. Believe that I am in my Divine Parent and my Divine Parent is in me but if you do not, believe because of the works themselves. Truly I tell you, whoever believes in me will also do the works which I do and will do even greater works because I go to my Divine Parent. I will do whatever you ask in my name, so that my Divine Parent will be glorified in the Son. I will do anything you ask for in my name.

15 If you love me, you will keep my commandments and I will ask the Sacred Father Who will give you another Comforter,[119] to abide with you forever, even the Spirit of Truth, whom the worldly cannot receive because they neither see Her[120] nor know Her. You know Her for She dwells with you and will be in you. I will not leave you orphans:[121] I will come back to you. Yet in a little while, the world will no longer see me but you will see me and because I live, you will live also. In that day you will know that I am in my Divine Parent, you are in me, and I am in you. Whoever has my commandments with them and keeps them is the one who loves me. Those who love me will be loved by my Divine Parent and I will love them and reveal myself to them."

22 Judas (not Judas Iscariot) said, "My Saviour, Why is it that you will reveal yourself to us and not to the worldly?" Jesus answered, **"Whoever loves me will keep my word and my Divine Parent will love them. We will come to them and make our home with them. Whoever does not love me will not keep my words and this word which you hear is not my own but the Divine Parent's Who sent me. I have spoken these words to you while I am present with you but the Comforter, Who is the Holy Spirit Whom the Sacred Father will send in my name; She will teach you everything and remind you of all that I have said to you.**

27 **Peace I leave with you, my own peace is what I give you. I do not give to you as the worldly give.[122] Do not let your heart be troubled and do not be afraid. You heard what I told you, 'I am going away and coming back to you.' You would rejoice if you loved me because I am going to my Divine Parent for my Divine Parent is greater than I. Now behold, I have told you before it happens so you may believe when it does happens. I will no longer talk much with you for the ruler of this world is coming and has no power over me. I do as my Divine Parent has commanded me so that the whole world may know that I love my Divine Parent. Arise, let us go away from this place.**

John 15:1–27

1 **I AM the true vine[123] and my Divine Parent is the gardener. Every branch in me that does not bear fruit is removed and the one who bears fruit is pruned to bear more fruit. You have already been cleansed by of the words that I have spoken to you. Abide in me and I abide in you. As the branch cannot bear fruit by itself, unless it shares the life of the vine; neither can you, unless you abide in me. I AM the vine and you are the branches. Whoever abides in me and I in them will bear abundant fruit for without me you can do nothing. Unless a person abides in me they are broken off like a branch which withers away and then picked up to be thrown into the fire to be burned. If you abide in me and my words abide in you, ask for whatever you wish and it will be done for you. My Divine Parent will be glorified when you bear abundant fruit and become my disciples.**

9 **Just as my Divine Parent has loved me, I also have loved you. Abide in my love. If you keep my commandments you will abide in my love**

---

just as I have kept my Divine Parent's commandments and abide in God's love. I have said these things to you so that my joy may be in you and that your joy may be full. This is my commandment: that you love one another as I have loved you. A person can have no greater love than to lay down their life for the sake of their friends. You are my friends if you do whatever I command you. Henceforth, I will no longer call you disciples because a disciple doesn't know what their teacher is doing. I call you friends because I have made known to you everything that I have heard from my Divine Parent. You did not choose me but I chose you and I have appointed you that you will go and produce fruit that will remain so that whatever you ask in my name the Divine Parent may give to you. I command these things to you so that you love one another. If the worldly hate you, know well that they hated me before you. If you were still of the world, the worldly would love their own but you are not of this world for I have chosen you out of the world which is why the worldly hate you.

20 Remember the saying that I told you, that no disciple is greater than their teacher. If they have pursued me, they will also pursue you and if they have kept my sayings, they will keep yours also. They will do all these things to you on my account because they do not know the One Who sent me. If I had not come and spoken to them, they would not have been guilty of sin but now they have no excuse for their sins. Whoever hates me hates my Divine Parent also.[124] If I had not performed works such as no other person has ever done before their eyes, they would be without sin. Now they have seen what I did and still they hated me and my Divine Parent, so the words which are written in the law may be fulfilled, *"19 Don't let those who are wrongfully my enemies rejoice over me or let them wink with the eye who hate me without a cause. For they do not seek peace but devise mischievous things against the meek of the earth. They opened their eyes wide against me, saying, 'Aha, aha, our eyes have seen it.'"*[125]

26 When the Comforter comes, Whom I will send to you from the Sacred Father; the Spirit of Truth, Who comes forth from my Sacred Father, will testify concerning me. You also will testify because you have been with me from the beginning.

John 16:1–33

1 I have spoken these things to keep you from falling away for they will put you out of their synagogues and the time will come when whoever kills you will think they are doing a service to God. They will do these things because they have not known the Divine Parent or me. I have told you these things so that when their time does come, you will remember that I told you of them. I didn't tell you these things before because I was with you.

5 Now I am going to the Divine Parent Who sent me, yet not one of you asks me, 'Where are you going?'[126] **Distress**[127] **has come and filled your hearts because I told you these things but I tell you the truth, it is better that I go away for if I do not go away the Comforter will not come to you but if I go, I will send Her to you. When She comes, She will convince the world concerning sin, concerning justice, and concerning judgment: concerning sin because they don't believe in me, concerning justice because I go to the Divine Parent so you will see me no longer, and concerning judgment because the ruler of the world has been judged.**

12 I still have many other things to tell you but you cannot grasp them now. When the Spirit of Truth[128] **comes, She will guide you into all truth for She will not speak from Herself but what She hears She will speak and She will make known to you things which are to come in the future. She will glorify me because She will take from what is mine and show this to you. All that the Divine Parent has is mine and this is the reason I told you that She will take from what is mine and show this to you.**

16 A little while and you will not see me and again a little while, you will see me because I am going to the Divine Parent." Then some of his disciples asked one another, "What does he mean by the saying, **'A little while and you will not see me and again a little while, and you will see me because I am going to the Divine Parent.'?"** "What does he mean by **'a little while'**? We can't understand what he is talking about." Jesus knew what they desired to ask him, so he answered, **"Are you discussing with one another my saying, 'A little while and you will not see me and again in a little while, and you will see me?' Very truly**

I tell you that you will weep and wail and yet the world will rejoice. You will be sorrowful but your sorrow will be turned into joy.

21 When a woman is giving birth she is in pain because her hour has come but when she has given birth, she no longer remembers the anguish for joy that a human being has been born into the world. So also you are in sorrow but when I will see you again, your heart will rejoice and no one will take your joy away from you. In that day you will ask nothing of me. Very truly, I tell you that whatever you ask my Divine Parent in my name will be given to you. Until now you have asked nothing in my name; now ask and you will receive so that your joy may be full.

25 I have been speaking of these matters in metaphors but the time is coming when I will stop speaking metaphorically and explain in plain words concerning the Divine Parent. When that day comes you will ask in my name and I do not say to you that I will ask the Divine Parent for you, for the Divine Parent God-self loves you, because you love me and believe that I came from God. I came from the Divine Parent and entered the world. Now I am going to leave the world and return to my Divine Parent."

29 His disciples responded, "Behold now you speak plainly without using metaphors! Now we understand that you know all things and do not even need to have anyone ask you questions. This makes us believe that you came from God." Jesus answered, **"Do you now believe? Behold, the hour is coming and has now come when you will be scattered each one to their own home and you will leave me alone. Yet I am never alone because the Divine Parent is with me. These things I have said to you that in me you may have peace. In the world you will have tribulation but be of good cheer for I have overcome the world."**

John 17:1–26

1 Jesus spoke all these things and looked up to heaven, saying, **"Oh my Divine Parent, glorify Thy Son so that Thy Son may glorify Thee. Since You have given me power over all flesh so that I may give eternal life to all whom You have given me. This is eternal life: that**

they may know Thee, the only true God and Jesus the Christ whom You have sent. I have finished the work which You have sent me to do and I have already glorified Thee on earth. So now, Oh my Divine Parent, glorify me in Thy Own Presence with the glory which I had with Thee before the world was made.

6 I have made Thy name known to the people whom You have given me out of the world. They were Yours, You have given them to me, and they have kept Thy word. Now they know that what You have given me is from Thee. They have accepted the words which You have given me and I gave them. These disciples truly know that I came from Thee and believe that You have sent me. I plead for them, not for the world, but for those You have given me because they are Yours. Everything which is mine is Yours and what is Yours is mine and I am glorified in them. Now I am no longer in the world but these are in the world while I am coming to Thee. Oh Holy Divine Parent,[129] protect them through Thy name, whom You have given me, that they may be one even as we are one. While I was with them in the world, I kept them in Thy name. Those whom You have given me I have kept and none of them were lost except the son of perdition[130] so that the scripture might be fulfilled.[131]

13 Now I am coming to Thee but I say these things while I am still in the world so that my joy may be complete in them. I have passed on Thy word to them and the worldly hated them because they don't belong to the world just as I don't belong to the world. I request that You would protect them from evil and not that You would take them out of the world. They don't belong to the world just as I don't belong to the world. Sanctify them in Thy truth because Thy word is truth. I have sent them into the world just as You have sent me into the world. I am sanctifying myself for their sakes so that they also may be sanctified in the truth.

20 I am not praying for these alone but also for those who believe in me through their word, that they may all be one; just as You, my Divine Parent are in me and I am in Thee. So they may also be one in us so the world may believe that You have sent me. I gave to them the glory which You have given to me so that they will be one just as we

are one. I in them and You in me, that they may become completely united and the world may know that You have sent me and that You have loved them as much as You have loved me.

24 Oh Divine Parent, I wish that those whom You have given me may also be with me where I am, to behold my glory which You have given me for You have loved me[132] before the foundation of the world. Oh my righteous Divine Parent, the worldly do not know Thee, but I know Thee and these disciples know that You have sent me. I have made known Thy name to them and I am still making Thy name known so that the love with which You have loved me may be in them and I may be in them."

John 18:1–40

1 Jesus said these things and went out with his disciples across the valley of Kidron where there was a garden which he and his disciples entered. Judas, who betrayed him, knew about this place for Jesus frequently gathered there with his disciples. So Judas brought a detachment of soldiers[133] together with some Temple guards from the chief priests and Pharisees who arrived with lanterns, torches, and weapons. Jesus who knew just what was going to happen to him, came forward and asked, "Who are you looking for?" They told him, "Jesus of Nazareth." He replied, "I AM." Judas, who betrayed him, was standing with them. When Jesus said to them, "I AM," they drew back and fell to the ground. He asked again, "Who are you looking for?" They said, "Jesus of Nazareth." Jesus said, "I have told you that I AM, so if you are looking for me, let these people go." This was to fulfill the word he had just spoken. "I have not lost even one of those whom you gave me."[134] Then Simon Peter who had a sword, drew it, struck the high priest's servant, and cut off his right ear. The servant's name was Malchus. Jesus told Peter, "Put the sword back into its sheath. Shall I not drink from the cup my Divine Parent has given me?"

12 Then the soldiers with their captain and the Temple guard arrested Jesus and bound him. First they took him to Annas,[135] the father-in-law of Caiaphas who was the high priest that year. Caiaphas was the one who counseled the Judean authorities that it was better for one man to die instead of the people.[136]

15 Simon Peter followed Jesus and so did another disciple. As this disciple was known to the former high priest he entered with Jesus into the courtyard but Peter stood outside near the door. The other disciple who was known by the former high priest went out, spoke to the woman who guarded the gate and brought Peter inside. The woman asked Peter, "Are you also one of this man's disciples? He said, "I am not!" Now the servants and the Temple guards were standing and had made a charcoal fire where they warmed themselves because it was cold. Peter stood with them and warmed himself.

19 Then the former high priest questioned Jesus concerning his disciples and concerning his teaching. Jesus answered, **"I have talked openly to everyone and said nothing in secret. I have always taught in the synagogues and at the Temple where all the Jewish people come together. Why do you ask me? Ask those who heard me concerning what I said to them, they know what I said."** When he said this one of the guards struck Jesus on his cheek[137] and said to him, "Is that any way to answer the high priest?" Jesus replied, **"If I have said something wrong, testify to the wrong but if I am right in what I said, why did you strike me?"** Then Annas sent him still bound to Caiaphas, the high priest.

25 Now Simon Peter stood warming himself when they asked him, "Are you also one of his disciples?" He denied it, saying, "I am not!" One of the servants of the high priest, a relative of the man whose ear Peter had cut off, asked, "Didn't I see you with him in the garden?" Peter again denied it and immediately a rooster began to crow.

28 Then, they took Jesus from Caiaphas' house to the Praetorium[138] and it was early in the morning. They did not enter into the headquarters to avoid ritual defilement[139] and to be able to share in the offerings of the Passover. Pilate then went outside to where they were and asked, "What charge do you have against this man?" They answered, " We would not have delivered him here if he wasn't a criminal." Pilate said, "Take him and judge him by yourselves according to your law." The Jewish authorities replied, "We are not allowed to put anyone to death." This fulfilled the words of Jesus when he signified what kind of death he was to die.[140]

33 Pilate entered his headquarters again, summoned Jesus, and asked him, "Are you the king of the Jews?" Jesus answered, **"Do you ask this question on your own or have others told you this concerning me?"** Pilate replied, "Am I a Jew? Your own people and the chief priests have handed you over to me. What have you done?" Jesus answered, **"My kin-dom is not of this world.**[141] **If my kin-dom were of this world, then my servants would have fought so that I would not have been handed over to the Jewish authorities but as it is, my kin-dom is not from here."** Pilate said, "So you are a king?" Jesus answered, **"You say that I am a king. The reason I came into this world is to testify concerning the truth and for this I was born. Everyone who belongs to the truth listens to my voice."** Pilate asked, "What is truth?" After he said this he went out to the Jewish authorities again and told them, "I find no case against him but you have a custom that I release someone for you during the Passover. Do you want me to release this "King of the Jews" for you?" They all cried out, "Not this man but Barabbas." Barabbas was a bandit.

John 19:1–42

1 Then Pilate took Jesus and scourged him[142] and his soldiers wove a crown of thorns which they placed on his head and dressed him in a purple robe. They came up to him, saying, "Peace be to you, Oh King of the Jews!" and struck him in the face. Pilate went outside again and told the crowd, "Behold, I bring him outside to you so you may know that I find no case against him. So Jesus came outside wearing the crown of thorns and the purple robe. Pilate told them, "See the mighty man! See the hero!"[143] When the chief priests and the Temple guards saw him, they cried out, "Crucify him, crucify him!" Pilate said, "I find no case against him. You take this man and crucify him."[144] The Jewish authorities answered, "We have a law and according to our law[145] he must be put to death because he claimed to be the Son of God.[146]

8 When Pilate heard this, he was more afraid than ever, so he entered his headquarters again and asked Jesus, "Where are you from?" but Jesus gave him no answer, Therefore, Pilate said, "Do you refuse to speak to me? Don't you realize that I have the authority to release you and I have the authority to crucify you!" He explained, **"You would have no authority over me if it was not given to you from above and for this reason the one who handed me over to you has the greater sin."**

12 When Pilate heard this he tried to release him but the Jewish authorities cried out, "If you release this man you are no friend of Caesar for whoever makes himself a king is a rebel against Caesar. When Pilate heard these words, he brought Jesus outside and sat down on the judgment seat at a place which is called the Stone Pavement but in Hebrew, Gabbatha. It was Friday of the Passover[147] and it was about noon. He said to the Jewish authorities, "Behold, here is your King!" They cried out, "Take him away, away with him, crucify him!" Pilate asked, "Shall I crucify your King? The chief priests answered, "We have no ruler but Caesar."

16 He handed him over to the soldiers to be crucified. So they took Jesus, brought him out carrying the cross by himself, and they went out to what is called the Place of the Skull which in Hebrew is called Golgotha. There they crucified him with two others; one on either side and Jesus between them. Pilate had an inscription prepared and fastened to the cross which read: Jesus of Nazareth, The King of the Jews. The place where Jesus was crucified was near the city, so many who visited this place of death read this notice written in Aramaic,[148] Greek, and Latin. Then the chief priests of the Jews said to Pilate, "Do not write that he is, The King of the Jews, but 'This man said, I am King of the Jews.'" Pilate replied, "What I have written, I have written."

23 Now when the soldiers had crucified Jesus, they took his clothes and divided them into four parts, a part for each soldier. Also the robe but the robe was seamless, woven from top to bottom so they said to one another, "Let's not tear it but cast lots to see who gets it. This fulfills the scripture, *They divided my clothes among them and cast lots for my robe.*"[149] While the soldiers were doing this, standing near the cross of Jesus were his mother, his mother's sister, Mary the wife of Clopas, and Mary Magdalene. When he saw his mother and the disciple, whom he loved, standing beside her, he said to his mother, **"Woman, behold your son!"**[150] Then he said to the disciple, **"Behold your mother!"** and from that hour, the disciple took Mary into her own home. After this Jesus realized that everything was now finished and said (that the scripture might be fulfilled[151]), **"I'm thirsty."** A bowl full of sour wine was sitting there so they soaked a sponge in the wine, put it on a hyssop branch, and placed on his mouth. When Jesus drank the sour wine, he said, **"It is finished!"** He bowed his head and gave up his spirit.

---

31 The Jewish leaders therefore, because it was Friday,[152] asked Pilate that their legs might be broken and that they might be taken away so that the bodies would not remain upon the cross on the Sabbath (for that Sabbath was a Passover day). The soldiers came and broke the legs of the first and of the other who had been crucified with him. When they came to Jesus, they saw that he had died already so they did not break his legs but one of the soldiers pierced his side with a spear and immediately blood and water came out. She who saw this testified and her testimony is true[153] for she knows well what she said is true that you also may believe.

36 These things happened that the scripture is fulfilled which was written: *"19 Many are the afflictions of the righteous but God delivers them out of all their troubles. He keeps all his bones, not one of them is broken."*[154] Another scripture is fulfilled which said: *"I will pour out a Spirit of compassion and supplication on the house of David and the inhabitants of Jerusalem; then they look on him whom they pierced. Yes, they will mourn for him as one mourns for an only child and grieve over him as one grieves over a first-born"*[155]

38 After this, Joseph of Arimathea who had been a secret disciple of Jesus for fear of the Jewish authorities, asked Pilate for permission to take away the body of Jesus. Pilate gave him permission so he came and removed his body. Nicodemus, who had come to Jesus at night,[156] also came bringing a mixture of myrrh and aloes weighing about a hundred pounds. They took the body of Jesus and wrapped it with the spices in linen cloths according to Jewish burial customs. Now there was a garden where he was crucified and in the garden was a new tomb in which no one had ever been laid. So they laid Jesus there because the Sabbath was approaching and the tomb was near.

John 20:1–31

1 Early on Sunday morning while it was still dark, Mary Magdalene came to the tomb and saw that the stone had been moved from the tomb. So she ran and went to Simon Peter and the other disciple, whom Jesus loved,[157] to tell them, "They have taken our Saviour's body out of the tomb and I don't know where they have laid him!" Peter and the other disciple came out and went to the tomb. They were both running together but the other disciple out ran Peter and reached the tomb first.

He bent down to look in, saw the linen wrappings lying there but didn't go in. Then Peter arrived, entered the tomb and saw the linen wrappings lying there. The facecloth, which had been wrapped around his head, was not with the other linen but was wrapped up and put in a place by itself. Then the other disciple entered in, saw, and believed for they did not yet understand from the scripture that he must rise from the dead. *"8 I shall not be moved because I am always thinking of my God who is so near. My heart is glad, my soul rejoices and my body rests in hope. For You will not leave me among the dead and You will not allow Your beloved one to rot in the grave. You show me the path of life. In Your Presence there is fullness of joy and pleasures forevermore."*[158]

10 Then those disciples returned to their homes but Mary stood weeping near the tomb and as she wept she stooped to look inside the tomb. She saw two angels sitting where the body of Jesus had lain; one at the head and one at the feet. They asked her, "Woman, why do you weep?" She answered them, "They have taken my Saviour away and I do not know where they have laid him!" She said this, turned around and saw someone standing there but she didn't know that it was Jesus. He said, **"Woman! Why are you weeping? Who are you looking for?"** She thought he was the gardener so she said, "Sir, if you are the one who has carried him away, tell me where you have laid him so I can go and get him." Jesus said, **"Mary!"** She recognized him and said to him in Aramaic, "Rabbouni" which means, "My Great Teacher!"[159] Jesus cautioned her, **"Do not hold on to me**[160] **for I have not yet ascended to my Divine Parent but go and tell my brothers and sisters**[161] **that I am ascending to my Divine Parent and your Divine Parent, to my God and your God."** Mary Magdalene went to the disciples with her good news, "I have seen the Saviour!" and told them that he had said these things to her.

19 That Sunday evening the disciples had locked the doors where they were hiding in fear of the Jewish authorities. Jesus came and stood in the midst of them, saying, **"Peace be with you!"** When he had said this, he showed them his hands and his side. His disciples rejoiced when they saw the Saviour. Then Jesus said again, **"Peace be with you, just as my Divine Parent has sent me so I send you."** Then he breathed on them[162] and said, **"Receive the Holy Spirit! If you forgive a person their sins, they are forgiven and if you do not forgive them they are not forgiven."**

24 Now Thomas, one of the twelve, called the Twin, was not with them when Jesus came. When the other disciples told him, "We have seen the Saviour!" he replied, "Unless I see the marks of the nails in his hands and put my fingers in them, and put my hand into his side, I will not believe!" Eight days later, the disciples were again indoors and Thomas was with them. Jesus came when the doors were locked and stood in the midst, saying, **"Peace be with you!"** Then he told Thomas, **"Look at my hands and put your finger here. Now, take your hand and put it into my side. Don't be faithless but believing!"** Thomas answered him, "My Saviour and my God!"163 Jesus taught, **"Now you believe because you have seen me. Blessed are those who have not seen me and have believed."**

30 Jesus did many other signs in the presence of his disciples which are not written in this book. Even these are written so that you may believe that Jesus is the Christ, the Son of God and when you believe you will have eternal life in his name.

John 21:1–25

1 After these things Jesus showed himself again to his disciples by the Sea of Tiberias [*Galilee*] and he appeared in this way. Those who gathered were Simon, Peter, Thomas "the Twin," Nathanael of Cana in Galilee, the sons of Zebedee and two others of his disciples. Simon Peter told them, "I'm going fishing." They said, "We will come with you." So they went out and climbed into the boat and they caught nothing that night. Jesus stood by the seaside in the morning but they didn't know him.

5 Jesus asked, **"Children, have you caught any fish?"** They answered, "No!' He directed them, **"You will find some if you throw your net on the right side of the boat."** They threw it out but they were unable to draw in the net because of the large number of fish. The disciple, whom Jesus loved, said to Peter, "This is the Saviour!" When Simon Peter heard that this was the Saviour, he put on his outer garment (for he had removed it) and jumped into the sea to come to Jesus. The other disciples came in the boat dragging the net full of fish for they were only about a hundred yards from shore.

9 When they reached shore, they saw a charcoal fire with fish laying on it and some bread. Jesus asked, **"Bring some of the fish you just caught."**

So Simon Peter went aboard and helped haul in the net to land, full of one hundred and fifty-three large fish, and in spite of the weight, the net didn't break. Jesus said, **"Come and eat breakfast!"** None of the disciples dared to ask who he was for they knew he was the Saviour. He came over and took the bread and gave it to them, then he took the fish and gave it to them. This was the third time that Jesus appeared to his disciples after he was raised from the dead.

15 After they finished breakfast, Jesus asked Simon Peter, **"Simon, son of John, do you love me more than these others?"** He replied, "Yes, Saviour, you know that I love you." Jesus told him, **"Feed my lambs."**[164] He asked him a second time, **"Simon, son of John, do you love me?"** He answered, "Yes, Saviour, you know that I love you. Jesus told him, **"Feed my sheep."**[165] He asked him a third time, **"Simon, son of John, do you love me?"** It grieved Peter the way that he asked a third time, **"Do you love me?"** so he replied, "Saviour, you know my heart, you know that I love you!" Jesus said, **"Feed my ewes.[166] Truly, I tell you, when you were younger, you used to fasten your own belt, and walk wherever you pleased but when you become old, you will stretch out your hands, and someone else will fasten a belt around you to take you where you do not wish to go."** He said this to show by what kind of death he would glorify God. After this he said to him, **"Follow me!"**

20 Peter turned around and saw the disciple, whom Jesus loved, following him; who leaned on the breast of Jesus at the supper and said, "Saviour, who is it that will betray you?" When Peter saw her, he said to Jesus, "Saviour, what about her?" Jesus answered, **"If it is my will that she remain until I come, what is that to you? You follow me."** Then the rumor went out among the community that the disciple, whom Jesus loved, would not die. Yet what Jesus said was not that she wouldn't die but, **"If it is my will that she remain until I come, what is that to you?"**

24 This is the disciple who testified concerning all these things and has written these things, and we know that her testimony is true.[167] There are many other things which Jesus said and did, which, if every one of them were to be recorded in detail, I suppose that the whole world could not hold the books that would be written. Amen

APPENDIX A

The Gospel According to Mary

The Gospel of Mary[1]
(Complete Text)

Page 1–6
Six manuscript pages and part of Mary 7:1 are missing.[2]

Page 7: Verse

1 "What is matter? Will matter then 2 be destroyed or not?" The Saviour replied, 3 **"All that is born, all that is created, and all the elements of nature 4 are interwoven and united with each other.**[3] **5 They will dissolve again to 6 their own proper root for the 7 nature of matter is dissolved into what belongs to 8 its origin.**[4] **Anyone with 9 two ears to hear, will understand."**[5] 10 Then Peter said to him, "Since you have been explaining everything to us, 11 tell us one other thing. 12 What is the sin of the world?" 13 The Saviour replied, **"There is no such thing as sin, 14 rather, you yourselves are what produces sin when 15 you act according to the nature of 16 adultery;**[6] **this is called sin. 17 For this reason the Good**[7] **came 18 into your midst, to the essence of every nature 19 to be restored 20 to its roots."**[8] Then he continued, 21 **"This is why you get sick and 22 die because you love what deceives you.**

Page 8

1 Anyone 2 who thinks, let them understand! Attachment to matter gave birth to 3 a passion which 4 has no form because it derives from what is contrary to nature. 5 Thus a disturbing confusion 6 occurs in the whole body. This is why I told 7 you, 'Become content at heart.'9 8 Do not be persuaded by what is opposite to nature. If you are discouraged, 9 take inspiration from the presence of other forms 10 of nature.10 Whoever has ears 11 to hear, will understand." 12 When the Blessed One had said this, 13 he embraced them all, saying, 14 **"Peace be with you, acquire my peace 15 within yourselves!11 Be on your guard 16 so that no one deceives you by saying, 17 'Look over here!' or 'Look 18 over there!' for the child of true Humanity12 19 exists within you.13 20 Follow him for those who seek him will 21 find him. Walk forth and preach 22 the Good News about the kin-dom.**

Page 9

1 Do not lay down any rule beyond that 2 which I have witnessed14 and do not give a law 3 like the lawgiver so that 4 you are not imprisoned by it." 5 After he said these things, he left them. The disciples were distressed 6 and shed many tears, 7 saying, "How are we going to go 8 out in the world and preach 9 the Good News about the kin-dom of the Son 10 of humanity? If they didn't 11 spare his life, how will 12 they spare us?" Then Mary 13 stood up, embraced them all, 14 and said to her brothers and sisters, "Do not 15 weep and be distressed nor let your hearts be 16 irresolute15 for his grace will be 17 with you and shelter you. 18 Rather, let us 19 praise his greatness for he 20 has prepared us for this and made us true human beings!"16 When 21 Mary said these things, she turned their hearts 22 inward, toward the Good and they began 23 to discuss the words of the Saviour.

Page 10

1 Peter said to Mary, "Sister, 2 we know that the Saviour loved you more 3 than all other women. 4 Tell us the words of our Saviour that you 5 remember, which you know 6 but we do not, because we haven't heard them." 7 Mary answered, saying, 8 "I will report to you as much as I remember of that which is unknown to you." 9 She began to speak to them 10 these words, 11 she said, "I saw the Saviour [*Lord*]17 in a vision and I 12 said to him, 'Saviour [*Lord*], I saw you 13 today in a vision!' He

answered, 14 saying, **'Blessed are you for not wavering 15 at seeing me for where the mind [*nous*]18 is, 16 there is the treasure.'19** Then I said 17 to him, 'Saviour [*Lord*], does a person who sees 18 a vision, see it with the soul 19 or with the spirit?' The Saviour replied, 20 **'A person does not see with the soul 21 or with the spirit but with the mind which exists 22 between the two, this sees the vision20 23 and it is [*this which makes us fully human.*]21'"**

Page 11–14
Part of Mary 10:23 and four manuscript pages are missing.

Page 15
122 " . . . it,' 2 and Craving23 said, 'I did not see you descend, 3 yet now I see you 4 rising. So why do you lie, since 5 you belong to me?' The soul answered, 6 'I saw you but you did not see me 7 nor did you recognize me. I was 8 like a garment to you and you did not know me.' 9 After she had said these things, the soul left rejoicing 10 greatly. Then she entered into the 11 third climate which is called 12 Ignorance.24 Ignorance 13 examined the soul closely, saying, 14 'Where are you going? 15 You are bound by evil inclinations. Indeed, you are bound, 16 do not judge!' 17 The soul asked, 'Why do you judge 18 me, since I have not passed judgment? I am bound 19 but I have not bound others. I am not recognized 20 but I have recognized that the universe is being dissolved, both the things of earth

Page 16
1 and those of heaven.' When the soul 2 overcame the third climate, 3 she went upward and found herself 4 in the fourth climate.25 This has 5 seven forms: the first form 6 is Darkness, the second 7 is Craving, the third 8 is Ignorance, the fourth is the Fear 9 of Death,26 the fifth is the Enslavement to the Body,27 10 the sixth is Foolish Wisdom 11 of the Flesh,28 and the seventh is 12 Wrathful Wisdom.29 These are the seven 13 forms of Wrath. They interrogated 14 the soul, 'Where are you coming from, 15 slayer of humans,30 and where are you going, 16 conqueror of space?'31 The soul answered, 17 'That which oppressed me 18 has been slain, that which surrounds me 19 has been overcome, my craving 20 has faded, and my ignorance 21 has died. I was released from this world

Page 17

1 through a world and from a model to a 2 model which is 3 from above[32] and freed from the chain of forgetfulness which 4 exists in time. Henceforth, 5 I travel toward Repose 6 where time rests in the Eternity of Time: I go now into 7 Silence.'"[33] When Mary had said 8 this, she became silent since it was up to this point that the Saviour 9 had spoken with her. 10 Then Andrew responded, addressing 11 the brothers and sisters, "What is your opinion 12 about the things she has said? 13 Indeed, I don't believe that 14 the Saviour said these things for what she said 15 appears to give views that are different from his thought."[34] Peter answered 16 and brought up 17 similar concerns and he 18 questioned them about the Saviour, "After all, he 19 did not speak with a woman in private 20 without our knowing about it. 21 Are we to turn around and all listen to her? 22 Did he choose her over us?"

Page 18

1 Then Mary wept and said to 2 Peter, "My brother Peter, what are you 3 thinking? Do you think that this is just my own imagination and that I 4 thought up these things by myself in my 5 heart or that I am telling lies about our Saviour?" 6 Levi answered, speaking to Peter, 7 "Peter, you have always been 8 a hot-tempered person.[35] Even now I see you 9 are questioning the woman just as 10 our adversaries do. For if 11 the Saviour made her worthy, who are you 12 indeed to reject her? Surely 13 the Saviour knew her 14 completely and that is why he loved her more 15 than us.[36] Rather let us be ashamed 16 and clothe ourselves with the perfect human being. 17 Let us bring him forth in ourselves as he 18 commanded us.[37] Let us walk forth to spread 19 the Good News without laying down 20 any other rule or law beyond 21 what the Saviour said."[38]

Page 19

1 After Levi said these words, they began 2 to go out to proclaim and to preach the Good News. 3 The Gospel 4 According to 5 Mary.

The Gospel of Mary
(Without Page, Verse and Note Numbers)

Six manuscript pages are missing.

"What is matter? Will matter then be destroyed or not?" The Saviour replied, **"All that is born, all that is created, and all the elements of nature are interwoven and united with each other. They will dissolve again to their own proper root for the nature of matter is dissolved into what belongs to its origin. Anyone with two ears to hear, will understand."** Then Peter said to him, "Since you have been explaining everything to us, tell us one other thing. What is the sin of the world?" The Saviour replied, **"There is no such thing as sin, rather, you yourselves are what produces sin when you act according to the nature of adultery; this is called sin. For this reason the Good came into your midst, to the essence of every nature to be restored to its roots."** Then he continued, **"This is why you get sick and die because you love what deceives you.**

Anyone who thinks, let them understand! Attachment to matter gave birth to a passion which has no form because it derives from what is contrary to nature. Thus a disturbing confusion occurs in the whole body. This is why I told you, 'Become content at heart.' Do not be persuaded by what is opposite to nature. If you are discouraged, take inspiration from the presence of other forms of nature. Whoever has ears to hear, will understand." When the Blessed One had said this, he embraced them all, saying, **"Peace be with you, acquire my peace within yourselves! Be on your guard so that no one deceives you by saying, "Look over here!" or "Look over there!" for the child of true Humanity exists within you. Follow him for those who seek him will find him. Walk forth and preach the Good News about the kin-dom. Do not lay down any rule beyond that which I have witnessed and do not give a law like the lawgiver so that you are not imprisoned by it."** After he said these things, he left them.

The disciples were distressed and shed many tears, saying, "How are we going to go out in the world and preach the Good News about the kin-dom of the Son of humanity? If they didn't spare his life, how will they spare us?" Then Mary stood up, embraced them all, and said to her brothers and sisters, "Do not weep and be distressed nor let your hearts be irresolute for his grace will be with you and shelter you. Rather, let us praise his greatness for he has prepared us for this and made us true human beings!" When Mary said these things, she turned their hearts inward, toward the Good and they began to discuss the words of the Saviour.

Peter said to Mary, "Sister, we know that the Saviour loved you more than all other women. Tell us the words of our Saviour that you remember, which you know but we do not, because we haven't heard them." Mary answered, saying, "I will report to you as much as I remember of that which is unknown to you." She began to speak to them these words, she said, "I saw the Saviour in a vision and I said to him, 'Saviour, I saw you today in a vision!' He answered, saying, **'Blessed are you for not wavering at seeing me for where the mind is, there is the treasure.'** Then I said to him, 'Saviour, does a person who sees a vision, see it with the soul or with the spirit?' The Saviour replied, **'A person does not see with the soul or with the spirit but with the mind which exists between the two, this sees the vision and it is** [*this which makes us fully human.*]**'"**

Four manuscript pages are missing.

" . . . it,' and Craving said, 'I did not see you descend, yet now I see you rising. So why do you lie, since you belong to me?' The soul answered, 'I saw you but you did not see me nor did you recognize me. I was like a garment to you and you did not know me.' After she had said these things, the soul left rejoicing greatly. Then she entered into the third climate which is called Ignorance. Ignorance examined the soul closely, saying, 'Where are you going? You are bound by evil inclinations. Indeed, you are bound, do not judge!' The soul asked, 'Why do you judge me, since I have not passed judgment? I am bound but I have not bound others. I am not recognized but I have recognized that the universe is being dissolved, both the things of earth and those of heaven.'

When the soul overcame the third climate, she went upward and found herself in the fourth climate. This has seven forms: the first form is

Darkness, the second is Craving, the third is Ignorance, the fourth is the Fear of Death, the fifth is the Enslavement to the Body, the sixth is Foolish Wisdom of the Flesh, and the seventh is Wrathful Wisdom. These are the seven forms of Wrath. They interrogated the soul, 'Where are you coming from, slayer of humans, and where are you going, conqueror of space?' The soul answered, 'That which oppressed me has been slain, that which surrounds me has been overcome, my craving has faded, and my ignorance has died. I was released from this world through a world and from a model to a model which is from above and freed from the chain of forgetfulness which exists in time. Henceforth, I travel toward Repose where time rests in the Eternity of Time: I go now into Silence.'"

When Mary had said this, she became silent since it was up to this point that the Saviour had spoken with her. Then Andrew responded, addressing the brothers and sisters, "What is your opinion about the things she has said? Indeed, I don't believe that the Saviour said these things for what she said appears to give views that are different from his thought." Peter answered and brought up similar concerns and he questioned them about the Saviour, "After all, he did not speak with a woman in private without our knowing about it. Are we to turn around and all listen to her? Did he choose her over us?"

Then Mary wept and said to Peter, "My brother Peter, what are you thinking? Do you think that this is just my own imagination and that I thought up these things by myself in my heart or that I am telling lies about our Saviour?" Levi answered, speaking to Peter, "Peter, you have always been a hot-tempered person. Even now I see you are questioning the woman just as our adversaries do. For if the Saviour made her worthy, who are you indeed to reject her? Surely the Saviour knew her completely and that is why he loved her more than us. Rather let us be ashamed and clothe ourselves with the perfect human being. Let us bring him forth in ourselves as he commanded us. Let us walk forth to spread the Good News without laying down any other rule or law beyond what the Saviour said." After Levi said these words, they began to go out to proclaim and to preach the Good News.

The Gospel According to Mary.

Appendix B

The Best Half of The Gospel According to Thomas[1]

Prologue:

These are the secret[2] sayings that the living Jesus spoke and that Judas Thomas the Twin[3] recorded.

Saying 1

Jesus said, **"Whoever finds the interpretation of these sayings will no longer experience death."**[4] [See Matthew 7:7.]

Saying 2: Verse

1 Jesus said, **"Let whoever seeks not cease from their seeking until they find; 2 and when they find, they will be troubled;[5] 3 and when they are troubled, they will marvel;[6] 4 and when they marvel, they will rule over all eternity;[7] and when they rule they will gain repose.** [See Matthew 7:7.]

Saying 3

1 Jesus said, **"If your leaders say to you, 'Behold, the kin-dom is in the sky,' then the birds will be there before you. 2 If they say to you, 'It is in the sea,' then the fish will be there before you. 3 Rather the kin-dom is within you and it is outside of you. 4 When you come to know yourselves, you will be known, and you will realize that you are children of the living Divine Parent.[8] 5 If you do not come to know**

yourselves than you dwell in vanity,9 **and you are that vanity.**" [See Luke 17:21, Mary 8:12–18, and Deuteronomy 30:11–14.]

Saying 4

1 Jesus said, **"The person advanced in days will not hesitate to ask a seven days old infant**10 **about the place of life and that person will live. 2 For many of the first will make themselves last and they will become a single one."**11 [See Mark 10:31, Luke 9:48, Luke 13:30, and John 1:29.]

Saying 5

1 Jesus said, **"Recognize what is right in front of your face and what is hidden will become clear to you. 2 For there is nothing hidden that will fail to be revealed."**12 [See Matthew 10:26, Luke 8:17, and Luke 12:2.]

Saying 6

1 His disciples questioned him: "Do you want us to fast? How shall we pray? Shall we give alms? What kind of diet shall we observe?" 2 Jesus said, **"Do not lie 3 and do not do what you hate 4 for all things are plain in the sight of heaven. 5 For there is nothing hidden that will not be revealed and there is nothing covered that will remain undisclosed."** [See Matthew 6:1–13, Matthew 10:26, Mark 4:22, Luke 8:17, Luke 12:2, Thomas 5:1–2, and Thomas 14:1–3.]

Saying 8

1 Jesus said, **"The human being is like a thoughtful fisher who cast their net into the sea and drew it up from the sea full of little fish. 2 Among the little fish the thoughtful fisher discovered a fine big fish.**13 **3 So the fisher threw all the little fish back into the sea and chose the big fish without hesitation. 4 Whoever has ears to hear, will understand."** [See Matthew 13:48.]

Saying 9

1 Jesus said, **"Once a sower went out to sow and sowed a handful of seeds. 2 Now some fell on the path and the birds came and gathered them up. 3 Others fell among the rocks and could not take root in the soil or produce any heads of grain. 4 Others fell among the thorns, which smothered their growth and the worms devoured them. 5 Others fell on fertile ground and their fruits grew up to heaven. These**

yielded sixty per measure and one hundred twenty per measure." [See Matthew 13:3–9, Mark 3:3–9, and Luke 8:5–8.]

Saying 10

Jesus said, **"I have sown fire upon the world and look, I am guarding it until it blazes."**14 [See Matthew 3:11, Luke 12:49, and Thomas 82:1–2.]

Saying 13

1 Jesus said, **"Compare me to someone and tell me whom I am like."** 2 Simon Peter replied, "You are like a just angel."15 3 Matthew replied, "You are like an intelligent lover of wisdom."16 4 Thomas replied, "Master, my mouth is utterly unable to say what you are like." 5 Jesus said, **"I am not your Master, you have become intoxicated because you have drunk from the bubbling source from which I spring."** 6 He took Thomas, they withdrew, and he spoke three sayings to him. 7 When Thomas came back to his friends, they asked him, "What did Jesus say to you?" 8 Thomas replied, "If I tell you even one of the sayings that he told me, you would pick up rocks and stone me. Fire would come out of those rocks and burn you up." [See Matthew 16:13–16, Mark 8:27–30, Luke 9:18–22, and Thomas 14:1–3.]

Saying 14

1 Jesus said to them, **"If you fast, you will bring sin upon yourselves; 2 if you pray, you will be condemned; 3 and if you give to charity, you will harm your spirits.17 4 When you go into any region and walk about in the country places; whenever people welcome you, eat what they set before you, and heal the sick among them. 5 Whatever goes into your mouth will not defile you; rather, it is what comes out of your mouth that defiles you."** [See Matthew 6:1–18, Mark 7:14–23, Luke 10:5–11, and Thomas 6:1–5.]

Saying 17

Jesus said, **"I will give you what no eye has seen, no ear has heard, no hand has touched, and no human mind has conceived."** [See Luke 1:77.]

Saying 18

1 The disciples asked Jesus, "Tell us, what will be our end?" 2 Jesus answered, **"What do you know about the beginning, so that you now seek the**

end? Where the beginning is, the end will also be. 3 Blessed are those who abide in the beginning for they will know the end and will not taste death."18 [See Matthew 24:3, Thomas 1, and Thomas 111:2.]

Saying 20

1 The disciples asked Jesus, "Tell us what the kin-dom of heaven is like." 2 He answered them: **"It is like a grain of mustard, 3 one of the tiniest of all seeds. 4 When it falls into prepared soil, it produces a large branch where the birds of heaven will come to rest."** [See Matthew 13:31–32, Mark 4:30–32, and Luke 13:18–19.]

Saying 21

1 Mary asked Jesus: "What are your disciples like?" 2 He answered, **"They are like little children living in a field that does not belong to them. 3 When the owners of the field come, they will say, 'Give us back our field!' 4 They will remove their clothes in front of them**19 **in order to give it back to them and leave the field to them. 5 Therefore I say, if the owners of a house know the thief is coming, they will keep watch and not let the thief break into the house of their domain and carry away their possessions. 6 You then must keep watch against the world. 7 Prepare yourselves with great strength or the thief will find a way to get to you for the trouble you expect will come. 8 Let there be among you a person who understands. 9 When the crop is ripe, the person came quickly with sickle in hand and harvested it. 10 Whoever has ears to hear, will understand."**20 [See Matthew 24:42–44, Luke 12:35–40, and Thomas 37:2–3.]

Saying 22

1 Jesus saw some babies being nursed and 2 said to his disciples, **'These nursing babies are like those who enter the kin-dom."** 3 They asked, "Then will we enter the kin-dom by becoming babies?" 4 Jesus answered, **"When you make the two into one, when you make the inner like the outer and the outer like the inner, when you make the above like the below and the below like the above, 5 when you make the male and the female into a single one so that the male will not be male nor the female be female.**21 **6 When you make an eye in place of an eye, a hand in place of a hand, a foot in place of a foot, an image in place of an image, 7 then you will enter the kin-dom."** [See Mark 10:15 and John 3:7.]

Saying 25

1 Jesus said, "Love your sister[22] like your own soul, 2 protect her like the pupil of your eye." [See Matthew 19:19.]

Saying 26

1 Jesus said, "You see the sliver in your brother's eye but you do not see the beam in your own eye. 2 When you remove the beam from your own eye, then you will see clearly enough to remove the sliver from your brother's eye." [See Matthew 7:3 –5 and Luke 6:41–42.]

Saying 28

1 Jesus said, "I stood in the midst of the world and appeared to them in the flesh. 2 I found them all intoxicated[23] but I did not find any of them thirsty. 3 My soul ached for the children of humanity because they are blind in their hearts and they do not see for they come into the world naked and they seek to depart of the world naked 4 but meanwhile they are drunk. When they have vomited their wine, then they will repent." [See John 1:9–11.]

Saying 31

1 Jesus said, "No prophet is acceptable in their own village. 2 Physicians do not heal those who know them well." [See Mark 6:4 and Luke 4:24.]

Saying 32

Jesus said, "A city built upon a high mountain and fortified cannot be taken, nor can it be hidden." [See Matthew 5:14.]

Saying 36

Jesus said, "Do not worry, from morning to evening and from evening to morning, about what you are going to wear." [See Matthew 6:26–34 and Luke 12:22–31.]

Saying 37

1 His disciples asked him, "When will you appear to us? When will we see you?" 2 Jesus replied, "When you strip naked without shame and trample your clothing underfoot just as little children do, 3 then you will look at the Son of the Living One without being afraid." [See Matthew 16:15–16, Matthew 18:3, and Thomas 21:2–4.]

Saying 39

1 Jesus said, "**The scribes of the Pharisees have received the keys of knowledge and have hidden them. 2 They did not go within and those who wanted to go there were prevented by them. 3 As for you, be as sly24 as the serpent and as simple as the dove.**" [See Matthew 10:16, Matthew 23:13, and Luke 11:52.]

Saying 41

1 Jesus said, "**Those who have something in hand25 will be given more, 2 and those who have virtually nothing will have what little they do have taken away.**" [See Mark 4:25 and Luke 8:19.]

Saying 42

Jesus said, "**Be passersby.**"26 [See Matthew 8: 20 and John 13:1.]

Saying 46

1 Jesus said, "**From Adam to John the Baptist there has been no one born of a woman who is greater than John the Baptist, so that his eyes should not be averted 2 but I have said that whoever among you becomes a child27 will know the kin-dom and will become greater than John.**" [See Matthew 11:11.]

Saying 47

1 Jesus said, "**A person cannot ride two horses or bend two bows at the same time. 2 A servant cannot serve two employers, otherwise the servant will respect the one and despise the other. 3 No one drinks aged wine and immediately desires to drink fresh wine. 4 Fresh wine is not poured into old wineskins for they will crack and aged wine is not poured into a new wineskin for it will spoil. 5 No one sews a patch of old cloth on to a new garment for it will create a tear.**" [See Matthew 6:24, Matthew 9:16–17, Mark 2:21–22, Luke 5:36–37, and Luke 16:13.]

Saying 48

Jesus said, "**If two make peace with one another within a single house, they will say to the mountain, 'Move from here!' and it will move.**"28 [See Matthew 21:21 and Mark 11:23.]

Saying 49

Jesus said, **"Blessed are the solitary ones**[29] **and the chosen ones for you will find the kin-dom, you will return there again because you come from it."** [See Matthew 19:11–12.]

Saying 50

1 Jesus said, **"If they ask you, 'Where are you from?' say to them, 'We were born of the Light, the place where the Light is born of Light. It came and revealed Itself through Their image.'**[30] **2 If they ask you, 'Who are you?' say to them, 'We are Its children, the beloved of the Living Divine Parent.' 3 If they ask you, 'What is the sign of the Divine Parent in you?' say to them, 'It is movement and it is repose.'"**[31] [See Matthew 11:28–29, John 3:8, John 8:12, John 12:35–36, Mary 17:4–7, and Thomas 51:1–2.]

Saying 51

1 His disciples said to him, "When will the repose of the [*living*] dead take place and when will the new world come?" 2 He answered them, **"The repose that you are waiting for has already come but you do not recognize it."** [See Matthew 1:28–30, Luke 17:20–21, John 5:25, Thomas 3:1–3, and Thomas 113:1–4.]

Saying 55

1 Jesus said, **"Whoever does not free themselves from their mother and their father cannot be my disciple. 2 Whoever does not free themselves from their sisters and their brothers and take up their cross as I have will not be worthy of me."** [See Matthew 10:37–38 and Luke 14:26–27.]

Saying 56

1 Jesus said, **"Whoever has come to understand the world has discovered a corpse 2 and the world is not worthy of the one who has discovered a corpse."**[32] [See Thomas 80:1–2.]

Saying 61

1 Jesus said, **"Two will lie on a couch; one will die, one will live."** 2 Salome asked him, "Who are you, man? You have climbed onto my couch and eaten from my table as if you are from someone." 3 Jesus replied, **"I**

AM³³ who comes into being from the One Who is whole.³⁴ What comes from my Divine Parent has been given to me." 4 Salome answered, "I am your disciple." 5 Jesus told her, "**For this reason I say that whoever is whole will be filled with Light but whoever is divided will be filled with darkness.**" [See Matthew 24:40–41, Matthew 11:27, Luke 10:22, Luke 17:34–36, and Thomas 77:1–3.]

Saying 63

1 Jesus said, "**There was a rich man who had considerable wealth. 2 He said, 'I will invest my wealth so that I can sow, reap, plant, and fill my storehouses with produce, that I will lack nothing.' 3 These were the things he was thinking in his heart but that very night he died. 4 Whoever has ears to hear, will understand.**" [See Luke 12:16–21.]

Saying 65

1 Jesus said, "**A usurer³⁵ owned a vineyard and leased it to tenant farmers so that they might cultivate it and he might collect its fruits³⁶ from them. 2 He sent his servant so that the tenant farmers might give the servant the fruits of the vine. 3 They grabbed him, beat him, and almost killed him and the servant returned and told the owner. 4 The owner thought, 'Perhaps they didn't recognize him.' 5 He sent another servant and they beat this one as well. 6 Then the owner sent his son and said, 'Perhaps they will show respect for my son.' 7 Since the tenant farmers knew that he was the heir to the vineyard, they grabbed him and killed him. 8 Whoever has ears to hear, will understand.**"³⁷ [See Matthew 21:33–46, Mark 12:1–12, and Luke 20:9–20.]

Saying 67

Jesus said, "**One who knows everything else, yet does not know oneself, lacks everything.**" [See Matthew 16:26, Mark 8:36–37, and Luke 9:25.]

Saying 69

1 Jesus said, "**Blessed are those who have been persecuted in their hearts for they have known the Divine Parent in Truth. 2 Blessed are those who are hungry, for the belly of the one in need will be filled.**" [See Matthew 5:6, Luke 6:21, and John 4:23–24.]

Saying 70

> 1 Jesus said, "**When you bring forth what is within you, what you have will save you. 2 If you do not have that within you, what you do not have within you will destroy you.**" [See Matthew 13:12, Luke 8:18, Luke 19:26, Mary 8:12–22, and Thomas 3:1–5.]

Saying 76

> 1 Jesus said, "**The kin-dom of the Divine Parent is like a merchant who had a supply of goods to sell and then found a pearl.**[38] **2 That merchant was wise and sold all her goods to buy the pearl. 3 You must also seek the unfailing and enduring treasures that do not perish; where no moth comes to eat and no worm destroys.**" [See Matthew 6:19, Matthew 13:45–46, Mark 9:48, Luke 12:33–34, and John 6:27.]

Saying 77

> 1 Jesus said, "**I AM**[39] **the Light that shines on everyone.**[40] **I AM everything. Everything came forth from me and everything reached me.**[41] **2 Split a piece of wood and I am there. 3 Lift up a rock and you will find me there.**" [See John 8:12 and Thomas 61:3.]

Saying 78

> 1 Jesus said, "**Why have you come out to the countryside? Did you expect to see a reed shaken by the wind?**[42] **2 To see a person dressed in elegant garments like your governors and your powerful ones 3 who wear expensive garments and cannot understand the truth?**" [See Matthew 11:7–8.]

Saying 79

> 1 A woman in the crowd said to him, "Blessed is the womb that bore you and the breasts that nursed you!" 2 He said to her, "**Blessed are those who listen to the Word of the Divine Parent and truly follow it. 3 For there will be days when you will say, 'Blessed is the womb that has not conceived and the breasts that have not given milk.'**" [See Matthew 24:19, Mark 13:17, Luke 11:27–28, and Luke 23:28–29.]

Saying 80

> 1 Jesus said, "**Whoever has come to known the world has discovered the body 2 and whoever has discovered the body, of that person the world is not worthy.**" [See Thomas 56:1–2.]

Saying 82

1 Jesus said, **"Whoever is near to me is near to the fire. 2 Whoever is far from me is far from the kin-dom."** [See Matthew 3:11, Luke 12:49–50, and Thomas 10.]

Saying 88

1 Jesus said, **"Angels and prophets will come to you and give you what belongs to you. 2 You, in turn, give them what you have and ask yourselves, 'When are they coming to take what belongs to them?'"** [See Matthew 10:8, Matthew 16:27, Mark 8:38, and Luke 9:27.]

Saying 90

Jesus said, **"Come to me: my yoke is easy, my rule is gentle, 2 and you will find repose for yourselves."** [See Matthew 11:28–30.]

Saying 91

1 They said to him, Tell us who you are so that we can believe in you. 2 He replied, **"You examine the face of the sky and the earth but you don't recognize the one who is before you and you do not know the nature of this present moment."** [See Luke 12:54–56 and John 14:8–10.]

Saying 93

1 Jesus said, **"Do not give sacred things to dogs, for they may treat them as dung. 2 Do not give pearls to pigs, for they might make mud of it.43"** [See Matthew 7:6 and Luke 14:35.]

Saying 100

1 They showed Jesus a gold coin and said to him, "Caesar's agents demand taxes from us." 2 He answered, **"Give to Caesar what belongs to Caesar, 3 give to God what belongs to God, 4 and give to me what is mine."** [See Matthew 22:21 and Mark 12:17.]

Saying 106

1 Jesus said, **"When you make the two into one, you will become children of humanity44 2 and when you say, 'Mountain, be moved!' It will be moved."45** [See Matthew 17:20, Luke 20:25, and Thomas 48.]

Saying 107

1 Jesus said, "**The kin-dom is like a shepherd who has a hundred sheep. 2 One of them, the largest, went astray. He left the ninety-nine and looked for the one until he found it. 3 After he had gone to such trouble, he said to the sheep, 'I love you more than the ninety-nine.'**"[46] [See Matthew 18:11–14 and Luke 15:4–6.]

Saying 108

1 Jesus said, "**Whoever drinks from my mouth will become like me. 2 I myself will become that person 3 and hidden things will be revealed to them.**" [See John 7:37.]

Saying 111

1 Jesus said, "**The heavens and the earth will be rolled up in your presence, 2 and whoever is living from the Living One will neither know fear nor see death.**" 3 Doesn't Jesus say, "**The world is not worthy of those who have found themselves.**"[47] [See Matthew 24:34–35, Luke 21:33, Mary 8:15–20, and Thomas 80:1–2.]

Saying 113

1 His disciples asked him, "When will the kin-dom come? 2 Jesus answered, "**It will not come by watching for it. 3 It will not be a matter of saying, 'Behold, it is over here!' or 'Behold, it is over there!' 4 Rather the kin-dom of the Divine Parent is already spread out upon the earth and people are not aware of it.**" [See Mark 13:21–22, Luke 17:20–21, and Mary 8:14–19.]

Saying 114

1 Simon Peter said to them, "Let Mary leave us because women are not worthy of eternal life." 2 Jesus responded, "**Look, I have been guiding her to make her into a human**[48] **so that she too will become a living spirit resembling you males** [human beings first].[49] **3 For every woman who becomes a human being will enter the kin-dom of heaven.**" [See Mary 9:18 and Thomas 22:1–7.]

The Gospel according to Thomas.

Appendix C

Jewish Life: Terms and Ideas Around the First Century, from A to Z

List of Jewish Life: Terms and Ideas

Contents

Page no.

Jewish Life: Terms and Ideas

Abomination of desolation

This is called *Churban Bayis Reshone* in Hebrew, which means the Greek-Syrian desecration the Jerusalem Temple in 168 BCE, where a pig was sacrificed to Zeus on the sacred Temple altar. In 175 BCE, the Seleucid ruler Antiochus IV overthrew the Hebrew high priest Onias and appointed his own while he tried to Hellenize Jerusalem. In 169 BCE, Antiochus IV rededicated the Temple to a Greek idol that Jews had to worship and eat pork that was sacrificed to it. "The decree was passed that pigs must be the usual animals to be sacrificed, even as part of the service in the Holy Temple in Jerusalem! Circumcision was banned, along with the celebration of the Jewish festivals and New Moon, observance of the Jewish Sabbath and the Jewish dietary and ritual purity laws, and the study of the Torah. All books of the Bible and the holy scrolls themselves were to be confiscated and burned. In short, any Jewish behavior was forbidden under pain of death."[1] Usually, the Greeks and Romans rule by encouraging local culture and religious freedom within limits. The Maccabees just said no to this and led the Jewish Revolt from 168 BCE to 165 BCE. They won and rededicated the Temple using a one day's supply of oil left by the high priest Onias, which lasted seven days, see Hanukkah below. The next "abomination of desolation" was the Roman destruction of the Temple in 70 CE and is called *Churban Bayis Shayne* in Hebrew. The Roman general Titus placed an idol on the site of the burned Temple.

Adonai

Name of G-d that that means "Master, Lord and lord" as in Psalm 110:1 and represents a substitute for the unsayable ineffable Name of God (*YHWH*, *YHVH*, the Eternal, Yahweh, Yahveh, and G-d), and *Adonai* (*YHWH*) is our God (*Elohim*) is often translated as "the Lord is our God" for "the Eternal is our God" (Deuteronomy 6:4). *YHWH* is often "LORD" while *Adonai* is "Lord." The plural of *Adon* meaning "lord" or "father" and can refer to men and angles. The Greek word for *Adonai*, *Kyrios* (*Kurios*), means God, lord (superior rank), master of women (including father, son, and brother), and sir. *Adonai* is from the Jewish oral tradition to respect and *Adonai* also means Compassionate One. See Appendix C, *Elohim* and *YHWH*.

Annas

The high priest from 6 CE to 15 CE was still called the high priest while his son-in-law Caiaphas served as high priest from 18 CE to 36 CE because, according to Hebrew law, the office of high priest was for life. The Romans sold the position every two years, but Annas was still a respected influential leader under Caiaphas.

Aramaic

A poetic Semitic language related to Hebrew, and both were spoken by Jesus. This language of Babylon was common language of second Temple era, 520 BCE to 70 CE and the language of the Babylonian Talmud. "Galilean, as well as Syriac, is a dialect of the Aramaic Language. Aramaic goes back to the Semitic family of languages, as does Hebrew and Arabic. The history of Aramaic goes back to the second millennium BC, and yet it still continues to be spoken and written by a variety of communities in the Middle East and elsewhere. At various times over the course of history, Aramaic has been spoken and written by people of many diverse faiths; Buddhists, Jews, Muslims, and Christians. The term *Aramaic* is derived from Aram, the fifth son of Shem, or Sem, who was the firstborn of Noah. The descendants of Aram lived in Mesopotamia (*Iraq*). The language of the people of Galilee shifted from Hebrew to Aramaic sometime between 700 and 500 BC. The differences in the regional dialects of Aramaic were not that great."[2]

Assarion

A copper coin worth one-sixteenth of a denarius, about $3.

Atonement

"The priestly atonement rituals of the Temple evolved into a private rite of intense introspection, prayer, and confession designed to elicit personal repentance. Atonement was still communal to some extent. The confessional prayers of the synagogue liturgy are in the plural, recited for the Jewish people as a whole. But Rosh Hashanah and Yom Kippur became the most individual and personal of Jewish holidays, relating to the psyche and one's personal relationship with God rather than to the events of Jewish History."[3] Yom Kippur is the Day of Atonement in the fall before the Jewish new year.

Beelzebul

Baalzubul, Beelzubul, Beelzebub, Beelzeboul, Beezeboul, "Baal [Lord] of the Flies" is from the Canaanite storm god worshipped by the Philistines of Ekron. In the Four Gospels, he developed into Beelzebul, "Prince of the demons," or Satan.

Blasphemy

The misuse of the name of God, *YHWH*. When accused of blasphemy, Jesus quoted Psalm 82, which discusses people as "gods." Jesus was the spiritually born anew adopted Son of God and did not make himself equal to God but became and preached the Christ, the consciousness of God in people.

Caiaphas, Joseph

The high priests from 18 CE to 36 CE. His father-in-law, Annas, was high priest from 6 CE to 15 BCE. The high priest had to buy the office every two years, and many became corrupt servants of the Romans. In Jesus' time, the high priest had to go every day to get his religious vestments kept by the Romans.

Chief priests

Highest ranking priests; see Sadducees.

Denarius

Roman silver coin that's worth a subsistence day's wage. In today's terms of $8 an hour times eight hours minus taxes, it's worth about $50. Worth about the same as a Jewish shekel, where thirty shekels is the price of a slave. Thirty pieces of silver was Jesus' selling price for Judas' betrayal.

Drachma

Greek silver coins were often worn as a ten-piece garland or headband. One drachma is equivalent to one denarius.

Elect

Chosen people. Those called by God to minister to others, righteous people in any religion or group, and those called to eternal life. A special group within a group. Often there is a ruling "elite" with their clergy supporters who falsely feel they are the "elect." Some felt that the worst people were the "elect" because they needed God the most.

Elohim

Elohiym in Hebrew. *Elohim* is basic with *YHWH* in Deuteronomy 6:4: Hear Oh Israel, *Adonai* [*YHWH*] is our God [*Elohim*], *Adonai* [*YHWH*] is One. *Adonai* substitutes for *YHWH* as "the Eternal" not as "the Lord." The name of God in the Hebrew Scriptures is *YHWH* without attributes and Adonai is often used in place of that unsayable name. *YHWH* includes all the other names of God with attributes such as *Elohim*. The Creator God of everything is *Elohim* in Genesis 1:1 and the Creator God of humankind, the male and female image of God in Genesis 1:26–27. *Elohim* is God in Exodus 3:14. "God said to Moses, 'I AM Who I AM. [I Am That I Am]' And God said, 'Thus you will say to the children of Israel, 'I AM has sent me to you.'" The "I AM" is *hayah* in Hebrew which is *YHWH*.

Elohim means "God as Creator and Judge," "God (*Elohim*) of the gods (*elohim*)" (Psalm 82), "One Who is also Many," "Nature of God," "Creator of Nature," "Divine Parent," "Mother-Father God" (Genesis 1:1–2:3. The image of God (*Elohim*) is male and female in Genesis 1:26.), or "Unity in Diversity." See Appendix C, *Adonai* and *YHWH*.

Essenes, Order of

"A strict sect of Judaism that existed from the middle of the second century BC until the destruction of Jerusalem by the Romans in AD 70. The Essenes insisted on strict observance of Old Testament Law, which they expanded and interpreted in their own commentaries. Some of this material was included in the Dead Sea Scrolls, documents that probably came from the library of an Essenes community at Qumran."4 "They thought of themselves as the true Temple priesthood in exile. The chief priests led the group and were seated at the head in communal meals, followed by the ordinary priests, then the laity. There was voluntary poverty, and all property was shared. Food was measured out to each member of the group in strict equality."5 They believed that God would visit (change history on) the earth with a mass slaughter of the forces of evil, which included most Jews. This is like the strict Revelation Christians who believe that God will visit the earth with a mass slaughter of the forces of evil, which will include most Christian and Jewish people. John the Baptist was said to be in the Essenes.

Gentiles

Goyim in Hebrew. People or nations who were not Jewish which included Syrians, Idumaeans, Canaanites, Greeks, Romans, pagans, heathens, and nonbelievers.

Hanukkah

Also, Chanukah. Festival of Rededication of the Temple. In 175 BCE, the Seleucid ruler Antiochus IV overthrew the high priest Onias and appointed his own while he tried to Hellenize (make it Greek) Jerusalem. In 168 BCE, he took the side of the Hellenized Jews in Jerusalem against the traditionalist Jews outside Jerusalem. Antiochus rededicated the Temple to a Greek idol, Zeus, which Jews had to worship and eat the pork that was sacrificed to it. He eliminated the high priesthood, outlawed the Torah, and made circumcision illegal. After the Maccabee victory in 165 BCE, they rededicated the Temple three years to the day of the Hurban, "Abomination of desolation," and declared an eight-day observance of Hanukkah.

A one day supply of oil sealed by the old high priest Onias was used to rekindle the menorah; the sacred seven-candle lamp in the Temple. Today, the menorah is a candelabrum used in Hanukkah for worship with eight candles to celebrate the miracle that the oil lasted eight days. An extra higher candle is used to light the others. "The message of Hanukkah is, as stated in the Jewish liturgy, 'the victory of the weak over the strong, the few over the many, the righteous over the arrogant' (Daily Prayer Book, addition to "Modim" prayer in the Tefilah)."6

Hebrew people

Semitic member or descendants from Abraham, Sarah, Keturah Isaac, Rebecca, Jacob, and Leah. Also called Israelites and Jews. "Abraham was an

Assyrian. Jacob's children were born in Assyria and later sojourned in Egypt and Palestine. The people of Palestine called them Hebrews which means, those who crossed over the river."7

Herod the Great

"Whatever Antipater was, his son Herod was more so. The oldest son of Antipater, he was Roman-educated and possessed of a terribly mercurial and volatile personality. He was vindictive to a fault, never forgetting an insult or slight, whether real or imagined. He was also a fierce warrior, seemingly oblivious to personal danger, an able administrator, and a charismatic leader. He was driven by insatiable ambition and was never burdened by any scruples whatsoever."8

He was ruler of Judah (Judea) and Galilee from 37 BCE to 4 BCE who enlarged the Temple mount and built many parts of the Temple over several decades. Herod was the builder of Caesarea, with its harbor and its pagan temples for his Roman and Greek subjects. He built a magnificent building on top of the Tomb of the Patriarchs near Hebron and many palaces, including the Masada. The Romans ruled through Herod, the Jewish aristocratic leaders (Sadducees), and the Pharisees, who maintained their own institutions of social control, which included the Temple and the Sanhedrin. "Perhaps Herod's greatest achievement was his ability to maintain the peace between his Jewish and Gentile subjects. No one after him was able to do this in all the regions of Judea, Samaria, Galilee, the Mediterranean Coast, and Trans-Jordan, all of which were calm once Herod pacified them early in his reign. Was Herod a Jew or a pagan? The best answer is that he presented himself as a Jew to his Jewish subjects, and as a pagan to his Gentile subjects."9

Herod Antipas

He ruled Galilee from 4 BCE to 39 CE while the Romans ruled Judea from 6 CE to 66 CE Antipas murdered John the Baptist by beheading him (Matthew 14:10), and Jesus called him "that fox." "'That fox' (Luke 13:32) has reference to his cunning, his subtle diplomacy, and his astute management of a difficult situation—qualities that enabled Antipas to retain his puppet position and petty royal power until AD 39."10

Herodians

Herod encouraged this group who supported the royal house and worked as allies of the Sadducees Temple priesthood. They promoted a Hellenized society while accommodating the Romans.

High priest

The priesthood was selected from a group of Jewish aristocrats, all of whom are direct descendants of Aharon (Aaron, Moses's older brother). Aharon was the first High Priest, *Hakoban,* and Caiaphas was high priest in Jesus' time. "Great bribes were paid to the Roman procurators to gain this office, and High Priests came and went at a dizzying pace, many times serving even less than a year in the post."[11] The high priest had to get his vestments every day as the vestments were kept by the Romans.

Hillel

This Hebrew teacher, woodcutter, and leader of the Pharisees (50–10 BCE) was known for his gentle, kind nature; his love for all people; and especially his concern for the poor. He founded the Bet (school) Hillel, also known as Bet Tannaim, which was in learned dispute the Bet Shammai Pharisees, a more conservative group. "Hillel, together with the Shammai, the Sanhedrin under them, and their yeshivah colleagues, built a Jewish life so rich in spiritual and social content that it allowed Jews to ignore and discount the government and ruler that nominally dominated them."[12] "In almost every case Hillel took the lenient position, Shammai the strict position. After their deaths their two schools continued in their separate paths. Disputes multiplied. The Mishnah and the Talmud record the disputes between Hillel and Shammai and their respective schools."[13]

History

The Greeks and the Romans usually rule by encouraging local culture and religious freedom within limits. The Maccabees led a successful revolt to teach the Greek ruler Antiochus IV respect for Hebrew culture and religion. Diverse Jewish religious sects flourished in response to Greek and Roman culture with the political stability they demanded from this time until the destruction of the Jerusalem Temple in 70 CE.

When the Maccabees led the Jewish Revolt from 168 to 165 BCE, they changed the Sabbath law to allow Jewish soldiers to fight on the Sabbath as their enemies would attack then. "'Let them desecrate one Sabbath so that they may sanctify many Sabbaths.' (See Talmud Yoma 85a–b, Sanhedrin 74a, Tanhuma Buber Masa'ey 81a, N. T. Mark 2:27.) This ruling of the Maccabees is important to our understanding of Judaism in the time of Jesus, for this may be our first sighting of the 'legal traditions of the Pharisees.' This became the 'Oral Torah' of rabbinic Judaism—a way of living by the Torah that was more flexible and liberal than the older priestly traditions."[14] After victory over Antiochus, Judas Maccabee decreed Hanukkah a holiday for all Jews, and when the Greek armies marched through Judea again, they never outlawed the Torah.

The Greek empire (Seleucids) was crumbling by 63 BCE and the Hasmonean King, Hyrcanus, invited the Roman General Pompeii to side with him in a civil war over the throne. When Julius Caesar became emperor, he made Judaism a legal religion. After he was assassinated, Herod the Great became King of Judea until he died in 4 CE. Judea was then split up, where Herod Antipas became King of Galilee until 39 CE, and a series of thirteen Roman prefects or governors ruled the rest until 70 CE.

Hokhmah, Chokmah

Also, *Khokhmah*. The Hebrew name for Holy Wisdom, while "Sophia" is the Greek name. "By a mystical reading, the roots of this word point to a breath of individuality (HO) which arises from a sense of innerness (KhM) and then expands to connect with Sacred Unity (A). The roots of *Hokhmah's* name, as well as the way she is depicted in Proverbs 8:22–24, show that her role in creation was to form the first integrated self, or 'I am.'"[15] "Another literal translation of the word *Hokhmah* could be 'Sacred Sense.' In the same way that Sacred Breath expresses the unity of all breathing, *Hokhmah* embodies the coming together of all senses and sense impressions to form a self or 'I.' Like the sound of thunder, which unites all of one's senses in an awareness of the moment, this Sacred Sense collect and galvanizes all senses every instant."[16] Jesus, meaning *YHWH* saves (I AM saves), claims this spiritual integration all through the Gospel of John, as in John 8:58: "Very truly I tell you, before Abraham lived; I AM." He also said in Matthew 11:19, "Wisdom is known by Her children" and in Luke 7:35, "Wisdom is justified by all Her children."

Jerusalem

Spiritual and cultural center of the Jewish people; inhabited since about 2800 BCE in the Early Bronze Age. It was a Canaanite town called Salem and in Jesus' time was the location of the Holy Temple or *Bais hamigdosh*.

Jewish authorities

The Jewish authorities governed the Jewish people under Roman rule in Jesus' time and included: 1) the ruling aristocrats, elders of the people, and the Sadducees; 2) the Sanhedrin, a supreme court for Jewish law; 3) the Sadducees priesthood (Levites) including the chief priests, and the high priest; 4) scribes, teachers of the law, and lawyers of the Pharisees; 5) the Publicans or tax collectors; 6) the Temple guards; and 7) the regional police. "Using their advantage as the majority of the Sanhedrin, the Pharisees oversaw the ritual functions of the high priests. The high priests were Sadducees but they dared not defy the rulings of the popular Pharisees. The Pharisees also appointed judges, teachers and civil administrators throughout the country who judged according to the Pharisee's interpretation of Torah law."[17] Power rested in a small group of hereditary aristocrats, and the Romans had power over this group.

The usual translation, in the Gospel of John, of the Greek *Ioudaioi* as "the Jews" ignores the context of *Ioudaioi* and sometimes meant "Jewish authorities," "Judeans," "scribes of the Pharisees," "Jewish people," or "the Jews" in a non hostile or hostile way. This lack of clarity in John's Gospel has contributed to the sad record of anti-Semitism among Christians, where the Romans, with help from some Jewish leaders, killed Jesus; but ordinary Jews were tragically blamed, persecuted, and murdered for 2,000 years. Of the seventy-one references to "the Jews" in John's Gospel, over half are hostile, even though most of Jesus friends, followers, and family were Jewish. Raymond E. Brown argues against using other terms for the hostile use of "the Jews" based on historical judgment.

"Because of this historical judgment, some would eliminate 'Jews' from the translation of John. Although their goal is good (preventing modern readers from developing a hostile attitude toward Jews), I would disagree with this solution. One is not translating a Greek Gospel written in Jesus' lifetime but a Gospel written some six decades later. Therefore, for those interested in the literal sense of the Gospel, the starting issue must be what the Johannine writer meant and what he wrote, not what Jesus meant during his lifetime."[18] "To translate some instances of *Ioudaioi* as 'the Jewish authorities' and other instances as 'Jewish people' or 'Jewish crowd' is unwarranted to clarify texts that John has left vague and cloaks that fact that by calling them both 'the Jews', John deliberately joins them together in their hostility to Jesus."[19] The translation in this book of John's Gospel uses the meaning of "the Jews" appropriate to the context of the situation.

Jews

Hebrew people throughout the world or those whose religion is Judaism. The term *Jew* came from Judah, the name of the southern Hebrew kingdom with its capital, Jerusalem. For a discussion of the use of "the Jews," *Ioudaioi* in Greek, see "Jewish authorities" above. "During the time of Jesus, there was quite a difference between the Jews, Samaritans, and Galileans. The latter were members of the Jewish religion, but their ancestors were the Assyrians, Babylonians, Persians, and other mixed races which the Assyrian King, Shalmaneser, had settled in Galilee (2 Kings 17:24). They adhered to their own ancient customs and traditions, but they worshipped the God of Israel. The Jews had no social dealings with the Samaritans, and they despised the Galileans because they did not strictly adhere to the traditions of the Jewish elders, such as washing hands before meals, fasting, and the strict observance of the Sabbath."[20]

Jubilee year

The year of God's favor is when every fifty years there is a redistribution of wealth where all property is returned to the original owners. There is the renewal of the earth, a forgiveness of debt, liberty for convicts, and the release of prisoners and slaves. Taken from Leviticus 25:8–17.

Judea

Land area around Jerusalem, including Samaria, Judah, and Idumaea. Jews in this area were required to give tithes of their agricultural products to the Temple.

Kosher

Pure foods that are prepared along guidelines found in Jewish dietary laws or *kashrut*.

Korban

Also Corban and Karban. Special sacrificial offering, usually an animal or agricultural sacrifice commanded by the Torah to draw closer to God. Various meanings are "my sacrifice," "an offering to God," "a gift to God, often through the Temple," "a sin offering." Korban can also be an oath, like "By God!" "By the life of the Temple!" and "By the life of the Temple service!" On Passover, there is a special one called the Korban Pesah.

Leptons

Small copper coins; the least valuable coin used.

Levites

Levites were from the tribe of Levi, who descended from Jacob and Leah's third son. Levites are not necessarily priests, but priests and Levites are both from the tribe of Levi. Aharon was the first high priest who happened to descend from Levi, and all his male descendants are priests. They live on land around the Holy Temple and serve as its "keepers." As their dues, they receive all first-born animals and children, but both can be redeemed through a ceremony called "Redemption of the first born"—*Pidyore Haber*. "A lower sacred cast, the Levites, preformed secondary service like singing in the Temple choir and maintaining a guard at the gates."[21] "When Israel conquered Canaan, no major territory was given to Levi. Instead, the Levites were given outlying strips of land belonging to forty-eight cities scattered throughout the districts belonging to the other tribes. This facilitated the teaching of the Law and the distribution of tithes to the Levites."[22]

Maccabees

The Maccabees were *Kohaniim*, priests who successfully revolted against Greek rule from Syria in 168 BCE when their king outlawed the Torah. They rededicated the Temple and established Hanukkah as a yearly festival for all Jews. They became the Hasmonean Dynasty in Israel, 166 BCE to 36 BCE.

Manna

Manna was the mystical food that looked white and powdery, fell from the sky, tasted like whatever you wanted, and would turn to insects if kept overnight. See Exodus 16:15 and John 6:31. BCE to 36 BCE.

Messiah

Mashiakh is the Hebrew term meaning "anointed one." "The Messiah was a king of the royal line of David. He was therefore a flesh and blood human being, divinely appointed like all Jewish kings but not divine nor angelic in any way."[23] When he comes he will bring all Jews from exile to Israel. The Samaritans and the Essenes waited for two messiahs; one was the ruler and the other was the high priest. Jewish monarchs were also anointed using a formula *"You are my son; today, I have begotten you."*[24] They were called messiah and the adopted Son of God. Jesus as the "Christ" (Greek for "Messiah") was a spiritual leader teaching the kin-dom of God in people's hearts but he was not a worldly ruler like a king, which he was accused of and crucified for being. Jesus was sent by God to live out and deliver "the Christ" which is the "consciousness of God" for all people given to him by God. "The Christ" is a spiritual state that Jesus made available to everyone who believed on him and is not limited to the Jewish people or the Messiah of the Hebrew Scriptures. When a woman of Canaan asked Jesus to heal her daughter, Jesus explained to his disciples, **"I am only sent to the lost sheep of the house of Israel."** The woman taught Jesus that he was also sent for her and he healed her daughter (Matthew 15:21–29).

Mikvah

Also, mikveh. A Jewish immersion bath in a large pool of water. All Jews can give themselves a mikvah as the need for ritual purification arises. The immersion without clothes in the waters of life, *mayim chayim* or living water, returns you to a ritually pure state. After a person would bathe, they washed their clothes and waited until nightfall to be ritually pure and clean. "'Pure' and 'impure' are also inadequate terms. A person or thing which was *tahor*-'ritually pure'—was suitable to enter the sacred precincts of the Temple, to approach the divine. A person or thing which was *tah-may*–'ritually impure,' could not come near to God and so could not enter the Temple precinct. The rabbis later replaced the biblical terminology of *tahor* and *tahmay* with their own preferred term–*kosher*."25 "Since sin generated distance from God and atonement generates nearness, just like impurity and purity, there was by analogy an aspect of penitence in the act of ritual purification. This correspondence between ritual purity and atonement was made explicit in the career of John the Baptist. We must remember that John was not a Christian but a Jew. His immersions in the Jordan River were not baptisms into faith in Christ but Jewish ritual immersions. He might better be called 'John the Mikvah-Man.'"26

Moses

Moshe in Hebrew. One of the greatest Prophets ever born, who freed the Jews from slavery in Egypt, received the Torah, and taught his people through God's help. The prophets have authority over the priests just as Moses did over his brother, Aharon, and his sons.

Nephesh

Soul, true Self, a person's consciousness, or spiritual self regarded as immortal. The only part of a human being to survive death, even a living death.

Nard ointment

Spikenard ointment. This rose-red perfume was a favorite of the ancients, which was packed pure in a clay or alabaster jar. Nard came from the Himalayas; it would cost about a year's wages for a laborer or $15,000.

Oral Torah

"The Oral Law (*Torah She'b'al Peh*) is the interpretation of the Hebrew Bible, the explanation of the commandments and the actual rituals of Judaism that God transmitted to Moses at Sinai. Moses, in turn, taught this law to his generation and to Joshua who transmitted it to later generations. This law was not written as a book or firmly codified but, rather, remained as a vital and creative study that was taught, analyzed through debate, and transmitted orally.

However, at the end of the second century CE, the process of transforming the Oral Law into a written code began with the editing of the Mishnah. This writing process continued for centuries, culminating in the final edition of the Talmud produced in Babylonia in the sixth century CE."[27] "What emerges is a world view steeped in holiness and buttressed by faith and goodness, that allows for a life of serenity and worth even under the worst physical circumstances of poverty and persecution. The Bible was fire, divine, and after a certain level of understanding, obviously beyond true human appreciation and understanding. The Talmud, however, was human, understanding, comforting, challenging, and personal."[28]

Passover

Pesach. The annual celebration of God's liberation of Israel from captivity in Egypt, which is conjoined with the seven-day Feast of the Matzov or Unleavened Bread for an eight-day festival. Israelites were exempted from the slaughter of the firstborn in Egypt (Exodus 12:21–28). This festival is highlighted with the Passover seder, and Jews celebrate God as the Redeemer Who established the nation of Israel through this event.

Passover Seder

Passover meal. "The seder evolved as a symposium on the topic of the Exodus from Egypt. There were four toasts, two before dinner and two after. These toasts were dedicated to the four terms for redemption found in Exodus 6:6–7. The banquet consisted of the required paschal lamb, matzoh—unleavened bread and bitter herbs, and Greek delicacies like lettuce dipped in sauce (haroset) and greens dipped in salt water. These delicacies also entered the ritual of the seder."[29] The *Haggadah* is the text of Jewish ritual acts and prayers to tell the children (*sons*) the story of the Exodus for the seder.

Pharisees

Perushim means "the pure," "those set apart," or "separate ones." An innovative Jewish religious sect during the Second Temple era from 536 BCE to 70 CE who lived by the Torah and the Oral Torah (see Oral Torah above). The Pharisees became Rabbinic Judaism. The Pharisees believed, "You shall be for Me a priestly kingdom and a holy nation" (Exodus 19:5–6). They lived among the people, interpreted the scriptures, instituted universal Jewish education, were spiritual leaders by example, had a program for Judaism, kept the Sabbath, ate only pure food, and kept ritual purity. From the time of the Maccabees until the destruction of the Temple in about 70 CE, diverse Jewish religious sects flourished under Greek and Roman rule. Many Pharisees followed Jesus and even some scribes (leaders) of the Pharisees.

"This is not to say that all Pharisees were perfect. Jesus was surely correct in criticizing those snobs who used knowledge and religious authority for public preening and social climbing instead of true divine service. We should not imagine, though, that Pharisees exhibited these human traits in any greater degree than other people, especially in light of the universal respect in which they were held. Even their worst opponents honored them for their virtues and conceded their popularity.30

Phylacteries

Tefillin. A headband with a box containing four compartments for scripture and bands of cowhide that flow over the shoulders. It became Jewish practice to remove their headband after worship. There is also another box with straps that is wrapped around the left or weaker arm and another box for the hand.

Pilate

There were thirteen Roman Prefects who ruled Judea from 6 CE to 67 CE. Pontius Pilate, the fifth Prefect over Jerusalem 26 CE to 36 CE, was a cruel sadistic tyrant who lived off excess Roman tax-collecting funds above the set amount for Rome.31 In Luke 13:1, "Then there came some men who told Jesus about the Galileans whose blood Pilate had mingled with their sacrifices." In the Gospel of John, Jesus was arrested and brought to Pilate who wanted him killed as the King of the Jews, a revolutionary who sets himself against Caesar.

In John 19:1–3, "Then Pilate took Jesus and scourged him, and his soldiers wove a crown of thorns which they placed on his head and dressed him in a purple robe. They came up to him, saying, 'Peace be to you, Oh King of the Jews!' and struck him in the face." Scourging alone could have killed him even before his crucifixion, but Pilate successfully blamed Jesus' death on the

Judeans, when only Pilate or Herod Antipas had the authority to kill him. The anti-Semitism in the Gospel of John minimizes Pilate's role and puts the blame for the persecution and death of Jesus onto every Jewish person and not the Jewish authorities and Pilate who were responsible.

Publicans

Tax collectors. Jewish bureaucrats who worked for the Romans and collected taxes from other Jews. They were considered traitors, usually corrupt, unclean from contact with pagans, and often charged double. "Government officials are indifferent to the methods employed to collect taxes. Thus the public, especially the poor, are at the mercy of dishonest publicans who extort bribes and collect unjust and undue taxes which they share with government officials. Taxes are generally extracted by force and violence. When the poor fail to pay the sums assessed or protest the confiscation of their crops or sheep by the tax collectors, they are stripped of their clothes, cruelly beaten, and made examples in order to make collections of taxes easier."32

Repentance

A person regrets past deeds, has a radical change of heart, and seeks forgiveness which is usually accomplished though prayer or animal sacrifice. Then they work at a changed lifestyle through a prophet, teachers, meditation, or therapy if needed to love themselves again and help achieve unity with God.

Rosh Hashanah

Time for cleansing and prayers to ask God for a Good New Year.

Sabbath

Shabat in Hebrew. A day of rest each week to commune with God from sunset Friday to sunset Saturday when three stars are observed. The Sabbath is a time of limited activity, loving God, feeling joy, spending the morning at the synagogue, sharing with your community, prayer–together and separate–to God, spiritual rejuvenation, Hebrew Scripture study, and eating special foods that are prepared beforehand. "The Hebrew people observed the Sabbath by resting from ordinary labor. Every Israelite with their slaves and even their animals was to refrain from work so that all might 'be refreshed' (Exodus 23:10–12). God cared for the physical as well as the spiritual state of his people."33

Sadducees

Zadokim means "righteous ones." An aristocratic and a conservative hereditary priesthood who maintained ancient priestly traditions. They date back to the time of King David and King Solomon when Zadok was their high priest. They rose to power after the Maccabean revolt (167 BCE–160 BCE) and lost it for a time under Queen Alexandra (76 BCE–67 BCE). They cooperated with the Romans in ruling Judea and controlled the Temple. They believed only in the first five books of the Hebrew Bible and denied the divine origins of the Oral Torah of the Pharisees. The Sadducees believed that God was above human affairs, and they didn't believe in the resurrection. The history of the aristocratic Sadducees with their priesthood and Elders ended about 70 CE with the Roman destruction of the Temple.

Samaritans

They worshiped at sacred shrines and had their own temple at Mt. Gerizim, which was 2,890 feet high. Jewish leaders would not recognize this as a second temple and this temple, which may have only been a large altar, was destroyed by Hycranus with a Judean group in 129 BCE. Samaria became a refuge for dissident Jews from Galilee to the North and Judea to the South. "The Samaritans were a mixed population made up of people which the king of Assyria had settled in Samaria in place of the ten tribes of Israel in 722 BCE. They were of the same stock as the people of Galilee, except that the Samaritans adhered more closely to the customs which their ancestors brought from Assyria. They adopted the Jewish faith in part but they carried on their own traditions and worship. (2 Kings 17:29)."34 "At the time of Jesus, the Jews despised the Samaritans more than the Galileans. Even though they had accepted the five books of Moses, the Jews looked upon them as pagans. The Samaritans resembled the Assyrians more than any other people in Palestine."35

Sanhedrin

Greek term *synhedrion*, meaning "council." The Hebrew name was *beth din* or "house of judgment" and included lower and higher courts based on

Deuteronomy 16:18. "The Mishnah says that the Sanhedrin was a court of seventy-one learned sages, under the leadership of the Pharisees. The Sanhedrin met in the Temple complex, in a room called the Chamber of Hewn Stones. This court was the highest Jewish authority. They supervised the high priest in all his activities and told him how to conduct the Temple worship. The Sanhedrin operated according to the highest principles of jurisprudence, appointing to membership only the most worthy, scrupulous and honest scholars who were completely dedicated to justice. Many historians doubt that a Sanhedrin like that described in the Mishnah ever existed in the Temple."[36]

The high priest Caiaphas had his own *beth din*, private council or sanhedrin, which met over Jesus in Matthew, Mark, and Luke but did not have to follow any judicial standards. The Sanhedrin never assembled during Passover, on the Sabbath, or at night, even for a capital crime which required at least two days to make a decision. In 70 CE, the Sanhedrin moved to the village of Yavneh near the Mediterranean coast, where members of the Yavneh Sanhedrin were called rabbis.

Scribes

Hachamin in Hebrew means "learned" or "sage." The sage was one who knew the Torah and how to interpret it: Moses, Aharon, Hillel, etc. The sage saw divine law as the principle of life. In Jesus' time, they were the teachers of the law, or canon lawyers. The scribes of the Pharisees in the Four Gospels were the leaders and misleaders of the Pharisees. All Pharisees considered themselves to be scribes, but Jesus was addressing the hypocritical leaders who were attacking him. Also, scribes were professional writers, copyists, scholars, students of scripture, bureaucrats, legal secretaries, lawyers, and high government officials. "The Scribes (*Hachamin* means "learned") became the interpreters of the Law of Moses and maintained oral traditions and requirements that had been added to the written commandments of the Pentateuch (the first five books of the Hebrew Bible). The Scribes originated about 440 BCE with the high priest Ezra, after the Jews returned to Palestine from the Babylonian captivity in 538 BCE. They regarded themselves as the authority and last word on interpretation of the Law and this stance was supported by the Jewish populace when they first returned to Palestine without their Temple or any remembrance of public worship. The Scribes served to reestablish a sense of national grandeur by founding a theocracy based on the Law of Moses."[37]

Sea of Galilee

Lake Kinneret, Lake Chinnereth, or Sea of Tiberius.

Shavuot

The Feast of Weeks on Pentecost on the fiftieth day after Pesach. A fall rainy season festival celebrating God teaching the Torah to the Jews.

Showbread

Consecrated bread or bread of the Presence was placed on special tables in the Temple every Friday and lasted until the next Friday when it was eaten.

Sukkoth

Sukkot. Feast of booths or Harvest festival when Jews came to Jerusalem with palm branches and etrogs (a citrus fruit) saying, "*Hosanna!* 'God save [deliver] Us!'" This is known as *zeman simhatenu* or "season of rejoicing." They brought offerings of grains and first fruits, thanking God for bringing the Jews out from slavery and into the land of plenty. "The purpose of these rituals, including the Hosanna's, was the prayer to God for abundant rain."[38]

Synagogue

Hebrew term is *beit k'nesset* or House of Assembly. *Assembly* in Greek. A Synagogue is a place for worship, Hebrew scripture study, public assemblies, mikvah purification, preaching, teaching, and prayer.

Temple

The Holy Temple is called *Bain Hamigdosh* in Hebrew, and it was the center of Hebrew worship and sacrifice in Jerusalem. The first Temple, 950 BCE to 586 BCE, was built by King Solomon and destroyed by the Babylonians. The second Temple, 520 BCE to 70 CE, was reconstructed under the leadership of Zerubbabel and renovated by Herod the Great from 37 BCE to 4 BCE. The Romans destroyed the second Temple in 70 CE.

Tithe

People give a tenth of the harvest or income to the Levites in the Temple, *Kobaniim,* or Synagogues, *Leviim* who distribute a tenth of the tenth to the priests. A tithe was an income tax to support the theocracy in Israel, and in Christianity, a tithe goes to support the church and their leaders.

Torah

The Pentateuch (five scrolls) or Law of Moses. The first five books of the Jewish Canon are Genesis, Exodus, Leviticus, Numbers, and Deuteronomy. The Torah or Law, in a broader use of the term, can come from all of Hebrew scripture. The Torah is not like a list of rules to be saved but a guide to respond to the salvation already given to the Jews. The Torah, like the Gospels of Jesus, is an aggregate of original written pieces of scripture combined with oral traditions, which later inspired religious literary schools, that are woven together as best they can to reveal spiritual and historical truth. They are rewritten over time by scribal copyists and later religious schools who ascribe an author or title.

YHWH

YHVH, Being, the Existing, or the Eternal represents the divine nature of God relating to people. This is called Tetragramammaton, meant to be unpronounceable, but with vowels becomes Yahweh. *YHWH* is also written as *YHVH,* Yahweh, Jah and Jehovah. *YHWH* is written and spoken as *Adonai, Hashem,* or G-d. This is the four letters of the personal name of God that was never to be pronounced except during worship in the Temple and on the Day of Atonement when it was pronounced ten times. *YHWH* is God without attributes (unmanifest) and other Hebrew names of God are God with attributes, like *Elohim* for God as Creator and Judge or *El Shaddai* for God Almighty. An example is Deuteronomy 6:4–5: "Hear Oh Israel, the Eternal is our God, the Eternal is One. You shall love the Eternal your God with all your heart, all your soul and all your strength." A complete version is: " Hear Oh Israel, *Adonai* [*YHWH*] is our God [*Elohim*], *Adonai* [*YHWH*] is One. You shall love *Adonai* [*YHWH*] your God [*Elohim*] with all your heart, all your soul and all your strength."

The name used in place of *YHWH* is *Adonai* which is translated into the Greek as *Kyrios* (*Kurios*) which is translated in to the English "the LORD." So "*Adonai* [*YHWH*] is our God [*Elohim*]" becomes "The LORD is our God" or "The LORD our God" in most Christian Bibles. The name of God of the second Creation Genesis 2:4–2:23) is *Adonai* (*YHWH*), God (*Elohim*) or "the Lord God." The other names for "God" in Judaism (included under *YHWH*) are God with attributes or roles like *Elohim* is the "One Who is also Many" and "God as Creator and Judge" (Genesis 1:1–2:3) whose image and likeness is male and female. Also *Elohim* is "God of the gods" (Psalm 82). See Appendix C, *Adonai* and *Elohim*.

Yom Kippur (See Atonement)

Zaken

Elders of the people; aristocratic rulers in Judea.

Zealots (Fourth Philosophy)

Kanna'im in Hebrew. Zeal for the law with no ruler but God. The Zealots became active in about 6 CE under the leadership of Judas of Galilee. One of Jesus' disciples was "Simon, who was called the Zealot" in Luke 6:15. The Zealot as Simon is also translated as a Patriot, Nationalist, and Revolutionary. In Matthew 10:4 and Mark 3:18, Simon is "the Cananaean," which is from the Aramaic *qan'an* meaning "the Zealot." "Their descent into violence coincided with a general breakdown of law and social convention at the end of the Second Temple era."[39] The Sicarii, whose name came from the small dagger they used, were a radical splinter group of the Zealots active under the Romans. They were the last holdouts at the Roman siege of Masada from 70 CE to 73 CE, and they all committed suicide rather than be captured by the Romans.

The Fourth Philosophy movement were people who believed that they had a right to overthrow invaders on their land with violent resistance to the foreign powers and their local agents. They were called Zealots, Sicarii, rebels, and revolutionaries. Jesus was a peaceful, spiritual revolutionary who wanted to change religion in his time by teaching the nonviolent kin-dom of God within you, here and now. This is a spiritual rebirth to develop the Christ or the consciousness of God within you.

APPENDIX D

Hebrew Scripture Quotes

List of Hebrew Scripture Quotes

Contents

Page no.

Hebrew Scripture Quotes

Quotes are from the many English language versions of the Hebrew Scripture (Hebrew Bible) or TaNaK, which includes *Torah* (Law of Moses), *Nebi'im* (Prophets), and *K'etubim* (Writings). Many Hebrew and Aramaic scripture references found in the Four Gospels are often paraphrased, shortened, and used out of context. Some quotes are expanded for greater context and placed in the text of the Four Gospels; see Appendix D: List of Expanded Hebrew Scripture Quotes. Hebrew Scripture quotes are in *italic* in the text of the Gospels. The use made of the Hebrew Scripture quote in the text of this book is referred to in brackets at the end of the quotes below: Genesis 1:1–3 . . . [See Proverbs 8:22–31.]; Genesis 1:26–27 . . . [See Matthew 19:4.]

Genesis

Genesis 1:1–3

1 In the beginning when God created the heavens and the earth, the earth was a formless void without form and darkness covered the face of the deep while the [*Holy*] Spirit of God moved over the face of the waters. God said, "Let there be light!" and there was light. [See Proverbs 8:22–31.]

Genesis 1:26-27

26 Then God said, "Let Us make humankind in Our image, according to Our likeness and let them have husbandry over the fish of the sea, over the birds of the air, over the cattle, over the wild animals of the earth, and over all the creatures that crawl on the ground." So God created humankind in Their (His)[1] own image; in the image of God They created them; male and female They created them. [See Matthew 19:4.]

Exodus

Exodus 3:6

6 God said further, "I am the God of your father, the God of Abraham, the God of Isaac and the God of Jacob." Then Moses hid his face for he was afraid to look at God. [See Matthew 22:32, Mark 12:26, and Luke 20:37.]

Exodus 3:14

14 God said to Moses, "I AM WHO I AM. [I AM THAT I AM.]" And God said, "Thus you will say to the children of Israel, 'I AM has sent me to you.'" [See Matthew 14:27.]

Exodus 15:26

26 I AM the God who heals you. [See Luke 4:18.][2]

Exodus 16:14–15

14 When the dew that lay was gone up, behold, upon the face of the wilderness lay a fine flaky substance as small as hoar frost on the ground. Then the children of Israel saw it saying to one another, "Manna-ho?" ("What is it?") They didn't know what it was. Moses told them, "This is the bread which God has given you to eat." [See John 6:31.]

Exodus 20:12

12 Honor your father and your mother that your days may be long upon the land which your God gives you.[3] [See Matthew 15:4 and Mark 7:10.]

Exodus 21:17

17 Whoever curses[4] your father or your mother shall [*may*] be put to death. [See Matthew 15:4 and Mark 7:10.]

Leviticus

Leviticus 19:9–10

9 When you reap the harvest of your land, you will not reap your field to the very corners or gather the gleanings of your harvest. You will not glean your vineyards or gather that which has fallen from your olive trees. Leave them for the poor and for those traveling through for I am God. [See Luke 6:1.]

Leviticus 19:17–18

19 You will not hate in your heart any one of your kin and you will reprove your neighbor or you will incur guilt yourself. You will not take vengeance or bear a grudge against any of your own people but you will

love your neighbor as yourself for I am God. [See Matthew 22:39, Mark 12:31, and Luke 10:27.]

Numbers

Numbers 28:9–10

28 On the Sabbath day; two lambs of the first year without blemish and two-tenths of an ephah of choice flour mixed with oil for a meal offering with its drink offering. This is the burnt offering of every Sabbath, besides the continual burnt offering and its drink offering. [See Matthew 12:5.]

Deuteronomy

Deuteronomy 6:4–5

4 Hear Oh Israel, the Eternal is our God, the Eternal is One. You shall love the Eternal your God with all your heart, with all your soul and with all your strength.[5] [See Matthew 22:37, Mark 12:29–30, and Luke 10:27.]

Deuteronomy 6:16

16 Do not involve the Eternal your God in a foolish test, as you did at Massah.[6] [See Matthew 4:7 and Luke 4:12.]

Deuteronomy 8:3

3 God humbled you, allowed you to hunger, and fed you with manna, with which neither you nor your ancestors were acquainted, to make you understand that one does not live by bread alone but by every word that proceeds from the mouth of God. [See Matthew 4:4 and Luke 4:4.]

Deuteronomy 10:20

20 You shall revere [fear][7] the Eternal your God, God alone you shall worship, to God you shall hold fast, and by God's name you shall swear. [See Matthew 4:10 and Luke 4:8.]

Deuteronomy 18:15–19

15 Your God will raise up from you a prophet like me from the midst of your people. Listen to him! Just as you asked of God at Horeb on the day

of the assembly, "If I hear the voice of my God any more or ever again see this great fire, I will die!" Then God replied to me, "They are right in what they have spoken. I will raise up for them a prophet like you from among their own people and I will put My words in the mouth of that prophet who will speak to them everything that I command him. I will hold accountable anyone who does not heed the words that prophet will speak in My name." [See Matthew 17:7, Mark 9:7, Luke 9:35 John, 5:46, and John 17:8.]

Deuteronomy 19:15–19

15 A single witness will not suffice to convict a person of any crime or wrongdoing with any offense that may be committed. Only on the evidence of two or three witnesses may the charge be established. If a false witness will rise up against any person and testify against that which is wrong; then both people between whom the controversy is, will stand before God, before the priests and the judges who are in office in those days. The judges will investigate the case diligently and behold, if the witness has deliberately testified against the person; then you will do to the witness as they had thought to do to the person. In this way you will you put out injustice away from you. [See John 7:51 and John 8:17.]

Deuteronomy 23:24–25

24 When you go into your neighbor's vineyard, you may eat as many grapes as you desire but do not put any in a container to go. When you go into your neighbor's standing grain, you may pluck a few handfuls but do not use a sickle to cut the grain. [See Luke 6:1.]

Deuteronomy 25:5–6

5 When brothers dwell together and one of them dies and has no son, the wife of the dead man shall not marry a stranger outside the family. Her husband's brother shall go into her, take her as his wife and perform the duty of a brother-in-law to her. And it shall be that the first-born son whom she bears shall be named after his brother who is dead so his name may not be forgotten in Israel. [See Mark 12:19 and Luke 20:28.]

Deuteronomy 30:11–14

11 Surely this commandment which I command you this day is neither hidden from you nor is it far off. It is not in the sky that you would say,

"Who will go up for us up in the sky and bring it to us, that we may hear it and do it?" Neither is it beyond the sea that you would say, "Who will go over the sea and bring it to us that we may hear it and do it?" The word is very near you, in your mouth and in your heart, that you may do it. [See Luke 17:21, John 1:1–5, Mary 8:17–19, and Thomas 3:1–3.]

Ruth

Ruth 4:11–12

11 All the people who were at the gate and the elders said, "We are witnesses." They blessed him and said to him, "God make the woman who is coming into your home like Rachel and Leah, the two who built the house of Israel; and may you prosper in Ephrathal and be famous in Bethlehem. May your house be like the house of Perez, whom Tamar bore to Judah because of the offspring which God will give you from this young woman. [See Matthew 2:6, Luke 2:4, John 7:42, and Micah 5:2–5.]

2 Samuel

2 Samuel 7:12–17

12 "When your days are fulfilled and you rest with your ancestors, I will raise up your seed after you who will come from your body and I will establish his kingdom [kin-dom]. He shall build a house for my name and I will establish the throne of his kingdom [kin-dom] forever. I will be a Father [Divine Parent] to him and he will be a Son to Me. When he does wrong, I will punish with a rod such as mortals use, with blows inflicted by human beings. I will not take My mercy from him as I took it from Saul, whom I put away from before you. Your house and your kingdom [kin-dom] shall be made sure before you, your throne shall be established forever." In accordance with all these words and with all this vision, Nathan spoke to David. [See Matthew 5:16 and Matthew 25:31.]

1 Kings

1 Kings 17:7–16

7 It happened after a while that the brook dried up because there had been no rain in the land. Then the word of God came to Elijah saying,

"Arise, go to Zarephath which belongs to Sidon and dwell there for I have commanded a widow there to feed you." So he set out and went to Zarephath. When he came to the gate of the town, a widow was there gathering sticks, he called to her and said, "Bring me a little water in a vessel so that I may drink." As she was going to fetch the water he called to her and said, "Bring me a morsel of bread in your hand!" She replied, "As your God lives, I have nothing baked, only a handful of flour in a pot and a little olive oil in a jug. Behold, I am gathering a few sticks that I may go in and bake some bread for my son and I, so we may eat it and die!" Elijah told her, "Fear not; go and do as you have said but first make a little cake of it and bring it to me. Then make some for yourself and your son. For the God of Israel says, 'The pot of flour will not be spent and the jug of oil will not diminish until the day that God sends rain down upon the earth.'" She went and did according to the sayings of Elijah so she as well as he and her household ate for many days. Neither was the pot of flour spent nor was the jug of oil diminished according to the word of God spoken by Elijah. [See Luke 4:25–26.]

2 Kings (A Condensed Version)

2 Kings 5:1–14

1 (Naaman, a successful Syrian army commander had leprosy and a maid, who was an Israeli captive serving his wife, suggested that the prophet Elisha in Samaria could cure him. So he had his king of Arman write a letter to the king of Israel. The king of Israel became upset and when Elisha heard, he asked the king to allow Naaman to come to him.) So Naaman came with his horses and his chariots and stood at the door of the house of Elisha. Elisha sent a messenger to him saying, "Go and wash in the Jordan River seven times, your flesh will come again to you, and you will be clean."

11 (Naaman became angry, offended by the secondhand message and left in a rage.) His servants came near to him saying, "Our lord, if the prophet had told you to so some great thing, would you have done it? How much more would you have done it when he says to you, 'Go, wash and be clean?'" So he went down and washed seven times in the Jordan River according to the saying of the prophet of God. His flesh came again like the flesh of a little child and he was clean. [See Luke 4:27.]

Job

Job 32:6–9

6 Elihu, son of Barachel the Buzite answered, "I am young in years and you are very old, therefore I was timid and afraid to declare my opinion to you." I said, "Age should speak and the multitude of years should teach wisdom. Surely, it is God's Spirit within people, the breath of the Almighty, that gives them understanding. It is not age that makes people wise nor do the aged always understand justice. [See Matthew 11:19, Luke 7:36, and John 14:16–17.]

Job 33:4

4 The Spirit of God has stirred me up and the breath of the Almighty has given me life. [See Matthew 11:19, Luke 7:35, and John 14:16–17.]

Psalms (Psalter)

Psalms 2:7–8

7 I will declare the decree: God said to me, "You are My son; today I have begotten[8] you. Ask of Me for I will give you the Gentiles for your inheritance and the uttermost parts of the earth for your dominion." [See Matthew 3:17, Luke 3:22, and John 1:18.]

Psalms 8:1–2

1 Oh God, Your majesty fills all the earth and Your glory overflows the heavens. Out of the mouths of babes and nursing infants You have established Your glory in their perfect praise because of your foes. May their example silence the enemy and the avenger. [See Matthew 21:16.]

Psalms 16:8–11

8 I have set God always before me; because God is at my right hand, I shall not be moved. My heart is glad, my soul rejoices, and my body rests in hope. For You will not leave me among the dead[9] and You will not allow Your beloved one to rot in the grave.[10] You show me the path of life. In Your Presence there is fullness of joy and in Your right hand are pleasures forevermore. [See John 20:9.]

Psalms 22:1–5

1 My God, My God, why have you forsaken me? Why are you so far from helping me and from the words of my groaning? Oh my God, I cry in the daytime but You do not hear and I cry in the night season but I find no rest. Yet You are enthroned as the Holy One in the praises of Israel. Our ancestors trusted in You; they trusted and you delivered them. They cried to You and were saved, they trusted in you and were not put to shame. [See Matthew 27:46 and Mark 15:34.]

Psalms 31:1–5

1 In Thee Oh God, I put my trust; let me never be put to shame; deliver me in Thy justice [*righteousness*].11 Incline Your ear to me, rescue me speedily. Be a rock of refuge for me and a fortress of defense to save me. For You are my rock and my fortress; therefore for Thy name's sake lead me and guide me. Pull me out of the net which they have secretly laid for me for You are my strength. Into Thy hands I commit my spirit; You have redeemed me, Oh God of truth. [See Luke 23:46.]

Psalms 34:19–20

19 Many are the afflictions of the righteous but God delivers them out of all their troubles. He keeps all his bones, not one of them is broken. [See John 19:36.]

Psalms 35:19–21

19 Don't let those who are wrongfully my enemies rejoice over me or let them wink with the eye12 who hate me without a cause. For they do not seek peace but devise mischievous things against the meek of the earth. They open their eyes wide against me, saying, "Aha, aha, our eyes have seen it!" [See John 15:25.]

Psalms 41:9

9 Even my own familiar friend in whom I trusted, who ate my bread, has lifted up his heal against me. [See Matthew 26:23, Mark 14:18, and John 13:18.]

Psalms 49:1–20

1 Hear this, all you peoples; give ear, all who inhabit the world; both low and high, rich and poor alike. My mouth shall speak Wisdom and

the meditation of my heart shall give understanding. I will incline my ear to a proverb and I will chant my dark saying[13] on the harp. I will not fear in the times of trouble, when the iniquity of my persecutors surrounds me; those who trust in wealth and boast of the abundance of their riches. Truly, no ransom avails for one's life nor can one give to God a ransom for oneself. Redemption does not come so easily for no one can pay enough to live forever and not experience corruption. Those who are wise[14] must finally die, just like the foolish and senseless, and leave their wealth behind. Their inner thought is that their graves shall be their houses forever for they may name their estates after themselves but they leave their wealth to others. For all their riches, mortals will perish like the animals if they do not understand. This is the way of those who are foolish for in the end, demented, they will graze like cattle,[15] though they will be remembered as being so wise. Selah.[16]

14 Like sheep, they are led into a living hell[17] where death is their shepherd. In the morning the upright will rule over them, their beauty will be consumed in their living hell and they will be cast out from their glory. As for me, God will redeem my soul from the power of a living hell for God will receive me. Selah. Do not fear when others becomes rich and when the wealth of their estates increases, for when they die they will carry nothing away and their wealth will not go down after them. Though in their lifetime they blessed themselves (for you are praised when you do well for yourselves) but they will join the company of their ancestors and they shall never see the light of life. For all their riches, if mortals do not have Wisdom, they perish like the animals. [See Mark 10:24.]

Psalms 51:10–12

10 Create in me a clean heart, Oh God, and renew a steadfast [*human*] spirit within me. Do not cast me away from Your Presence and do not take Your Holy Spirit from me. Restore to me the joy of Your salvation and sustain in me a generous spirit. [See John 14:16–17.]

Psalms 69:8–12

8 I have become a stranger to my kinfolk and an alien to my mother's children. It is zeal for Your house that has made me courageous.[18] The insults of those who have insulted You have fallen on me. When I wept and found my soul through fasting, they reproached me for doing so. In

sorrow, I made sackcloth my outfit but I became an object of scorn. I am the subject of gossip by those who sit in judgment and alcoholics make up songs about me. [See Matthew 12:49, Mark 3:21, Luke 8:19, and John 2:17.]

Psalms 78:1–4

1 Give ear, Oh my people, to my teaching; incline your ears to the words of my mouth. I will open my mouth in parables; I will utter dark sayings of old which we have heard and known, that our ancestors have told us. We will not hide them from their children; telling to the coming generation: the praises of God, the strength of God, and the wonderful works that God has done. [See Matthew 13:34–35.]

Psalms 82:1–8

1 God stands in the congregation of the mighty:[19] God judges among the gods. "How long will you judge unjustly and show favor to the evil acting people? Selah! Defend the weak and the orphan; do justice to the afflicted and destitute. Deliver the poor and the needy; free them from the hands of evil acting people. These don't know or understand for they walk about in darkness. All the foundations of the earth are unstable, changing. I said, "You are gods! All of you are children of the Most High but you will die like other people, and fall like one of these rulers." Arise, Oh God, judge the earth; for You will inherit all people. [See John 10:34–35.]

Psalms 89:3–4

3 God said, "I have made a covenant with My chosen one, I have sworn to David My servant, I will establish your offspring forever and build up your throne [rule] to all generations." Selah. [See John 7:42.]

Psalms 91:11–12

11 God will give angels over you to keep you in all your ways. They will bear you up in their hands, so you will not dash your foot upon a stone. [See Matthew 4:6 and Luke 4:10–11.]

Psalms 110:1

1 God said to my lord, "Sit at my right hand until I make your enemies your footstool." [See Matthew 22:43, Mark 12:36, and Luke 20:42.]

Psalms 118:19–29

19 Open to me the gates of righteousness that I may go into them and praise God. This is the gate into the presence of God through which the righteous will enter. I will give thanks to Thee because You have answered my prayer and have become my salvation. The stone which the builders rejected has become the headstone of the corner. This is God's doing; it is marvelous to our eyes. This is the day which God has made; we will rejoice and be glad in it. Hosanna! Blessed is the one who comes in the name of God! We have blessed you from the house of our God. The Eternal is God Who has given us light. Bind our festival processions as an unbroken chain, even to the horns of the altar. You are my God and I will give thanks to You; You are my God and I will exalt You. Oh give thanks to God Who is wonderful for God's mercy endures for ever. [See Matthew 21:9, Matthew 21:42, Mark 11:9, Mark 12:10–11, Luke 20:16, and John 12:12.]

Proverbs

Proverbs 1:20–23

20 Wisdom cries out in the street; She raises Her voice in the public square. At the busiest corner She cries out: at the entrance of the city gates She speaks Her words. "How long will you naive ones love your naivete? How long will you mockers delight in your mocking and how long will fools hate knowledge? Give heed to My reproof; I will pour out My Spirit upon you; I will make my wisdom known to you." [See Matthew 11:19, Luke 7:35, and John 14:16–17.]

Proverbs 3:15–18

15 She [*Wisdom*] is more valuable than precious stones and there is nothing to be compared to Her. Length of days is in Her right hand and in Her left hand, riches and honor. Her ways are ways of pleasantness and all Her paths are peace. She is the tree of life to those who lay hold of Her and blessed are those who wait for Her. [See Matthew 13:44–46.]

Proverbs 7:1–5

1 My child, keep My words and treasure; My commands within you. Keep My commands and live; keep My teachings as the apple of your eye. Bind them on your fingers; write them on the tablet of your heart. Say to

Wisdom, "You are my Sister," and call understanding your nearest kin, that they may keep you from the stranger, from the seducer who flatters with their words. [See Matthew 11:19, Luke 7:35, and John 14:16–17.]

Proverbs 8:1–36

1 Does not Wisdom cry out and understanding lift up Her voice. On the top of the high hill along the road, at the crossroads, She takes her stand. By the gates at the entry to the city, in the doorways She cries aloud, saying, "To you, Oh people, I call and My cry is to the children of humankind, so you naive ones may learn prudence [*balanced judgement*][20] and you fools may be of an understanding heart. Listen, for I will speak of noble things and from the opening of My lips will come honesty. For My mouth will speak truth for lying lips are an abomination before me. All the words of My mouth are just and nothing crooked or perverse is in them. They are all plain to one who understands and right to those who are willing to find knowledge. Receive My instruction and not silver and choose knowledge rather than fine gold; for Wisdom is more valuable than rubies and all the possessions you may desire cannot be compared with Her.

12 I, Wisdom, dwell with prudence and possess knowledge and reason. Reverence of God despises evil; pride, arrogance, corruption, and the perverted speech do I hate. Counsel and sound wisdom are Mine; I am understanding, I have strength. By Me, monarchs reign and lawgivers establish justice. By Me, princes [princesses] and rulers govern, even all the righteous judges of the earth. I love those who love Me and those who seek Me diligently will find Me. Riches and honor are with Me; yes, enduring wealth and justice. My fruit is better than gold, even fine gold, and My yield is better than choice silver. I walk about in the way of righteousness, along the paths of justice, that I may cause those who love Me to have hope and I will fill their treasuries.

22 God possessed Me at the beginning of His way, before the first of His works of long ago. I [*Wisdom*] have been established from everlasting, from the beginning, before there was ever an earth. When there were no depths I was brought forth, when there no fountains abounding with water. Before the mountains were settled into place, before the hills were formed, I was brought forth while He had not yet made the earth or the valleys or the primal dust of the world. When God established the

heavens, I was there. When He drew a circle on the face of the deep, when He set the clouds above, when He strengthened the fountains of the deep, when He assigned to the sea its limits so the waters would not transgress His command, when He laid down the foundations of the earth, then I was beside Him as a master Craftswoman. I was His delight, day by day, rejoicing in His presence always. Rejoicing in His inhabited world and My delight was with the children of humankind.

32 So now listen to Me, My children, for blessed are those who keep My ways. Hear instruction, be wise and do not go astray. Blessed is the one who listens to Me, watching daily at My gates, waiting at the posts of my doors for whoever finds Me finds life and obtains favor from God, but one who sins against Me wrongs their own soul and all those who hate Me love death." [See Matthew 11:19, Luke 7:35, John 14:16–17, and Genesis 1:2.]

Proverbs 9:1–6

1 Wisdom has built Her house, She has hewn out Her seven pillars. She has slaughtered Her animals, She has mixed Her wine and She has prepared her table. She has sent out Her servants to invite everyone to come. She cries out from the highest places of the city to say, "Whoever is simple, let them come to Me!" As for one who lacks understanding, She says to them, "Come, eat of My bread and drink the wine I have mixed. Forsake foolishness that you may live and walk in the way of understanding for by Me your days will be multiplied and the years of your life increased." [See Matthew 11:19, Luke 7:35, and John 14:16–17.]

Isaiah

Isaiah 6:8–10

8 Also, I heard the voice of God, saying, "Whom will I send and who will go for Us?" Then I said, "Here I am; send me!" God said to me, "Go and tell this people, 'You listen carefully but you will not understand; you look intently but you will not perceive.' For the heart of this people is hardened, their ears are closed, and their eyes are shut; so that they may not look with their eyes, hear with their ears, understand with their heart, turn to Me, and be healed." [See Matthew 13:14–15, Mark 4:12, Luke 8:10, and John 12:40.]

Isaiah 7:14–15

14 Therefore, God will give you a sign; Behold, a young woman will conceive and give birth to a son who will be called Immanuel.[21] He will eat butter and honey that he may know how to refuse the evil and choose the good. [See Matthew 1:23, Luke 1:31, and John 1:45.]

Isaiah 9:1–2

1 There will be no gloom for those who were in anguish. At first God brought contempt and judgment into the land of Zebulun and Naphtali. Though in the future these lands: the way of the sea and the land beyond the Jordan and the Galilee of the Gentiles, will be made glorious. The people who walked in darkness have seen a great light. This light will shine on those who dwelt in the land of the shadow of death. [See Matthew 4:15–16.]

Isaiah 9:6–7

6 For unto us a child is born, unto us son is given and the government will be upon his shoulders. His name is called; Wonderful, Counselor, Mighty One, Everlasting Father, and Prince of Peace. His authority will grow continually and there will be no end to his peace upon the throne of David and his kingdom [kin-dom]. He will establish it and sustain it with judgment and justice from this time onward and forevermore. The zeal of the God of hosts will perform this. [See John 12:34.]

Isaiah 11:1–2

1 A shoot shall come out from the stump of Jesse [*David's father*] and a branch shall grow out of his roots. He shall be at peace and the Spirit of God shall rest upon him, the Spirit of wisdom and understanding, the Spirit of counsel and might, the Spirit of knowledge and reverence of God. [See Matthew 11:19, Luke 7:36, and John 14:16–17.]

Isaiah 12:3

3 Therefore with joy you will draw water out of the spring of salvation. [See John 4:10–14 and John 7:38.]

Isaiah 29:13

13 God said, "These people draw near to Me with their mouths, honor Me with their lips but have removed their hearts far from Me. They

worship Me by teaching the precepts and doctrine of people." [See Matthew 15:8–9 and Mark 7:6–7.]

Isaiah 40:1–5

1 "Comfort, give comfort to my people." Says your God. "Speak tenderly to the heart of Jerusalem. Cry out to her that her warfare is ended and her penalty is paid for she has received from Me double for all her sins." The voice of one crying in the wilderness, "Prepare the way of our God. Make directly in the desert a highway for our God. Every valley will be filled up, every mountain or hill will be leveled, the crooked ways will be made straight, and the rough places smooth. Then the glory of God will be revealed and all people will see it together for the mouth of God has spoken." [See Matthew 3:3, Mark 1:3, Luke 3:4–6, and John 1:23.]

Isaiah 41:4

4 Who has performed and done this, calling the generations from the beginning? "I, God, am the first and I will be the last; I AM." [See Matthew 14:27.]

Isaiah 42:1–4

1 Behold, My servant, whom I uphold, My chosen in whom My Soul delights. I have put My Spirit upon him; He will bring forth justice to the Gentiles.22 He will not cry out or lift up his voice; nor will he cause his voice to be heard in the street. He will not break a bruised reed and he will not put out a flickering lamp; he will faithfully bring forth justice. He will not fail nor be discouraged until he has set justice in the earth: the coast lands wait for his teaching. [See Matthew 3:17, Matthew 12:18–21, Matthew 17:5, Mark 1:11, and Luke 3:22.]

Isaiah 43:10

10 "You are My witnesses," God says, "and My servant whom I have chosen, so that you may know and believe Me and understand that I AM. Before Me no god was formed, nor shall there be any after Me." [Matthew 14:27.]

Isaiah 46:3–4

3 Listen to Me, Oh house of Jacob and all the remnant of the house of Israel, who have been borne by Me from your birth, who have been

carried from the womb; even to your old age, I AM. Even when your hair is grey I will carry you! I have made you and will bear you; even I will carry and will deliver you. [Matthew 14:27.]

Isaiah 53:1–12

1 Who has believed our report? To whom is the arm of God revealed? He grew up before God as an infant like a tender green shoot sprouting from a root in the dry ground. He was not attractive in our eyes so we denied him. We despised and rejected him; a man of sorrows and aquatinted with grief. We turned away from him as he came by us. He was despised and we didn't care. It was our grief that he bore and our sorrows that weighed him down. We considered him stricken, afflicted, and struck down by God for his own sins. He was stricken that we might be healed, afflicted that we might have peace, and struck down for our transgressions; the punishment that made us whole.

6 We are all like sheep who have strayed; each going our own way. So God laid the sins of all of us on him. He was oppressed and he was afflicted but never opened his mouth; like a lamb led to the slaughter and as an ewe before her shearers is silent. So he did not open his mouth. By a perversion of justice he was taken from prison to suffer punishment for their transgressions. He was cut off from the land of the living and beat up by some men of my own people. He was buried as a criminal but in a rich man's grave, although he had done no violence and there was no deceit in his mouth.

10 Yet it pleased God to afflict him, put him to grief, and lay down his life as an offering for sin so that posterity will see him, his days will be prolonged, and the pleasure of God shall prosper in his hand. Out of anguish he will see light and he will find satisfaction through his knowledge. As the servant of many, he will make them righteous for he will bear their iniquities. Therefore, I will divide him a portion with the great and he will divide the spoil with the strong because he poured out his soul unto death.23 He bore the sins of many and made intercession for the transgressors so he was numbered with the transgressors. [See Matthew 8:17, 26:54, 26:63, 27:12–14, 27:30, 27:57–60, Mark 14:61,15:3–5, 15:28, Luke 18:31–33, 22:37, 23:9, 23:33–34, John 1:11, 12:38, and 19:9.]

Isaiah 54:13–15

13 All your children shall learn from God and great will be the peace of your children. In righteousness will you be established: you will be far from oppression for you will not fear. You will be far from terror for it will not come near you. If anyone stirs up strife, it is not because of Me. Whoever stirs up strife with you will fall because of you. [See John 6:45.]

Isaiah 56:7

7 I will even bring the children of strangers to My holy mountain and make them joyful in My house of prayer. Their burnt offerings and their sacrifices will be accepted on My altar for My house shall be called the private prayer place for all peoples. [See Matthew 21:13, Mark 11:17 and Luke 19:46.]

Isaiah 61:1–2

1 The Spirit of God is upon me because God has anointed me to bring good tidings to the oppressed. God has sent me to heal the brokenhearted; to proclaim liberty to the captives and release to the prisoners;24 to proclaim the year of God's favor25 and the day of the salvation26 of our God; to comfort all who mourn. [See Luke 4:18–19.]

Jeremiah

Jeremiah 7:11

11 Has this house, which is called by My name, become a den of robbers in your sight? "Behold, even I have seen it," says God. [See Matthew 21:13 and Mark 11:17.]

Jeremiah 31:15

15 A voice is heard in Ramah, lamentation and bitter weeping. Rachel is weeping for her children and refused to be comforted because they are not. [See Matthew 2:17–18.]

Jeremiah 31:31–34

31 "Behold, the days are coming when I will make a new covenant with the house of Israel and with the house of Judah. It will not be like the covenant I made with their ancestors when I took them by the hand to

bring them out of the land of Egypt—a covenant which they broke and I turned away from them," said God. "This is the covenant which I will make with the house of Israel after those days," said God. "I will put my law within them, I will write it upon their hearts, I will be their God and they will be My people. No longer will they teach one another or say to each other, 'Know God!' for they will all know Me, from the least of them to the greatest," said God. "I will forgive their iniquity and remember their sin no more." [See Mark 14:24 and Luke 22:20.]

Lamentations

Lamentations 4:20

20 God's anointed, the breath of our life was taken in to their pits. The one of whom we said, "Under his shadow we shall live among the nations." [See Matthew 26:56.]

Daniel

Daniel 5:14

14 I have heard of you, that the Spirit of God is in you and that enlightenment, understanding, and excellent wisdom are found in you. [See Matthew 11:19, Luke 7:36, and John 14:16–17.]

Daniel 7:13–14

13 As I watched in the night visions and behold, one like a son of humanity [*human being*] coming with the clouds of heaven. He came to the Ancient of Days and was presented before the Ancient One. Then to him was given dominion, glory, and a spiritual leadership that all peoples, nations, and languages will serve him. This dominion is an everlasting domain that will neither pass away nor be destroyed. [See Matthew 24:30, Matthew 26:64, Matthew 28:18, Mark 13:26, Mark 14:62, Luke 21:27, John 3:35, and John 12:34.]

Hosea

Hosea 6:6

6 I desired mercy, not sacrifice and the knowledge of God more than burnt offerings. [See Matthew 9:13, 12:7.]

Hosea 10:7–8

The king of Samaria will perish like a chip on the face of the water. The idol altars of Aven, where Israel sinned, will be destroyed. Thorns and thistles will grow up on their altars and they will say to the mountains, "Cover us!" and to the hills, "Fall on us!" [See Luke 23:30.]

Hosea 11:1

1 When Israel was a child, I loved him and called my son out of Egypt. [See Matthew 2:15.]

Micah

Micah 5:2–5

2 But you Bethlehem of Ephrathah, who are one of the little clans of Judah, from you shall come forth for Me a ruler in Israel whose origin is of old, from Ancient Days. Therefore God will deliver them until the time when she who was in labor gives birth; then the rest of his kindred will return to the children of Israel. He will stand and feed his flock in the strength of God, in the majesty of the name of the Eternal his God. They will live secure for now his dominion will extend to the ends of the earth, and he will be the one of peace. [See Matthew 2:6, Luke 2:4, John 7:42, and Ruth 4:11–12.]

Zechariah

Zechariah 9:9–10

9 Rejoice greatly Oh daughter Zion! Shout, Oh daughter Jerusalem! Behold, your ruler [king] comes to you. He is just and having salvation. Lowly and riding on a colt, the foal of an ass. I will disarm all peoples of the earth, including My people in Israel. The battle bow will be broken and he shall bring peace among the nations. His realm shall stretch from sea to sea, from the river[27] to the ends of the earth. [See Matthew 21:5, Mark 11:7, Luke 19:35, and John 12:14–15.]

Zechariah 11:12–13

12 I said to the leaders of the sheep merchants, "If you like, give me my pay, whatever I am worth but only if you want to." So they weighed out thirty shekels of silver as my wages. God told me, "Use it to buy a field

from the pottery makers for this considerable sum they value you at." So I took the thirty coins and put them into the Temple for the pottery makers. [See Matthew 27:9–10.]

Malachi

Malachi 3:1

1 "Behold, I send My messenger and he will prepare the way before Me. He for whom you are waiting shall suddenly come to the Temple of God. The messenger of the covenant in whom you delight; behold he is coming" says the God of hosts. [See Matthew 11:10 and Mark 1:2.]

Malachi 4:4–6

4 Remember the teaching of Moses my servant, which I commanded to him with the statutes and judgments at Horeb for all Israel. Behold, I will send you the prophet Elijah before your judgment day. He will turn the hearts of the parents back to their children and the hearts of the children back to their parents for if they do not repent I will come and bring judgment on their land. [See Matthew 11:14, 17:11, and Mark 9:12.]

List of Expanded Hebrew Scripture Quotes In Gospel Text

Gospel Text	Usual Quote	Added Text
Matthew 1:23	Isaiah 7:14	Isaiah 7:15.
Matthew 2:6	Micah 5:2	Micah 5:3–5.
Matthew 3:3	Isaiah 14:3	Isaiah 14:4–5.
Matthew 8:17	Isaiah 53:5	Isaiah 14:4.
Matthew 13:14–15	Isaiah 6:9–10	Isaiah 6:8.
Matthew 13:35	Psalm 78:1–2	Psalm 78:3–4.
Matthew 15:4	Exodus 20:12 (*part*)	Exodus 20:12 (*all*).
Matthew 21:5	Zechariah 9:9 (*part*)	Zechariah 9:9 (*all*)–10.
Matthew 27:46	Psalm 22:1 (*part*)	Psalm 22:1 (*all*)–5.
Mark 14:49	(*after*) "scriptures might be fulfilled."	Isaiah 53:7.
Mark 15:28	Isaiah 53:12 (*part*)	Isaiah 53:12 (*all*).
Luke 2:23	Exodus 13:2 (*part*)	Exodus 13:1–2 (*all*).
Luke 2:24	Leviticus 12:8 (*part*)	Leviticus 12:8 (*all*).
Luke 3:4–6	Isaiah 40:3–4, 5(*part*)	Isaiah 40:1–6 (*all*).
Luke 22:37	Isaiah 53:12 (*part*)	Isaiah 53:12 (*all*).
Luke 23:46	Psalm 31:5 (*part*)	Psalm 31:1–5 (*all*).
John 5:46	(*after*) "he wrote about me."	Deuteronomy 18:15–19.
John 6:45	Isaiah 54:13 (*part*)	Isaiah 54:13 (*all*)–14–15.
John 10:34	Isaiah 82:6 (*part*)	Isaiah 82:1–8 (*all*).
John 12:14	Zechariah 9:9 (*part*)	Zechariah 9:9 (*all*)–10.
John 12:38	Isaiah 53:1	Isaiah 53:2–12.
John 12:40	Isaiah 40:10	Isaiah 40:9.
John 15:25	Psalm 35:19	Psalm 35:20–21.
John 19:36	Psalm 34:20	Psalm 34:19.
John 19:37	Zechariah 12:10 (*part*)	Zechariah 12:10 (*all*).
John 20:9	(*after*) "he must rise from the dead."	Psalm 16:8–11.

Notes

Preface Notes

1 Usually, "kingdom of heaven" or "kingdom of God." The "kin-dom of heaven" is a family centered term coming from liberation theology in Latin America. The term *king* is a gender-specific expression that was completely dishonored by European royalty. It became a symbol of tyranny and corrupt feudalism to most people, especially Americans (see Declaration of Independence). Jesus was not a king and refused to become one but is kin to all people (see Matthew 25:34, Note no. 308). The kin-dom of heaven within includes everyone who receives the Light and is born anew spiritually with the faith of a little child. Jesus showed the way, for those who believed in him, to be adopted as a child of God through the Holy Spirit and the Sacred Father in the kin-dom of heaven within to experience eternal life now.

Referenced by Lasma in Matthew 13:24, "kin-dom of heaven." "Kingdom of heaven. A universal state, a reign of peace and harmony." George M. Lasma, *Idioms In the Bible Explained and A Key to the Original Gospels*, (New York, New York: HarperSanFrancisco, A Division of HarperCollinsPublishers, 1985) 53.

2 See Matthew 5:37.

3 Matthew 19:4. Jesus' words are in **bold** type, **"Let the little children come to me!"**

4 Usually "Son of man," *bar nasha* in Aramaic, which also means Son of Adam, human being or I. Here *man* means "humanity" and *mankind* means "humankind." Matthew 16:13 . . . **"Who do people say that I, the Son of humanity, am?"** The Son of humanity (the child of true Humanity in Mary 8:18) is a person who is transformed by the Light of God. Jesus the Christ is

a divine being who shows the way to follow him for all people to become the spiritual sons and daughters of God. John 1:12–13 "To those who received the light and believed in his name, were given the right to become children of God. They are born not of blood, nor the will of the flesh, nor the will of people but of God."

5 Also **drunk, drunkard** and **winebibber**.

6 For many people their "sin" is in not following the doctrines of people (synagogue or church leaders) even when they follow the Truth of God like Jesus.

7 The following gives an idea of the great variety of choices in the many translations of the gospels. The following list is from the Matthew 11:19 (last sentence) and Luke 7:35 (For Luke's version, "all" is added in most translations).

God's wisdom, however, is shown to be true by all who accept it. God's Wisdom, however, is shown to be true by its results. God's Wisdom is proven right by all who are Her children. God's Wisdom is proven right by its results. Sophia is justified by Her children. Sophia is justified by all Her children. (*Sophia* is the Greek name for *Wisdom* while Her Hebrew name is *Holkmah, Chokmah,* or *Khokhmah* and *Asherah*.) **Wisdom always was vindicated by all of its offspring. Wisdom has been proven right by Her actions. Wisdom has been proven right by all Her children. Wisdom is justified by Her children. Wisdom is justified by Her deeds. Wisdom is justified by Her offspring. Wisdom is justified by Her works. Wisdom is justified by its works. Wisdom is known by Her children. Wisdom is proven right by Her actions. Wisdom is proven right by Her children. Wisdom is shown to be right by the lives of those who follow it. Wisdom is shown to be right by what results from it. Wisdom is vindicated by Her children. Wisdom is vindicated by Her deeds. Wisdom is vindicated by Her offspring. Wisdom is vindicated by Her works. Wisdom sends forth Her children. Wisdom stands or falls by Her results. Wisdom will be justified by the events that follow.** For more on Wisdom see Appendix D, Proverbs 1:20-23, Proverbs 7:1-5, Proverbs 8:1-36 and Proverbs 9:1-6.

Matthew Notes

1 Descendant.

2 Jesus is the Son of humanity (man), Son of Adam, first born anew adopted Son of God, unique Son of God. He is also the Anointed, the Messiah, the Lamb of God, and the true seed of humanity. Christ is the consciousness of God in human beings, known to many prophets and some of their followers.

3 There are eighteen generations in Chronicles 3:10–16: (1) Solomon, (2) Rehoboam, (3) Abijah, (4) Asa, (5) Jehoshaphat, (6) Joram, (7) Ahaz, (8) Joash, (9) Amaziah,(10) Azariah,(11) Jotham, (12) Ahaz, (13) Hezekiah, (14) Manasseh, (15) Amon, (16) Josiah, (17) Jehoiakim, and (18) Jechoniah. The names that are missing in Matthew 1:6–11 are included.

4 Bride price; *Makhirta* in Aramaic.

5 Usually translated as "virgin," which would be *bethlah* in Hebrew, but here *alma* in Hebrew means "young woman" or "unmarried woman."

6 Jesus was only called Immanuel in Matthew 1:14. Matthew's words in parenthesis were added to the original text before Isaiah 7:15 of the expanded quote.

7 Or "curds."

8 "butter and honey" is referenced by Lasma in Isaiah 7:15, "Wisdom, harmony, prosperity." George M. Lasma, *Idioms In the Bible Explained and A Key to the Original Gospels*, (New York, New York: HarperSanFrancisco, A Division of HarperCollinsPublishers, 1985) 28.

9 Isaiah 7:14–15. Hebrew Scripture quotes are in *italic* and expanded Hebrew Scripture quotes are added to give fuller context to the often brief citations usually found paraphrased in the Four Gospels. See Appendix D: List of Expanded Hebrew Scripture Quotes. Most quotes like Isaiah 7:14–15 referred to in Notes are found in Appendix D. Some like Luke 4:18–19 and Isaiah 61:1–2 each have an additional quality not found in the other so both are available. The Gospel Verse and Note numbers are not in *italic*.

10 Also Magi, astrologers, or monarchs.

11 The star Sirius "Star of the East" is aligned with three stars called "The Three Kings" on the Orion's belt during the Winter Solstice on December 25. "Some say this star may have been a conjunction of Jupiter, Saturn and Mars in 6 CE" *Life Application Study Bible*, (Wheaton, Illinois: Tyndale House Publishers, 1996) 1400 Note 2:2.

12 A class of learned men who studied the law, teachers of the law or canon-lawyers, as in scribes of the Pharisees, see Appendix C, scribes.

13 "Beth—In proper names 'Beth-' means 'house' or 'place.' Thus Bethlehem means 'house of bread,' and Bethel 'House of God.'" *The Revell Concise Bible Dictionary*, (Tarrytown, New York: Flemming H. Revell Company, 1991) 86.

14 Micah 5:2–5. Also, see Ruth 4:11–12 in Appendix D.

15 Hosea 11:1.

16 Jeremiah 31:5.

17 "Nazareth sat in a hilly area of southern Galilee near the crossroads of great caravan trade routes. The people of Nazareth had contact with people from all over the world so world news reached them quickly. The town itself was rather small. The Roman garrison in charge of Galilee was housed there, making Nazareth despised by many Jews. This may have been why Nathanael commented, 'Can anything good ever come out of Nazareth!'" *Life Application Bible*, (Wheaton, Illinois: Tyndale House Publishers, 1986) 1324 Note 2:22.

18 This prophecy is not recorded in any of the known Hebrew scriptures. May refer to a "Nazirite," a "Holy One," or "wisdom keeper." "Nazirite: A person under a 'special vow, a vow of separation to the Lord' (Numbers 6:1). During the period of this vow, the Nazirite was not to cut their hair, touch a dead body, drink any fermented beverage, or consume any product of the grapevine. Requirements and procedures of this vow appear in Numbers 6:1–21. Samson is probably the best known Nazirite of the Bible (Judges 13:1–5), though Samuel (1 Samuel 1:11) and John the Baptist (Luke 1:15) were similarly dedicated." *Revell* 398.

19 Usually "kingdom of heaven," See Preface Note no. 1 about "kingdom of heaven."

20 Isaiah 40:1–3.

21 "John ate not 'locusts and wild honey' but 'garlic and byrony' or 'ramesones (broad-leaf garlic) and wilde-nepes.'" Matthew Black, *An Aramaic Approach to the Gospels and Acts*, (Peabody, Massachusetts: Hendrickson Publishers Inc., 1967) 294.

22 These are two of the sects of the Jewish religion of this time, and the Pharisees included the School of Hillel and the School of Shammai. Others were; "Essenes," "Zealots" (Fourth Philosophy), and the "Herodians"; see Appendix C. In Judaism, Christianity, Islam, Hinduism, etc., there are sects and divisions within each sect.

23 Also used are "generation of vipers" and "spawn of Satan." "It is an Oriental belief when a scorpion is conceived, its father dies and when it is born, it eats its way out of the side of its mother causing her death. A scorpion thus comes into the world without father or mother to protect or guide it and it is

exposed to danger from other hostile insects." George M. Lasma, *Gospel Light*, (Nashville, Tennessee: Holman Bible Publishers, 1967) 16.

24 "Baptism of fire. A thorough cleansing." Lasma, *Idioms* 50. See Luke 12:49–50 and Appendix B, Thomas 10, and Thomas 82:1–2.

25 Matthew 3:15. Frank Zimmermann, *The Aramaic Origin of the Four Gospels*, (New York, New York: KTAV, 1979) 53. "Replete" means "fill up."

26 Also "the Spirit of God came down upon him directly." Zimmermann 171. In the ancient Near East, the dove is the symbol of the Goddess.

27 This quote is a combination of Psalms 2:7 and Isaiah 42:1 with "beloved" added to Psalm 2:7 by Matthew and Mark. Mark 7:11 *"You are My beloved Son in you I am well pleased!"* The older version is Luke 3:22: "You are My Son, today I have begotten you!" The term *begotten* means "adopted" in this spiritual rebirth; see Luke 3:22, Note no. 30.

28 Also Satan, divider, obstacle, and prosecuting attorney.

29 Jesus, a man, became the first born anew Son of God, spiritually adopted by God through the Holy Spirit in the baptism by John the Baptist. In Matthew 1:18 Mary was pregnant by an unknown father and blessed of the Holy Spirit as are all children conceived outside of marriage. Many believe that the fertilized egg that became the human being called Jesus was miraculously conceived in Mary by the Holy Spirit.

30 Deuteronomy 8:3.

31 Psalm 91:11–12.

32 Deuteronomy 6:16.

33 Deuteronomy 6:13 and Deuteronomy 10:20. Usually "the Lord your God" but "the Eternal" is a more accurate term for *YHWH* than "the Lord" which is the English translation for the Greek *Kyrios*. *Kyrios* is a translation of *Adonai* which is a substitute term for unsayable, ineffable *YHWH* Who is more Eternal than just a Lord. See the fourth paragraph of Matthew Note no. 41 referenced to Matthew 5:16 and Appendix C, *Adonai* and *YHWH*.

34 "Being comforted by God's thoughts through God's messengers." Lasma, *Idioms* 50.

35 Isaiah 9:1–2.

36 Usually "poor in spirit" or "beggars in spirit." Lasma, *Gospel*, 24. "Blessed" can also be "Ripe with fruit [*spiritual*]" or "Happy."

37 See Appendix B, Thomas 69:1–2.

38 See an Aramaic version the Beatitudes in Neil Douglas-Klotz, *Prayers of the Cosmos*, (San Francisco, California: Harper San Francisco, 1990) 75–76.

39 Zimmermann 71.

40 See Appendix B, Thomas 32.

41 Mother-Father God. Usually "your Father in heaven." "Divine Parent" is the Sacred Father, the Christ in Every Child, and the Holy Spirit (Divine Feminine). The Sacred Father and the Holy Spirit are in Unity for the children of God and the creation. The children of God are made in the male and female image and likeness of the Divine Parent (*Elohim* in Genesis 1:27). This term is used for the usual "Father" as "God" unless both "Sacred Father" and "Holy Spirit" are used together in the same context (Examples are Matthew 28:19 and John 14:26). Christ is the consciousness of God or the God essence that manifests in every person and was fully realized in Jesus. God's role as Sacred Father to his spiritually adopted Son is emphasized in 2 Samuel 7:14: "I will be a Father to him and he will be a Son to Me." See Appendix D, 2 Samuel 7:12–17 for the context of this quote.

The same term for God, *Lord,* is also used for Jesus, the human being spiritually adopted by God as the Son of God. Divine Parent is the "Father-Mother God" in Christian Science; see Matthew 6:9, Note no. 70 for Mary Baker Eddy's use of "Father-Mother God." Divine Parent is "S/he" in Hindu thought for "All" or "Mother-Father God" where God the Father's masculinity is a feminine force. Swami Veda Bharati, ed., *Night Birds; A Collection of Short Writings*, (Kanpur, India; Himalayan International Institute of Yoga Science and Philosophy, 2000) 237 and 239.

From the beginning to now, the Divine Parent attribute or role of God nurtured, sustained, and healed the creation as the Good. God is also Absolute (without attributes or not manifested), All, the Eternal, Being, I AM, the Infinite, Unity, No Name, Transcendent, Oneness, Sacred Unity, One Being, One Reality, and the Source of the Source. The united Divine Parent is greater than the Sacred Father and the Holy Spirit, just as God is greater than the male and female image of God in creation, including the children of God. The united human parent, where the two spouses become one flesh and raise a child, is greater than two divided spouses who raise a child (Genesis 2:24 and Mark 10:8).

In the second century BCE in the Septuagint translation of the Hebrew scriptures into Greek, the translation for *Adonai* was *Kyrios* (*Kurios*) meaning; God, highest ranking, Lord, and master (father, son, brother, and uncle) of women. *Adonai* (Lord) was the male Hebrew substitute for the "the name of *YHWH* (*YHWH* is *YHVH*, Yahveh, Jehovah, or The Eternal) which was not to be pronounced except on certain occasions by the high priest. The Semitic word *adon* which means "lord, master, sir" developed into the Canaanite and Greek god Adonis and the Hebrew name used instead of *YHWH*; *Adonai*. *Adonai* is a title of deity (Lord, applied to *YHWH*, Lord God) while *Adown* is a royal title (lord applied to messiah in Psalm 110:1). Jesus is also called *Kyrios* but in this book, it is "Saviour" for believers; "Sir" for nonbelievers.

Some of the many Hebrew names for God: *YHWH* (also *YHVH*, the Tetragrammaton which is spoken on rare Jewish celebrations as *Ya*.) which means the ineffable unsayable "Name of God" or "The Eternal;" *Ehyeh-Asher-Ehyeh* which means "I AM that (Who) I AM" or "I will be Who I will be;" *Hashem* means the "Sacred Name" or "Ineffable Name;" *YHWH Elohim* and *Adonai YHWH* both mean "the Eternal God;" *Adonai Elohim*" which is a substitute for the *YHWH Elohim*; *Adonai* also means the "Compassionate One" and "Lord;" *El Elyon* which means "Most High God;" *Elohim* which means "God of the gods," "One Who is also Many," "Nature of God," "Creator of Nature," "Holy Spirit" (*Ru'ah Elohim*), "Divine Parent" (Genesis 1:27), or "Unity in Diversity;" *El Shaddai* which means "God Almighty" or "All Sufficient God;" and *El Elohe Yisrael* means "God, the God of Israel."

The Canaanite most high god is *El* whose wife is *Asherah*. *Asherah's* husband became *YHWH* in Hebrew until the 7th Century BCE. *YHWH* alone came to mean "*YHWH* (the Eternal) is our *Elohim* (God)," Deuteromomy 6:4, or the Eternal One. The Aramaic *Alaha*, also spelled *Elaha*, means "Sacred Unity" and the Arabic "Allah" means "Unity." The English *God*, German *Gott*, Spanish *Dios*, French *Dieu*, Italian *Dio*, Latin *Deus*, Aramaic *Alaha*, Arabic *Allah*, and Hebrew *YHWH* and *Elohim* are all names for the same God.

42 Moses gave the law in the Torah or "Instruction" (Pentateuch; Genesis, Exodus, Leviticus, Numbers, and Deuteronomy) along with the "Oral Torah" or oral interpretations (in the tradition of the elders) but the law is found all through the Hebrew Scriptures. The Hebrew Bible or Hebrew Scriptures is called "TaNaKh" which included: the Law or Torah; the Prophets or Nevi'im and the Writings or Ketuvim. See Psalm 119, the longest Psalm with 176 verses, which is a wisdom Psalm on the Torah and the love of God's law.

43 Also **dot or comma**.

44 See Appendix C, scribes. Usually "scribes and Pharisees" but Mark 2:16 has "scribes of the Pharisees" which reflects Jesus criticism of the leaders of the Pharisees and not all Pharisees.

45 Exodus 20:13. War and occupation are the domain of rationalized murder or Satan's paradise. Here demons thrive, grow, and bear bad fruit in the warriors and the civilian population of both those who destroy and those who support destruction. Jesus' gift is spiritual peace when you love yourself and love one another in the midst of permanent war and worldly peace. Twenty-first century war means destroying people's lives, land, air, water, livelihood, and culture so that their resources are easier to covet and steal. War is no longer about killing an enemy but killing everyone who may support, may be, or may become the "enemy." See Herod's collective punishment of infants and toddlers through mass murder in Matthew 2:13–18.

46 "'Raca' in Aramaic means to spit in one's face!" Lasma, *Idioms* 94.

47 Opponent in the law.

48 Unless proven innocent and even then you may not be released.

49 Also, until you have done your time and completed your community service in probation or parole.

50 Exodus 20:14.

51 "If you have a habit of envying, cut it out. Stop it." Lasma, *Idioms* 51. "The counsel of Jesus is to pluck out the eye of lust, covetousness, envy, and greed, so that the life might be clean and wholesome." Lasma, *Gospel* 36. This is a spiritual act and not a mutilation because the idea is to stop error in the beginning before it grows into a living hell.

52 "Stop stealing." Lasma, *Idioms* 51.

53 Deuteronomy 24:1.

54 Usually "fornication" as in the Lasma text; see Matthew 5:32 Note no. 55 below. "Like adultery, fornication is used figuratively to represent spiritual and moral unfaithfulness to God." *The Revell Concise Bible Dictionary*, (Tarrytown, New York: Flemming H. Revell Company, 1991) 228. Fornication is the adulterous union of the soul with the cravings of the flesh or sex with another outside of a spiritual union which includes rape and incest.

55 Adapted from Matthew 5:32. "But I say to you that whoever divorces his wife, except for fornication, causes her to commit adultery; and whoever marries a woman who is separated but not divorced, commits adultery." George M. Lasma, *Holy Bible: From the Ancient Eastern Text*, (San Francisco, California; HarperSanFrancisco for A. J. Holman Company, 1968) 955.

56 Deuteronomy 23:23 and Leviticus 19:12.

57 Under God's control.

58 Deuteronomy 19:21.

59 Also **evil, evil one**, or **Satan**. Lasma, *Gospel* 40.

60 "Do not start a quarrel or a fight. Be humble." Lasma, *Idioms* 51.

61 Leviticus 19:18 and Psalm 139:21–22.

62 "The Aramaic word *gmera* means perfect, comprehensive, complete, thorough, and finished. In this verse it does not mean perfect in character as God is perfect but perfect or complete in understanding. Jesus knew that no one could be perfect like God." Lasma, *Gospel* 43. See Appendix B, Thomas 3:4.

63 Alms that comes from your heart are gifts to share with the poor who can't give back and serving the needy, not for a tax deduction. Gifts to under-regulated tax exempt charities often corrupt the people working for them like when Judas stole from the early Jesus movement (John 12:3–6). Tithes are different from alms in that they go to support the synagogue, the church, the congregation, the temple, or other place of worship. See Appendix C, tithes.

64 Also churches, mosques, temples, and charity events.

65 Also TV shows.

66 "Don't advertise your giving." Lasma, *Idioms* 51.

67 "Inner heart or mind." Lasma, *Idioms* 51.

68 Another version of Matthew 6:6 **"When you meditate, enter into thy soul and when you have shut thy door of your external senses, pray to thy Father in secret."** Franz Hartmann, *The Life Of Jehoshua*, (Montana, U.S.A.; Kessinger Publishing Company, 1998) 113.

69 People who are not Jewish; like pagans, Syrians, Greeks, and Romans but applies to pretenders found in every religious, political, ethnic, social, or peace group.

70 Also **"Our Father in heaven"** and **"Our Father who art in heaven."** **"O Birther! Father-Mother of the Cosmos,"** is another version of this phrase from an Aramaic translation of the Saviour's Prayer [the Lord's Prayer]. Neil Douglas-Klotz, *Prayers of the Cosmos: Meditations on the Aramaic Words of Jesus*, (San Francisco, California: Harper San Francisco, 1990) 41. The Aramaic words for this phrase, ***Abwoon d'bwashmaya***, is discussed in of *Prayers of the Cosmos* (Douglas-Klotz Prayers p. 12–14.) Forty-one pages are devoted to the Saviour's Prayer based on the Aramaic in that book. The term ***Abwoon d'bwashmaya*** by itself has thousands of websites. In Mary Baker Eddy's version of the Saviour's Prayer, **Father-Mother God** also has the meaning of **Divine Parent**. "Here let me give what I understand to be the spiritual sense of the Lord's Prayer: **Our Father-Mother God, all-harmonious, Adorable One. Thy kingdom is come; Thou art ever-present. Enable us to know—as in heaven, so on**

earth—**God is omnipotent, supreme. Give us grace for today; feed the famished affections. And Love is reflected in love. And God leadeth us not into temptation but delivers us from sin, disease and death. For God is infinite, all-power, all Life, Truth, Love, over all, and All.**" Mary Baker Eddy, *Science And Health With Key To The Scriptures,* (Boston, Massachusetts: The Christian Science Board of Directors, 1906) 16–17.

71 Black 207.

72 Matthew 6:12. Lasma *Holy Bible* 956.

73 Also **evil, evil one,** or **Satan.** See Matthew 5:39, Note no. 59. Stated positively; **deliver us to be in justice.** Jesus embraced the side of justice, overcoming the oppression of the poor and downtrodden (especially women) by the worldly patriarchy. He showed and lived, the Christ and the kin-dom of God, within each person to help us come through injustice without fear; living with dignity as spiritually whole human beings. Also see Matthew 5:6–10, Matthew 5:38–39. Matthew 12:18–21 (Isaiah 42:1–4), Matthew 25:41, Luke 18:1–8, Luke 23:46 (Psalm 31:1–5), John 7:24, John 10:34 (Psalm 82:1–8), and John 16:33. In some translations **"for Thine is the kin-dom, the power, and the glory forever. Amen."** is a part of verse 13.

74 Matthew 6:1–18, see Appendix B, Thomas 6:1–5 and Thomas 14:1–3.

75 See Appendix B, Thomas 76:3.

76 Matthew 6:22–23. Zimmermann 37. Also for Matthew 6:22: "**If your eye be single . . .**" can refer to the spiritual eye (inner eye, eye of faith or third eye) in the middle of the forehead between the eyebrows as a focus concentration in meditation. In meditation the spiritual eye needs to be stilled by using a mantra (sound or short prayer) so that slowly you mentally release thoughts of your body and material attachments. This lets God or the universal consciousness of inner peace fill you up to build spiritual awareness and health. Psalm 46:10: "Be still and know I am God."

77 Syrian god of riches, wealth, profits, and ego or the piling up of outer appearances to define one's self; see Appendix B, Thomas 47:1–2.

78 See Appendix B, Thomas 36.

79 Usually **Gentiles.** Lasma, *Gospel* 51.

80 Also **brother's, neighbor's,** and **friend's.**

81 See Appendix B, Thomas 26:1–2.

82 "**Don't speak words of wisdom to fools.**" Lasma, *Holy Bible* 957.

83 Another Aramaic translation, "**Do not hang precious rings on dogs or adorn the snout of swine with your pearls,**" Black 201.

84 See Appendix B, Thomas 93:1–2.

85 See Appendix B, Thomas 1 and Thomas 2:1–4.

86 Also, "Then a man came to Hillel. 'I will convert' he repeated 'if you can teach me Judaism on one foot.' Hillel said to the man, 'What is hateful to you do not do to anyone else. (Rephrasing the verse from Lev. 19:18 "'Love your neighbor as yourself.'") All the rest is commentary. Go and learn it!'" Stephen M. Wylen, *The Jews in the Time of Jesus: An Introduction*, (Mahwah, New Jersey; Paulist Press, 1996) 153. See Appendix C, Hillel.

87 Repeatedly.

88 On their first attempt. An Aramaic version of verse "Narrow is the gate,": **"Subtle and delicate is the door that lets us float between the worlds, over our boundaries and beyond. Compelling and urgent is the way that shows the light connecting us with the energy of the cosmos. It is not a way for the feint-hearted, for those who do not use their full inner fire of passionate desire to find it."** Douglas-Koltz, *Hidden Gospel* 155.

89 Even after manure, pruning, and care.

90 Usually translated as **My Lord, My Lord.**

91 Also **preach.**

92 Hanson's disease is caused by a bacteria, although leprosy can mean one of several skin conditions.

93 A Roman officer commanding a "century" or one hundred foot soldiers which is a division in the Roman legion. In the same story in John 4:48, he was a royal government official serving under Herod Antipas who could have been attached to the Roman legion.

94 Also with **Sarah** and **Hajira** (Hagar), **Rebecca**, and **Leah.**

95 Zimmermann 47.

96 Until they participate in their own salvation. The kin-dom of heaven is not hereditary for the Jewish people or for the followers of Jesus.

97 Possessed with devils and suffering from mental diseases.

98 Isaiah 53:4–5. See Appendix D, Isaiah 53:1–9 for context.

99 See Appendix B, Thomas 42.

100 "Jesus knew what this man meant, 'Let me go and bury my father,'" if translated into English would mean 'My father is an old man, over seventy years of age. I have to support him until he dies.'" Lasma, *Idioms* 100.

101 "Usually '**let the dead bury their own dead.**' It seems more likely that the early copyists and translators confused the word *matta* (town) for the word *metta* (dead) and what Jesus meant was, let the town bury their own dead." Lasma, *Idioms* 100.

---

102 Pigs who are not possessed by demons do not stampede. See Mark 5:13, Note no. 30.

103 "However, in the Eastern Aramaic *hanaq* means not only 'strangle, hang,' but also 'drown, be overwhelmed by waves, be submerged in the water,' the only appropriate meaning here." Zimmermann 58.

104 Used as a bed.

105 See Appendix C, Publicans.

106 Social and moral outcasts can be people who are unhappy, unbalanced, corrupted, missed their mark, cut off from the Holy Spirit, and/or entangled in mental problems.

107 Hosea 6:6.

108 "New teachings mixed with old teachings." Lasma, *Idioms* 52.

109 See Appendix B, Thomas 47:3–5.

110 Also called a Zealot, see Appendix C, Zealot.

111 "Pagan practices." Lasma, *Idioms* 52.

112 "The lost tribes of Israel. Lost men and women." Lasma, *Idioms* 52. The lost out of any religion, group, family or gang. Now it is also the lost sheep of the house of Christianity.

113 See Appendix B, Thomas 88:1–3.

114 "In the Near East a traveling man is killed only when the bandits find money in his purse. This is done to hide the identity of the murderers in order to escape punishment. A man traveling without money has nothing to fear. If he should be in need and is met by robbers they will offer to help and let him go in peace." Lasma, *Idioms* 96–97.

115 "Peace be to this house and family." Luke 10:5. In Hebrew, *Shalom*; in Aramaic, *Shalama*; and in Arabic, *Salaam*.

116 Also **sand**.

117 "Have nothing to do with them; leave them alone." Lasma, *Idioms* 52.

118 "Avoid trouble and be pure in heart, sincere, and trustful." Lasma, *Idioms* 52. See Appendix B, Thomas 39:1–3.

119 Also **monarchs** and **tribal heads**.

120 See Matthew 5:16, Note no. 41 about **Sacred Father."**

121 Zimmermann 118. For another discussion, see Zimmermann 35–36 about Matthew 24:13. Usually **"those who endure to the end will be saved."**

122 A deity of the Philistines.

123 See Appendix B, Thomas 5:1–2.

124 Usually **him**. Also **Rather, fear yourself who is able to destroy both body and soul in a living hell.**

125 Usually **Gehenna**. Gehenna is a valley near Jerusalem where human sacrifices and then rubbish were burned. Also known as **hell**.

126 "To bring division." Lasma, *Idioms* 52. Jesus came to bring a spiritual peace in the kin-dom of heaven within you by the sword of truth. The temporary worldly peace brought by people through a sword or a gun will not deliver you to the kin-dom of God Who is Spirit. See Matthew 11:12, Note no. 136.

127 Micah 7:6.

128 "Willing to die, risk your life." Lasma, *Idioms* 52. Also, take responsibility for your actions.

129 See Appendix B, Thomas, 55:1–2.

130 Young children or young born anew children of God.

131 Lasma, *Holy Bible* 963. Also, "**the poor are sustained.**" Black 250. Usually, "**the poor have the Good News preached to them.**"

132 "Or as one frenzied/agitated by a spirit?" Zimmerman 51. Usually translated as "**A reed shaken by the wind?**"

133 Also **wealthy estates**. See Appendix B, Thomas 78:1–3.

134 Malachi 3:1.

135 A spiritual birth is greater than a physical birth; see Appendix B, Thomas 46:1–2.

136 The usual translation is Matthew 11:12 **From the days of John the Baptist until now, the kin-dom of heaven has suffered violence and the violent take it by force.** "The force that is mentioned in the verse does not refer immediately to the kingdom of God, where one would enter violently, or seize violently, but to the violation of the Torah laws." Zimmermann 131. The kin-dom of heaven is a spiritual reality not subject to violent people using force to get in or control it. You need to be humble like a child to get in.

137 See Appendix D, Malachi 4:5–6. Matthew 17:10–13, Mark 9:11–13, and Luke 1:17 agree that Elijah is John the Baptist, but John the Baptist disagrees in John 1:21.

138 "'He who has ears to hear will understand,' or 'will comprehend it.'" Zimmermann 154. Also Matthew 13:13: **Therefore I speak to them in parables because they see but do not perceive and they hear but they neither listen nor do they understand.**

139 People were called "sinners" who don't obey the human made rules and regulations of the scribes of the Pharisees. Jesus was a sinner to the scribes of

the Pharisees because he didn't follow their law and the scribes of the Pharisees were sinners to Jesus because they were hypocrites.

140 Also, **"Wisdom will be justified by the events that follow."** Zimmermann 49. See Luke 7:35 (in Preface), Preface Note no.7 for the many variations on this quote. Often written in the Hebrew Scriptures is, "The fear of God is the beginning of wisdom" (Proverbs 1:7, Proverbs 9:10, Psalm 111:10), but "The reverence of God" or "The fear of separation from God" is the beginning of wisdom. Jesus taught people to love and receive the love of God, the Son of humanity, and one another.

141 Psalm 8:2.

142 See Appendix B, Thomas 61:3.

143 Also "repose" and to "repose in silence" is another name for the "kin-dom of heaven" within you. See Appendix A, Mary 17:5–7, Appendix B, Thomas 50:1–3, and Thomas 51:1–2.

144 Also **gentle** and **patient**.

145 Also **lowly**. Ranking low in a hierarchy and the absence of egotism certainly describes a Saviour not a Lord or *Kyrios* as Jesus is often called.

146 "My rule is easy." Lasma, *Idioms* 53. Like yoga, in Hindu thought, takes you from your gross worldly body to your subtle spiritual body where you feel the Holy Spirit and realize God, so the yoke of spiritual discipline or the Christ of Jesus is required to guide you to realize God and to fulfill your own personal Christ.

147 "My religion is simple and easy. My demands are few." Lasma, *Idioms* 53. For Matthew 11:28–30, see Appendix B, Thomas 90:1–2.

148 A day of rest with prayer, meeting, and study for spiritual rejuvenation; special foods and certain rules apply between sunset Friday and sunset Saturday. See Appendix C.

149 Bread offering or showbread.

150 Exodus 29:32.

151 See Appendix D, Numbers 28:9.

152 Hosea 6:6.

153 Also My Breath and the Holy Spirit.

154 Another version of Matthew 12:20. He does not crush the weak or quench the smallest hope. He will end all conflict with his final victory. *Life Application Bible*, 1353.

155 Isaiah 42:1–4.

156 Another version is in Mark 9:39–40: **Jesus said, "Do not forbid them for no one who performs a miracle in my name can lightly speak evil of me for whoever is not against us is for us."**

157 "The Aramaic word translated as 'sin' could also mean that which misses the mark or falls into error as well as a failure or a mistake." Douglas-Klotz, *Hidden Gospel* 45.

158 "The Aramaic word for 'blasphemy' can also mean a reviling, or more literally from the word's roots, a cutting off, incision, irruption, or furrow. To blaspheme would be to cut oneself off from the object of blasphemy." Douglas-Klotz, *Hidden Gospel* 45.

159 An Aramaic version of Matthew 12:31: **"All types of tangled behavior, the missing and falling, the rips and tears—all the ways you cut yourself off, break your connection or disrupt the pattern—can and will be mended. Sooner or later, you will be freed from error, your mistakes embraced with emptiness, your arrhythmic action returned to the original beat. But your state cannot be mended or repaired, when you cut yourself off from the Source of all rhythm—the inhaling, the exhaling of all air, wind and atmosphere, seen and unseen—the Holy Breath."** Neil Douglas-Klotz, *The Hidden Gospel*, (Wheaton, Illinois: Quest Books—Theosophical Publishing House, 1999) 45–46. They will not be forgiven until they admit their error and ask forgiveness.

160 Often "in this age" or "in the age to come" is used here. Others believe that this refers to the "second coming" found in Revelations. The "second coming" is usually Jesus coming into your heart when, after a change of heart, you ask him.

161 Also **generation of vipers, brood of vipers,** and **spawn of Satan**. See Matthew 3:7, Note no. 23.

162 "A meaningless word; gossip." Lasma, *Idioms* 53.

163 Today, tonight, tomorrow, or any time.

164 Usually translated as "scribes and Pharisees" but correctly translated in Mark 2:16. When the scribes of the Pharisees saw that he was eating with sinners and tax collectors, they said to his disciples, "Why does he eat and drink with tax collectors and sinners?" Here, Jesus is criticizing the leadership of the Pharisees, not all "Pharisees." Just as in the Gospel According to John, Jesus is critical of the "Jewish authorities," not all "Jews."

165 Usually, **An evil and adulterous generation seeks for a sign . . .** , but Jesus wasn't speaking to the entire generation but the scribes of the Pharisees

(and their followers) whose words make them guilty. The basic meaning of adultery is when people worship other gods in the world, like material wealth (gold, money, and possessions); addictions (drugs, alcohol, and sex); or a person before God alone.

166 Jesus was in the heart of the earth for one full day, parts of two days, and two nights. Using sunset to sunrise as a day, he was in the heart of the earth two full days and nights and small parts of two days. Jesus was a human being who was also wrong about God sending him only to the lost sheep of the house of Israel, when a Canaanite woman furthered his glory and reach. See Matthew 15:21–28.

167 The African Queen of Sheba.

168 Also **demon, devil,** and **evil inclination**.

169 Besides ruins, demons also inhabit bars, drug stores, malls, and the Internet.

170 Zimmermann 40. Usually "**empty, swept, and put in order.**"

171 This saying speaks to the unclean spirit of craving (addiction or chemical dependency) in the twenty-first century for meth-amphetamines, alcohol, cocaine, heroin, opioids, and prescription drugs that cover up symptoms with grave side effects. Also, the gateway drug for infants and young children is refined white sugar, like high fructose corn syrup, which introduces this unclean spirit of craving. Chemically adulterated, highly processed fast food is a close second because a person's body knows that it is not getting nutrition from this type of food. Addiction or the compulsive use of drugs despite harm is different from physical dependence like in cancer pain management. Taking prescription drugs with serious side effects that mask symptoms which return without the drug are addressed in Mark 5:25–29 where a woman suffered under many physicians and only grew worse. Addiction can take the form of an attachment to destructive lifestyles like constant greed for money, wrath that harms others, and compulsive shopping for possessions that are not needed.

Often in a crisis, those in a living hell separated from God can change and start healing by welcoming Jesus into their heart, abiding in the spiritual path of another prophet, receiving the unconditional love of a friend, and/or following their own path of truth. Live a real (I AM) life nourished by the Holy Spirit in the kin-dom of God within you, instead of filling the unneeded cravings of your alienated body. Develop your own version of "the Christ," and become an unwelcome place for the return of the demon with seven more evil unclean spirits. Heal yourself with the Infinite Mind of God through your awakened human spirit. Believe in and value Jesus or your guide, commit to practice your faith in God, take inspiration from nature, pray, and live your life in hope. Follow the directions of healing people, including physicians who try to do no harm. Restore the temple of your body by following simple healing procedures, like regular washing with scripture, using positive thinking to replace negative thinking, breathing deeply through your nose, going through a cleansing or purification program, praying, loving and forgiving yourself, and receiving God's healing power directly or through others in a place of worship.

A productive way to deal with the emotional stress of addiction and even post traumatic stress syndrome is to practice the Emotional Freedom Technique (EFT) where you tap on various acupuncture meridians on the body, especially the head. While tapping on a sequence of meridian points you say, "Even though [*say your specific stress problem*], I deeply and completely accept myself." The website, TheTappingSolution.com is complete with instructions and videos for this free, easy to learn method of releasing your emotional blocks quickly without drugs and their side effects.

Practice prayer, yoga, tai chi, martial arts, dancing, or meditation for a spiritual awakening. There are a variety of meditation experiences available through different techniques from many spiritual disciplines. Experience a deeper level meditation through the process of a regular learned standard of practice for Self- and God-realization. This is possible by sitting up straight, closing your eyes, letting go of all your attachments, and focusing on your spiritual eye. Empty the thoughts and feelings of your mind and body to enter the silence to experience spiritual peace. Let still small voice of Spirit enlighten you with solutions to your problems. Persistence in the process will begin the healing of your whole self. Psalm 46:10: "Be still and know that I am God."

172 Spiritual kinship in the kin-dom of God inside and outside yourself comes before worldly kinship. Jesus may have visited with his family later when he wasn't so busy.

173 Teaching or wisdom stories.

174 See Appendix B, Thomas 9:1–5.

175 This is about having an abundance spiritually, not about the wealthy taking from the poor. See Appendix B, Thomas 70:1–2.

176 Genesis 1:26. The "Us" corresponds to a Hebrew name for God, *Elohim*, which means "One Who is also Many" and "Unity in Diversity." "The

word for God used in Genesis 1:1 is not YHWH, but Elohim (literally 'gods'). God, in the myth is not an individual, but a collective. God says, 'Let us make man, in our image, after our likeness'(Genesis 1:26). Elohim, then, represents a Godhead, not an individual deity." Richard J. Hooper, *The Crucifixion of Mary Magdalene*, (Sedona, Arizona; Sanctuary Publications, 2005) 74. See Appendix C, *Elohim*. "As a term for God, 'Elohim' appears far more times in the Bible (2,500 times to be exact) than the term *Yahweh*. Although Elohim is a plural form, it is usually singular in construction. Most uses of the word in the Bible, in other words, are meant to represent a single deity." Hooper, 75.

Genesis 1:26 Then God said, "Let Us make humankind in Our image, according to Our likeness and let them have husbandry over the fish of the sea, the birds of the air, over the cattle, over the wild animals of the earth, and over all the creatures that crawl on the ground.

177 Isaiah 6:8–10. Also **forgiven** or **saved** for **healed.**

178 Mustard is considered a weed in Galilee, it grows freely, spreads without being sown, and enriches the soil. See Appendix B, Thomas 20:1–4.

179 This is 1.125 bushels of flour, which produces about sixty loaves of bread, so the kin-dom of God is like a woman who wants to feed the village.

180 Psalms 78:1–4.

181 Or **close of the age.** The Age of Pisces 1 CE to 2150 CE.

182 In their own living hell.

183 Also **she.**

184 "A great truth." Lasma, *Idioms* 53. Also, see Appendix B, Thomas 76:1–3, Note no. 38 about a "pearl."

185 See Appendix B, Thomas 8:1–4.

186 The scribes were looking for a kingdom of God in the physical world of Israel led by a ruler and spiritual leader, while Jesus' kin-dom of God is a spiritual second birthplace in your heart now.

187 Herod Antipas, the Tetrarch of Galilee and Peer from 4 BCE to 39 CE, was the son of Herod the Great by his wife, Maltase. Herod Antipas was Herodias' second spouse and half-uncle. Her first spouse was Herod, the son of Herod the Great and his wife, Marianne II.

188 Leviticus 18:16.

189 Salome is the daughter of Herodias and her first spouse, Herod.

190 Two fish is the symbol of the astrological Age of Pisces, 1 CE to 2150 CE.

191 Morsels of bread. Zimmermann 41.

192 3:00 a.m. to 6:00 a.m.

193 Usually translated as "It is I" or "I am he" in the gospels, and this is *ego eimi* in Greek. Also, in the Septuagint translation (LXXM) of the Hebrew Scriptures into Greek, *ego eimi* is in Exodus 3:14 God said to Moses, "I AM WHO I AM. [I AM THAT I AM.]" And God said, "Thus you will say to the children of Israel, 'I AM has sent me to you.'" "I AM" is *hayah* in Hebrew which here means *YHWH*.

Also, in Isaiah 41:4: "Who has performed and done this, calling the generations from the beginning? 'I, God, am the first and I will be the last; I AM.'" See Appendix D for Isaiah 43:10 and Isaiah 46:3–4. "It may be remarked here that the name Jesus is the English version of Joshua, which in turn comes from the Hebrew Yehoshua. This literally means 'Yahweh saves.' Although it is not completely clear what precisely Yahweh, or the more traditional form without the vowels, YHWH, means, it may well signify I AM—the very name of God. The name Jesus would then literally mean 'I AM saves.'" Ravi Ravindra, *The Gospel of John: In The Light Of Indian Mysticism*, (New York, New York; Inner Traditions, Rochester, 2004) 74.

194 Lack of faith causes you to sink back into the world you left before you found Jesus.

195 From oral traditions that were given to Moses on Mount Sinai along with the written law, the Torah. See Appendix C, Oral Law.

196 Exodus 20:12.

197 Exodus 21:17.

198 A gift to God, see Appendix C, Korban.

199 Isaiah 29:13.

200 "Teaching, doctrine." Lasma, *Idioms* 53.

201 Sex without a spiritual union, which includes incest and rape.

202 "Sharing the truths of Judaism with the pagans." Lasma, *Idioms* 53.

203 See Appendix B, Thomas 13:1–8.

204 See Appendix B, Thomas 37:1–3.

205 "Upon this truth." Lasma, *Idioms* 53.

206 "Spiritual authority." Lasma, *Idioms* 53.

207 For more on Peter, the stumbling block, see Appendix B, Thomas 114:1–3 and Appendix A, Mary 17:3–4.

208 Take responsibility for yourself and your actions (karma).

209 See Appendix B, Thomas 67.

210 See Appendix B, Thomas 88:1–3.

211 "One who wishes to taste the taste of death, let them put on their shoes and sleep." Zimmerman 80.

212 His appearance was transformed to reveal his future glory.

213 Combination of Psalm 2:7, Isaiah 42:1 and Deuteronomy 18:15, 18. "You are My beloved Son [Psalm 2.7 with 'beloved' added by Matthew] in whom My Soul delights! [Isaiah 42:1] Listen to him! Hear him! [Deuteronomy 18:15, 18.]" Also, see Mark 9:7 and John 17:8.

214 Implied, so Verse 11 makes sense with Verse 12.

215 See Appendix D, Malachi 4:5–6. Matthew 11:11–13, Mark 9:11–13, and Luke 1:17 agree that Elijah is John the Baptist but John the Baptist disagrees in John 1:21.

216 "Epilepsy is quite prevalent in eastern countries and its victims are exposed to unfortunate accidents by fire or water. When this epileptic boy was seized with spells, he fell into the fire place. Such accidents are quite common because an oriental house contains one or several ovens, dug into the floor, for cooking of food and the baking of bread. The ovens are left uncovered and sometimes members of the household as well as strangers fall into them and are severely burned. This is what happened to the epileptic boy in his own home." Lasma, *Gospel*, 103–104.

217 See Appendix B, Thomas 48, and Thomas 106:1–2.

218 "A fish worth a shekel." Lasma, *Idioms* 54. One shekel = one denarius = about $50.

219 Also **sin**.

220 "Stop stealing. Stop trespassing." Lasma, *Idioms* 54.

221 Aramaic idiom, see Matthew 5:29, Note no. 51.

222 Or **abuse**.

223 See Appendix B, Thomas, 107:1–3.

224 Also **neighbor, sister, brother**, or member of your synagogue (congregation, church, mosque, or temple).

225 Deuteronomy 19:15.

226 Also **congregation, synagogue,** or a member of your group.

227 Also **heathen, Gentile,** or **nonbeliever**.

228 Usually, one talent is described as worth about fifteen to twenty years of wages for a laborer; that now would be about $50 per day. At $50 per day or $250 per week or $12,500 per year or $187,500 per fifteen years, times 10,000 talents, is 1,875,000,000. For twenty years, it is $2,500,000.

229 About $5,000, as a denarius is a day's wage for a laborer. See Appendix C, denarius.

230 Genesis 1:27.

231 Genesis 2:24.

232 Deuteronomy 24:1.

233 Adapted from **Matthew 9:9: "But I say to you that whoever leaves his wife without a charge of adultery and marries another commits adultery, and he who marries a woman thus separated commits adultery."** Lasma, *Holy Bible* 973.

234 Usually **eunuch** which means a castrated male but both male and female can be incapable of marriage. **Celibate** is also used and means abstaining from marriage and sexual relations but people who choose not to marry or be joined as a couple can still take care of their needs alone.

235 See Appendix B, Thomas 49.

236 Exodus 20:13–16.

237 Exodus 20:12 and Deuteronomy 5:16.

238 Leviticus 19:18. See Appendix B, Thomas 25:1–2.

239 "All inclusive, thorough in every way." Lasma, *Idioms* 54.

240 Lasma, *Gospel* 112.

241 Usually **a rich man.** "The Aramaic did not have on this occasion the usual *atir* but [The word in Aramaic meaning *meyattar.*] *meyattar* 'one who has abundance of things, who has more than he needs,' who has excess baggage, so to speak, which will prevent him from entering the kingdom of God." Zimmermann 61. Many people who are not rich have an abundance of things, but the attachment to these possessions is the problem that keeps one from the kin-dom of God.

242 "The Aramaic word *gamla* means *rope* and *camel.*" Lasma, *Holy Bible* 974.

243 "With great difficulty. (The rich man must give up something.)" Lasma, *Idioms* 54.

244 Usually **a rich man.** See Matthew 19:23, Note no. 241 above.

245 Regeneration or new world.

246 Refers to the throne of David, see Appendix D, 2 Samuel 7:13–16. Jesus' spiritual throne of glory is made of the Good News of the kin-dom of God within, his example, his resurrection, and the rebirth of the living dead to spiritual life. He rejected being an earthly ruler of the Jewish people, John 6:15, and was sent by God to bear witness to the truth, John 18:37, as kin to all people.

247 Not all Jewish people but those given by God to Jesus (the new Moses according to Matthew), most were still given to Moses and the prophets. See Luke 16:29–31 and John 17:6.

248 **"Many are called for work, but only a few collect fully for work done."** Zimmerman 50.

249 See Mark 10:35–41 for the sons of Zebedee version of this story.

250 Jesus taught about a spiritual kin-dom of heaven within and not an earthly kingdom complete with a male hierarchy.

251 Zechariah 9:9–10. "The Hebrews used the mule on such occasions, as a symbol of strength (1 Kings 1:33). An ass is a symbol of disgrace and humiliation in Eastern countries; it is never used by princes or nobleman, but only by the very poor." Lasma, *Gospel* 119.

252 Matthew 21:7 is from Lasma, *Holy Bible* 975. Usually "They brought the ass and the colt and they laid their clothes on them and he sat him on them." Jesus is mocking the attempt to have him be declared a "king of the Jews" through a form of ancient protest march. Jesus was sent by God to save the lost sheep of the house of Israel but his mission was expanded by a woman of Canaan (Matthew 15:21–28) so that he became the spiritual kin to all peoples rather than just an earthly king of the Jews.

253 "Power." Zimmermann 38.

254 Psalms 118:26.

255 Isaiah 56:7.

256 Jeremiah 7:11.

257 Psalms 8:2.

258 Jesus' curse in Matthew worked faster than Jesus' curse in Mark, which took place before the next morning. Matthew gave Jesus more faith than Mark did.

259 See Appendix B, Thomas 48, and Thomas 106:1–2.

260 Aristocratic leaders.

261 Usually refers to women but most sex industry workers of today could be included.

262 Others are settlers, indentured servants, refugees, slaves, peasants, poor people, and survivors—even today.

263 Matthew 21:33–41. "The listeners understood the symbolism: God, of course, is the owner of the vineyard, and the vineyard is Israel or the covenant, or more broadly, the whole creation. It is all that God entrusts to the leaders of his people and what is in question is their stewardship of this bounty. In the parable, the tenants are the leaders of Israel. They hoard the fruits of the vineyard for themselves instead of sharing the fruits as the covenant teachers, according to God's holy purposes. And the holiest of God's purposes, ancient tradition taught, is helping the poor, and the fatherless, and the widow, and

the stranger—all who do not have the resources to live in a manner befitting their dignity as creatures made in God's image, as children of God." From Bill Moyers, "A Parable For Our Time" 1. TomPain.com., http://www. commondreams.org/views06/1222-24.htm . See also Mark 12:1–12, Luke 20:9–20 and Appendix B, Thomas 65:1–8, Note no. 37.

264 "Truth which religious people rejected." Lasma, *Idioms* 54.

265 Psalms 118:22–23. See Appendix D, Psalms 118:19–29 for the larger context.

266 Isaiah 8:14–15.

267 Usually "**outer darkness**." Zimmerman 47.

268 The scribes of the Pharisees were usually against the Herodians and their allies, the Sadducees, but only Herod or Pilate could legally execute Jesus.

269 See Appendix B, Thomas 100:1–3.

270 An ancient hereditary priesthood; see Appendix C, Sadducees.

271 Deuteronomy 25:5.

272 Exodus 3:6. The other longer version: "I am the God of your mother and father, the God of Sarah, Hajari, Keturah and Abraham, the God of Ribah and Ishmael, the God of Rebecca and Isaac and the God of Leah and Jacob!"

273 For the resurrection the living dead, see the Gospel of Mary in Appendix A. There, the soul is resurrected from its attachment to the body to the realization, nourished by the Holy Spirit, of their mind (enlightened mind, nous, or human spirit) in the kin-dom of God within. Guided by their Saviour Jesus, they ripen through this process into a true human being ruled by their Christ, united with God in the present like Jesus.

274 The complete version is: ***You shall love Adonai [YHWH] your God [Elohim] with all your heart, with all your soul and with all your might.'*** Usually *Adonai* is translated as "The LORD," see Note no. 5 from Deuteronomy 6:4–5 in Appendix D. *Adonai* is a substitute for *YHWH* meaning "the Eternal" and God is *Elohim.* Deuteronomy 6:5 has "***with all your strength***" not "***with all your mind***" added, See Appendix C, *Adonai, Elohim,* and *YHWH.*

275 Leviticus 19:17–18.

276 The promised Messiah. The Jewish rulers and the high priests were also called messiah as in "anointed one." King David was anointed by Nathan as ruler and Aharon was anointed by Moses as high priest. The long awaited Jewish "Messiah" would be a triumphant ruler-priest on earth who would expel all foreigners from Israel and bring all Jews from exile back to Israel so that all

will live by the Torah in peace. A Jewish ruler was also called a spiritual "Son of God."

277 This "lord" was the "the Christ" in Spirit and King David's version of the messiah but the spiritual "Christ" as fully expressed in Jesus, was greater than the earthly Jewish Messiah and includes both female and male in all children (Sons and Daughters) of God.

278 Power of God.

279 Psalm 110:1. Putting your enemies under your control is making them your footstool.

280 From Mark 2:16. When the scribes of the Pharisees saw that he was eating with sinners and tax collectors, they said to his disciples, "Why does he eat and drink with tax collectors and sinners?" Usually translated as **scribes and Pharisees,** but Jesus was talking to the leaders, not the common people of the Pharisees. Other terms are "teachers of the law (canon-lawyers) of the Pharisees" and "leaders (misleaders) of the Pharisees." The chief priests and the high priest from the Sadducees also sit on Moses' seat. In the twenty-first century, it would be "The misleaders of the Christians sit on Jesus' seat."

281 "**Teacher**"; a Rabbi is a teacher of the Torah.

282 The consciousness of God in the Good News (Gospels) is within you.

283 They interpret the Torah so strictly that no one could obey all of it. Only hypocrites could be so strict (perfect). See Appendix B, Thomas 39:1–3.

284 "A corrupt person." Lasma, *Idioms* 54.

285 A tenth part. See Appendix C, tithe.

286 "**ye have abandoned the more precious matters of the Torah: justice, mercy, and honesty!**" Zimmermann 59.

287 "**fathers**"

288 2 Chronicles 24:20–22. Usually a different "**Zachariah, son of Barachiah**" from Zechariah 1:1.

289 And every generation.

290 Psalm 118:26.

291 See Appendix B, Thomas 18:1–3.

292 Also **trade group** and **kingdom.**

293 Zimmermann 35–36. For another discussion, see Zimmermann 119 about Matthew 10:22. Usually "**endures to the end will be saved.**"

294 Daniel 9:27, 11:31, 12:11. See Appendix C, abomination of desolation.

295 Daniel 9:23.

296 See Appendix B, Thomas 79:1–3.

297 See other variations in Matthew 24:4–5, Mark 13:21, Luke 17:21–23, Luke 21:33, Appendix A, Mary 8:7, and Appendix B, Thomas 113:3–4. The Gospels of Luke, Mary, and Thomas have Jesus coming within you for your rebirth in the kin-dom of God.

298 "Vultures are powerful nations and the carcass is a weak nation." Lasma, *Idioms* 55.

299 Isaiah 13:10.

300 See Appendix B, Thomas 111:1–3.

301 "During the persecutions and wars when a town is conquered by an enemy the young girl at the house and the young boy in the field are taken captive, but the old woman and the old man are left." Lasma, *Idioms* 101. See Appendix B, Thomas 61:1–5 for a different view.

302 See Appendix B, Thomas 21:1–10.

303 By agreement, they were given wages, shelter, meals, and benefits.

304 This will happen in their own living hell, probably in the darkness of the dungeon. See Matthew 22:13 and Matthew 25:30.

305 See Matthew 18:24, Note no. 228 about "talent."

306 Zimmermann 50.

307 Refers to the throne of David, 2 Samuel 7:13–16: "He shall build a house for my name and I will establish the throne of his kingdom [kin-dom] forever. I will be a Father [Divine Parent] to him and he will be a Son to Me. When he does wrong, I will punish with a rod such as mortals use, with blows inflicted by human beings. I will not take My mercy from him as I took it from Saul, whom I put away from before you. Your house and your kingdom [kin-dom] shall be made sure before you, your throne shall be established forever." Also, Psalm 89:3–4: God said, "I have made a covenant with My chosen one, I have sworn to David My servant, 'I will establish your offspring forever and build up your throne [rule] to all generations.'" Selah!

Jesus did build a house (see 2 Samuel 7:16 above) in three days, which is the temple of God that is in each person who practices their belief in Jesus and God. The kin-dom of God is within you forever in your eternal life that begins when you believe in Jesus and love God. Jesus' Good News, the example of Christ, and the resurrection of the living dead are the throne he rests on.

308 Usually **King** but Jesus was not a king and in the Gospel of Matthew (27:11), the Gospel of Mark (15:2), and the Gospel of Luke (23:3); when Pilate asked him if he was the king of the Jews, he answered, "You say so."

Pilate asked the same question in John 18:33: Pilate entered his headquarters again, summoned Jesus, and asked him, "Are you the king of the Jews?" Jesus answered, **"Do you ask this question on your own or have others told you this concerning me?"** Pilate replied, "Am I a Jew? Your own people and the chief priests have handed you over to me. What have you done?" Jesus answered, **"My kin-dom is not of this world. If my kin-dom were of this world, then my servants would have fought so that I would not have been handed over to the Jewish authorities but as it is, my kin-dom is not from here."** Pilate said, "So you are a king?" Jesus answered, **"You say that I am a king. The reason I came into this world is to testify concerning the truth and for this I was born. Everyone who belongs to the truth listens to my voice."**

The leadership of Jesus is described by "kin to all people" where the least of his followers are the last who become first. Jesus is a spiritual Saviour, a divine Teacher, and a leader as the kin of all people given to him by God, not the king of Israel. The commandment of Jesus is to love one another unconditionally as he loves us and he calls people his friends who become like their Teacher. This is not what a king would do and a more accurate image of a "king" takes up most of the American Declaration of Independence directed against King George of Great Britain.

309 Passover. This is a Jewish holiday celebrating the Hebrews' liberation from slavery in Egypt and the establishment of nation of Israel through this event of God's redemption. Israelites were exempted from the slaughter of the firstborn in Egypt (Exodus 12:21–28.) The festival joins Passover day with the seven days of the Feast of the Unleavened Bread. See Appendix C, Passover.

310 See Appendix C, Caiaphas.

311 The Roman silver coin, "Denarius" and the Greek silver coin, "drachma," are both worth a day's wage for a laborer or about $50 today. The total, about $1,500, is the price of an uninjured slave's life and the indemnity for a slave who had been gored by an ox.

312 Besides these twelve, Jesus had many other disciples that included women, some of whom probably served supper and ate with the twelve and Jesus. See Matthew 27:55–56.

313 Forgiveness that was bought and paid for by Jesus' blood on the cross to set us free.

314 Zechariah 13:7.

315 Of offering and death.

316 Usually "least you enter into temptation." Zimmerman 81.

317 An Aramaic version of Matthew 26:42, "Thy will be done": "**Let Your delight be, Your desire be, Your whole unfolding harmony be and move through me, as individual as a moment of pleasure, as cosmic as my place in the stars.**" Douglas-Klotz, *Hidden Gospel* 153–154.

318 Usually "**Are you still sleeping and resting?**" Zimmermann 74.

319 Malchus.

320 Isaiah 53:8–12.

321 Also **revolutionary leader**.

322 Lamentations 4:20. See Appendix D.

323 This "whole council" is the high priest's private council and not the Jewish Supreme Court or Sanhedrin as many interpret this. Trials during Passover, night trials, and single sessions for capital offenses were all illegal. The Sanhedrin would have to set aside the Torah to behave as this "whole council" does in Matthew 26:67–68. See Appendix C, Sanhedrin.

324 "Coming with glory, honor and victory." Lasma, *Idioms* 55.

325 Blasphemy only refers to *YHWH* not "Son of God," which is also a title given to Jewish monarchs when they are enthroned (Psalm 2:7). Jesus didn't blaspheme against the name of God but against the corrupt high priest's misconception of blasphemy. The scribes of the Pharisees in Matthew 9:3 also accused Jesus of blasphemy, but forgiving sins is not blasphemy but a violation of their mistaken tradition of the elders.

326 Also "lying."

327 Rome reserved the right to capital punishment except that Herod Antipas could also use capital punishment.

328 For use as korban (corban), which is an offering to God. See Appendix C.

329 Usually Jeremiah, but it is the quote from Zechariah that follows.

330 Rephrased from Zechariah 11:12–13.

331 From the Greek *su legeis*.

332 A "bandit" or "revolutionary" who led a rebellion against Rome.

333 Usually translated as "envy." "Nor do other words used in the various translations at Mt. 27:18, as 'spite,' 'jealousy,' 'malice,' represent the real motives that spurred Jesus arraignment. The motivation must be sought from another viewpoint. Jesus not only advocated an examination and renewal of Jewish ethical ideals and a reversal and change in Jewish law but he manifestly was a political danger to the state. Overtly Jesus was considered a king and this was the charge inscribed as the reason in the titulus on the cross." Zimmerman 62.

334 He is playing games to manipulate this crowd of Jewish authorities and shift the blame from the Romans, who had the authority to kill Jesus, to the Jewish people, through this group of corrupt leaders. See John 19:6, Note no. 144. Pilate was known for his brutal reprisals and disdain for local religious practices. In Luke 13:1, "Then some men came and told him about the Galeleans whose blood Pilate had mingled with their sacrifices." His soldiers reflected Pilate's true feelings in Matthew 27:27–31 after he had Jesus scourged in Matthew 27:26.

335 Washing hands is not a Roman custom but a Jewish one.

336 Also "lying." See Matthew 27:26-31.

337 Usually "all the people then answered," which condemned all the Jewish people for the death of Jesus, when Pilate and the Jewish authorities was responsible. This error was corrected in Luke after Jesus died in Luke 23:48.

338 The Romans attached pieces of metal and bone to their lashes for scourging captives.

339 Pilate's headquarters.

340 The color of the Roman warrior's cloak. In Mark 15:17 and John 19:2, the robe was purple.

341 Gall is a poisonous herb with a bitter taste.

342 Psalm 22:18.

343 Psalm 22:8.

344 Psalm 22 is a Psalm praising and thanking God. The first five verses give more context. Psalm 22:1–5: "My God, My God, why have you forsaken me? Why are you so far from helping me and from the words of my anguish? Oh my God, I cry in the daytime but You do not hear and I cry in the night season but I find no rest. Yet You are enthroned as the Holy One in the praises of Israel. Our ancestors trusted in You; they trusted and you delivered them. They cried to You and were saved, they trusted in you and were not put to shame."

345 The curtain was an eighty-foot-high Babylonian tapestry representing the visible universe. "Jesus, however, rendered the curtain obsolete, along with the old temple traditions. Indeed, it was his firsthand knowledge of the God who dwells within the human heart—the true holy of holies—that illuminated his opposition to every form of superstitious nonsense, especially the Old Testament belief in a vindictive God." Mark H. Gaffney, *Gnostic Secrets of the Naassenes*, (Rochester, New York: Inner Traditions, 2004) 202–203.

346 Mary from "Magdala," called Mary Magdalene. "Magdala is the Hebrew name of a fortified mercantile town at the west shore of the Sea of

Galilee, between Tiberias and Capernaum. The town was favorably located for different international trade routes and its strategic situation was also strong. The Greek name was Tarichea which refers to the drying and salting of fish. There was also trade in dyed fabrics and in a variety of agricultural products. The town was a hotbed of opposition against the Romans and a sanctuary for fugitives. It had a Hellenistic hippodrome, but also a small Jewish synagogue." Esther A De Boer, *The Gospel of Mary: Listening to the Beloved Disciple*, (New York, New York: Continuum Books, 2005) 118.

"I suspect that the epithet 'Magdalen' was meant to be an allusion to the 'Magdaleder' found in Micah, the promise of the restoration of Sion following her exile. Perhaps the earliest verbal references attaching the epithet; 'Magdalen' to Mary of Bethany's name had nothing to do with an obscure town in Galilee, as is suggested, but were deliberate references to the lines in Micah, the 'watchtower' or 'stronghold' of the daughter of Sion who was forced into political exile." Margaret Starbird, *The Woman With The Alabaster Jar: Mary Magdalen and the Holy Grail*, (Santa Fe, New Mexico; Bear & Company Publishing, 1993) 51. Micah 4:8 And you, Oh tower of the flock [Magdal-eder], hill of the daughter of Zion, to you it will come, the former dominion will be restored to the daughter of Jerusalem.

347 **Matthew 20:19: "Then they will hand him over to the Gentiles to mock, scourge, and crucify him and on the third day he will rise again."**

348 Matthew 26:32.

349 Remember; you know.

350 Usually "Jews to this day." The term *Jews* fails to distinguish between the Jewish authorities and the Jewish people who may not have believed the corrupt Jewish authorities. "This day" would be in the last part of the first century when the Gospel of Matthew was written. "To this day" is also at the end of Matthew 27:8. See Appendix C, Jewish authorities and Jews.

351 Or "they paid him homage." Usually "they worshipped him," but in Judaism (and in the later Islam), it is wrong to worship a human being as God. Jesus the Christ, the son of a builder who became the Lamb of God, built the temple of his body in three days to make real the kin-dom of heaven in the temple of your body where you can worship God in spirit and in truth. John 2:18–21: The Jewish authorities asked Jesus, "What sigh can you show to us, since do these things? He answered, **"Destroy this Temple and I will raise it up in three days!"** They said, "It has taken forty-six years to build this Temple

and you will raise it up in three days?" but he was speaking of the temple of his body.

352 Jesus, the Christ or the Anointed, is the Son of God; but the Christ, which is the consciousness of God, includes the Son of God and the Daughter of God as the Children of God. The Sacred Father, the Christ in Every Child, and the Holy Spirit as the Divine Mother completes the spiritual Holy Family. In the Unity movement, the Trinity is described metaphysically, "Trinity. God, threefold in Being. *Metaphysical.* The divine Trinity is known as Father, Son and Holy Spirit. Metaphysically we understand these to refer to mind, idea, and expression or thinker, thought, and action. Man is also threefold—spirit, soul, and body; spirit relating to I am, soul to consciousness (I am conscious), and body to manifestation (I appear)." Charles Fillmore Reference Library, ed. *Metaphysical Bible Dictionary,* (Unity Village, Missouri; Unity House, 2007) 664.

353 Usually "**the end of the world**" or "**the end of the age.**" The end is the beginning in the present where God is forever "I AM" here and now.

354 "An oral seal; faithful, sincere and truthful." Lasma, *Idioms* 56. "And when people join their voices together in worship to chant 'Amen" (Hebrew "May it be so."), their unanimous voice anticipates how all that exists finally shall be restored into a single, harmonious whole." Elaine Pagels, *Beyond Belief: The Secret Gospel of Thomas*, (New York, New York; Random house, 2003) 96–97. Another way to say Amen is to say, Om (*Aum*), which is the Cosmic Vibration of God or the name of God. "The deeper meaning of 'name' is a reference to Cosmic Vibration (the Word, *Aum*, Amen). God as Spirit has no circumscribing name. Whether one refers to the Absolute as God or Jehovah or Brahman or Allah, that does not express Him. God the Creator and Father of all vibrates through nature as the eternal life, and that life has the sound of the great Amen or *Aum*. That name most accurately defines God." Paramahansa Yogananda, *The Yoga of Jesus; Understanding the Hidden Teachings of the Gospels*, (Los Angeles, California; Self-Realization Fellowship, 2007) 29.

Mark Notes

1 "Son of God" was a later addition to earlier texts to reflect Mark's emphasis on "Jesus the Christ" being "the Son of God."

2 Malachi 3:1.

3 Isaiah 40:3.

4 See Matthew 3:4, Note no. 21 about his diet.

5 Combination of Psalm 2:7 with "beloved" added to "Son" and Isaiah 42:1. See Luke 3:22 and Luke 3:22, Note no. 31.

6 Also "kin-dom of heaven." "God's counsel, a reign peace and harmony." George M. Lasma, *In the Bible Explained and A Key to the Original Gospels*, (New York, New York: HarperSanFrancisco, A Division of HarperCollinsPublishers, 1985) 55. More on kin-dom of God (heaven) in Preface Note no. 1.

7 Simon, Peter, and Andrew were called before John the Baptist went to prison. John 1:40–42 and John 3:22–24.

8 Also demons, devils, and mental illness.

9 Leprosy can mean a variety of skin diseases.

10 Usually "feeling compassionate." Bart D. Ehrman, *Misquoting Jesus*, (New York, New York; Harper One—HarperCollins Publishers, 2005) 133. Jesus was a good judge of character and his feelings were justified by the rest of the story.

11 See Appendix C, scribes.

12 See Appendix C, publicans.

13 The Sabbath day goes from Friday evening at sundown to Saturday evening upon seeing three stars. See Appendix C, Sabbath.

14 Usually **Abiathar**, see 1 Samuel 21:1.

15 **Showbread** is a consecrated bread.

16 1 Samuel 21:1–6.

17 The Pharisees and the Herodians were usually adversaries, but if the scribes of the Pharisees really wanted to have Jesus killed, they would need to consult with the Herodians because only Herod Antipas or the Romans could inflict capital punishment. See Appendix C, Pharisees and Herodians.

18 Also **government**, **village**, and **business**.

19 See Matthew 12:31, Note no. 159.

20 Also "He has lost his mind" or "He is crazy."

21 They were concerned, confused, and trying to help him because people were saying, "He has gone out of his mind" (Mark 3:21). Also, "He has an unclean spirit" (Mark 3:30). Jesus' love for God was greater and came before

his love for his disciples who came before his love for his family. He also expects his disciples to love him more than their family (Matthew 10:37, Luke 14:26, and Thomas 55:1–2). If they stayed until after the crowd left, he probably met with them.

22 Also **mystery**.

23 Isaiah 6:10. See Appendix D, Isaiah 6:8–10 for the full context.

24 Usually "**desires for other things**." Frank Zimmermann, *The Aramaic Origin Of The Four Gospels*, (New York, New York; KTAV Publishing, 1979) 88.

25 For making bread. Zimmermann 57. Also "**under a meal-tub**" but usually "**under a bed**."

26 See Appendix B, Thomas 5:1–2, 6:5.

27 See Appendix B, Thomas 41:1–2.

28 "That which is . . . nothing and which consists of nothing, inasmuch as it is indivisible—a point—will become through its own reflective power an incomprehensible magnitude. This . . . is the kin-dom of heaven, the grain of mustard seed, the point which is indivisible within the body. And . . . nobody knows this point save the spiritual only." (From *Refutation of All Heresies*, 5.9.4–6) in Mark H. Gaffney, *Gnostic Secrets of the Naassenes*, (Rochester, New York: Inner Traditions, 2004) 204. The mustard seed can be compared to the Pinpoint of Light, which transforms into the entire universe as a meditation focus in Hindu thought to realize God.

29 "I have many wrong ideas; I am a hopeless case." Lasma, *Idioms* 55. A *legion* is a Roman attack force of about six thousand soldiers. The demons may be from Roman torture and the horrors of war or Post-traumatic Stress Disorder demons. PTSD is a normal reaction to a person's internal demons from being around or forced into the unjust killings of war and other horrible events.

30 "Since the story most likely arose on Palestinian soil or adjoining territory, and since presumably the native storyteller would have known that Gerasa was nowhere near the Sea of Galilee, our decision that, "Gerasenes" belongs to the earliest form of the story confirms the view that the original story of the Gerasene demonic did not include the incident of the pigs rushing into the Sea of Galilee. In other words, what has often been claimed on form-critical grounds (namely, that the pig incident is secondary) is likewise supported by our text-critical decision that the primitive story was located near Gerasa—from which not even possessed pigs can jump into the Sea of Galilee. Since the self-destructive pigs do not belong in the original story, we may

dispense with rationalizing theories about how the swine were panicked into stampeding by the paroxysms of the demoniac in the throes of his exorcism." John P. Meier, *A Marginal Jew: Rethinking The Historical Jesus, Volume Two: Mentor, Message and Miracles*, (New York; Doubleday, 1994) 651–652.

31 See Matthew 8:32, Note no. 103.

32 This league of ten cities on both sides of the Jordan River was mostly Greek.

33 "All in all, the linguistic oddities noted in the story, plus the possible Sitz im Leben ["setting in life"] that Annen sketches, incline me to the view that an exorcism performed by Jesus near Gerasa lies at the basis of the Gospel narrative in Mark 5:1–20. I readily admit, though, that there is no hard proof in the matter. Beyond this, I doubt that much can be said about the historical event; too many layers of literary activity and theological imagination have been superimposed." Meier 653.

34 Power from God. Also "virtue" which is used in Luke 6:19 and Luke 8:46 in place of "power."

35 An insult that implies an illegitimate birth, or they would say, "son of Joseph."

36 See Appendix B, Thomas 31:1–2.

37 Coat.

38 Herodias is the spouse of Herod Antipas's half-brother Herod and the granddaughter of Herod the Great. Herod is the son of Herod the Great by his wife, Mariamme II. Herod and Herodias had a daughter named Salome who married another half-brother of Herod Antipas named Philip, who was the son of Herod the Great and his wife, Cleopatra of Jerusalem. Herodias divorced her first spouse, Herod, to marry her second spouse, Herod Antipas. Herod Antipas was the son of Herod the Great by another of his ten spouses, a Samaritan woman called Malthace.

39 Usually translated as, "the leading men of Galilee." Zimmermann 88.

40 Or "at." "The Aramaic expression similarly means 'On/at the sea shore.' Probably the story received amplification, expansion and editing to make it into a miracle and even more pronouncedly so with the rescue of Peter, Mt. 14." Zimmermann 89. For *"by* the sea" See John 6:19, Note no. 53.

41 Usually "all the Jews."

42 Oral Torah; see Appendix C.

43 *Adonai* in Hebrew. See Appendix C.

44 Isaiah 29:13; see Appendix D.

45 Exodus 20:12.

46 Exodus 21:17; They are already dead to the blessings of the relationship.

47 This was true in the time of Jesus; but today, even more strict dietary laws along with repeated cleansing is needed to purify the body and be healthy for all the factory-made, genetically engineered, toxic, highly processed, chemically adulterated food that is eaten in the twenty-first century.

48 See for Matthew 5:21, Note no. 45, for the **"Thou shall not murder."**

49 Joining things that don't belong, like a spouse and one who is not their spouse or God and mammon.

50 Usually **fornication;** see Matthew 5:32, Note no. 54, on sexual immorality.

51 The usual lies and false witness, but TV and print advertising set the standard for deceit in the twenty-first century.

52 "Wicked, wickedness. Evil expressed in the harm a person does to others; criminal acts. All sin involves some violation of divine standards. However, the words typically translated 'wicked' and 'wickedness' focus attention on those sinful acts that violate God's standards for the treatment of others. Among these acts are violence, oppression, fraud, theft, extortion, and dishonesty. Thus, wickedness not only causes individuals harm but distorts the very fabric of society itself." *The Revell Concise Bible Dictionary*, (Tarrytown, New York: Flemming H. Revell Company, 1991) 558. Wickedness acts to destroy the underlying structure of society and includes domestic male violence (wife torture), child abuse, rape, torture, collective punishment, slavery, and war.

53 Sex and lust without love or responsibility.

54 See Appendix B, Thomas 14:5.

55 The people of Israel.

56 See Matthew 15:26, Note no. 202 about bread and dogs.

57 Aramaic versions of **"Be opened!" "Be opened to the healing power of Sacred Unity!"** and **"Expand! Give up your small identity as a person without sound."** Neil Douglas-Klotz, *The Hidden Gospel*, (Wheaton, Illinois: Quest Books—Theosophical Publishing House, 1999) 33.

58 Also Magdala or Mageda.

59 "I suggest that Mark's double story might draw on the early tradition of the seven and twelve disciples. Mk 8:14–21 underlines that the disciples do not need the leaven of the Pharisees or the leaven of Herod. Through Jesus they each individually, the twelve and the seven, male and female disciples, have their own basket of bread to share, to feed themselves (8:14–21) and to feed all the needy people (6:30–44; 8:1–10), even the non-Jewish (7:24–34)."

Ester A. De Boer, *The Gospel of Mary: Listening to the Beloved Disciple*, (New York: Continuum Books, 2005) 115–116 footnote no. 96. Jesus set the example of sharing, and all the people were inspired to share the food that they had but usually kept for themselves.

60 See Appendix B, Thomas 13:1–8.

61 An Aramaic version of Mark 8:36: **"For how does it help a human being to know diversity and abundance outside but lack an inner life."** Douglas-Klotz, *Hidden Gospel* 115. "Like breath-spirit, the soul-self is really a continuum that connects the 'heavenly' or vibrational aspect of being with the 'earthly' or particular aspect. The *naphsha* represents the aspect of the soul-self that usually feels itself more on the 'earth' side of the continuum. For most of us, our sense of spiritual guidance feels separate from our subconscious self, where many emotional dramas and traumas get played out. Just as Sacred Breath connects our personal breath to cosmic spirit, Sacred Sense or Hokhmah links our individual sense of 'I' to the 'I Am.' In this view, the journey of life asks us to fully realize our connections with Unity. We do not so much purge or empty our *naphsha* of all its problematic elements as we allow each element to find its place at the table of Hokhmah and Alaha." Douglas-Klotz, *Hidden Gospel* 116.

62 Jesus is teaching about the spiritual kin-dom of God that did come within people's hearts with the power to change their lives. Many scholastic theologians see Mark 9:1 and Mark 13:30 as failed apocalyptical messages because they didn't take place in the physical world. The spiritual transformation of people, knowing God directly through the Good News in the kin-dom of God within, spread rapidly with power. Then the early church fathers set up themselves as the saved person's leaders instead of the Christ within that Jesus gave to the saved person as their leader. Jesus' second coming here and now was moved from a changed heart to a change happening up in the sky and in the future through their doctrines of men.

63 Psalms 2:7 and Deuteronomy 18:15.

64 See Appendix D, Malachi 4:5–6. Matthew 11:11–13, Matthew 17:10–13, and Luke 1:17 agree that Elijah is John the Baptist; but John the Baptist disagrees in John 1:21.

65 Isaiah 53:3. For the larger context, see Appendix D, Isaiah 53:1–12.

66 See Matthew 17:15, Note no. 216, about falling in fire.

67 Aramaic idiom; see Matthew 5:30, Note no. 52.

68 Isaiah 66:24. There are always problems in the worldly life from inside and from outside.

69 Aramaic idiom; see Matthew 18:8, Note no. 220.

70 Aramaic idiom; see Matthew 5:29, Note no. 51.

71 Refining sea salt removes its quality; the flavor, and the minerals that satisfy your needs.

72 "Have good manners; good conduct." Lasma, *Idioms* 56.

73 Genesis 1:27. This is in the image of God which here is *Elohim* in Hebrew, see Appendix C, *Elohim.*

74 Genesis 2:24.

75 Matthew 5:32: **"but I tell you that whoever divorces their spouse, except for sexual immorality, causes them to commit adultery and whoever marries a spouse who is separated but not divorced, commits adultery."**

76 See Appendix B, Thomas 22:1–7.

77 Exodus 20:12–16 and Deuteronomy 5:16–20.

78 Usually **those who have riches**. See Matthew 19:23, Note no. 241. A person attached to their possessions includes the rich and wealthy.

79 See Appendix D, Psalm 49 for the problems of "those who trust in riches."

80 "The words, 'with persecutions' are mistranslated from the Aramaic, *rdopia* derived from *rdap* which means, 'to follow, to pursue, to persecute.'" George M. Lasma, *Gospel Light,* (Nashville, Tennessee: Holman Bible Publishers, 1967) 195.

81 See Appendix B, Thomas 4:1–3.

82 The Jewish authorities could "condemn him to death," but only the Romans or Herod Antipas could order capital punishment.

83 See Matthew 20:21–22 for the mother of the sons of Zebedee's version.

84 The Hebrew *Rabbi* means "Teacher," and the Aramaic *Rabbouni* means "My Teacher," but it also means "My Great One." 51 (Center Note for Mark 10:51) 1Lit. *My Great One, The Holy Bible: New King James Version,* (Nashville, Atlanta, London, Vancouver; Thomas Nelson Publishers, 1994) 1444.

85 Psalm 118:26.

86 Isaiah 56:7.

87 Jeremiah 7:11.

88 See Appendix C, Jewish authorities.

89 In John 2:14–21, Jesus cleanses the Temple at the beginning of his ministry.

90 An Aramaic version of "If you have faith in God": **Remain within yourselves—live in a place of rooted confidence in Sacred Unity.** Douglas-Klotz *Hidden Gospel* 27.

91 See Appendix B, Thomas 48.

92 Isaiah 28:16. Also **keystone**; the "rejected stone" symbolizes Jesus.

93 Psalm 118:22–23. See Vineyard Parable variations in Matthew 21:33–46, Luke 20:9–20, and Thomas 65:1–8.

94 The Gospel of Matthew, at the end of vineyard parable, clears up why this parable was against the Jewish authorities. Matthew 21:43: **"Therefore I tell you, the kin-dom of God will be taken away from you and given to a people bringing forth the fruits of it."**

95 See Appendix B, Thomas 100:1–3.

96 See Appendix D, Deuteronomy 25:5–6.

97 Exodus 3:6.

98 See Note no. 5 for Deuteronomy 6:4-5 in Appendix C. Usually *"the LORD"* and not *"the Eternal"* is a translation of *Adonai* which is a place name for the name of God, *YHWH*. Deuteronomy 6:4–5 is without *"with all your mind."* See Appendix C, *Adonai, Elohim*, and *YHWH*.

99 Leviticus 19:17–18.

100 The Christ of David, the messiah. See Matthew 22:42, Note no. 276 for "Christ" of Jesus, the Christ.

101 Put your enemies under your feet or control; Psalm 110:1.

102 Fund-raisers.

103 Widows often entrusted their property to pious men.

104 Daniel 9:27, Daniel 11:31, and Daniel 12:11. See Appendix C, Abomination of desolation.

105 Daniel 9:23.

106 The chosen people and righteous people in any religion or group. Those who need God the most can also be the elect.

107 See Appendix B, Thomas 113:1–4.

108 Pesach, the annual celebration of God's liberation of Israel from captivity in Egypt, which is conjoined with the seven-day festival of the Matzoh or Unleavened bread. See Passover in Appendix C.

109 This rose-red perfume was a favorite of the ancients.

110 Annoyed or irritated.

111 Jesus had many disciples, male and female (Mark 14:3–9 and Mark 15:40–41), who followed him besides the twelve mentioned in Mark 14:17

and in Mark 14:20 where Jesus pointed out one of the original twelve disciples out of all his disciples.

112 "Share my suffering. Make my teaching a part of you. Think of me when you celebrate Passover." Lasma, *Idioms* 56.

113 "Make my teaching a part of your life. Be willing to suffer for my truth. Think of me when you celebrate Passover." Lasma, *Idioms* 56.

114 See Appendix C, Jeremiah 31:31–34 on the new covenant.

115 "The Aramaic language provides only one word for 'blood.' This is *dama*, a word which, like the Hebrew word *dam*, must also stand for juice, wine, sap, essence. So Jesus may have been saying, this is my blood, juice, wine, sap or essence. The reference in the above sentence to 'fruit of the vine' emphasizes the multiple meanings of *dama*." Douglas-Klotz, *Hidden Gospel* 166.

116 Zechariah 13:7.

117 "The word for father (*abba*) can also mean parent, ancestor or founder." Neil Douglas-Klotz, *Hidden Gospel*, (Wheaton, Illinois: Quest Books—Theosophical Publishing House, 1999) 130.

118 Zimmerman 75.

119 Isaiah 53:7.

120 "The high priest's sanhedrin, as a private council, did not have to follow any judicial standards. It could meet when it wanted to and do as it wished. The sequence of events in the Synoptic Gospels may then be essentially correct. The High Priest called together his council in emergency session on the night of Passover, had Jesus brought to him, and sentenced him." Stephan M. Wylen, *The Jews in the Time of Jesus*, (Mahwah, New Jersey; Paulist Press, 1996.) 127. Often referred to as the "Sanhedrin" or the "Jewish Supreme Court," but they never assembled during Passover or at night. See Appendix C, Sanhedrin.

121 John 2:18–19: "The Jewish authorities asked Jesus, 'What sigh can you show to us, since do these things?' He answered, **'Destroy this Temple and I will raise it up in three days!'**"

122 "**the Power**" is a name for God. See Appendix D, Daniel 7:13–14.

123 Usually "blasphemy." "Mark's 'blasphemy' must be read in context: the Greek word need only mean 'insolence,' not specific 'insolence to God.' Above all, Mark is presenting the hearing as a shambles." Robert Lane Fox, *The Unauthorized Version: Truth and Fiction in the Bible*, (New York, New York; Alfred A. Knopf Inc., 1991) 290.

124 Fox 291. Usually "They all condemned him to be guilty of death." Joseph of Arimathea, a respected member of the council (see Mark 15:43), would not have decided that Jesus was guilty of death; so the high priest's

"whole council" was a private one, not the Sanhedrin, the Jewish Supreme Court, which met for judgment, not torture. See Appendix C.

125 A crowd who was friendly with the Jewish Authorities.

126 "In short, *qina'ah* cannot be translated by a single word; 'angry zeal' would be more appropriate. The translation should not, however, be 'envy.'" Zimmerman 63. See more in Matthew 27:18, Note no. 333.

127 Cyrene is a city in present day Libya, Africa.

128 This mix was to help relieve pain.

129 Isaiah 53:12. See Appendix D, Isaiah 53:1–12 for a larger context.

130 Psalm 22:1. See Appendix D, Psalm 22:1–5 for a larger context, which is not one of abandonment by God.

131 The curtain was an eighty-foot-high Babylonian tapestry representing the cosmos. Jesus shows us that the "Temple" is in your body and the kin-dom of God is within you. No need for everyone to pay a tithe tax for a cast of priests hiding behind a curtain just to realize God and live in the Spirit.

132 A time of limited activity and no food preparation from sunset Friday to Saturday evening upon seeing three stars.

133 This council was the Sanhedrin, the Jewish Supreme Court, and not the high priest's "whole council." See Mark 14:55,64 and Mark 15:1.

134 Mark 14:28.

135 Verse 8 was the original ending of Mark's gospel. "The Longer Ending of Mark," Mark 16:9–20 in double brackets, was added by the end of the second century. "The Shorter Ending of Mark" was added by the fourth century: [[Mark 16:21–22: "The women went to Peter and those with him and gave them a brief account of all they had been told. After this, Jesus himself sent out through his disciples, from the east to the west, the sacred and imperishable message of eternal salvation."]]

136 The seven demons, which are also mentioned in Luke 8:2, match up with the seven forms of wrath that the soul of Mary Magdalene went through under Jesus' guidance toward Repose or the kin-dom of heaven within. Appendix A, Gospel of Mary 16:5–13: **"the first form is Darkness, the second is Craving, the third is Ignorance, the fourth is the Fear of Death, the fifth is the Enslavement to the Body, the sixth is Foolish Wisdom of the Flesh and the seventh is Wrathful Wisdom. These are the seven forms of Wrath . . ."**

137 George M. Lasma, *Holy Bible: From the Ancient Eastern Text*, (San Francisco, California; HarperSanFrancisco for A. J. Holman Company, 1968) 1011.

138 See Appendix A, Mary 18:1–6 and Appendix B, Thomas 114:1–3 for more on Mary Magdalene's relationship to Peter.

139 Also **Gospel**.

140 John 3:18: "**Whoever believes in him will not be condemned but whoever does not believe is condemned already for not believing in the name of the unique Son of God.**" See John 1:14, Note no. 7 about **the unique Son of God**. John 6:65: He "[*Jesus*] said, '**Therefore I have told you that no one can come to me unless it is given to them by my Divine Parent.**'" Many are given by God to other prophets in other religions, many are enlightened to realize God by themselves, and many are righteous without a formal God. Luke 5:31–32: "Jesus answered, '**Those who are sick need a physician not those who are well. I have come to call sinners to repentance, not the righteous!**'"

141 "You will learn foreign languages wherever you go." Lasma, *Idioms* 56.

142 "Handle an enemy; overcome opposition." Lasma, *Idioms* 56.

143 "To be able to withstand any attacks against your character." Lasma, *Idioms* 56.

Luke Notes

1 "Theopilus" means "Lover of God."

2 See Appendix D, Malachi 4:5–6. Matthew 11:11–13, Matthew 17:10–13, and Luke 1:17 agree that Elijah is John the Baptist, but John the Baptist disagrees in John 1:21.

3 Usually "to make ready for the Lord a people prepared." Frank Zimmermann, *The Aramaic Origin of the Four Gospels*, (New York, New York; KTAV Publishing, 1979) 98.

4 Luke 1:24–25, Zimmermann 99.

5 "The translator chose the wrong meaning at this point, and translated *rabba* as 'great.'" Zimmermann 127.

6 "The translation of our phrase should run, 'a saintly man, a godlike person,' ['divine being' - Luke Note 8] not son of the Most High." Zimmermann 126.

7 Zimmermann 100.

8 "And proleptically even in v. 35 'son of God' may be explained as (four words in Aramaic) 'an angelic being, a divine being.'" Zimmermann 126. "Proleptically" means assuming a future act as already existing, like Jesus becomes the Son of God after John the Baptist's baptism when he is adopted by God, Luke 3:22.

9 Usually "Lord." Jesus is referred to as "Saviour" for the word "Lord" when the person is a believer, and God is referred to as "Savior" in Luke 1:47. Jesus is referred to as "Sir" when the person is not yet a believer.

10 Mary's speech (Luke 1:46–55) parallels the Song of Hannah (1 Samuel 2:1–10) where Hannah was the mother of Samuel.

11 "Strength and triumph." George M. Lasma, *Idioms In the Bible Explained and A Key to the Original Gospels*, (New York, New York: HarperSanFrancisco, A Division of HarperCollinsPublishers, 1985) 57. Also, Mighty Saviour.

12 See Luke 2:36, Hanna. The term "prophets" includes women and men.

13 See Appendix B, Thomas 17.

14 Zimmermann 102. Also translated as dayspring, daybreak, shining, shining one, rising sun, morning sun, dawn, and ray. Jesus is the "Christ" based on the narrower Jewish term "Messiah."

15 Usually "while."

16 Micah 5:2–4 and Ruth 4:11–12.

17 By dowry arrangement.

18 Leviticus 12:3.

19 Leviticus 12:2–8.

20 Exodus 13:1–2.

21 Leviticus 12:8.

22 Also Messiah or the Anointed.

23 The "law" can come from the "Torah" or "Law" given to Moses by God; Genesis, Exodus, Leviticus, Numbers, and Deuteronomy; from the prophets, the writings, or from the oral traditions and customs of the elders. See Appendix C, Oral Torah.

24 "Wrongs righted, injustices removed." Lasma, *Idioms* 57.

25 "Proud and arrogant people humbled." Lasma, *Idioms* 57.

26 "Crooked teachings replaced by the truth." Lasma, *Idioms* 57.

27 They will see Salvation or the Saviour.

28 Isaiah 40:1–5.

29 "Subtle and deceptive people." Lasma, *Idioms* 57. Also brood of vipers.

30 Means "adopted," because this is a spiritual birth, not a physical birth.

31 Usually, this quote is the same as Mark 1:11 and similar to Matthew 3:17. This is the older version of Luke 3:22, which is the formula that is used when Jewish royalty takes the throne. Jesus is the first born anew adopted Son of God, not a God born as a God or a king: John 18:37: "Pilate said, 'So you are a king?' Jesus answered, **'You say that I am a king. The reason I came into this world is to testify concerning the truth and for this I was born. Everyone who belongs to the truth listens to my voice.'"** See for Appendix D, Psalm 2:7, Note no. 8, about the adoption of kings in Israel. Jewish kings were also called "Son of God" as well as "Messiah."

"A place to begin is with textual corruptions that appear to suppress adoptionistic understandings of Jesus' baptism. One of the most intriguing occurs in early witnesses of Luke's account, in which the voice from heaven is said to proclaim 'You are my Son, today I have begotten you' (Luke 3:22). This is the reading of the codex Bezae and a number of ecclesiastical writers from the second century onward. I will argue that it is in fact the original text of Luke and that orthodox scribes who could not abide its adoptionistic overtones 'corrected' it into conformity with the parallel in Mark, 'You are my beloved Son, in you I am well pleased' (Mark 1:11)." Bart D. Ehrman, *The Orthodox Corruption of Scripture*, (New York, New York; Oxford University Press, 1993) 62.

32 Or Sala.

33 Deuteronomy 8:3.

34 Deuteronomy 6:13 and Deuteronomy 10:20.

35 Psalms 91:11–12.

36 Deuteronomy 6:16.

37 Usually "**He**."

38 **Good News** with healing as in Exodus 15:26. Also **Gospel** with healing.

39 Also **the acceptable year of God** or **a year of jubilee,** but many feel that this is not the same as the Jubilee year in Leviticus. The Year of Jubilee is explained in Leviticus 25:8–17. Every fifty years, there is a redistribution of wealth, the renewal of the earth, a forgiveness of debt, and the release of slaves, prisoners, and captives.

40 The text of Jesus reading of Isaiah 61:1–2 is significantly different from the text of Isaiah 61:1–2 in Appendix D, so both are included.

41 To remind his neighbors of his outcast status in the law as an illegitimate child by questioning the parenthood of Joseph. In Mark 6:3, the insult was "Isn't this is the builder, the son of Mary" to recall his illegitimate status.

42 See Appendix B, Thomas 31:1–2.

43 See Appendix D, 1 Kings 17:8–16 for the larger context.

44 See Appendix D, 2 Kings 5:1–14 for the larger context.

45 "Many insane were restored." Lasma, *Idioms* 57.

46 Luke 5:17 is usually translated "Pharisees and teachers of the law," but "teachers of the law" are the "scribes," and they are leaders of the Pharisees just as in Luke 5:21, where it is usually translated as "scribes and the Pharisees." The correct translation is in Mark 2:16 as "scribes of the Pharisees," because Jesus is very critical of the leaders of the Pharisees and not the common people of the Pharisees. See Appendix C, scribes, Pharisees.

47 Usually, "Who is this who speaks blasphemies?" Matthew Black, *An Aramaic Approach to the Gospels and Acts*, (Peabody, Massachusetts: Hendrickson Publishers Inc. 1967) 122.

48 Also includes healers, who practice alternative medicine, besides the usual physicians, many of whom are like the physicians in Jesus' time. Mark 5:25–26: "Now there was a women who had sick from hemorrhages for twelve years. She suffered much at the hands of many physicians, had spent all her money and was not helped at all but rather grew worse."

49 "Old and new wine." "Judaism and Jesus teaching." Lasma, *Idioms* 57. Jesus wasn't sent by God just to the lost sheep of the house of Israel or to patch up Judaism but to form a new universal spiritual religion within and among all people given to him by God.

50 Deuteronomy 23:24: "If you go in to your neighbor's standing grain, you may pluck a few handfuls; but do not use a sickle."

51 1 Samuel 21:1–6.

52 The prophets have authority over the priests, just as Moses did over Aharon and his sons.

53 Center.

54 Other translations are "filled with madness," "filled with mindlessness," "filled with insane fury," "furious," "beside themselves with anger," and "wild with rage."

55 Also "Judas brother of James." The Greek does not indicate son or brother. In Matthew, he is called "Lebbaeus, whose surname is Thaddaeus"; and in Mark, he is called Thaddaeus.

56 Zimmermann 109. Usually **"For you have received your consolation."**

57 See Matthew 6:1–4 and Appendix B, Thomas 6:1–5.

58 Also **robe**. "Easterners carry wheat from house to house in their robes." George M. Lasma, *Holy Bible From the Ancient Eastern Text*, (San Francisco, California; HarperSanFrancisco for A. J. Holman Company, 1968) 1022.

59 A real blind person today with training and a cane can teach another blind person, and they will not fall in the ditch, but Jesus means the spiritually blind and the ditch is error.

60 Zimmermann 109.

61 Usually **brother's eye**.

62 Not even poured concrete footings.

63 Coffin.

64 Black 110. Usually translated "In that very hour he healed," but the sense of the context is sooner.

65 Usually **"the poor have the Good News preached to them."** Lasma, *Holy Bible* 1022. Also see Luke 4:18–19 and Isaiah 61:1–2.

66 See Matthew 11:7, Note no. 132.

67 Malachi 3:1. See Appendix D for the rest of verse Malachi 3:1.

68 Jewish baptism, purification, see Appendix C, mikvah.

69 Usually "The Pharisees and the lawyers" or "the Pharisees and the teachers of the law" as in Luke 5:17, Note no. 46.

70 Possessed by an evil spirit or devil.

71 See Matthew 11:19, John 14:16–17, Proverbs 1:20–23, 7:1–5, Proverbs Chapter 8, Proverbs 9:1–6, and Psalm 139:7–12 for more on Wisdom.

72 "The usual gestures of Near Eastern hospitality (water for my feet, a kiss, and oil) are extravagantly outdone by the woman." Wayne A. Meeks ed. *The Harper Collins Study Bible* (New York, New York; Harper Collins Publishers, 1993) 1972, Luke 7:44–46 Footnote.

73 Isaiah 6:9. See Appendix C, Isaiah 6:8–10 for context.

74 Also self-deception, which results from your attachment to possessions or privileges.

75 Usually **pleasures of life**. Zimmerman 88.

76 See Mark 4:21, Note no. 25.

77 See Appendix B, Thomas 5:1–2.

78 Like one who "has understanding," "gets it," or "catches on."

79 See Appendix B, Thomas 41:1–2.

80 Your spiritual family is a priority over your birth family or any social group. Jesus would visit with his birth family when he had spare time from his spiritual family.

81 This story is in greater detail in Mark 5:1–20.

82 A legion is a Roman regiment of about 6,000 soldiers. The demons could be physical and mental problems from Roman torture or Post Traumatic Stress Syndrome from being in war.

83 Described as the bottomless pit for God's enemies, the prison for evil spirits in the burning depths of the earth, or the world of the dead disobedient spirits. Demons prefer to exist on earth in people, ruins, cemeteries, alcoholic drinks, addictive drugs, and swine (an unclean food for Jews and Muslims), rather than in hell.

84 See Mark 5:13, Note no. 30 about the swine story.

85 See Matthew 10:9–10, Note no. 114 for more about traveling.

86 Zimmerman 46. Usually translated as "desert place" or "solitary place."

87 See Appendix B, Thomas 13:1–8.

88 Your worldly self before you were born anew to become your true self.

89 An Aramaic version of Luke 9:25: **"For how does it help a human being to know diversity and abundance outside but lack an inner life?"** From Neil Douglas-Klotz, *The Hidden Gospel*, (Wheaton, Illinois: Quest Books—Theosophical Publishing House, 1999) 115.

90 See Appendix B, Thomas 88:1–3.

91 "Tents" or "booths." A portable sanctuary that embodied all that was necessary for the worship of God.

92 Isaiah 42:1 and Deuteronomy 18:15.

93 You become like the least as a child to enter the kin-dom of God and realize your oneness with everyone in Sacred Unity to become the greatest. See Appendix B, Thomas 4:1–3.

94 Usually **"You do not know what manner of spirit you are."** George M. Lasma, *Gospel Light*, (Nashville, Tennessee: Holman Bible Publishers, 1967) 251.

95 See Matthew 8:21, Note no. 100.

96 See Matthew 8:22, Note no. 101.

97 See Appendix B, Thomas 14:4.

98 Lasma, *Holy Bible* 1028. Usually translated as "**rejects.**"

99 Deuteronomy 6:5 without *with all your mind.* See Appendix D for the expanded quote of Deuteronomy 6:4-5 and see Hebrew Scripture Note No. 5. See Appendix C, *Adonai, Elohim,* and *YHWH.*

100 Leviticus 19:18. For the expanded quote of Leviticus 19:17–18, see Appendix D.

101 "Luke had mistakingly translated *zakutha*, probably in one of the verbal forms, to mean 'justify' instead of 'merit'." Zimmermann 128.

102 Hearing the word is "**the good portion.**" The realization of God through being Jesus' disciple is a higher priority than household chores or even family.

103 "Anything contrary to the truth, evil." Lasma, *Holy Bible* 1030. Also, "**and deliver us from the evil one.**" but this is not added to most versions. For an Aramaic version of the Saviour's Prayer (The Lord's Prayer) in Matthew 6:9–13, see Neil Douglas-Klotz, *Prayers of the Cosmos*, (San Francisco, California: Harper San Francisco, 1990) 41.

104 From the old Canaanite god; also Satan, the Enemy, Lord of the Flies.

105 Luke 11:19. Zimmermann 110.

106 Also **power of God**; see Exodus 8:19.

107 A similar version is in Matthew 12:30: **"Whoever is not with me is against me and whoever does not gather with me will be dispersed."** However, a different version is in Mark 9:38–40: "John said, 'Teacher, we saw someone casting out demons in your name and we forbad him because he didn't follow us.' Jesus said, '**Do not forbid him because no one who performs a miracle in my name who can lightly speak evil of me for whoever is not against us is for us.'"** Also, in Luke 9:50: "Jesus said, '**Do not forbid him, for whoever is not against us is for us!'"**

108 See Matthew 12:44, Note no. 170.

109 See Matthew 12:45, Note no. 171 for a discussion of the unclean spirits of addiction or chemical dependency.

110 See Appendix B, Thomas 79:1–3.

111 Queen of Sheba.

112 Also **in a cellar**.

113 See Matthew 6:22–23 and Matthew 6:23, Note no. 76. In Iridology, the iris of the eye reveals your body constitution through nerve connections to every part. This includes tissue conditions, inherent weaknesses, levels of health, and transitions that take place according to how a person lives. Among other signs, the iris will darken at the nerve endings connecting the unhealthy area of your body and as that area heals, the iris reflects this process by changing back to its normal color.

114 Zimmermann 40.

115 People give a tenth of the harvest as an income tax to the Levites in the Temple for supporting the theocracy associated with the Temple. They distributed a tenth of that to the priests.

116 Usually "**mint and rue and all manner of herbs.**" Lasma, *Holy Bible* 1031.

117 Luke 11:42. Zimmermann 28.

118 2 Chronicles 11:24–25.

119 See Appendix B, Thomas 5:1–2.

120 See Matthew 10:28, Note no. 125.

121 A copper coin worth one-sixteenth of a denarius, about three dollars.

122 See Matthew 12:31, Note no. 158, for blasphemy and Matthew 12:32, Note no. 159, about not being forgiven by the Holy Spirit.

123 See Appendix B, Thomas 63:1–4.

124 The length of your forearm, from your elbow to the tip of your middle finger, about eighteen inches.

125 Usually "**Do not fear, little flock.**" Taken from (Divine Parent for Father and kin-dom for kingdom). **Luke 12:32: "Fear little this decree for your Father has chosen you to give you the kingdom."** Zimmermann 113.

126 Give alms to the poor and needy, but for the true gift, subtract the amount of your tax write-offs. Also, **Luke 11:41: "So give for alms those things which are from within and behold, everything will be clean for you."** See Matthew 6:1–4 for instructions.

127 See Appendix A, Mary 10:15–16.

128 See Appendix B, Thomas 21:1–10.

129 Taken from (**employer** for **master**) Luke 12:43–44: **"Fortunate is the steward whom the master of the house finds doing his work conscientiously, for the master will appoint him all his possessions."** Zimmerman 130.

130 "Upsetting the order of the day; revolutionizing the world." Lasma, *Idioms* 58. See Matthew 3:11, Note no. 24 and Appendix B, Thomas 10, 82:1–2.

131 Zimmermann 124. Usually "**I have a baptism to be baptized with.**"

132 John 19:30: "When Jesus drank the sour wine, he said, '**It is finished!**' He bowed his head and gave up his spirit."

133 Micah 7:6.

134 See Appendix B, Thomas 91:1–2.

135 Luke 12:58, Zimmermann 115.

136 "Slain at the same time with their animal offerings." Lasma, *Idioms* 58.

137 Luke 13:9. Zimmermann 130.

138 About a bushel which makes about sixty loaves of bread, enough to feed a village.

139 Matthew 8:11–12 is similar.

140 See Appendix B, Thomas, 4:1–3.

141 "Shrewd and subtle person." Lasma, *Idioms* 58.

142 Usually **perfected.**

143 In Luke 13:33, "**I must do my work.**" Lasma, *Holy Bible* 1035.

144 "**one day soon pass on.**" Black 207.

145 Psalm 118:26.

146 Edema, a condition of severe fluid retention resulting in swollen arms and legs.

147 Lasma, *Gospel* 271. Usually **ass,** not **son.**

148 An Aramaic version of Luke 14:11: "**But you seek from little to become great and not from great to become small.**" Black 17.

149 Also **righteous.**

150 Usually "**compel.**" Lasma, *Gospel* 272.

151 Lasma, *Holy Bible* 1036. Usually "**hate,**" but Jesus sets the example in Matthew 12:46–50, Mark 3:31–35, and Luke 8:19–21 when he puts his spiritual family first before his mother, sisters, brothers, and father. He probably met with them later after he put his spiritual family first, but he didn't hate them—he loved them. John 15:12: "**This is my commandment: that you love one another as I have loved you.**"

152 Giving up your attachment to possessions is a key idea in Hindu thought for the realization of Self (soul) and God.

153 Luke 15:3–7; see Appendix B, Thomas 107:1–3.

154 The coins are usually a wedding gift, which are often worn as a ten-piece garland or headband.

155 Usually translated as "**sweep the house.**" Black 291.

156 Recklessly extravagant living or lavish, wasteful spending. This son is called the Prodigal Son.

157 Pods of the carob tree. Rabbi Aha, "When the Jew is reduced to eating the wretched fruit of the carob tree, then they repent." Bamidbar Rabbah, 13:4 in Louis Browne, ed. *Wisdom of Israel,* (New York, New York; Random House, Inc., 1945) 247.

158 Zimmermann 117. Usually this is translated as "**devoured your livelihood with prostitutes.**"

159 Has come to life.

160 "The Qur'an describes the soul as made by God with the capacity to do right and wrong and also the wisdom to recognize both: 'By the Soul, the proportion and order given to it and its enlightenment as to its wrong and its right. Truly he succeeds that purifies it and he fails that corrupts it!' (91:7–10). Because we are programmed to do some wrong, we can take comfort when we make a mistake to know that we are simply manifesting how God made us. I would even argue that by recognizing why we have made a mistake, we are already starting to manifest that part of our soul that God made for 'right.' If we can keep from making the same mistake again, we are also still engaging in 'right.' In making a mistake we also give God a chance to show us forgiveness." Asma Gull Hasan, *Why I Am A Muslim,* (San Francisco, California; Harper Collins Publishers, 2004.) 70.

161 Zimmermann 116.

162 Usually Luke 16:9 begins with "**I say to you**" or "**I tell you**" and ends with a period, not a question mark. Jesus would not tell someone to use their earthly wealth from being dishonest to secure eternal life in the kin-dom of heaven within. However, this quote without a question mark is a handy tool for church or charity fundraising from dishonest people.

163 Wealth, riches, materialism. You don't have to be wealthy as you can also serve mammon by being completely attached to possessions that you don't need. "New luxuries are invented every day and they become indispensable necessities for existence tomorrow but still there is no contentment. The gratification of desires merely begets new desires as long as the power to enjoy that gratification exists and thus the chains which bind people to matter are growing stronger every day, while the claims of the imprisoned spirit are laughed at and neglected. Christ, being looked upon as being merely a historical person, a thing of the past, is sent away to the garret, and that higher state of

consciousness which constitutes the true Christ in people is a thing equally unknown to the lay person as it is to the priest." Franz Hartmann, *The Life Of Jehoshua: The Prophet Of Nazareth*, (Montana, U.S.A.; Kessinger Publishing Company, 1998) 191. See Appendix B, Thomas 47:1–3.

164 Usually translated as "The Pharisees, who were lovers of money," but this is an untrue stereotype. From the time of the Maccabees until the destruction of the Temple about 70 CE, diverse Jewish religious sects flourished under Greek and Roman rule. Many Pharisees followed Jesus, even some scribes of the Pharisees. See Appendix C, Pharisees, Hillel, Oral Torah, Essenes, Sadducees, Sanhedrin, and Zealots for a larger view than this stereotype.

165 Usually "**everyone forces their way in.**" Black 116. It is not possible to violently enter the spiritual kin-dom of God found in your heart. God is always adding new scripture to light the way for humankind to develop spiritually. Jesus teaches that you shall not murder, but in addition, you shall not be angry with your sister without a cause. See Matthew 5: 20–21

166 Also, Luke 21:33: "**Heaven and earth will pass away but my words will not pass away.**"

167 See Matthew 5:32 for another version of Luke 16:18.

168 Or **sister**.

169 "In America and Europe laborers and servants work by hours. Even though they are required to be on duty they are given certain hours for rest, and when their work is done they are free to go home. This is not so in the East where servants are hired to work throughout the year and be at their task every hour, ready whenever their lord may want them. They are assigned to perform various duties, both at home and in the field, and they must not remain idle." Lasma, *Gospel* 285–286.

170 "Paid him homage." Lasma, *Idioms* 60.

171 Also **saved thee** or **healed thee**.

172 "The Aramaic version of Luke actually uses two prepositions to express a range of meanings beyond what the Greek *entos* (translated as 'within' or 'among') can offer. These words are *legue men*. The first derives from a word that means inside, inward, or the belly, and can refer to the viscera of an individual or a community. The second word can mean within, among, from, out of, at, on, or by—a range of relationships that all point to the image or definite outline of a being, its "mien" in the antique usage. Placed together, the two Aramaic words indicate a process that happens 'from inside out,' or as an inner community expresses itself outwardly." Douglas-Klotz, *Hidden Gospel*,

87. See Appendix A, Mary 8:7–8, Appendix B, Thomas 3:1–3 and Appendix D, Deuteronomy 30:11–14.

173 Genesis 19:26.

174 See Matthew 24:28, Note no. 298.

175 Luke 18:7–8. Zimmermann 105. "For faith in the next verse, really 'persistence, endurance.'" Zimmermann 105. The "next verse" above refers to Luke 18:8.

176 Exodus 20:12–16.

177 The highest rate in Jewish law.

178 Zimmermann 179. Usually "**to receive a kingdom.**"

179 Also **pounds**. A "mina" was worth about three months wages for a laborer or about $3,000.

180 "The Aramaic word *Kakra,* talent, is similar to the word *karkha,* province or city, as in some other versions. A talent was the largest coin, equal to many pounds." Lasma, *Holy Bible* 1042. See Matthew 18:24, Note no. 228, about talents.

181 Also **the ground** as in Matthew 25:25. Zimmermann 25.

182 Young donkey.

183 Reprimand or yell at.

184 Keep silent.

185 Isaiah 56:7.

186 Jeremiah 7:11.

187 Psalm 118:22. Jesus explains in Matthew 21:43: "**Therefore, I tell you, the kin-dom of God will be taken away from you and given to people bringing forth fruits thereof.**"

188 Isaiah 8:14–15. See Vineyard Parable variations in Matthew 21:33–46, Mark 12:2–12, and Thomas 65:1–8.

189 Pontius Pilate, the Roman governor who had the authority to use capital punishment.

190 Denarius.

191 See Appendix B, Thomas 100:1–4.

192 Exodus 3:6.

193 Psalm 110:1.

194 Collection boxes in the Temple near the Court of the Women.

195 Mite or lepton in Greek. This is the least valuable coin used, worth less than a penny.

196 "adorned with beautiful and heavy stones." Zimmermann 117.

197 Lasma, *Holy Bible* 1045.

198 Usually translated as **"In your patience you possesses your soul."** Zimmermann 118.

199 Deuteronomy 32:35, Hosea 9:7.

200 Zimmermann 121. Usually **"Look at the fig tree and all the trees."**

201 An Aramaic version of Luke 21:33 is **"Heaven and earth, wave and particle, individual and community may cross boundaries, go beyond themselves and transgress their limits: form may pass into light and light back to form. But the story I am telling you will not: the fullest expression of the purpose of my life, from beginning to end will continue."** Douglas-Klotz, *Hidden Gospel* 99. Luke 16:17: **"It is still easier for heaven and earth to pass away than for one letter of the Torah to pass away."**

202 Lasma, *Holy Bible* 1046.

203 Some omit part of Luke 22:19–20 as a later addition. Luke 22:19–20 **" . . . which is given for you; do this in memory of me."** Likewise, he took his cup after supper, saying, **"This cup which is poured out for you is the new covenant in my blood which will be shed for you.**

204 Friends of the people.

205 "Test you and purify you." Lasma, *Idioms* 58.

206 Learn self-defense and practice nonviolence like Jesus. In Luke 22:38, his disciples showed their misunderstanding by giving Jesus two swords, which he rejected as futile.

207 Isaiah 53:12.

208 Usually **"It is enough."** "The reply is couched in the familiar rhetorical trope of the talhin (1) Two swords will be futile. (2) It is futile to talk to you. You do not understand. (3) Resistance will be of no avail as the end is near." Zimmermann 137. The phrase "trope of the talhin (cantalation)" means "style of the chant" or "recite in musical terms."

209 Zimmermann 81.

210 Luke 22:43–44 were added later.

211 More like being in a struggle to be ready than agony.

212 Zimmermann 119.

213 Luke 22:45. Zimmermann 133.

214 Caiaphas.

215 This was a private council, not the Sanhedrin or Jewish Supreme Court that many commentaries suggest. "The court could not convict on the day of the trial. They had to hear evidence one day and vote on the next day. Jewish courts did not meet on festival or Sabbath days according to the Mishnah. Since a capital case required a two-day trial, no capital trial was initiated on

the eve of a festival. This contradicts both the synoptics' timetable and John's." Stephen M. Wylen, *The Jews in the Time of Jesus: An Introduction*, (Mahwah, New Jersey: Paulist Press, 1996) 125–126. See Appendix C, Sanhedrin.

216 "Trust and power." Lasma, *Idioms* 58.

217 Jesus avoided being a king in John 6:14–15 and John 18:33–37.

218 In Luke 13:1, "Then some men came and told him about the Galileans whose blood Pilate had mingled with their sacrifices."

219 Flogging with the Roman scourge (scraps of metal and bone are embedded in the thongs) can lead to death and is used before crucifying to hasten hang time. Herod had already punished him, and Pilate wants to flog him, when they both claim him to be innocent.

220 Pilate succeeded in getting rid of Jesus and blaming the Jewish people for it because the crowd was selected by the chief priests. Luke separates the Jewish people from the Jewish authorities in Luke 23:48. As a political revolutionary attacking Temple business, Jesus was a threat to Rome and the Jewish authorities, but Pilate played the game to shift the blame from himself. See John 19:6, Note no. 144, for more on Pilate's character.

221 The Jewish authorities' will was also Pilate's will as he ordered Jesus crucifixion, got to have him flogged (Verse 16 and 22), became friends with Herod, and got rid of Jesus, while the Jewish people—even now—still take the blame.

222 Usually "to carry it behind Jesus." Lasma, *Holy Bible* 1049.

223 Those days have arrived in the overpopulated twenty-first century with over seven billion people.

224 Hosea 10:8.

225 "Green tree is an innocent person and a dry tree is a guilty person." Lasma, *Idioms* 58.

226 The Skull.

227 Some ancient authorities omit this part of Luke 23:34.

228 Luke 23:43, Lasma, *Gospel* 304. Paradise. "A Persian word for a beautiful garden; a place of harmony and tranquility." Lasma, *Idioms* 59.

229 Veil. A Babylonian tapestry representing the visible universe.

230 Usually "**Father, into Your hands I commit my spirit.**" Psalm 31:1–5.

231 Joseph of Arimathea was a member of the Sanhedrin, the Jewish Supreme Court. See Mark 14:55, Note no. 120, about the whole council and Appendix C, Sanhedrin.

232 Exodus 20:10.

233 "and there were other women with them." Lasma, *Holy Bible* 1050.

234 Also foolish talk, fairy tale, and nonsense.

235 Luke 24:12 was not included in other texts and believed to have been added later.

236 Also **"Peace be with you; it is I; do not be afraid."** Lasma, *Holy Bible* 1051.

237 Also **Remission.**

238 Also **Nations.**

239 **The Holy Spirit** or **the Comforter**.

240 Some ancient authorities add "and was carried up to heaven."

241 Some ancient authorities add "they worshipped him and."

John Notes

1 The "Word" in Greek is *Logos* which means the divine reason and creative order principle that controls and develops the universe.

2 Usually "he" but the Word manifested as the Christ or the "consciousness of God" is neither male or female. Jesus was the human person who became the Christ. Jesus the Christ was sent by God to deliver the Word through the Good News into people's hearts to reopen the kin-dom of God within them. This is the renewed "commandment" or "word" in Deuteronomy 30:11–14. "Surely this commandment which I command you this day is neither hidden from you nor is it far off. It is not in the sky that you would say, 'Who will go up for us up in the sky and bring it to us, that we may hear it and do it?' Neither is it beyond the sea that you would say, 'Who will go over the sea and bring it to us that we may hear it and do it?' The word is very near you, in your mouth and in your heart, that you may do it."

3 John 1:1–3. Another version of this beginning of John 1:1–3 "In the beginning was the Lamb, the Lamb was with God and the Lamb was God. He [The Lamb] had been in the beginning with God. The Lamb became a man and he dwelt among us." Frank Zimmermann, *The Aramaic Origin of the Four Gospels*, (New York, New York; KTAV Publishing, 1979.) 170. The Aramaic word "meaning both 'lamb' and 'child, child of God' was played upon." Zimmermann 169.

4 "He" is Jesus the Christ, the true Light.

5 See Appendix B, Thomas 28:1–4.

6 This happened when God spoke in Luke 3:22: "the Holy Spirit descended upon him in bodily form like a dove and a voice from heaven said, *'You are My Son, today I have begotten [adopted] you!'"* This is a formula for the adoption of a ruler when they take the throne; see Appendix D, Psalms 2:7, Note no. 8.

7 Usually translated as "The only begotten Son," which comes from Psalms 2:7. The choice is between the unique Son and the unique God. "The Gospel of John uses the phrase 'the unique Son' (sometimes mistranslated as 'only begotten Son') on several other occasions (see John 3:16, 18); nowhere else does it speak of Christ as 'the unique God.' Moreover, what would it even *mean* to call Christ that? The term *unique* in Greek means 'one of a kind.' There can only be one who is one of a kind. The term *unique God* must refer to God the Father himself—otherwise he is not unique. But if the term refers to the Father, how can it be used of the Son?" Bart D. Ehrman, *Misquoting Jesus*, New York, New York; Harper One—HarperCollins Publishers, 2005) 162.

8 See Matthew 5:16, Note no. 41, on Divine Parent.

9 Also "ahead of me."

10 Torah; see Appendix C, Torah and Oral Torah.

11 Usually "The only begotten Son." "The first one who recognized the fatherhood of God. The only God-like man; hence, a spiritual son of God." George M. Lasma, *Idioms In the Bible Explained and A Key to the Original Gospels*, (New York, New York: HarperSanFrancisco, A Division of HarperCollinsPublishers, 1985) 59.

12 Matthew 5:8: **"Blessed are the pure in heart, for they shall see God."**

13 See Appendix D, Malachi 4:5–6. Matthew 11:11–13, Matthew 17:10–13, Mark 9:11–13, and Luke 1:17 all agree that Elijah is John the Baptist.

14 Isaiah 40:3.

15 "Dedicated to God, innocent and blameless." Lasma, *Idioms* 59. "Jesus did not come to eat the Paschal Lamb: he is the Paschal Lamb. He did not come to save the Jewish people. He came to save mankind. He is the Lamb who will be sacrificed, and whose blood will be shed to redeem humanity. So important did the author of the Fourth Gospel consider Jesus in this role of the lamb and its sacrifice, that he focuses on this motif at the crucifixion itself, where Jesus did not have his bones broken John 19:36 (as he was a political offender). In contrast, the thieves had their legs broken. This was of prime significance to the Johannine narrator. Jesus as the Paschel Lamb was intact, not disqualified by a broken bone. He was symbolically the true Paschel Lamb, as the Scripture has it, 'A bone ye shall not break in it' Exodus 12:46; Numbers 9:12. It is this motif that unites the beginning and the end of this Gospel. Such an unblemished sacrifice now becomes acceptable to God." Zimmermann 169.

16 "The proof that the writer of this Gospel wished to impress his readers with this concept of Jesus as a lamb, is brought home to us immediately after the prologue, and his emphasis on the lamb in John 1:36. John sees Jesus on the street coming to him, and proclaims in sudden designation, 'Behold the Lamb of God.'" Zimmermann 169–170.

17 Jesus, the Lamb of God (John 1:36), is a spiritual Messiah, the Christ.

18 *Cephas* or *Keptar* is the Aramaic word for "stone." "Peter" comes from *Petra*, the Greek word for "rock."

19 See Matthew 2:23, Note no. 17, about Nazareth.

20 "Understanding and reconciliation between God and people." Lasma, *Idioms* 59. Genesis 28:10–12: "Now Jacob went out from Beersheba and went

toward Haran. So he came to a certain place and stayed there all night because the sun had set. He took one of the stones of that place, he put it at his head and he lay down in that place to sleep. Then he dreamed and behold, a ladder was set up on the earth and its top reached to heaven. There the angels of God were ascending and descending on it."

21 Also **miracle!** Taken from, **"They invited me and not my miracle!"** Zimmermann 142. In the text **sign** is used instead of **miracle**.

22 Including the mikvah; see Appendix D.

23 John's seven miracles are called signs that are to help people believe in Jesus, the Christ, Son of God; see John 4:48 and John 20:30–31. Doing signs to get people to believe didn't always work; see discussion in John 12:37–43.

24 Psalm 69:9.

25 Usually translated as "the Jews," which doesn't discriminate between the Jewish leaders and the Jewish people. The Jewish authorities governed under Roman rule and included the elders of the people (of the aristocrats), Sadducees, Sanhedrin (council, court), high priest, chief priests, Pharisees, Herodians, scribes (canon-lawyers, teachers of the law), Publicans (tax collectors), Temple guards, and the police. See Appendix C, Jewish authorities.

26 In John 2:13–18. In Matthew 21:12–16, Mark 11:15–18, and Luke 19:45–46, Jesus cleanses the Temple at the end of his ministry.

27 Usually "signs that he did," and the sign that he did is the first sign at Cana because the second sign is referred to in John 4:54.

28 John 2:23–25. Zimmermann 152.

29 Born anew is a spiritual birth. Also **born from above** and **born again**. "To become like a child, to start all over." Lasma, *Idioms* 59.

30 Usually "born of water and the Spirit." Zimmermann 156.

31 See Appendix B, Thomas 22:1–7.

32 A real life, immortality, eternal life, living every moment knowing God and Jesus here and now. Also means being in God's Presence after your body's death.

33 See John 1:14, Note no. 7.

34 John 6:65: "He [Jesus] said, **'Therefore I have told you that no one can come to me unless it is given to them by my Divine Parent.'"** Many are given by God to other prophets in other religions, many are enlightened to realize God by themselves, and many are righteous without a formal God. Luke 5:31–32: "Jesus answered, **'Those who are sick need a physician not those who are well. I have come to call sinners to repentance, not the righteous!'"**

35 See John 1:14, Note no. 7.

36 Their own living hell separated from God. The Jewish people, not given to Jesus, have Moses and the prophets, while other faiths also have their own prophets to help them realize God. See John 3:18, Note no. 34. To obey the Son, you must follow John 15:12: **This is my commandment: that you love one another as I have loved you."**

37 In John 3:22 and John 3:26, Jesus is baptizing.

38 "True teaching." Lasma, *Idioms* 60. Living water usually means "fresh water" or "flowing water" used in part or for all the water in a mikvah for purification.

39 Mount Gerizim. Their temple there was destroyed in 129 BCE; see Appendix C, Samaritans.

40 Isaiah 12:3: "Therefore with joy will you draw water out of the spring of salvation."

41 John 4:26. Ravi Ravindra, *The Gospel of John: In The Light Of Indian Mysticism,* (New York, New York; Inner Traditions, Rochester, 2004) 53.

42 Also means **burden**. "Here in the Aramaic, the double meaning, repeated in **food** and **burden** would be understood in a palpable fashion by the Aramaic reader." Zimmermann 160.

43 Baptismal pool for purification, especially before entering the Temple; see Appendix C, mikvah.

44 Covered walkways supported with columns.

45 The words in brackets were added later to explain "when the water is stirred up" in John 5:7.

46 Usually translated as "Jews," and here, it probably means Pharisee leaders or scribes of the Pharisees.

47 He also attacked the Temple merchants, bringing fear of Roman intervention.

48 See Appendix A, Thomas 1.

49 The living dead are separated from God by the worldly and their own actions in the world, so that their human spirit is dead. See Appendix B, Thomas 50:1–3, and Thomas 51:1–2.

50 Also **their own living hell, Sheol, Ghenna, hell,** or **outer darkness.**

51 This is true under Hebrew law where at least two witnesses are needed (Numbers 35:30, Deuteronomy 17:6, and Deuteronomy 19:15), but Jesus adds that God is his witness in John 5:32, John 8:14, and John 8:18.

52 Deuteronomy 18:15–19.

53 "The Aramaic 'al' means "on" or 'by' and the disciples were going from Tiberias to Capernaum which are both on the same side of the Sea of Galilee." George M. Lasma, *Holy Bible From the Ancient Eastern Text*, (San Francisco, California; HarperSanFrancisco for A. J. Holman Company, 1968) 1059. See Mark 6:48, Note no. 40.

54 Also **affirmed** or **attested to**.

55 See Appendix D, Exodus 16:14–15.

56 "Jesus was the sacred bond between God and people. He was the true bread, the bread of the spirit, because he offered his life as spiritual food and for an everlasting covenant. No bond is sacred without him. No earthly bread is holier than his body. He is the bread of life and truth and those who eat never hunger nor lack in understanding." George M. Lasma, *Gospel Light*, (Nashville, Tennessee: Holman Bible Publishers, 1967) 342. Also, from an Aramaic reading: **"Simple Presence is the food of understanding, giving life to all."** Neil Douglas-Klotz, *The Hidden Gospel* (Wheaton, Illinois: Quest Books—Theosophical Publishing House, 1999) 112. Bread of life is "Eternal truth." Lasma, *Idioms* 60.

57 Isaiah 54:13–15.

58 Also, Matthew 5:8: **"Blessed are the pure in heart, for they shall see God."**

59 The body of Jesus is the truth of the Good News, and the blood of Jesus is the power of the Holy Spirit, which flows through his body. The Lamb of God is Jesus the Christ, the Son of humanity, and the Son of God.

60 "The Aramaic *satana* (Satan) is derived from *sta* which means to slide, to slip, or to miss the mark and applies to one who causes these results." Lasma, *Holy Bible* 1061. Satan also means accuser, adversary, divider, and obstacle. Besides "Satan" entering Judas Iscariot in John 13:27, Simon Peter is called "Satan" in Matthew 16:23.

61 Festival of Booths. The Sukkoth was a seven-day harvest festival in October; see Appendix C, Sukkoth.

62 John 7:6. "In effect, Jesus declares **Your time is fixed by the calendar to go regularly to the feasts. My time is not ordered that way.**'" Zimmermann 159.

63 "Let him come and learn from me." Lasma, *Idioms* 60. See Appendix B, Thomas 108:1–3.

64 "Abundant and eternal truth. Spiritual satisfaction." Lasma, *Idioms* 60. Also, Isaiah 12:3: "Therefore with joy will you draw water out of the spring of salvation."

65 See Appendix D, Psalm 89:3–4, Mica 5:2, and Ruth 4:11–12.

66 Also authorities.

67 See Appendix D, Deuteronomy 19:15–19.

68 Galilee was the land of the Gentiles and mixed races.

69 John 7:53–8:12 was absent in earlier manuscripts but added centuries later (fourth century CE at the earliest), and the writing style is different.

70 Leviticus 20:10. The law says that both spouses shall be put to death.

71 "Ignorance and superstition." Lasma, *Idioms* 60.

72 From the oral tradition of Sophian Gnosticism (Sophia is Wisdom) in "The Secret Gospel of St. Mary Magdalene;" Verse 52, "Mary taught, 'Once you come to the light and know the light is in you, you cannot continue to walk in the ways of darkness, lest you fall into a greater darkness. You must walk in the light and enter the light, and bring forth the light from within you, for only then will you be established in the Way of Life.'" Tau Malachi, *St. Mary Magdalene: The Gnostic Tradition of the Holy Bride*, (Woodbury, Minnesota: Llewellyn Publications, 2006) 137.

73 Usually translated as **"You judge after the flesh but I judge no one."** Zimmermann 162.

74 Deuteronomy 17:6.

75 Jesus was born anew or born from above. John 3:5–7: Jesus answered, **"Very truly, I tell you, If a person is not born in the likeness of the Spirit they cannot enter the kin-dom of God. That which is born of the person is human but that which is born of Spirit is spirit. Don't be surprised that I told you that, 'You must be born anew!'"**

76 Usually "Jews," which is used in an anti-Semitic argument to prove that the Jewish people are against Jesus and are not of God. Jesus is referring to the scribes or misleaders of the Pharisees and not to the Jewish people. In John 8:48, "They" is followed by [*The Jewish leaders*] in brackets to correct this error. After the destruction of the Temple in 70 CE, the teachings of the true leaders of the Pharisees centered Judaism away from Temple worship to the hearts and minds of the Jewish people. The legacy of the Pharisees is the Mishna, the Gemara, and two Talmuds. See Appendix C, Pharisees.

77 John 8:35, Zimmermann 159.

78 John 8:44. "he is a liar and the father of lies." Zimmermann 165. Usually "murderer."

79 Jesus is not talking about a physical death but spiritual immortality as in reborn in the Spirit. John 1:12–13: "To those who received the light and believed in his name, were given the right to become children of God. They

are born not of blood, nor the will of the flesh, nor the will of people but of God."

80 For "I AM," see Appendix C, *Hokhmah* (Wisdom). Jesus as the first born anew adopted Son of God is "I AM." Anyone, female or male, who becomes their own Christ through the example and guidance of Jesus (I AM saves) will receive the I AM, in their kin-dom of God within, as a born anew spiritual daughter or son of God.

81 "We have good reason for thinking that something of this sort did happen later in the first century—but not during the days of Jesus, when Jewish leaders had not in fact passed legislation concerning Jesus and his followers. It is likely, then, that the story as narrated in the Fourth Gospel is not historically accurate." Bart D. Ehrman, *Jesus: Apocalyptic Prophet of the New Millennium* , (New York, New York; Oxford University Press Inc., 1999) 95.

82 See John 8:15–16 about Jesus' way of judgement.

83 An Aramaic version of "**I AM the good Shepherd.**" "**The 'I am' leads us to the right experiences at the right time and place.**" Douglas-Klotz, *Hidden Gospel* 112.

84 Also Festival of Lights and Feast of the Maccabees. See Appendix C, Hanukkah.

85 The Sacred Unity that is *Alaha* (God in Aramaic which is also spelled *Elaha*.)

86 Jesus is quoting this Psalm to show God judging the Jewish authorities, the congregation of the mighty (gods who represented God as judges), for being unjust, especially when they falsely judged him for being the spiritual Son of God.

87 Psalm 82:1–8.

88 Blasphemy only refers to *YHWH*, the Eternal. Jesus is the spiritual Son of God, spoken of in 2 Samuel 7:14, "I will be a Father to him and he will be a Son to Me." See Appendix D, Samuel 7:12–17 for the context.

89 The Didymus.

90 The usual translation is "Let us also go, that we may die with him." Zimmermann 147.

91 They have eternal life in Spirit.

92 See Luke 17:16, Note no. 170, "homage."

93 Usually "deeply moved in spirit" or "he raged in spirit." Matthew Black, *An Aramaic Approach To The Gospels And Acts*, (Peabody, Massachusetts: Hendrickson Publishers Inc., 1967.) 243.

94 Lasma, *Holy Bible* 1068.

95 The high priest and his allies needed the Romans or Herod Antipas to legally kill Jesus.

96 Nard (spikenard) is imported from the Himalayas in India, and a pound costs about a year's wages of a laborer or about $15,000. A Roman pound is about twelve ounces.

97 Psalm 118:26, see Appendix D, Psalm 118:19–29 for full context.

98 Zechariah 9:9–10.

99 Usually translated "Greeks." "The Aramaic *Ammey* means *Gentiles* that is Syrians, Idumeans, and other neighboring peoples. The word for Greeks is *yonaey*." Lasma, *Holy Bible* 1070.

100 John 12:24, Zimmerman 163.

101 Usually "hates their life." Lasma, *Holy Bible* 1070.

102 Or "**will begin their real life.**" Those who have no concern for their life in this world have already been born anew in the Spirit and trust the process of God's will for them. Some drugs can also induce this lack of concern until the drug wears off or side effects take over. In Hindu thought, there is the idea of giving up your attachment to people, things, and the outcome of what happens but not your responsibility for what you do. Then you begin your real life in the will of God.

103 Satan, sin, or error. Truth rules in the spiritual world and drives away error. Error is not real in your mind but rules without knowledge of the Truth.

104 "Accordingly it appears that the translator bethought himself of the fundamental meaning, and rendered too literally, 'be lifted up from the earth' whereas he should have rendered 'disappear,' i.e., die, which is the sense quite explicit here." Zimmermann 155.

105 See Appendix D, Isaiah 9:6–7.

106 Isaiah 53:1–12.

107 Isaiah 6:8–10.

108 See John 9:22, Note no. 81, for doubts about being put out of the synagogue in the time when Jesus lived.

109 John 8:15: "**You judge in a human fashion; I do not judge as a man.**" See John 8:15, Note no 73.

110 "Usually "disciple" and "teacher" are translated as; "servant" and "master," "servant" and "lord," or "slave" and "master."

111 Psalm 41:9.

112 "This article makes a case for ascribing authorship of the Fourth Gospel (the Gospel of John) in the New Testament to Mary Magdalene. As far

as I know — no previously published work has made an argument in support of this hypothesis. Most biblical scholars today assert that the Fourth Gospel was authored by an anonymous follower of Jesus referred to within the Gospel text as the Beloved Disciple. It is posited here that, in an earlier tradition of the Fourth Gospel's community, the now "anonymous" Beloved Disciple was known to be Mary Magdalene. It is further posited that Mary Magdalene is the true founder and hero of what has come to be known as the Johannine Community (i.e., Mary Magdalene was one of the original apostolic founders and leaders of the early Christian church)." Raymond K. Jusino, "Mary Magdalene: Author of the Fourth Gospel?" http://ramon_k_jusino.tripod.com/magdalene.html 1998. 1 (Out of 14 pages).

"What does it mean to see Mary Magdalene as: 'the disciple whom he loved'? Because here we have a man and a woman, the first thought to arise is, 'Indeed, so Mary Magdalene was Jesus beloved!' It should be clear that in the Gospel of John we do not have erotic love, since the bond of love is a relationship which Jesus has with all his disciples, as emerges from the texts above. The word used for love is agape, comparable not to the love between lovers, but to the love between parent and child and between brothers and sisters. As the Father loves Jesus, so Jesus loves Mary Magdalene. As Jesus reclines in the bosom of the Father, so does Mary Magdalene remain on the bosom of Jesus. In the Jewish tradition this staying on the bosom of the teacher symbolizes the handing on of an authoritative tradition. In the Gospel of John, the fact that Mary Magdalene is seen as 'the disciple whom he loved' means that she is the anonymous figure on whom the gospel leans. She is the eyewitness who has told of Jesus. The Gospel of John is based on her story." Ester De Boer, *The Mary Magdalene Cover-Up*, (New York, New York: T & T Clark, 2006.) 64.

113 The fourteen pronoun changes from "him" and "he" to "her" and "she" allow the following passages from The Gospel of John to flow more dramatically with deeper meaning than the usual patristic version. The changes make sense concerning the rivalry between Peter and Mary Magdalene in the Gospel of John, the Gospel of Mary, and the Gospel of Thomas.

Mary Magdalene is clearly identified in John 19:25-26 as "the disciple, whom he [Jesus] loved." "While the soldiers were doing this, standing near the cross of Jesus were his mother, his mother's sister, Mary the wife of Clopas, and Mary Magdalene. When he saw his mother and the disciple, whom he loved, standing beside her, he said to his mother, **'Woman, behold your son!'**" Mary

Magdalene in John 20:3, is mentioned as being with "Simon Peter and the other disciple, whom Jesus loved," where the other disciple is probably John. Two passages from the Gospel of Mary (Appendix A) confirm that Mary Magdalene was the disciple whom Jesus loved. Page 10:1–3: "Peter said to Mary, 'Sister, we know that the Saviour loved you more than all other women.'" Page 18:6–15: "Levi answered, speaking to Peter, 'Peter, you have always been a hot-tempered person. Even now I see you are questioning the woman just as our adversaries do. For if the Saviour made her worthy, who are you indeed to reject her? Surely the Saviour knew her completely and that is why he loved her more than us.'"

114 Usually translated as **"The Jews"** as before in the Temple. See John 7:14–15 and John 34–35.

115 "See the Light of God in each the other and love it and love the human who it resides in." Joan Norton, *The Mary Magdalene Within*, (Lincoln, Nebraska; iUniverse, 2005) 54.

116 House of many mansions (many rooms—Lasma). "A kingdom [*kin-dom*] for all races and peoples." Lasma, *Idioms* 60.

117 See Appendix B, Thomas, 91:1–2.

118 Of those given to Jesus by God but many are given to other prophets and forms of worship by God to realize God. Jesus is also given the lost sheep of any religion.

119 Comforter names: Spirit of Truth, Holy Spirit, Paraclete, Advocate, Counselor, Helper, Guide, Protector, Wisdom of God, Wisdom, Sister Wisdom (Proverbs 7:4), Sophia, and *Hokhmah* (*Chokmah*).

120 **Her** is the Comforter Who is the Holy Spirit and the Holy Spirit is feminine, but The Comforter is usually translated as **Him** or **He** in the Gospel of John. God is usually translated as "Him," "He," and "Lord," even though the image of God is female and male in Genesis 1:27 and God is Being, the Existing, the Eternal, not a Lord but beyond gender. In this version of John's Gospel, the Comforter is referred to as **Her** and **She** by sixteen pronoun changes. The Hebrew word for Holy Spirit is *Ruach* (*Ruah, Ru'ah*) *Ha-Kodesh* (*Hakkodesh*) where Spirit (*Ruach*) is a noun of female gender. *Ruach Elohim* is the Spirit of God. "Wisdom" is a word with a female ending known as *Holkmah* or *Chokmah* in Hebrew and the female *Sophia* in Greek. The following Scripture quotes confirm the idea that the Holy Spirit is She and Wisdom is She. Matthew 11:19, Matthew 12:27–28, Mark 1:7–12, Luke 4:18–19, 7:35, 11:11–13, 11:49, John 3:5–8, 14:15–18, 14:24–26, 15:26–27,

16:5–15, Genesis 1:1–3, Job 32:6–9, 33:4, Psalm 51:10–12, 139:7–12, Proverbs 1:20–23, 3:15–18, 7:1–5, 8:1–36, 9:1–6, Isaiah 11:1–2, and Daniel 5:14.

121 Usually **comfortless**. Lasma, *Gospel* 368.

122 See Appendix A, Mary 8:14–15.

123 "I am the true religion." Lasma, *Idioms* 60. The vine is the symbol for Israel, the people of God, and how some of these people have become false. See Psalm 80:8–13, Isaiah 5:1–7, Jeremiah 2:21, and Hosea 10:1.

124 Originally "He who hates me hates my Father also." Martin Luther of the Protestant movement used this passage to justify his anti-Semitism.

125 Psalm 35:19–21.

126 Peter asked "Where are you going?" in John 13:36; and Thomas asked, "Saviour, we don't know where you are going so how can we know the way?" in John 14:5.

127 Usually translated as **Sorrow**. Zimmerman 133.

128 Holy Spirit and Wisdom. In Hindu religious thought, one way to realize God is to keep following your own path of truth.

129 Usually "Holy Father," but in the Catholic Church, the Pope uses this name and the Priests use the name "Father" which usually means "God" in the Four Gospels. See Matthew 5:16, Note no. 41 about Divine Parent.

130 Also **Son of destruction, the one who chose to be lost, the one destined to be lost, son of corruption**, and **man of lawlessness**.

131 See Appendix D, Psalm 41:9.

132 The Word before it became flesh as the true Light, which is the consciousness of God in the Christ of Jesus, the Lamb of God.

133 Roman soldiers.

134 See John 17:12, Note no. 130 about the son of perdition.

135 The former high priest from 6 CE–15 CE who was still referred to as "high priest" because according to Hebrew law, the office of high priest was for life; however, the Romans sold the position every two years. See Appendix C, Annas.

136 See John 11:50.

137 "The eastern text reads 'struck Jesus on his cheek.' This is in accordance with eastern custom." Lasma, *Gospel* 380.

138 Pilate's headquarters included the governor's palace, a military barracks, and an outdoor courtyard used as a court of judgment.

139 Those who were unclean had to wait a month to celebrate Passover; Numbers 9:10–11.

140 See John 12:32–33.

141 The spiritual kin-dom is in the world, in your heart, but hidden under layers or veils of error that hide the kin-dom from the worldly.

142 The Romans scourged a prisoner only after he was condemned to death because the scourging alone may kill them.

143 Usually "Behold the man!" Zimmermann 150.

144 "The background to those events was that Pilate was playing a cat and mouse game. We know, from Josephus and Philo independently, that he was a bitter, barbarous, and ferocious tyrant, who disregarded both the solemn feelings of the Jews and Roman precedent, by bringing images and standards into Jerusalem. He threatened to murder those who protected others, confiscated money from the Temple treasury, and sadistically mingled the blood of Galilean Jews with their sacrifices (Luke 13:1). He put to death so many of the Samaritans (of a religious movement only, and nonpolitical) that they appealed to the Syrian governor, Pilate's superior." Zimmermann 150.

145 Leviticus 24:16. This was their interpretation the law because blasphemy only refers to *YHWH*. A Jewish king is called a spiritual "Son of God" after they are begotten (adopted) by God and enthroned in a sacred ritual.

146 See Jesus defense in John 10:31–38 and John 10:36, Note no. 88, about "the Son of God."

147 Usually, "It was the day of Preparation of the Passover." Lasma, *Holy Bible* 1078.

148 Usually translated as "Hebrew." "*Hebrew* here refers to nationality but the language of the inscription was Aramaic." Lasma, *Holy Bible* 1079.

149 Psalm 22:1.

150 "But, more important, I would like to argue that the word 'son' in John 19:26 does not primarily refer to the disciple Jesus loved, but rather refers to Jesus himself. For the reader who does not know the flow of the story beforehand, the word 'son' directed to the mother of Jesus designates her own son: the dying crucified Jesus himself." Ester A. De Boer in *The Gospel of Mary: Listening to the Beloved Disciple*, (New York, New York: Continuum Books, 2005) 185.

151 Psalm 22:15: "My strength has dried up like sun baked clay, tongue cleaves to my jaws and they have thrown me into the dust of death."

152 "The eastern text reads 'because it was Friday' instead of 'preparation day.' The Passover was eaten on Thursday. The preparation day was the day before, which would be Wednesday when all preparation for the Passover was

completed. Friday was the day after the Passover, when the crucifixion took place." Lasma, *Gospel* 388.

153 See John 21:24.

154 Psalm 34:19–20. The Passover Lamb of God was sacrificed and had no broken bones, just as required in Exodus 12:46 and Numbers 9:12.

155 Zechariah 12:10.

156 See John 3:1–21.

157 Mary Magdalene is "the disciple, whom Jesus loved," so here, she couldn't be "the other disciple, whom Jesus loved." This identifies the other beloved disciple with Peter who was probably John.

158 Psalms 16:8–11. This scripture is about being among the living dead or the worldly who are corrupted spiritually and cannot know God because they worship their possessions and can't let go. Jesus gave us the guide to resurrection from out of the corruption of the living dead to be alive in the Spirit. A person is born anew before the death of their physical body, not after. The Gospel of Mary (Appendix A) shows the path of the soul in a person's new life out of their living death and the details of escaping the corruption from that person's attachment to the world and the worldly.

"A person sets milk in a quiet place to curdle and then they extract butter from the curd. After once extracting the butter of Devotion and Knowledge from the milk of the mind; if you keep that transformed mind in the water of the world, it will float in the world unattached. But if the mind in its 'unripe' state—that is to say, when it is just like liquid milk—is kept in the water of the world, then the milk and water will get mixed. In that case it will be impossible for the mind to float unattached in the world." Gupta, Mahendranath—"M," Swami Nikhilananda, (From Bengali) trans. *The Gospel of Sri Ramakrishna*, (New York, New York; Ramakrishna—Vivekananda Center, 1977) 627.

159 The Aramaic *Rabbouni* means "My Teacher" and "My Master." In Mark 10:50, it means "My Great One," so "My Great Teacher" seems appropriate here. See Mark 10:51, Note no. 84, where Bartimaeus told him, "Rabbouni, I want to receive my sight!" Jesus, the humble builder's son who became the Lamb of God, has just finished building the temple of his body in three days (John 2:19–21) for each person who believes, so they have the temple in their body to be with God in their kin-dom of heaven.

160 Also **Do not cling to me, Stop holding on to me, Do not hold me, Do not hold me now,** or **Touch me no more**.

161 The usual translation is **brethren**. "The Greek word here can also mean 'brothers and sisters'. I adopt this translation because in the Gospel of John women play a clear role as disciples of Jesus." Ester De Boer, John Bowden trans. *Mary Magdalene: Beyond the Myth*, (Harrisburg, Pa: Trinity Press International, 1997) 136, Note no. 47. "While it is true that John 20:17 cannot be understood without John 13–17 (Jesus farewell discourses at the Passover meal), here, the proclamation is broadened. In John 15:15 the disciples are no longer servants of Jesus but friends. Now they are brothers and sisters, together children of one Father. Those who believe in Jesus and are born in the spirit can become children of God (John 1:12–13; 3:5, cf 14:26–27)." De Boer, Mary M. *Beyond* Note no. 48, p. 136. John 1:12–13 "To those who received the light and believed in is name, were given the right to become children of God. They are born not of blood, nor the will of the flesh, nor the will of people but of God."

This is where Mary Magdalene becomes the apostle to the apostles or *apostola apostolorum* in Latin. See John 13:23, Note no. 112 about the handing on of an authoritative tradition. Jesus selected Mary Magdalene to replace Judas as the twelfth apostle, but the other eleven didn't believe her (Mark 16:9–11 and Luke 24:10–11).

162 "He gave them courage." Lasma, *Idioms* 61.

163 Jesus said to Thomas in John 14:7–9, **"If you had known me, you would have also known my Divine Parent. From this moment on, you know God and have seen God."** Philip said, "My Saviour, show us the Divine Parent and we will be satisfied." Jesus taught, **"All this time I have been with you and you do not know me, Philip? Whoever sees me has seen the Divine Parent. How can you say, 'Show us the Divine Parent?'"** See John 14:5–12 for context.

164 "Feed my young people, take care of them." Lasma, *Idioms* 61.

165 "Feed the adults!" Lasma, *Idioms* 61.

166 "Feed the young women!" Lasma, *Idioms* 61.

167 "If we look upon Mary Magdalene as concealed in the grammatically male anonymous disciple Jesus loved, this will affect our perspective on her as well as on the Gospel of John. Not only Mary Magdalene's testimony about the Lord's resurrection would have been important to the Johannine community, as we concluded earlier, but Mary Magdalene would also have had disciples, who preserved her accounts of Jesus' life and teachings, which later received the title: The Gospel of John. Moreover, through the canonization of The Gospel of John, Mary Magdalene's accounts of Jesus would have been canonized and taught through the ages, and spread over the world." De Boer *Gospel* 190.

Mary Notes

1 The Gospel of Mary was translated from early second-century manuscripts, some fragments in Greek and a fuller version in Coptic—a form of native Egyptian language written during the Roman period. This version is from the many translations of the Gospel of Mary in English. Most translations use different "Page: Verse" numbering systems so this book uses a rational composite of several systems. Words in the text are translated into a variety of meanings, with many of the alternatives here in Mary Notes.

2 The missing pages 1–6 and part of page 7:1 with part of Page 10:23 and Pages 11-14; have been revealed and published in Claire Nahmad & Margret Bailey, *The Secret Teachings of Mary Magdalene*, (London, Great Britain; Watkins Publishing, 2006) 190–196 and 203-209.

3 Mary 7:3–4, Jean-Yves Leloup, Joseph Rowe, trans. *The Gospel of Mary Magdalene*, (Rochester, Vermont; Inner Traditions, 2002) 25. Also Mary 7:3–4: "**All natural phenomena, all that has been moulded, all that has been brought into being exists in and with each other.**" De Boar, *Gospel* 19.

4 Also **roots** or **nature**. "While everything material is interconnected, in the end all things will dissolve back into their constituent natures." Robert J. Miller ed., The Gospel of Mary in *The Complete Gospels*, (Sonoma, California; A Polebridge Press Book, HarperSanFrancisco, A Division of HarperCollinsPublishers, 1994) 361. Footnote; 2:1–5.

5 Also Mary 7:8–9: "**Anyone with two ears able to hear should listen.**" King, Karen, *The Gospel of Mary of Magdala: Jesus and the First Woman Apostle*, (Santa Rosa, California; Polebridge Press, 2003) 13.

6 "The original meaning of adultery is betrayal of the Real, of lying to oneself by knowingly allowing a reflection to usurp the place of the Light itself or, in other words, idolatry." Leloup, *Gospel of Mary* M. 88. Adultery is the habit of a corrupted nature, where one joins things that don't belong, like worshiping God and worshiping mammon, having sexual relations with both a spouse and one not their spouse, working in a job you hate, or being overwhelmed by abundance but still greedy.

7 God the Good. See Mark 10:17–18. "According to the Gospel of Mary, the Teacher came to help free us from the ignorance that is identification (corruption). For he is the very continence, the incarnation, and the practice of this Good. The Good is the manifestation of the famous triad of the ancient philosophers: goodness, truth, and beauty." Leloup, *Gospel of Mary* M. 55. Also **Good One**, from Esther A. De Boer, *The Gospel of Mary: Listening to the*

Beloved Disciple, (New York, New York: Continuum Books, 2005) 19. **Christ Light**, from Nahmad, *Secret* 227.

8 The spiritual nature of people is separated from them by attachment to their body and the material world.

9 Also "**this is why I tell you: Be in harmony . . .** ' To be in harmony is to be in a conscious and loving relationship with what is. Here, there is no willing or desiring of particulars, for that would imply a fixation on an illusory, separate part of the flowing totality in which we live. Harmony means to have a musical relationship with the world, to be in resonance, to be in tune with all that is." Leloup, *The Gospel of Mary M.* 62.

10 Also, **Mary 8:10–11: [9] "go out into nature and take heart from the manifestations [10] of beauty and harmony with the Divine nature."** Nahmad, *Secret* 228. [9] and [10] are from a different numbering system. Walk to be near a stream in the woods, spend time in the company of wise and holy people, visit special places where the Presence of the Good is felt, cleanse your body, or meditate on the kin-dom of God inside you and outside you in other people.

11 Also, Mary 8:14–15: **"Peace be with you, bring forth my peace from yourselves"** from Esther De Boar, *Mary Magdalene: Beyond the Myth*, (Harrisburg, Pa: Trinity Press International, 1997) 83.

12 King, Gospel 14. Also **Son of Man, Human One, Blessed One,** and **the Christ**.

13 To compare with "the kin-dom of God is within you," see Luke 17:21, Thomas 3:3, Thomas 70:1–2, and Thomas 113:4.

14 De Boer, *Gospel* 19. "This single unknown rule the Saviour gave in the Gospel of Mary may have alluded to the one law Jesus gave according to the New Testament writings: the law of love." De Boer, *Gospel* 90. Another version of Mary 9:1–4, **"Do not add more laws to those given in the Torah, lest you become bound by them."** Leloup, *Gospel of Mary M.* 29. John 15:12–14, **"This is my commandment: that you love one another as I have loved you. A person can have no greater love than to lay down their life for the sake of their friends. You are my friends if you do whatever I command you."**

15 Mary 9:14–17. King, *Gospel* 15. **"do not be in two minds."** De Boer, *Gospel* 19.

16 Also "fully human" or anthropos. "I prefer the term *anthropos* to *androgyne* (not *eunuch*) because the former word still leads to confusion today, in spite of a widespread contemporary appreciation of the value of spiritual integration and balance of male and female polarities in us." Leloup, *Gospel of Mary M.* 104.

The fully human being or "Anthropos" is the essential inner person, not the male or female roles. See Gospel of Thomas, 22:5, 49, 114:1–3.

17 Saviour is used for Jesus everywhere else in the Gospel of Mary except Mary 10:11, Mary 11:12, and Mary 11:17, where Mary addresses Jesus as "Lord."

18 The **nous** is a person's part the Infinite Mind of God. Also **nous** can mean **human spirit, mortal mind, enlightened mind, higher mind, spiritual heart, inner nature of a person, creative imagination, consciousness, magic door,** and **mirror.**

19 In Matthew 6:21 and Luke 12:34; **"For where your treasure is, there will be your heart also."**

20 "Therefore, the soul (beauty) leads forth our unrealized self (the beast) through the magic door or mirror (the nous) so that it becomes the glorious God-being." Nahmad, *Secret* 232.

21 The other revealed part of Mary 10:23, *"this which makes us fully human."* Nahmad, *Secret* 203.

22 The four spiritual climates or atmospheres ("Climate" is usually translated as "Power") are what the soul passes through during the soul's resurrection from its worldly body. The soul, attached to its body and materialism in a living hell separated from God, undergoes a change of heart. Guided by Jesus (Mary, another prophet, a loved one, or friend), the soul is helped by the awakened mind (nous, human spirit) to begin healing what is opposite to its nature. The soul will be nourished by the Holy Spirit in the process of welcoming the Light. Dissolving into or returning to their original goodness, a person begins to know their true self and become alive in eternal life as a true human being like Jesus, the true child of Humanity. The person goes through a process of detaching from their old worldly self to become alive, loving, full of light, and united with the Spirit in their true self as a fully human being.

"I. FIRST CLIMATE *Darkness or Absurdity* The sterile void.—> II. SECOND CLIMATE *Craving* The desire to possess.—> III. THIRD CLIMATE *Refusal of knowledge* Willful ignorance, refusal of awareness.—> IV. FOURTH CLIMATE *Sevenfold Wrath* Darkness, craving, ignorance, lethal jealousy, enslavement to the body, intoxicated wisdom, guileful wisdom." Leloup, *Gospel of Mary M.* 130.

23 Or "Desire." See Matthew 12:43–45 and Matthew 12:45, Note no. 171, about addicted people.

24 "We prefer not to know, for knowing would imply a conscience and responsibilities. 'We didn't know,' or 'We were just following orders,' have now

become familiar excuses given by those judged for crimes against humanity." Leloup, *Gospel of Mary M.* 133.

25 "The fourth climate, containing seven levels, we will call Wrath. This was considered by some ancient traditions to be the worst of all demons, because of its power to thoroughly alienate the soul, which can then no longer own or recognize itself. The soul is no longer accessible—it is *possessed*, in the true sense of the term." Leloup, *Gospel of Mary M.* 139. The seven forms of Wrath are related to the seven demons that Jesus cast out of Mary Magdalene; see Mark 16:9 and Luke 8:1–3.

26 Also Excitement of Death, Jealousy of Death, Lethal Jealousy, and Zeal for Death.

27 Also Power of the Flesh, Realm of the Flesh, and Kingdom of the Flesh.

28 Also Intoxicated Wisdom, Foolish Learning of the Flesh, and Impure Wisdom.

29 Also Hot-tempered Wisdom, Guileful Wisdom, Wisdom of the Wrathful Person, and Self-righteous Materialism.

30 Also murderer. "*Human-killer* refers to the soul having cast off the flesh." Miller, *Complete Gospels* 364.

31 Also vagabond? "They shout 'murderer!' at the soul because it has slain the phantoms of Darkness, Desire, and Ignorance, and address it as 'vagabond' and 'slayer of space' because it has freed itself from the vacuum or imprisonment in the lower planes and, no longer having roots in its corrupt nature, has no home there anymore." Nahmad *Secret* 240.

32 Mary 16:21–17:3: "I left the world with the aid of another world: a design was erased by virtue of a higher design . . ." Leloup, *Gospel of Mary M.* 37. John 3:6–7: "That which is born of the person is human but that which is born of Spirit is spirit. Don't be surprised that I told you that, 'You must be born anew!'" John 8:23: "He said, 'You are from below and I am from above. You are of this world but I am not of this world.'"

33 Mary 17:4–7: "Henceforth, I travel toward Repose where time rests in the Eternity of Time; I go now into Silence." Leloup, *Gospel of Mary M.* 37. "Repose in Silence" is another name for the kin-dom of God within you. The soul has reached immortality or eternal life here and now, where the person, Jesus, and the God of the living are One in Sacred Unity.

34 Also "are strange ideas" and "according to another train of thought."

35 Also, "Peter, you have always been a wrathful person," "Peter, you are always ready to give way to your perpetual inclination to anger." King, *Gospel* 17.

36 See Mary 10:1–3.

37 Or another version of Mary 18:15–18 (part of 15 and part of 18) is "Therefore let us atone and become fully human (*Anthropos*) so that the Teacher can take root in us. Let us grow as he demanded of us." Leloup, *Gospel of Mary M.* 39. "Anthropos," see Mary 9:20, Note no. 16.

38 Mary 18:19–21, De Boer, *Gospel* 21. Also, "In The Gospel of Mary, Peter and Andrew do not heed the Saviour's warning against rules and laws which are other than the one he himself has made. They add an extra law, even two: 1. In their view the brothers need not listen to a woman. 2. In their view only the knowledge and interpretation of the brothers should determine the truth content of what others add about their contacts with the Redeemer. The Gospel of Mary resolutely rejects both claims." De Boer, *Mary M. Beyond* 100. John 13:34 **A new commandment I give you, that you love one another; just as I have loved you, that you also love one another.**

Thomas Notes

1 This version is from the many versions available in English, and Thomas Notes reflect the variety of choices for many words and ideas in the text. References to the text of the Gospels are cited in brackets [See Matthew 7:7] after Saying 1. The "Best Half" are those fifty-seven Sayings that are closer in meaning to the Four Gospels but not those with the same words as the Four Gospels.

2 Also hidden, obscure, or mystery. These sayings are like when Jesus teaches the multitude in parables but reveals the "secret" meaning to his disciples (Matthew 13:10–17 and Mark 4:10–12). "The God of Love who dwells in the depths of human beingness is a secret, and it is from these hidden depths that we can act, think, and speak in true freedom." Jean-Yves Leloup, Joseph Rowe (English) trans., *The Gospel of Thomas*, (Rochester, Vermont; Inner Traditions, 2005) 60.

The "secret" is the true connection between the Divine and the human, leading to Sacred Unity. Jesus teaches the secret sayings that reveal to the believer the "secret place" in Matthew 6:6 and Luke 17:21. The kin-dom of God within everyone is hidden from us by barriers or veils that people create which separate them from God like greed, possession worship, theft, lies, and adultery. The experience of knowing that Jesus, the Holy Spirit, and the kin-dom of God are within you is the Glory that Jesus made for you in the Christ. Repent, believe in Jesus, understand his sayings, be born anew spiritually, and realize the kin-dom of heaven within as a spiritual child adopted by God. A person becomes alive with the Spirit in eternal life where they forgive themselves, love themselves, forgive others, and love one another.

3 Didymus Judas Thomas.

4 "Immortality is said to be the reward of anyone who successfully decodes Thomas's enigmatic sayings. The correct interpretation of the sayings is not the final goal but the means to the goal, the discovery of the kingdom of Heaven. Thomas's Gospel is an exercise book, a list of riddles for decoding. The secret lies not in the final answers but in the effort to find the answers. This Gospel's Christianity is not based on grace, on salvation given as a gift by God, but on active individual effort." Stevan Davies trans., Andrew Harvey ed. *The Gospel of Thomas: Annotated & Explained*, (Woodstock, Vermont; Skylight Paths Publishing, 2002) 2.

5 Also **disturbed**.

6 Also **be astounded** and **be astonished**.

7 Also **will reign over All, will reign over the All, will rule over all,** and **will reign over everything**.

8 For Divine Parent, see Matthew 5:16, Note no. 41. Usually "Father" as in Elaine Pagels, *Beyond Belief*, (New York, New York; Random House, 2003) 227.

9 Leloup, *Gospel of Thomas*, 67. Also, **poverty**. This is a spiritual vanity or poverty that is overcome through self-knowledge or "gnosis" when you know that your immortal essence is united with God or everybody, everything, everywhere.

10 "The specific symbolism of a 'seven-day-old' infant suggests a time before circumcision, which was performed on the eighth day. The infant of seven days may also refer to the Image of God who existed on the seventh day before the second round of creation brought Adam into being. The old person probably represents the ordinary person who has not sought or found the Kingdom." Davies, *Gospel* 6.

11 Also **undivided** or **One**.

12 "Thomas declares that it is all very obvious and easy to comprehend, once one has found the key to seeing things in the new way Jesus recommends." Davies, *Gospel* 6.

13 "What is the 'big fish'? It is your Neshamah, heavenly soul, and the Christ-self that dwells in it. Indeed, the fundamentalist would say it is Yeshua Messiah, the Son of God and Savior, yet what the fundamentalist would not understand is that the only begotten Son, the child of the Living God, is that Divine self within each and every person. This, the Master has revealed through himself, though what is revealed is not exclusive to himself; it is the Truth of one and all in attainment. You must understand that faith in Yeshua Messiah is faith in the Divine potential within yourself and that to follow him is to follow the way of the Spirit of the Christ within yourself. The path he has revealed is the path to enlightenment, a conscious development and evolution of the soul into Messianic consciousness or Christhood." Tau Malachi, *The Gnostic Gospel of St. Thomas*, (St. Paul, Minnesota; Llewellyn Publications, 2004) 26.

14 "Here, when he throws fire upon the world we probably should understand that he has come to reveal knowledge of the Kingdom that is spread out upon the world." Davies, *Gospel* 10.

15 Also righteous messenger and righteous angel.

16 Also wise philosopher and intelligent philosopher.

17 Thomas 14:1–3 may be the answer to the three questions of Thomas 6:1 and the three sayings Jesus spoke to Thomas in 13:6. Fast in secret from others so that only God knows, not people (see Matthew 6:17). Pray secretly in words that have meaning, not vain repetitions (see Matthew 6:7). Give to charity in secret, do not blow your horn for others to notice or give to receive a tax deduction (see Matthew 6:3–4). Your Divine Parent Who sees you fast, pray, or give to charity in secret will reward you openly.

18 The beginning and the end are one in God's Presence, here and now. To return to the beginning is to find your original goodness in the present, naked but not ashamed. This is the same present as in the beginning of time (Genesis 1), where you are born anew in this beginning, which ended your worldly life and begin your eternal life (immortality).

19 "The motif of stripping naked refers to the ideal primordial time before the fall, prior to which Adam and Eve were naked and unashamed (Genesis 2:25). Subsequently, they became aware of their nakedness and were ashamed (Genesis 3:7). The Gospel of Thomas advocates return to the time of the Beginning, and so also to the nakedness symbolic of that time." Davies, *Gospel* 30.

20 "Through vigilance and attention, these children can mature and become wise. It is then that they will harvest the promised fruit. They will no longer be naked strangers in the field of knowledge. They will be masters along with the Master, sons and daughters along with the Son." Leloup, *Gospel of Thomas*, 98.

21 "The image of God is essentially one, male and female, perfect, immortal, ever present, and yet it is human. Therefore the image of God has hands and eyes and feet and so forth. To find it is to find oneself and to be reborn back in to the seventh day of creation. Then one enters the Kingdom." Davies, *Gospel* 32. Changing the eye that envies to an eye that loves or the hand that hits to a hand that gives is a process where you transform the image of Satan in the living hell that you want to leave behind into the image of God that you want to become. This is the unity of female and male, the fully human being like the Sacred Unity that is Alaha. Also, see Appendix A, Mary 9:20 and Mary 9:20, Note no. 16.

22 Usually **brother** but also **friend, neighbor,** and **little one**.

23 "The theme of the 'intoxicated' man in Gnostic literature is opposed that of 'the man of light,' set here as the opposite of 'divine drunkenness,' for it is a condition in which mind and heart are blurred, dense and intoxicated by the world of appearances." Leloup, *Gospel of Thomas*, 108.

———

24 Also **alert, wise, clever,** and **shrewd.**

25 "It is based on the fundamental law that the more we give, the more we receive. Thus the meaning of having "something in hand" has nothing to do with material wealth but instead concerns the capacity to give of ourselves. It also means having love and self-knowledge or gnosis." Leloup, *Gospel of Thomas* 128.

26 Also **Mind your own business.** Jesus is a passerby. Time passes by where the world changes, reality changes, and a person changes. Don't hang on to your life in this temporary moment but become grounded in the eternal kin-dom of God within. Let go, let God.

27 One who chooses rebirth in the Spirit with a childlike faith.

28 "In the canonical gospels it is faith that moves mountains. Yet what is faith if not the unity of mind and heart? When the "two" of intellect and emotion are united in one house, mountains can indeed be moved." Leloup, *Gospel of Thomas* 140.

29 Also **whole ones, simple ones,** and **undivided ones.**

30 John 8:12: "Later Jesus spoke to the people again, '**I AM the light of the world. Whoever follows me shall not walk in darkness but shall find in yourselves the light of life.**'"

31 Also **rest.** "Repose in Silence" is another name for the kin-dom of God within you. Psalms 46:10: "Be still and know that I am God." The soul has reached immortality or eternal life where you and Jesus and God are One. This is the spiritual birth anew of the living dead.

32 The worldly are those who exist but are not alive. They are the living dead because their soul is attached to the worldly life in a living hell separated from God.

33 Usually, **"I am he."** See Isaiah 41:4. "Jesus" means "*YHWH* saves" or "I AM saves." **I AM the way, the truth and the life. I AM the light of the world. Very truly I tell you, before Abraham lived; I AM. I AM the good shepherd. Be of good cheer, I AM, do not be afraid. I AM the bread of life. I AM the resurrection and the life.**

34 Also **undivided, undifferentiated, integrated,** and **open.**

35 Meyer, *Gospel* 108. Usually **good man.**

36 Also **the fruit, its crop,** or **its produce.**

37 "This parable presents the same problems as several others do for the landlord acts in an incompetent and ultimately disastrous manner. What sane man would discover that his tenants violently refuse to pay up, that they have beaten his first agent nearly to death and a second agent also, and then send

his son and heir into the same situation? But this is what the landlord does in this case. His reward is to have his son murdered. This is a man who does not learn from experience. The idea that the landlord represents God and the son represents Christ is not present in Thomas's Gospel." Davies, *Gospel* 86.

38 "In many gnostic texts (see the Gospel of Philip), the pearl is used as a symbol of the Self or uncreated Being. This may derive from Iranian gnostic teachings, for the Persian word *gowhar* means both "precious stone" and "quintessence." One of the pearl's characteristics is that it is filled with light but also reflects it. In the beginning, in Paradise, a human being was a pearl, filled with light inside and outside. Thus the pearl also signifies the state of grace to which we can return through love and gnosis." Leloup, *Gospel of Thomas* 175.

39 This is the gift of God (Exodus 3:14, God said to Moses, "I AM WHO [That] I AM.") through *Holkmah* to Jesus. This is the integrated self, the "I AM" of *Holkmah* (See Appendix C, *Holkmah* and Appendix D, Proverbs 8:22–24.), the Holy Wisdom of God, Who became the "I AM" in Jesus. All people who become a true human being like Jesus the Christ and realize their own Christ, go from "I should be" to "I AM."

40 Also **that shines above everything, that shines over all things,** and **which is above them all.**

41 Also **came into me** and **returned to me.**

42 "Yes, a reed shaken by the wind! That is the very nature of the prophets. They are moved by the Spirit and being empty of themselves, they are Spirit-filled." Malachi, *Gnostic* 243. See Matthew 11:7, Note no. 132 for "**One frenzied by the spirit?**"

43 See Matthew 7:6 for another ending.

44 "Like saying 22, the two becoming one refers to men and women returning to the androgynous state enjoyed by Adam before the fall." John Dart & Ray Riegert, *Unearthing the Lost Words of Jesus*, (Berkeley, California; Seastone—Ulysses Press, 1998) 88.

45 "Faith is the intuition of an experience we have not yet had and therefore the invocation of that spiritual or mystic experience. Faith is the certainty of things not seen and the awareness that with God, nothing is impossible. It is a great and awesome magic-power and a most significant part of what makes us truly human. By nature, a human being is a creature of faith and worship, and until faith is born in us, as with certain other innately human qualities, it may be rightly said that we are not yet human beings in the fullest possible sense. A little faith can move mountains and make great wonders transpire, and through faith, we are redeemed from our ignorance and forgetfulness. One

might say that faith is the holy remembrance that we are children of the Light, sons and daughters of the Living God." Malachi, *Gnostic* 329.

46 "It was the rare lamb that was lost in first century Israel. Each shepherd had a unique whistle known only to their flock. If two flocks became hopelessly intermixed at a watering spot, the shepherd needed simply to whistle softly for their flock to immediately part from the other sheep and follow them." Dart, *Unearthing* 88.

47 Also Thomas 111:3: "For it is said, 'Whoever has self-knowledge, the world cannot contain them.'" Leloup, *Gospel of Thomas* 216.

48 Usually **male**. From a version of Thomas 114:1–3 found in Jean-Yves Leloup, *The Gospel of Mary Magdalene*, (Rochester, Vermont; Inner Traditions, 2002) 102.

49 Males who have become fully human, where their male role is of a lower priority than their humanity, like the Son of humanity.

Jewish Life Notes.

1 Rabbi Berel Wein, *Echoes of Glory*, (Brooklyn, New York: Shaar Press, 1995) 63.

2 Joseph Pashka, *The Aramaic Gospels & Acts Companion*, (Longwood, Florida: Xulon Press, 2003) ii (introduction).

3 Stephen M. Wylen, *The Jews In The Time of Jesus*, (Mahwah, New Jersey; Paulist Press, 1996) 100.

4 *The Revell Concise Bible Dictionary*, (Tarrytown, New York: Flemming H. Revell Company, 1991) 199.

5 Wylen, *Jews* 139.

6 Wylen, *Jews* 56.

7 From George M. Lasma, *Gospel Light*, (Nashville, Tennessee: Holman Bible Publishers, 1967) 385.

8 Wein, *Echoes* 125–126.

9 Wylen, *Jews* 74.

10 J. D. Douglas and Merrill C. Tenney, *New International Version Compact Dictionary of the Bible*, (New York, New York; Harper Paperbacks for Zondervan Publishing House, 1989.) 249.

11 Wein, *Echoes* 144.

12 Wein, *Echoes* 133.

13 Wylen, *Jews* 151.

14 Wylen, *Jews* 53.

15 Neil Douglas-Klotz, *The Hidden Gospel*, (Wheaton, Illinois: Quest Books—Theosophical Publishing House, 1999.) 108.

16 Douglas-Klotz, *Hidden Gospel* 110.

17 Wylen, *Jews* 71.

18 Raymond E. Brown, Francis J. Moloney, ed. *An Introduction to the Gospel of John*, (New York, New York; Doubleday, 2003.) 160.

19 Brown, *Introduction* 165–166.

20 Lasma, *Gospel* 394-2 & 394-3.

21 Wylen, *Jews* 85.

22 *Revell* 351.

23 Wylen, *Jews* 170.

24 See Psalm 2:7, Note no. 8 in Appendix D.

25 Wylen, *Jews* 88–89.

26 Wylen, *Jews* 89–90.

27 Wein, *Echoes* 7, Footnote no.15.

28 Wein, *Echoes* 285.

29 Wylen, *Jews* 102.

30 Wylen, *Jews* 143.

31 See John 19:6, Note no. 144 for a larger view of Pilate's record.

32 Lasma, *Gospel* 174–175.

33 *Revell* 481.

34 Lasma, *Gospel* 349.

35 Lasma, *Gospel* 349.

36 Wylen, *Jews* 126–127.

37 Richard Kieninger, *The Hidden Christ*, (Quinlan, Texas; The Adelphi Organization, 1989) 18–19.

38 Wylen, *Jews* 99.

39 Wein, *Echoes* 145.

Hebrew Scripture Notes

1 Usually the pronouns for the Hebrew name for God, *Elohim*, are, "His" and "He," not "Their" and "They"; but this comes from the same "Us" and "Our" as in Genesis 1:26.

2 See Luke 4:18, Note no. 38 as the healing by God is part of the Good News.

3 Deuteronomy 5:16 has a longer version.

4 Or strikes.

5 The completed version is Deuteronomy 6:4–5: "Hear Oh Israel, Adonai [*YHWH*] is our God [*Elohim*], *Adonai* [*YHWH*] is One. You shall love *Adonai* [*YHWH*] your God [*Elohim*] with all your heart, with all your soul, and with all your strength." *Adonai* is used in place of *YHWH* which means "the Eternal" but the usual English translation of *Adonai* is The LORD, so you have: "Hear Oh Israel, the Eternal [*LORD*] is our God, the Eternal [*LORD*] is One. You shall love the Eternal [*LORD*] your God with all your heart, with all your soul, and with all your strength." The name used in place of *YHWH* is *Adonai* which is translated into the Greek as *Kyrios* which is translated in to the English as "The LORD." "The LORD" is used as a place name for *YHWH* which is unsayable and unpronounceable and unknowable as the God without attributes; "the Eternal," "Existing," or "Being." So in most Christian Bibles *YHWH* becomes the royal male "LORD" who is often referred to as "He." The other names for God with attributes or roles in Judaism are included under *YHWH*. Examples are: *Elohim* (God as Creator and Judge), *Adonai* (God as Lord or Compassionate One) and *El Shaddai* (God Almighty). See Appendix C, *Adonai, Elohim,* and *YHWH*.

6 Numbers 14:22 and Psalm 95:8–9.

7 Usually "fear." The use of the phrase "fear of God" or "fear of the Lord" usually means being in awe of God, the reverence of God, the fear of separation from God, and the awesome respect of God.

8 Means "adopted" because this is not a human birth but a spiritual birth. "Decree, the royal protocol legitimating the king at the time of enthronement. 'You are my son; today I have begotten you.' is a formula of the adoption of the king, who from that point on is then viewed as God's son (Psalms 89:26–27; 2 Samuel 7:14)." Wayne A. Meeks, ed. *Harper Collins Study Bible: New Revised Standard Edition*, (New York, New York; Harper Collins Publishers, 1993.) 801 Footnote no.2:7.

9 "*Sheol*, the abode of the dead. The one praying seems to be near death. Death is seen as a condition in which one is removed from God's presence and the possibility of worship and praise (cf. Job 10:21–22; Isaiah 38:18). That fact is given." Meeks, *Harper* 804. Footnote no. [Psalm] 6:5 is referenced page from 812 Footnote no. [Psalm] 16:10.

10 Also, "suffer thy Holy One to see corruption," and "let your faithful servant to see the pit."

11 Usually "righteousness."

12 "Insincere, deceptive." George M. Lasma, *Idioms In the Bible Explained and A Key to the Original Gospels*, (New York, New York: HarperSanFrancisco, A Division of HarperCollinsPublishers, 1985) 18.

13 Also riddles, obscure sayings, and proverbs.

14 Wise in the ways of the world.

15 "in the end, demented, they will graze like cattle." George M. Lasma, *Holy Bible: From the Ancient Eastern Text*, (San Francisco, California; HarperSanFrancisco for A. J. Holman Company, 1968) 610.

16 Interlude or Pause and consider.

17 Usually "Shoel" or "to the grave." See Psalm 16:8, Note no. 9.

18 Usually "eaten me up" or "consumed me." Lasma, *Holy Bible* 619.

19 Also "divine council," "the great assembly," "judges appointed by God to represent God before people," and "assembly of *El*." *El* is the most high god in the Canaanite religion whose wife is *Asherah*. *Asherah's* husband became *YHWH* in Hebrew until the 7th Century BCE. *YHWH* evolved into God without attributes; meaning Eternal, Being, I AM, or Existing.

20 Also "practical wisdom."

21 God within us.

22 Also "Nations" and "all peoples."

23 The Lamb of God.

24 The nonviolent ones first.

25 The acceptable year of God or the year of Jubilee, but many see these two years as not the same. The year of Jubilee in Leviticus 25:8–17 states that every fifty years, there will be a renewal of the earth, a redistribution of wealth, and the release of slaves, captives, as well as prisoners.

26 Lasma, *Holy Bible* 750. Usually "the day of vengeance of our God."

27 Euphrates River.

BIBLIOGRAPHY

Scriptures

Beers, Ronald A., ed. *Life Application Bible: The Living Bible*, Wheaton, Illinois; Tyandale House Publishers, Inc. and Youth for Christ; 1988.

Browne, Lewis, ed. *The Wisdom of Israel: An Anthology*, New York, New York; Random House, Inc., 1945.

Dart, John and Ray Riegert, *Unearthing the Lost Words of Jesus: The Discovery and Text of The Gospel of Thomas*, Berkeley, California; Seastone—Ulysses Press, 1998.

Davies, Stevan trans., Andrew Harvey ed., *The Gospel of Thomas Annotated & Explained*, Woodstock, Vermont; Skylight Paths Publishing, 2002.

De Boer, Esther A., *The Gospel of Mary: Listening to the Beloved Disciple*, New York, New York: Continuum Books, 2005.

_____, *The Mary Magdalene Cover-Up: The Sources Behind The Myth*, John Bowden, trans. New York, New York: T & T Clark, 2006.

_____, *Mary Magdalene: Beyond the Myth*, John Bowden, trans. Harrisburg, Pa: Trinity Press International, 1997.

Dowling, Levi, Transcribed from the Akashic Records, *The Aquarian Gospel of Jesus the Christ*, Kempton, Illinois; Adventures Unlimited Press, 1996.

Eddy, Mary Baker, *Science And Health With Key To The Scriptures*, Boston, Massachusetts: The Christian Science Board of Directors, 1906.

Eight Translation New Testament: King James Version; The Living Bible; Phillips Modern English: Revised Standard Version; Today's English Version; New International Version; Jerusalem Bible and New English Bible, Wheaton, Illinois; Tyndale House Publishers, Inc., 1974.

Gaus, Andy, trans., *The Unvarnished New Testament*, Grand Rapids, Michigan; Phanes Press, 1991.

Gupta, Mahendranath—"M", Swami Nikhilananda, (From Bengali) trans. *The Gospel of Sri Ramakrishna*, New York, New York; Ramakrishna—Vivekananda Center, 1977.

Hayford, Jack W., ed., *Spirit Filled Life Bible for Students: New King James Version*, Nashville, Tennessee—Atlanta, Georgia; Thomas Nelson Publishers, 1995.

The Holy Bible: New King James Version, Nashville, Tennessee—Atlanta, Georgia; Thomas Nelson Publishers, 1994.

Irving, Thomas B., (Arabic text and English) trans. *The Noble Qur'an*, Brattleboro, Vermont; Amanda Books, 1992.

Johnson W. J., trans. *The Bhagavad Gita*, Oxford, Great Britain; World's Classic Paperback for Oxford University Press, 1994.

King, Karen, *The Gospel of Mary of Magdala: Jesus and the First Woman Apostle*, Santa Rosa, California; Polebridge Press, 2003.

Kroeger, Catherine Clark, Mary Evans and Elaine Storkey, ed., *Study Bible for Women: The New Testament—New Revised Standard Version*, Grand Rapids, Michigan; Baker Book House Company, 1995.

Lasma, George M., *Gospel Light*, Nashville, Tennessee: Holman Bible Publishers, 1967.

——————————, (From the Aramaic of the Peshitta) trans. *The Holy Bible: From the Ancient Eastern Text*, San Francisco, California; HarperSanFrancisco for A. J. Holman Company, 1968.

——————————, *Idioms in the Bible Explained and A Key to the Original Gospels*, New York, New York: HarperSanFrancisco, A Division of HarperCollinsPublishers, 1985.

——————————, *The Kingdom on Earth*, Covington, Georgia; The Aramaic Bible Society, Inc., 2002.

Layton, Bentley, trans. *The Gnostic Scriptures: Ancient Wisdom for the New Age*, New York, New York; Doubleday, 1987.

Leloup, Jean-Yves, Joseph Rowe, trans., *The Gospel of Mary Magdalene*, Rochester, Vermont; Inner Traditions, 2002.

——————————, trans., Joseph Rowe (English) trans., *The Gospel of Thomas: The Gnostic Wisdom of Jesus*, Rochester, Vermont; Inner Traditions, 2005.

Life Appreciation Bible: The Living Bible, Wheaton, Illinois: Tyndale House Publishers, 1986.

Life Application Study Bible, New Living Translation, Wheaton, Illinois: Tyndale House Publishers, 1996.

Ludwig, Emil, trans., *The Son of Man*, Garden City, New York; Garden City Publishing Company Inc., 1928.

Malachi,Tau, trans., *The Gnostic Gospel of St. Thomas: Meditations On The Mystical Teachings*, St. Paul, Minnesota; Llewellyn Publications, 2004.

_____, *St. Mary Magdalene: The Gnostic Tradition of the Holy Bride*, Woodbury, Minnesota: Llewellyn Publications, 2006.

Meeks, Wayne A., ed. *The Harper Collins Study Bible: New Revised Standard Version*, New York, New York; Harper Collins Publishers, 1993.

Meyer, Marvin, (English) trans. *The Gospel of Thomas: The Hidden Sayings of Jesus*, New York, New York; HarperSanFrancisco, A Division of HarperCollins Publishers, 1992.

Meyer, Marvin W., trans. *The Secret Teachings of Jesus: Four Gnostic Gospels*, New York, New York; Vintage Books, 1984.

Miller Robert J., ed. *The Complete Gospels: Annotated Scholars Version*, Sonoma, California; A Polebridge Press Book, HarperSanFrancisco, A Division of HarperCollinsPublishers, 1994.

Nahmad, Claire & Margret Bailey, *The Secret Teachings of Mary Magdalene*, London, Great Britain, Watkins Publishing, 2006.

The New American Bible, Catholic Parish Edition, Wichita, Kansas; Catholic Bible Publishers, 1991.

The New International Reader's Version New Testament: Young Reader's Edition, Grand Rapids, Michigan; Zondervan Publishing House, 1995.

Nikhilananda, Swami, ed., *Vivekananda: The Yogas and Other Works*, New York, New York; Ramakrishna—Vivekananda Center, 1953.

Pagels, Elaine, *Beyond Belief: The Secret Gospel of Thomas*, New York, New York; Random House, 2003.

Pashka, Joseph, *The Aramaic Gospels & Acts Companion*, A Text Transliteration (In Aramaic from the Aramaic Peshitta Version.), Longwood, Florida; Xulon Press, 2003.

Price, Reynolds, trans. *Three Gospels*, Touchstone—Simon and Schuster Inc., New York, New York; 1996.

Ravindra, Ravi, *The Gospel of John: In The Light Of Indian Mysticism*, New York, New York; Inner Traditions, Rochester, 2004.

Robertson, James M., ed. *The Nag Hammadi Library In English*, San Francisco, California; HarperSanFrancisco, 1988.

Szekeley, Edmond Bordeaux, Translated from the third century Aramaic and Old Slavonic Texts, *The Essene Gospel of Peace*, San Diego, California; Academy Books: Publishers, 1973.

Ziegler, Julie H. and B. L. Green, (English) trans. Ira Rashid and Eduard Albert Meier, (German) trans., *The Talmud of Jmmanuel: The Original Book of Matthew*, Newberg, Oregon; Wild Flower Press, 1992.

Scripture Studies

Ashcroft, Mary Ellen, *The Magdalene Gospel*, Minneapolis, Minnesota; Augsburg Fortress, 2002.

Bharati, Swami Veda, ed., *Night Birds; A Collection of Short Writings*, Kanpur, India; Himalayan International Institute of Yoga Science and Philosophy, 2000.

Black, Matthew, *An Aramaic Approach to the Gospels and Acts*, Peabody, Massachusetts: Hendrickson Publishers Inc., 1967.

Boyde, James P., *Bible Dictionary*, Ottenheimer Publishers, Inc., New York, New York; 1958.

Brown, Raymond E., Francis J. Moloney, ed. *An Introduction to the Gospel of John*, New York, New York; Doubleday, 2003.

Butz, Jeffrey J., *The Brother of Jesus and Lost Teachings of Christianity*, Rochester, Vermont; Inner Traditions, 2005.

Crossan, John Dominic, *The Historical Jesus: The Life of a Mediterranean Peasant*, San Francisco, California; Harper San Francisco, 1991.

_____, *Jesus: A Revolutionary Biography*, San Francisco, California; Harper San Francisco, 1994.

Davis, Roy Eugene, *An Easy Guide To Meditation: For Personal Benefits and Spiritual Growth*, Lakemont, Georgia; CSA Press, 1995.

Douglas, J. D. and Merrill C. Tenney, *New International Version Compact Dictionary of the Bible*, New York, New York; Harper Paperbacks for Zondervan Publishing House, 1989.

Douglas-Klotz, Neil, *The Hidden Gospel*, Wheaton, Illinois: Quest Books—Theosophical Publishing House, 1999.

_____, *Prayers of the Cosmos: Meditations on the Aramaic Words of Jesus*, San Francisco, California; Harper San Francisco, 1990.

Eddy, Mary Baker, *Christ and Christmas A Poem*, Boston Massachusetts, Published under the Will of Mary Baker G. Eddy, 1925.

Ehrman, Bart D., *Jesus: Apocalyptic Prophet of the New Millennium*, New York, New York; Oxford University Press Inc, 1999

_____, *The Orthodox Corruption of Scripture*, New York, New York; Oxford University Press, 1993.

_____, *Misquoting Jesus*, New York, New York; Harper One—HarperCollins Publishers, 2005.

Freke, Timothy and Peter Gandy, *Jesus and the Lost Goddess: The Secret Teachings of the Original Christians*, New York, New York; Three Rivers Press, 2001.

Fox, Robert Lane, *The Unauthorized Version: Truth and Fiction in the Bible*, New York, New York; Alfred A. Knopf Inc., 1991.

Gaffney, Mark H. *Gnostic Secrets of the Naassenes: The Initiatory Teachings of the Last Supper*, Rochester, New York: Inner Traditions, 2004.

Gottlie, Lynn, *She Who Dwells Within: A Feminist Vision of a Renewed Judaism*, San Francisco, California; Harper San Francisco, 1995.

Hartmann, Franz, *The Life Of Jehoshua: The Prophet Of Nazareth*, Montana, U.S.A.; Kessinger Publishing Company, 1998.

Hasan, Asma Gull, *Why I Am A Muslim*, Element, San Francisco, California; Harper Collins Publishers, 2004.

Haskins, Susan, *Mary Magdalene, Myth and Metaphor*, Riverhead Books, New York, New York; The Berkley Publishing Group, 1993.

Hooper, Richard J. *The Crucifixion of Mary Magdalene*, Sedona, Arizona; Sanctuary Publications, 2005.

Jenkins, Philip, *Hidden Gospels*, New York, New York; Oxford University Press, 2001.

Jones, Timothy Paul, *Misquoting Truth: A Guide to the Fallacies of Bart Ehrman's Misquoting Jesus*, Downers Grove, Illinois; InterVarsity Press, 2007.

Jusino, Ramon K., "Mary Magdalene: Author of the Fourth Gospel?", (14 pages), copyright 1998, Viewed 12/25/06, http://Ramon_K_jusino.tripod.com/magdalene.html

Kieninger, Richard, *The Hidden Christ*, Quinlan, Texas; The Adelphi Organization, 1989.

Leloup, Jean-Yves, trans., Joseph Rowe (English) trans., *The Sacred Embrace of Jesus and Mary*, Rochester. Vermont, Inner Traditions, 2006.

Longfellow, Ki, *The Secret Magdalene*, New, York, New York; Crown Publishers, a division of Random House Inc., 2007. (ISBN 978-0-307-34666-7)

Martin, Edward T., *King of Travelers: Jesus' Lost Years in India*, Lampass, Texas; Jonah Publishing Company, 1999.

Meier, John P., *A Marginal Jew: Rethinking the Historical Jesus—Volume Three: Companions And Competitors*, New York, New York; Doubleday, 2001.

_____, *A Marginal Jew: Rethinking the Historical Jesus—Volume Two: Mentor, Message And Miracles*, New York, New York; Doubleday, 1994.

Metaphysical Bible Dictionary, Charles Fillmore Reference Library, ed., Unity Village, Missouri; Unity House, 2007.

Mish, Frederick C. ed., *The New Merriam—Webster Dictionary*, Springfield, Massachusetts; Merriam-Webster Inc., Publishers, 1989.

Moyers, Bill & Lev Daly, 1 "A Parable For Our Times", (4 pages), <TomPaine. com> 12/22/06. http://www.commondreams.org/views06/1222-24. htm

Norton, Joan, *The Mary Magdalene Within*, Lincoln, Nebraska; iUniverse, 2005.

Pagels, Elaine, *The Gnostic Gospels*, New York, New York; Random House, 1979.

_____, *The Origin of Satan*, New York, New York; Random House, 1995.

Raskin, Jay, *The Evolution of Christs and Christianities*, Printed in the United States; Xlibris Corporation, 2006.

Roberts, Mark D. *Jesus Revealed*, Colorado Springs, Colorado; WaterBrook Press, 1996.

The Revell Concise Bible Dictionary, Tarrytown, New York; Flemming H. Revell Company, 1991.

Ridge, Milan, ed., *Jesus; The Unauthorized Version*, New York, New York; New American Library, 2007.

Seymore-Smith, Martin, *Gnosticism: The Path of Inner Knowledge*, Hong Kong, China; Labyrinth Publishing Ltd. for Harper San Francisco, 1996.

Sprong, John Shelby, *This Hebrew Lord: A Bishop's Search for the Authentic Jesus*, San Francisco, California; Harper San Francisco, 1993.

Standard Process Purification Program, Palmyra, Wisconsin; Standard Process Inc., 2008.

Starbird, Margaret, *The Woman With The Alabaster Jar: Mary Magdalen and the Holy Grail*, Santa Fe, New Mexico; Bear & Company Publishing, 1993.

Torjesen, Karen Jo, *When Women Were Priests*, San Francisco, California; Harper San Francisco, 1993.

Watchtower Bible and Tract Society of Pennsylvania, *The Greatest Man Who Ever Lived*, Brooklyn, New York; Watchtower Bible and Tract Society of New York Inc., Publishers, 1991.

Webster's Ninth New Collegiate Dictionary, Springfield, Massachusetts; Merriam-Webster Inc. Publishers, 1987.

Wein, Rabbi Berel, *Echoes of Glory*, Brooklyn, New York: Shaar Press, 1995.

Winston, William, trans., *Jesophus Complete Works*, Grand Rapids, Michigan; Kregel Publications, 1978.

Wouk, Herman, *This Is My God: The Jewish Way of Life*, Boston, New York; Little Brown and Company, 1987.

Wylen, Stephen M., *The Jews in the Time of Jesus: An Introduction*, Mahwah, New Jersey; Paulist Press, 1996.

Yogananda, Paramahansa *The Yoga of Jesus; Understanding the Hidden Teachings of the Gospels*, Los Angeles, California; Self-Realization Fellowship, 2007.

Zimmermann, Frank, *The Aramaic Origin of the Four Gospels*, New York, New York; KTAV Publishing, 1979.

Index

Y

Edwards Brothers Malloy
Thorofare, NJ USA
June 28, 2013